Praise for *Grand Obsession*

"Mesmerizing . . . her gift for sound exten̲̲̲̲̲̲̲̲̲̲

"In the best tradition of the memoir, Perri̲̲̲̲̲̲̲̲̲̲̲̲̲̲̲̲
simple shopping expedition and ends in total existential collapse. . . . It's a mark
of her deftness that despite the esoteric subject matter, it reads at the pace of a
mystery and the pitch of a love story. . . . By the end of the story, when Knize
is told she 'fell in love with an illusion,' it has the weight of tragedy."
— *The New York Times*

"Fascinating insights emerge as she strives to understand the metaphysics of
music: how vibrations influence us, how music heals us, how indulging our
desire for beauty seems to feed our very soul. She examines such esoteric
concepts as sympathetic frequencies—for example, in a room filled with
pianos, if you play just one note on one of them, the others will play that
note too if their dampers are raised—and what it all means to us, musicians
and nonmusicians alike. To follow Knize on this crazy-quilt quest is to engage
some of the deepest of life's questions: not just why and how music moves
us but why and how we respond to beauty, to the world, to each other—and
how a soul learns to thrive."
— *Los Angeles Times*

"Lucid yet lyrical, analytical yet deeply affecting. From the opening of her
'prelude,' you know you're in the hands of an observant naturalist with an
artist's sensibility."
— *The Washington Post*

"Exquisite . . . those who've never touched the keys will find themselves lost
in the poetry of the hammers, the strings, the fallboard, the felting, the idea
of the Schubert concert tuning."
— *The Times-Picayune* (New Orleans)

"Intimately powerful: It changed the way I look at the world . . . it reminded
me of my own unfulfilled search for music, self, harmony."
— *Missoula Independent*

"I was hooked from the first page. The longing ache of playing a really beautiful instrument is a familiar one, and there is fascination in the complexity
and elegance of piano mechanics and a cornucopia of piano lore. Add passionate writing and a long metaphor for self-realization, and this book travels beyond the sphere of mere music."
— *The Buffalo News*

"Knize writes in a wonderfully evocative, lushly romantic style, and music lovers will resonate to her mad pursuit of a gorgeous sound."
—*Publishers Weekly*

"Articulating precisely the way music makes us feel may be nearly impossible, but Knize makes a commendable attempt, combining synesthetic flourishes of language with a journalistic attack on the experience. A well-written, heartfelt, classy paean to a singular instrument."
—*Kirkus Reviews*

"The quest seems straightforward; having heard the voice of her beloved, Perri Knize sets out to possess it. But what has she heard, the action of hammers on strings or the murmurings of her own heart? *Grand Obsession* begins as a book about finding the right piano and becomes more than that, a search for the sublime that poses a question essential to every reader, musical or not: How do we recognize, much less capture, the always fleeting object of desire?"
—Kathryn Harrison

"Occasionally a book appears that is sui generis. It is so intense, so passionate, so powerfully and cleanly written that it changes the way the reader sees the world. Perri Knize's *Grand Obsession,* the story of her quest for the perfect piano, is such a book."
—*Magellan's Log*

"Knize's writing soars throughout this account of her musical journey. It gives her nonfiction a structure and sustains the suspenseful inevitability that propels the narrative. . . . From first line to last, *Grand Obsession* maintains a marvelous consistency of tone, never hitting a false note."
— *The Free Lance-Star* (Fredericksburg, Virginia)

"Knize has crafted a poetic tribute to the piano. We rejoice upon her discovery of Marlene and sympathize when the instrument she loved in New York changes on its trip through blizzards to Montana where she makes her home. . . . Warmly recommended for all collections."
—*Library Journal*

"The book reads like a detective story, one that will totally pull the reader in, and the passage of time in the narrative is handled so masterfully that it's easy to forget how long the author's quest took. But the obsession and passion of Perri Knize and her unflinching determination to recreate that sound . . . is truly inspiring.

"Any listener who has ever been transfixed by the otherworldly sound of a truly magnificent piano will find an articulate kindred spirit in this author and in this story, and anyone who doubts the ability of music to touch and enrich the human spirit will have those doubts erased upon reading *Grand Obsession.*"
—*American Music Teacher* magazine

GRAND OBSESSION

A Piano Odyssey

PERRI KNIZE

Scribner
New York   London   Toronto   Sydney

SCRIBNER
A Division of Simon & Schuster, Inc.
1230 Avenue of the Americas
New York, NY 10020

This work is a memoir. It reflects the author's present recollections of
her experiences over a series of years. Some identifying characteristics
have been changed. Some dialogue has been re-created from memory.
Some scenes are composites of events. Events have been compressed
and in some cases their chronology has been changed.

First Scribner trade paperback edition June 2009

SCRIBNER and design are registered trademarks of
The Gale Group, Inc., used under license
by Simon & Schuster, the publisher of this work.

For information about special discounts for bulk purchases,
please contact Simon & Schuster Special Sales:
1-866-506-1949 or business@simonandschuster.com.

The Simon & Schuster Speakers Bureau can bring authors
to your live event. For more information or to book an event
contact the Simon & Schuster Speakers Bureau at
1-866-248-3049 or visit our website at www.simonspeakers.com.

DESIGNED BY KYOKO WATANABE
Text set in Bembo

Manufactured in the United States of America

1   3   5   7   9   10   8   6   4   2

Library of Congress Control Number: 2007048098

ISBN 978-0-7432-7638-2
ISBN 978-0-7432-7639-9 (pbk)
ISBN 978-1-4165-4600-9 (ebook)

for Wendell

8

CONTENTS

III

GRAND OBSESSION

PRELUDE

From a Tree in the Forest

"In life I was mute; in death I sing."

—A MAPLE'S LAMENT

Maier Christian sits on a log in the sun, his boots half-buried in slushy snow, and examines his forest plan. It's a shining April day in the Alps: the Dachstein Mountains swell up, sparkling white, beyond ridges of towering spruce. They cut a jagged stencil across the sky, mottled with wisps of clouds. Before Christian's feet is a narrow logging road, transformed by winter's melting snow into a conduit of mud. Several yards farther down that road, four loggers take their mid-day nap atop the trunk of a felled giant, warming themselves like a family of painted turtles, their orange-and-green Forest Service uniforms garish in the brilliant sun.

Christian, head forester of the 12,000-acre Austrian Forest Service district known as 381F1, bends back the sewn binding of his management plan and unfolds a corresponding topographic map covered in erratic shapes of many colors. Together, the ten-year plan and the map tell him all he needs to know to decide what, and when, and where to harvest trees in this stand.

These trees are about 120 years old, the map's colors tell him. The elevation is about 4,300 feet, with a 25-degree slope. A rare wild-flower, the *sauerklee,* grows here, says the plan. Ninety percent of the trees are European spruce, an estimated 73,000 cubic feet of wood standing on more than 700 acres. The plan is to cut about 19,000 cubic feet of wood over the next ten years. At that rate the forest's supply of old-growth lumber can be sustained indefinitely.

The forester chooses carefully which trees to cut. They must be the very oldest, and the hole they make in the forest canopy must let in light for the greatest number of baby trees. These young trees are difficult to see, as the snow is still deep. And yet, any logging must take place in deep snow, so that skidding logs do no harm to the forest floor or the *sauerklee*.

The need for snowpack keeps the logging season short, from November through April. All winter, trees are felled and stacked like hedgerows alongside the rough logging roads, until they have dried enough for truck travel. Then the logs must be removed from the forest quickly, before insects infest them. Trees must also be cut before their sap rises in spring. Running sap stains black the pure white wood of European spruce, rendering it useless to the best-paying and most-demanding customers.

A round-wood dealer, Reinhard Kirchner, walks into the logging site, balancing atop the stacked logs, his arms waving to steady himself. Kirchner drove into the forest in an old Volkswagen sedan, but had to abandon his car when it would go no farther up the mud-swollen road. The loggers rouse themselves from their naps to greet him. Christian rises, claps Kirchner on the shoulder, and shakes his hand. Kirchner is here in search of spruce for his best customer. His sawmill is in Filzmoos, a nearby Alpine village of 1,200 people, where he grew up. He's a lanky, athletic man of thirty-nine, with a cherubic face and a mop of curly hair.

The forester's first responsibility is for the forest's health, and this alone determines the size, location, and age of the trees he orders cut. The dealer's first concern is the quality of the wood, and that wood must be grown under exacting conditions.

The trees must have germinated naturally where they grow, from seeds dropped by the parent trees directly onto this forest floor. Transplanted seedlings, even if they are also European spruce, grow too fast, and fast-growing wood, with its wider-spaced growth rings, will not be strong enough.

These indigenous trees are the genetic product of a very particular microclimate: Summers are short, and winters long; the soil is poor, and so the trees grow slowly, forming tight, uniform growth rings, twenty or more to the inch. The range of elevation is narrow, from 3,600 to

4,600 feet. They grow on slopes facing west, preferably northwest, so their trunks will not twist too much nor too little toward the sun. Too much sun will produce too much pitch in the wood. The trees must also grow out of the wind, because movement compresses their grain. The ground must be as level as possible, or the trees, in growing upright against a slope, will have compressed growth rings on their uphill sides. Only a few special places grow just the right subspecies of European spruce in just the right microclimate, and they are in the mountains of Switzerland, Bavaria, Austria, and Italy.

Trees from eighty to 280 years old are suitable, but the very best trees are 130 to 140 years old. In their lifetimes, they must not have been affected by insects, disease, or fire. However, if they were sick only when they were very young, that is the best, as they will have grown even more slowly during their earliest years.

Kirchner wanders among the winter's harvest, eyeing the closeness and regularity of the growth rings, the straightness of the trunks, the number of branches. A good tree is very straight, perfectly cylindrical, and has no limbs for the first dozen feet of its trunk. Only three to five percent of the trees grown under even the most favorable conditions will be suitable for Kirchner's customer. He is a very tough customer.

The forester closes his manual and enters the dark of the forest. Shafts of light dapple Christian's shoulders. He throws back his broad-domed head, turns his face upward, and his heavy features, grizzled with a three-day growth of beard, squint into the canopy, studying it. He turns about, his boots circling the forest floor; fallen boughs snap under them.

Christian looks at the branches above, then the slush-covered ground, then the canopy again. Which tree?

"This one," he says, pointing his arm straight as an arrow to a spruce more than two feet across.

A logger standing by steps forward. He carries a chainsaw and wears a bright orange helmet with a mesh visor and protective yellow ear cuffs. Josef Hacki has cut trees in the forests of the Pongau region of Austria most of his fifty-nine years. Like many who choose to work in the mountains, he possesses an almost reckless love for the outdoors. Hacki and the other loggers spend their summers paragliding, their winters extreme telemark skiing in the ungroomed Alpine backcountry. Hacki moves toward the designated tree lightly, gracefully, with an athlete's swift sureness.

Christian points to the ground where he wishes the tree to fall. Hacki rests the engine of his chainsaw against one thigh and yanks the pull cord. The saw snarls to life. Hacki bites a pie-shaped notch out of the side of the tree facing the fall line, and the chips and sawdust fly. Then, on the trunk's opposite side, he makes a deep back cut toward the point of the notch, removing the chainsaw just before the weight of the tree pinches it. Only a quarter of the trunk now remains unsevered from its roots. The air is thick with the smell of pitch.

Next, Hacki inserts an orange-painted steel wedge, drawn from a leather pocket on his belt, into the back cut, and pounds it toward the heart of the tree with the butt of his axe. His swings are swift, certain, and powerful, landing precisely on the wedge each time with a vigorous clang. The tree rocks and sighs, her boughs sough the air, making an ethereal music in her final moments. The wedge is driven true one last time, and there is a crack, the first sounding of the voice of the tree, a voice heard only in death.

Yet the tree does not fall. Hacki raises his visor and looks up. In the narrow shafts of light, his face is grayed with stubble. His searching eyes are tranquil, as if they have borne witness to the secrets of the mountains. Hacki points his axe handle to the problem—the tree is entangled in the arms of a neighbor spruce.

The logger retrieves his wedge from the new stump, and with his chainsaw severs the tree's last, splintered hold on life. One hundred and twenty years. Now over. The forester and the logger step back. The giant collapses, almost softly, onto her boughs, into the snow, first with a whisper, then with a delayed and reverberant cry, a cannon boom that echoes through the mountains.

A tree dies. A piano is born.

I

I

Epiphany

In the autumn of my forty-third year, I remembered, quite unexpectedly, that I was meant to be a pianist.

I was alone in my car, on my way to spend a weekend with friends. I fumbled through a box of cassette tapes I kept on the front passenger seat and found one my brother gave me: pianist Arthur Rubinstein performing Chopin waltzes. This might make a good soundtrack for the trip, I thought, and I pushed the cassette into the tape deck.

From the opening notes of Opus 18—quick, percussive repetitions of B-flat—the car seemed to rock in sympathy to the driving three-quarter-time beat, taken at a wildly joyous tempo. Rubinstein's complete freedom within the music astonished me, and his abandonment to it was contagious—the music seemed to enter my pulse and carbonate my blood.

Meanwhile, through the windshield, Montana's luminous Indian summer performed a fitting accompaniment: a sapphire sky hung behind the Elkhorn Mountains, where tawny grasses gleamed in the lowering sun. Quaking aspen lined the banks of the Boulder River; their burnished leaves turned up their bellies to the wind and trembled in unison, a ribbon of gold threading its way up the valley.

I found myself gripping the steering wheel, as if I were hanging on for the ride, gripped myself by a piano-induced rapture that was as sweet as it was searing.

This is all that I want to do with my life. These words arose as if from nowhere in my mind, astonishing me. *This is all that I want to do with my life.* They hit with the force of an inner directive that cannot be questioned. They arose again and again, as if rising on the swells of the music itself.

The beauty of the day intensified the heartbreak: I felt as if I'd missed an urgent and critical appointment that could never be rescheduled. I had reached my own autumn, and the leaves would soon fall. How then could I devote my life to the piano?

I recognized this inner voice—it was that of the child I had been, eight years old and asking for piano lessons that were not forthcoming.

✦

"Which instrument will you choose?" my father asked one spring evening. He peered at me from beneath his knotted brow, heavy with an ever-present intensity that always suggested an impending storm. That day my third-grade class had attended a presentation of all the band and orchestra instruments; they were available to rent for school music lessons in the coming fall.

Some people are passionate about music. My father was ferocious about it. Until I came along, he was a professional musician. In the 1940s, he played first clarinet with the Denver, Columbus, Chicago Civic, and Ballet Russe de Monte Carlo orchestras. During the war years, while undergoing army intelligence training at Yale, he studied with the great German neoclassical composer Paul Hindemith, and dreamed of becoming a conductor. In the early 1950s, at the end of his still-youthful music career, he played first clarinet in the Metropolitan Opera Orchestra and with the Metropolitan Quintet.

Though he gave up professional performing at the age of thirty-five for a more lucrative career as a design manager at a stereo company, his life and our home remained saturated in music. When I was a child, his love of music penetrated my every cell and pore. Each night I fell asleep listening to the sonorous sounds of his clarinet as he accompanied recordings of his favorite works. A clarinet was never just a clarinet to me, and never will be: it is the sound of my father's voice.

There is no time I can remember when he was not training me to have a musician's ear. I had my own high-fidelity component system before I was two, and my own collection of classic children's records: *The Carnival of the Animals* by Saint-Saëns, *Peter and the Wolf* by

Prokofiev, *The Nutcracker Suite* by Tchaikovsky, and the opera *Hansel and Gretel* by Englebert Humperdinck (the composer, not the pop star).

But the stereo was never just on—no!—this was not background music! We were, rather, to always listen closely: "See how the theme from the beginning comes in again now, except in a different key?" my father would point out.

Nor was the radio ever just on when we drove somewhere in the car. The dial was tuned to a classical station, and I listened with all my being as my father described the qualities of the soloist—"He has a 'juicy' sound," my father would say—or noted the tempo: "See? He's rushing. You must never rush. You must play each note for its full value."

I listened closely because there would be a quiz—before the work ended my father would ask me to identify the composer, the conductor, the orchestra, and the soloist. Then, when the announcer came on, we would see how well I did. My father, with great deliberation, was teaching me how to listen.

This was not a wasted effort on his part—I had a very good ear, good enough that my father often used me as his rehearsal coach, and took my judgment of his playing seriously. I did not reject the gifts he shared with me, but embraced them, and worshipped him as one might an Old Testament–style god—with an equal mixture of fear and admiration. I took his theology, his only religion—music—as my own.

My father applied this sort of rigorous training to my intellectual upbringing as well. He taught me to question all assumptions, to carefully read between all lines, to always think for myself. Each Sunday we applied critical analysis to the stories in the newspaper—to both the content and the caliber of the writing. What questions went unasked? Where was the reader misled? And in every conversation with my father, no matter how serious or trivial, these skills were honed to a high polish: suspect, question, investigate, skewer. He taught them as contentiously as I imagine a rabbi might grill a Yeshiva boy over the Talmud. It is no wonder I ultimately became an investigative reporter and put those powerful tools to work.

Meanwhile, I plundered his vast record collection with his tacit approval. I wore out his copies of Nathan Milstein playing the Tchaikovsky violin concerto, the Vienna Octet playing the Schubert Octet, and Karl Böhm conducting the Berlin Philharmonic's rendition of Brahms's first symphony. This last became a kind of personal anthem, and I would spend hours alone listening to it in my room, conducting before a mirror.

Yet the enormous musical universe I inhabited was isolating. I could not play the music I loved for my friends—they would not have understood, and I would have become an outcast. As vast as this music was, as exalted as it made me feel, it also induced claustrophobia: it belonged only to me, my father, and, infrequently, my father's musical friends.

Some Sunday mornings, his friends would arrive with their instruments—strings, or other woodwinds—and they would have a few rousing hours playing chamber music in our living room. Mozart, Hindemith, Beethoven, Couperin, Brahms, Schubert. My father's musician friends were always relaxed, full of jokes and witticisms that went over my head. They were nothing like other parents I knew: they laughed loudly, told dirty stories, and winked at me frequently. I loved to be near them.

My mother served what she called "Jewish breakfast": bagels and lox and cream cheese, smoked whitefish, and jelly donuts. My younger brother and I could partake of the food, and we could sit quietly and listen, but we were not to interrupt or ask questions.

My father's question was really a series of questions: Which instrument would I choose to join him on his musical journey? Which instrument would be mine when we played duets together? Which instrument would I contribute to his chamber music gatherings? And finally, with which instrument would I fulfill the musical promise he himself had abandoned?

In my father's universe, music was a serious business, and so, by deduction, the choice of one's instrument could not be a casual thing, but rather was fraught with larger implications for one's ultimate destiny. I was too young to think this consciously, but I sensed it, I felt its heft, and it felt too heavy for me, too dark, and too oppressive. For I was growing up not only in the shadow of my father's musical achievements, but also under the long, dark pall of his abandoned musical ambitions and the force of his enormous, deeply frustrated, and explosive personality.

Answering my father was rarely easy. He was an intimidating giant of a man, a former high school football player, six foot two and a swollen

245 pounds, with thick, meaty hands, every finger broken and bent. His once luxuriantly curly hair was mostly gone now, his dark, handsome face puffy from intemperance, worry, and overwork. His expression was often a scowl, his voice brusque, the tone irritated and angry, even when he said he wasn't. Sometimes, at the sound of that voice, his children would burst into tears.

I had an idea of the answer my father wished to hear, but for just a moment I heard instead my own small, inner voice whisper to me: *the piano.*

Our piano was a beat-up, turn-of-the-century upright player my mother bought at an auction when I was three. When we moved to a spacious colonial home in Annapolis, Maryland, the following year, she painted it white, with house paint, to make it fit in with the décor of the 1830s plantation house. When I lifted the fallboard to reveal the yellowed ivories, the original mahogany finish still showed. There was no name on the fallboard. This was one of millions of nameless pianos produced during the instrument's Golden Age, in the early years of the twentieth century, when every middle-class home aspired to own a piano. At that time, pianos were the family hearth, the center of home entertainment. Soon they were replaced by the phonograph, the radio, television, and now the computer.

This old upright was to become my longtime friend. The day it arrived, as soon as it was placed in our den, my mother sat down before the keyboard, pulled me onto her knees, and began working the foot treadles behind the open doors of the piano's lower compartment. The treadles cranked and creaked and thunked, working the bellows that sucked air through a pneumatic player mechanism that turned a spool upon which a paper roll was wound. The paper had holes punched through it, in a perforated pattern like a ticker tape.

The doors of the upper panel were parted so we could see the paper roll turn on the spool. As the paper passed over a tracker bar, air was sucked through the perforations, each representing a note on the piano. The vacuum activated a pneumatic striking mechanism, which then activated the hammers. As the hammers struck the strings they pulled the ivory keys along with them.

The sight of the keys moving up and down, depressed and released as if by ghostly invisible hands, mesmerized me. The creaking and groaning of the treadles, the wheezing of the bellows in the belly of the old player were spooky. The music was a turn-of-the-century standard, "Daisy, Daisy," silly and fun and bright. I shrieked with delight as my beautiful, young mother sang along with the music and held me on her rollicking lap, in her arms, her legs pumping under me as if she were using a bicycle to wind an enormous music box.

When my mother's father came to visit, he always played the piano for us. Grandpa Joe had never learned how to read music, but he was a natural, with big hands and an unerring ear. You could sing him anything and he could sound out the melody and make up a chord accompaniment on the spot, and then he was off and running. But mostly he played the same kind of music that was on the piano rolls, songs recalling the summers he spent as a lifeguard at the beach on Coney Island in the 'teens, and his time as a soldier in World War I. He'd play "Take Me Out to the Ball Game," "Who's Sorry Now?" "Shine On, Harvest Moon," and "Baby Face," and my grandmother would sing along, rocking in the rocking chair, tapping her foot, grinning, no doubt remembering the days of their youth.

Grandpa Joe was an unpretentious man with a goofball, faintly racy sense of humor. When my mother was a girl, during the Great Depression and World War II, he went to the record store once a week to pick out the silliest recording he could find. I inherited his record collection because none of his children wanted it—my uncle Carl put all the 78 rpm records together in one album and labeled it "Junk" and gave it to my mother. My mother passed it on to me. Playing the collection now reminds me of my grandfather's irreverence: Spike Jones singing "Der Fuehrer's Face" with its fart noises, and "The Sheik of Araby" with its obscene gargling sound effects; Eddie Cantor singing "I'm Hungry for Beautiful Girls." There are World War I popular tunes: "I Don't Want to Get Well—I'm in Love with a Beautiful Nurse," which includes the coy lyric "I always get a Band-Aid every time she feels my pulse."

My friends and I beat on the old upright often; it was the center of our playtime, with hyperkinetic renditions of "Chopsticks" and "Heart and Soul" the order of the day. Babysitters entertained us on it, and once, after I had watched one of my friends play "Für Elise" by Beethoven on her family's console, I went home and furiously tried to play it by ear for hours on our old upright. My friend got piano lessons, and I remember feeling jealous, but until now, I had never thought to ask for them myself.

And so, by the time my father asked his question, I already had a deep affection, an affinity for a particular instrument.

"I want to play the piano," I replied to my father, startling myself with the clarity and rightness of the request.

My father didn't answer right away, but looked aside. "Why don't you pick an instrument they are teaching at school?" he said at last. His voice sounded pinched, as if he were wincing. "Then we don't have to pay for private lessons."

This was a surprise. I didn't know we couldn't afford lessons. We seemed to have everything we could ever need or want. Had I resisted at all, insisted that the piano was important to me, my father probably would have relented, and then the rest of this story would have been different. But I did not yet know how to trust my own inner promptings. That was not something I was to learn at home.

The next day at school, I chose the cello. It was my father's favorite instrument, the one he wished he had studied himself. I knew he would be pleased. He spent an evening in his basement workshop, fashioning me a wooden brace to keep the cello's prop stick in place on the floor. He talked of the wonderful pieces we would play together. In the following months, dismayed at how difficult it was to carry a heavy cello the half mile to school, I switched to the more portable flute. By the time I was fifteen, I had abandoned the flute as well; I was bored with its limited repertoire and overwhelmed by my father's expectation that I become a professional musician.

And yet, I remained in music's thrall. For my sixteenth Christmas, my father gave me the Canadian pianist Glenn Gould's recording of Bach's *The Well-Tempered Clavier*. Soon, on my own, I discovered Gould's 1955 recording of Bach's *Goldberg Variations*. This work became my private solace, a circle of light I stood in when I sought refuge from the dark chaos my family had become. Bach soothed me, but Gould, with his breathtaking virtuosity, his use of the piano as if it were his own voice, speaking as clearly of the composer's contrapuntal designs as if they were words, stoked my desire to play the piano until it became a burning, furious passion.

By now, there was no use in asking for piano lessons. My family was too broken, my parents grieving and coping as best they could with my youngest brother's diagnosis of a degenerative brain disease, and the years-long crises that ensued. Besides, I knew my father well: I'd had my chance, and had broken faith with him by abandoning the flute. There would be no more lessons.

✦

A decade later, still inspired by Glenn Gould, and finding myself with the time and the means, I began piano lessons with the first of a series of teachers. My goal, I told each of them, was to play the *Goldberg Variations*. When I moved to New York City in 1981, I became a piano student at Mannes College of Music, in their nondegree program. But within just a few short years, the struggles and complications of my young adult life unraveled my commitment to the piano. There were more urgent and pressing demands weighing on me such as food, shelter, and establishing a career. My last piano teacher, pleading with me to honor my talent, demanded more of me than I believed I could give, and so I moved on.

Fifteen years passed.

✦

When I arrive home in Missoula after my epiphany along the Boulder River, I telephone the office of the music school at the University of Montana, and ask for a referral to a local piano teacher. The secretary transfers my call to a Dr. Jody Graves, the head of the school's keyboard department.

Dr. Graves asks a lot of questions. She has only recently arrived in Missoula from New York herself, she says, and she knows my last teacher. She asks me to come in to play for her. I do not know how to play anymore, I say, but Dr. Graves insists. "If you don't want to play, then we will just talk," she says. "How about tomorrow?"

When I arrive at her office, Dr. Graves is demonstrating a demanding passage to a young man seated before one of two grand pianos. She is a robust blonde, perhaps in her forties, petite yet powerful. As I listen to her play Rachmaninoff, I cannot help but think that I will never be able to play anything so difficult.

I feel an old, paralyzing fear—stage fright. I have a book of Chopin nocturnes with me; some of them I used to play, but suddenly I wish I had left the music at home.

Dr. Graves dismisses her student and turns her attention to me. "Well, why not come here," she says, patting the vacated piano bench. Reluctantly, I take the seat. "I see you brought some music. Why not play a little for me?" Her voice is light, undemanding, as if to say "No big deal if you do or you don't." This gives me courage. I put the book on the music desk and begin.

Though my hands are unsteady and shaking, they amaze me—they still know the nocturne. My fingers return to their old places with shocking familiarity. The sensation of the keys beneath them and the tones they produce hit me hard.

What have you been doing with your life? It is the inner voice again. *How could you have let this get away?* I let both hands fall fully into the keyboard. Oh, how I have missed that touch, the feel of the keys under my fingers! How had I ever been able to stop touching them? Suddenly this fact, once unremarkable, seems incredible.

The keyboard's black-and-white topography floods me with tactile memories. I want this contact. I have to have it. The rush of intoxication, of certainty, of destiny I felt when listening to Rubinstein fills me again. This time, I resolve, I won't let it get away.

"That was very, very good!" Dr. Graves crows. "I think you will do well with one of my master's students. And then, of course, you can come to the school to practice."

My lessons with the master's student begin the very next week, and she and I spend the winter reviving the repertoire I learned some twenty years before. But in the spring, my new teacher graduates and moves away, leaving me with the name of her former high school piano teacher, a woman who has many adult students. Lessons won't begin with this teacher until the fall.

In the meantime, I am to spend a month at Point Reyes, California, at the Mesa Refuge, a retreat for environmental writers. And there, when it comes to maintaining what little I have regained at the piano, I will be on my own.

2

A Lesson with Mozart

"Too easy for children; too difficult for adults."

—ARTUR SCHNABEL ON MOZART'S SONATAS

The Mesa Refuge is a modern, asymmetrical house perched high on a bluff, nested in a luxuriant hillside garden. A winged muse poised on a gatepost greets new arrivals. The vast entry doors open to a cathedral-like foyer and a wall of windows looking northwest, framed by clambering roses, providing an unimpeded view of Tomales Bay and the seashore beyond. When I arrive, several cartons of research files I shipped from home are waiting for me, stacked neatly on the foyer's tile floor. I made notes and gathered documents for a decade to write a book about wilderness management; now I have the gift of time and support to begin it.

But first I must find a piano. Just as soon as I am settled in my upstairs room, I walk back down the hill a short distance to the village of Point Reyes Station, where I remember, on my taxi ride here, seeing a large church. I knock on the church office door, but no one answers. A small sign posted in the window lists the telephone number of the interim pastor. I return to the house and call her, and she directs me to a church elder, an attorney originally from Montana, who just happens to share my professional interest in public lands policy. He invites me to stop by his office to borrow his key to the church sanctuary, where a grand piano sits in state. The key is mine to use for the month. I have only been in Point Reyes a few hours, and I have a practice instrument! I return to the church and let myself in.

The sanctuary has a high, beamed ceiling, making the room pleasantly alive for music. Casement windows look out toward the parking lot on one side, and toward the sea on the other. Left open, they let in the salty smell of the bay and the pungent odor of dairy farms.

With my music under one arm, I walk down the aisle between the long columns of pews to the piano. It is covered in a heavy brown quilt tailored to its shape. I peel the quilt back only far enough to expose the keyboard and the music desk; the body remains cloaked like a patient on an operating table. I lift the fallboard. The name on it is too worn and scuffed to read. The keys are chipped and yellow. I press a few, listening. Out of tune. The mechanical action is as worn as old slippers, sloppy under my fingers, hard to control. For a few moments, I relish the silence and privacy of the sanctuary. Then I pull back the bench, sit before the keyboard, and begin to play the one piece I have memorized: the first prelude of Bach's *The Well-Tempered Clavier.*

The patient, it seems, needs rehabilitative surgery: the action clacks, some keys do not respond, and it has the insubstantial voice of an elder. I wish I could thank the church by giving them a new piano, or at least the services of a good technician. Still, this piano will do for a re-beginner struggling on her own. Out of my accordion file I pull the score for my self-assigned summer project, Mozart's G major piano sonata, and set to work.

I first began this piece some seventeen years ago, with my last teacher, Robert, whom I studied with at Mannes College. I never mastered the sonata, but this summer I hope to make it performance ready, or at least play it well enough to favorably impress my new teacher in the fall. So I keep to a daily habit: at the end of each afternoon I leave my desk at the Refuge, stroll beneath the eucalyptus trees, past high, fragrant hedges and magnificent bungalows, down the hill to town, with my music under my arm and the sanctuary key in my pocket.

Two weeks go by, and though I practice daily, my rendition of the Mozart gets no better—not even a *little* better. In fact, I reflect with mounting frustration, it seems the harder I strive to play the piece note perfect, the *worse* my performance becomes. What am I doing wrong? Every time I play a wrong note, I stop and start over from the beginning. When it is clear that does not work, I just keep playing, and then whole handfuls of notes go awry, my fingers stutter and stumble until the entire architecture of the piece collapses in a muddle on the keyboard. So I bring out the mental lash, grit my teeth, and *will* this piece to yield to me. But it yields nothing. By now, playing even a single wrong note makes me want to hurl the score across the room. This is not fun.

Why do I want to play piano, anyway? What a miserable, unforgiving experience it is. I feel betrayed by my dreams, by the siren song of the Rubinstein recording that led me back into this absurd and embarrassing venture. I should give up. I berate myself: *Who do you think you are?*

Inflamed with humiliation, I turn from the keyboard and look out the casement windows toward the bay. A storm is boiling up from the west, high winds sing in the tree branches; they saw and scratch at the windowpanes. The air in the sanctuary is heavy with the feel of dropping air pressure, oppressive with humidity.

Such a simple, beautiful, uncomplicated work is this Mozart, full of serenity and love and play. I hear the melodic lines in my mind's ear the way Robert taught me to hear them, like a miniature opera: First the young ingénue enters stage right, singing of love. Then her little brother, a rascal, scampers to stage left, his governess after him in a lower octave. Then out of nowhere, the fat village burgher runs up and down the stage steps, his cap set with a bouncing feather atop his askew powdered wig, his belly shaking as he gallops up and down the keyboard, pounding his cane along with the beat. What is he doing there? His part arrives for no apparent reason, other than perhaps Mozart's whim.

How ironic that such silliness, such lightness of heart, is being ground down into turgid constipation by my insistence on getting every note right. I do see that my reverence is killing my love for the piano, my desire to play, the music itself. I think: I bet Mozart would not care a whit if every note is right. And then I think: *So why should I?*

A small revolution lights up my brain. Why, indeed, should I care? Who am I playing for, if not for me? If playing is not fun, then why am I doing it? What would a few wrong notes cost me, anyway? It's not like the empty pews paid $50 each to hear me play.

The sky cracks open with lightning and a torrent comes down in a sudden rush, breaching the windowsills, sending me running to staunch the flood, slamming the windows shut as fast as I can. Thunder booms and shakes the church; the sky becomes a sheet of water. The charge of negative ions refreshes me, lifts my mood. I shudder with delight.

Suddenly I feel electrified. I have nothing to lose by playing Mozart in the spirit of Mozart, that is, with love, playfulness, irreverence. Give up the idea of right notes. *Just play! Be playful in your playing!* I almost say aloud.

I begin the sonata again, this time at a swift tempo, the way I hear the work in my head, launching myself into the music with verve and feeling. My fingers fly—I throw them at the keyboard as a painter might dash pigment against a canvas, willing to see whatever magic might arrange itself on its own. Thunder crashes again. The music sweeps me up into its arms, spins me about. Mozart and I, alone in this church, we are having a blast together. My hands know these notes, as well they should; all I have to do is get out of the way. I feel infected with a new attitude, a thrilling bravado. I laugh aloud. And I play not a single wrong note.

As I play the last chord of the pages I have worked through so far, I am overtaken with wonder. Why were all the notes right this time? An idea creeps into my mind: *You have been living your life the same way you have been learning this sonata.* I've been dour, self-denying, punitive for any infraction, withholding joy, chaining myself to a perfectionistic ideal. Just as I get in the way of my hands, I realize, so too do I get in the way of my soul. Hands know how to play, and soul knows how to live, if only I will trust them. What happens if I get out of my own way? I don't yet fully trust myself. But for just a moment, I trusted Mozart.

The storm is over now. I re-cover the piano, turn out the lights, and leave the sanctuary. The evening air is cool and fresh and I walk back to the house slowly, enjoying the play of clouds in the darkening sky.

That night I dream of my father. He arrives in Point Reyes by bus, a small, whining boy of five. His need for comfort is insatiable, more than I want to give. After walking about with him clinging to my hand, he becomes a man again. He sits in a canoe in a swift river, while I stand on shore, holding the rope from the bow. We say nothing. My father is still and silent in the canoe, a cutout, two-dimensional. I let go the rope, and stand and watch as the river carries my father off, the canoe diminishing in size, until finally, it rounds a bend in the river and disappears.

In the morning, I push all my boxes of wilderness research into a corner of my room and cover them with a tablecloth. Something in me is reclaimed, and I am ready to be as unfettered as that Mozart sonata. I am also ready for a new approach to the piano.

3

Piano Lessons

*"Whoever is moved by music to the depths of his soul,
and works on his instrument like one possessed . . .
will acquire virtuoso technique."*

—HEINRICH NEUHAUS, *THE ART OF PIANO PLAYING*

Molly Morrison's teaching studio sits high on a hill overlooking the Missoula Valley. Even before I reach the door of her walk-out basement, at the rear of her house, I can hear music. Through the glass I see two women sitting side by side at a glossy black grand piano. One of them rises at my knock, and pulls aside the sliding door. She's a matronly figure, dressed all in brown—a sweater set and a knee-length skirt—and her hair is a soft brown pageboy tinseled with gray. Her round blue eyes, set in a moonlike face, meet my gaze. She seems about to speak, but just then a tangle-haired shih tzu dog leaps out from between her brown pumps, yapping fiercely.

"Charles! Shush!" She waves the dog away, then wraps her cardigan about herself. "Don't mind him. Come on in and have a seat. We're just finishing a lesson."

The other woman, still seated at the piano, seems about my age. She beams a big smile at me and waves a jaunty hand, then turns back to the keyboard.

I sit on the sofa dividing the room, facing away from the grand piano. There's a Yamaha vertical to my right, its lid covered in piano trinkets, no doubt gifts from students. Floor-to-ceiling bookcases, holding music scores and books about the piano, cover the walls.

The student is struggling through a piece I do not recognize. "Nice work!" Molly exclaims when the music stops. "That is coming along well. Yes." The lesson is over. The student rises from the bench, and we turn to greet each other.

"Sandy, this is Perri, a new student," says Molly. Sandy takes my hand. "Good for you," she says, grinning. "But watch out for Molly." She winks. "She's a tough one!"

"Yeah, right!" says Molly, mock scorn in her voice. They laugh. Then Sandy lets herself out, and I am alone with my new teacher.

"Would you like to play something for me?" Molly and I settle before the piano, me on the adjustable artist's bench, and she in her straight-backed chair beside me. Every movement she makes is just enough in view to distract me. She smoothes her skirt across her lap and tugs her cardigan sweater closed again. I put Bach's first book of *The Well-Tempered Clavier* on the music desk and open to the first prelude.

"I get very nervous playing in front of people," I stall.

"That's okay," Molly says kindly. "Just do what you can."

I take a deep breath, and am about to touch the keys, when she stops me. "Here, I think the bench is a bit close to the keyboard, don't you? Let's move it back. And is it the right height for you? Sandy is shorter than you are, let's lower the bench." She turns the knob on one side before I have a chance to stand up. She stops when my elbows are just slightly higher than the keyboard, making a gentle inclined plane toward the keys. "That's better."

I begin the piece, but despite Molly's soothing words, I let my nerves get the better of me. I feel like I'm poised on a high wire, and can hardly breathe. I stop and restart several times. At last, I limp through to the end, relieved it is over, but disappointed in my poor performance. *I can play much better than that!* I want to protest.

"Okay, not bad! Very nice, really!" Molly says as I shake my head. Her big blue eyes gaze at me with bright compassion. "Let me show you something." She stands up and shoos me off the bench, sliding onto it herself. "Watch my hands. See how relaxed they are? See how I transfer all of my arm weight to the note I am playing, and then let go? Notice my wrists? See how they rebound, how flexible they are?"

Her soft, round hands float over the keys, fluid, almost boneless. The prelude is luminous under her touch.

"Now here's how you were playing." Abruptly her hands become stiff and flat, rigidly gripping the keyboard like claws. "See how *notey* that sounds? You can't move anywhere like that, holding yourself so stiff. You have to get up off the keys, let your hands float in the air. Think of tossing your hands back and forth."

"But how will I find the right notes if I lift off the keyboard like that?"

"Oh, you will. Your hands already know where to go. Just trust them. Here." She gets up and returns to her chair. "You try it now. Just the first line."

I sit down and begin again, and immediately I do notice the rigidity of my hands. I consciously soften and release them, but then I can no longer find my way.

"Just think of the music," Molly coaxes. "Your hands have this memorized."

I try it again with just the right hand, then with the left, then I put the hands together. Patiently she works with me on several repetitions of the first line. As my movement gradually relaxes, my hands do find their own way across the black-and-white landscape. Once the tension is gone, my fingers go right where they belong, startling me.

"You see? Much better! Try the next line."

I do, and it happens again. My hands can fly. The sense of effortlessness is deeply pleasurable. It sounds better, too, more like music, less like an exercise.

"That's it!" says Molly. "Let's work on some arpeggios this week." Sitting at the bench again, she shows me how to block the notes into chords, teaching the hands where to go, and assigns me C major. "Use your ear. Make them sound musical and connected." She puts my hand on her arm as she demonstrates, so I can feel her weight shift, her muscles tighten and release.

Uplifted by Molly's sincere encouragement, I leave her studio that first day feeling eager and determined.

In the days that follow, I work on the arpeggio, and on playing the Bach prelude with relaxed hands. It takes a lot of patience and concentration. I feel lazy and distracted, and don't really apply myself as well as I think I could. Perhaps the problem is how humble my assignment is. I want a grander, more ambitious goal, one that better fits my fantasy of possessing an innate, neglected talent that will surge to prominence, overcome all odds and my handicap of a late start, and surprise everyone by achieving greatness.

What exactly are my prospects, the prospects of an adult beginner? What should I expect from myself, given my age, given my abilities? These questions bear down on me. And even more, as I continue to study with Molly, week after week, I wonder, is she going to take me seriously? Will she put me on a program that will nurture my promise, just as she would if I were a precocious eight-year-old, or am I doomed to forever be on the "hobbyist" track, someone for whom real mastery, and therefore preparation for it, is not even up for consideration?

And I do want to master the piano. There have been, I learn, famous concert artists who got a late start: Ignaz Paderewski at the age of twenty-two, and Harold Bauer, at the age of twenty, began studying the piano as college students, and then went on to tour Europe as soloists the very next year. Sviatoslav Richter didn't seriously begin piano studies until he reached the Moscow Conservatory, at the age of twenty-seven. Heinrich Neuhaus, his teacher there, did not have to teach him much, and served mostly as a coach. But this level of virtuosity is not exactly the destiny of most adult beginners. Why not? Is it something mysteriously called "talent" alone that makes the difference?

I broach these questions to Molly, but this turns out to be a mistake. She says she won't let her students use words like "talent" and "gifted." Sometimes I think she must find my preoccupation with becoming a great pianist presumptuous and annoying.

"You can play anything you can hear," she tells me many times. "But you must hear deeply, and you must be infinitely patient." The only difference between a virtuoso and the rest of us, she maintains, are vast and innumerable hours and years of practice, more practice than most of us will ever devote ourselves to, if we wish to have a life besides. Her tone carries a gentle rebuke. "It's not enough to love the music," she says. "You have to learn to love the process. It's hard work, even for the gifted."

The first goal of our lessons is rehabilitating my stilted keyboard habits. Molly loans me a video, *Freeing the Caged Bird,* which uses film clips of Arthur Rubinstein to demonstrate good piano body mechanics. Rubinstein at the piano reminds me of Montana cowboys on horseback: they become a part of the animal, as easy in the saddle as if they are in a rocking chair. Rubinstein's body becomes an extension of his instrument; his spine grows out of the bench, each vertebra resting atop the next, a flexible spire with his head balanced on top, eyes cast down rather than neck bent to see the keyboard. His arms fall unrestricted from his shoulders, and he allows gravity to depress the piano keys, rather than using muscle power. This conscious relaxation grants him an obvious, effortless freedom. I study this video closely, sketching what I see in my lesson notes, to imprint it in my mind.

At first, Molly lets me select my own pieces. I want to finish the Mozart G major sonata, and I want to learn the first of the Mendelssohn *Songs Without Words*. After all, it is important, I feel, to play music that inspires me. Otherwise, it is too hard to find enough motivation to practice.

But after several months, my progress on the Mendelssohn is abysmal. I can only play what I have memorized through painstaking, endless repetition of the score. And this score is far too complex, with inner and outer voices like the parts of a choir, to learn in this way. I know it should not take so long, or be so difficult to learn this work, but I know no other way.

Molly lets me hit the wall on my own before she says a word.

"You aren't reading," she announces one day when I finally break down and ask why I'm not making progress. I'm sitting before the piano, with Charles, Molly's shih tzu, curled up in his accustomed place against the small of my back. "You aren't reading," she repeats. "You are playing by ear and by memory."

"I never really learned how to read." I blurt this out, before I have a chance to stop myself. *Now what? Will she dump me?*

"What is this note?" Molly asks, pointing to one in the bass line of the score. I have to stare at it and think it through before I can answer. "You should know that on sight, just like you know a letter of the alphabet when you see it, instantly, without thinking."

She gets up and pulls a folder of loose sheets from one of her many shelves. These are flashcards and pictures of random notes on clefless staves. "Take these home and practice recognizing the notes on sight by name, and then find them instantly on the keyboard. Keep changing the clef from treble to bass and back again. We're going to work

on your reading. From now on you will only play pieces you are able
to read, and instead of taking a year to learn one piece, you are going
to learn a new piece every week."

I know it is useless to protest, but I really do not like the idea of
giving up advanced repertoire. I've taken up the piano to play *this*
music, not baby pieces. How will I find my motivation? Meanwhile,
Molly is searching through another bookcase filled with sheet music.

"Here, you can borrow this." She presents me with a book of
beginning piano studies. I flip through them, feeling discouraged and
mortified. I've been demoted. I envision listless weeks of halfhearted
practice because to study such easy pieces is too humiliating.

"Let's try one and see if you can read it," Molly says. She puts the
book on the music desk, over the Mendelssohn score.

The piece looks so incredibly basic, I can't imagine I won't be able
to read it, but it collapses quickly under my fingers. I decide I am playing too fast, so I begin again, very slowly. But even with very slow
playing, I cannot read this music through on sight. I stop after only a
few bars. With a single blow, my musical illiteracy is laid bare. I feel
devastated. All my pianistic fantasies implode before my eyes.

"Okay, here's how you sight-read," says Molly, not granting me so
much as a moment of self-indulgence. Her protocol: Observe the key
signature, the time signature, the note patterns, the big leaps, and read
the music through in your head while counting. Then, when you play
it, hands together, play as slowly as necessary to play every note correctly in time. "Let's try it."

Now I find I can play the right notes if I go very, very, very slowly,
but then the notes do not have the correct value in time.

"You aren't counting."

"I-I don't know how to count." My admission brings back my
father's voice to my ear in an instant, as if he were in the room with
us: *"Count! Count!"* I hear him exhort me with an edgy ferocity as I
struggle to keep up with him while we play duets. Yet he never showed
me how to count. I have always cheated with my ear, just as I have
cheated with it to find the right notes instead of reading. Like my
grandfather, I am all ear and musical intuition. But a good ear alone is
not a ticket to advanced classical repertoire.

"What beat is this note on?" Molly demands, pointing to a random note in the midst of the score. This is even harder than naming the pitch of the note. I have to really study the score, count with my pencil on the notes to figure it out. There are *so many* notes in that measure! "You should always know what beat you are on, instantly."

"But why?" I wail. "What difference does it make?" Molly explains, but her explanation makes no sense to me.

"It's great that you have such a good ear." Her tone turns gentle when she sees my bafflement and distress. "Many people can't hear, so you have an important tool. But hearing is only one tool. You must also be able to read and count. It's like reading whole words and sentences, instead of just the individual letters. We'll spend some time every week on reading, counting, and theory."

My choices in this moment are really quite simple: I can protest, in a vain attempt to persist with my illusions. I can decide that playing the piano is just too difficult and humiliating, and quit. Or, I can take a third tack.

"Okay," I concede. I decide to embrace the unknown, the frightening, my own incompetence. My previous teachers, if they realized I was playing by ear instead of reading, must not have known what to do about it. But this time, with this teacher, I will get to the bottom of my impairment. I feel my appetite for this enterprise quickening. My piano studies have finally truly begun. "Take me back to the beginning," I say. "Give me the foundation I never got."

And so, week by week, I take copious notes at my lessons and practice diligently, giving up learning by ear. My reading improves; soon I can play all the pieces in the book Molly loaned me. I ace the tests in my piano theory workbook. I begin to gain confidence, and as my confidence builds, my attitude changes. My focus shifts away from the fantasy of what I might become, to the now of who I am, the present reality of my actual abilities. It's only by working with that present reality, Molly assures me, by learning to enjoy the process, in the moment, of just being with the piano, that I can make real progress. And my progress proves her right.

One day, after two months of work on reading and counting, Molly says I can return to learning *Songs Without Words*.

We begin by blocking chords and separating the inner and outer voices—the soprano, alto, tenor, and bass lines—then put them back together in varied combinations. The piece is tonally complex, and though my ear continues to help me out, when it comes time to play the piece as written, I can't do it.

"What beat are you on?" Molly suddenly calls out when I am halfway through the first line.

"Um," I hesitate.

"Count out loud while you are playing. Here's the beats." She writes them over the notes with a pencil, gouging the marks into the score: 1 + 2 + 3 + 4. "Focus on the beats."

I squirm on the bench. How can I play those complicated four voices if I am concentrating on counting? I won't be able to read.

"Just try it." She sounds encouraging. "Read from beat to beat, know which beat you are on and which note belongs to which beat. It's like having a map to the music. The beats are anchors. Just let the other notes be filler, you don't have to read them."

There is no escape. I close my eyes and take a deep breath, as if preparing to leap off a cliff. "It's okay," she coaxes, as if talking to a small, timid animal. "Just let it happen."

I exhale and put my hands to the keys. "One and two and three and four. One and two and three and four." We count aloud together, and then I begin to play. And something strange happens. The music simply *emits* from my hands. The beat is an oncoming locomotive, its wheels clacking in time; my hands leap aboard as it passes, and are carried along for the ride. The beat is the engine of the music, carrying my hands to the right notes. Focusing on the beats eats up so much of my attention, there is no room to read notes, too. I play through the first page, accurately, in time. I am making music with a piece I have never been able to play before. What just happened?

As with the Mozart sonata, I got out of my own way, but this time, counting beats was the vehicle. With my focus diverted to counting, my hands became free to do what they already know how to do. It felt exactly like reading aloud in full sentences for the first time. Your eyes move ahead to see the sentences coming, and the story flows instead of stutters from your tongue. I realize that I looked ahead to the emerging "sentences" of the music.

"I'm reading! I'm reading!" My glee is utterly childlike. "I want a gold star!"

Molly finds a sheet of gold stars she keeps for her young students, and puts one in my composition book under my notes for the lesson. Then she writes *Excellent!* and underlines it. My inner fourth grader is ecstatic.

"I'm going to make you the poster child for my adult students," Molly says. She sounds subdued, perhaps surprised. It occurs to me then that it must be very difficult to teach an ambitious, stubborn adult who can't read. My accomplishment belongs as much to Molly as to me. I start to castigate myself for being such a difficult student, but Molly stops me. She says it can easily take ten years before a student is able to read the bass and treble lines of a piano score at the same time.

"I think we can put this piece away now," Molly says. "Let's concentrate on your Mozart sonata. We have a piano party coming up in a month and I want you to have it ready."

4

The Piano Party

*"Every courageous act we commit in life transforms us in
some way. When we take our place onstage, shaking with
fear, and dare to make music, we re-create not only
a musical composition, but also ourselves."*

—MADELINE BRUSER, *THE ART OF PRACTICING*

Stage fright has always plagued me, even as a child. Once, when I
was fourteen, my father, who believed I could become a professional flautist, drove me to an audition for the all-state orchestra, and
I was so stricken with fear I refused to get out of the car. My father
carried me bodily into the auditorium, but he could not force me to
go onstage and play, and we returned home in bitter silence. When I
studied piano at Mannes, if I knew people were standing in the hall
near my practice room, I would freeze, unable to concentrate. These
reactions are actually normal and universal—playing in front of others
causes a rush of adrenaline that sends us into a "fight or flight" mode,
and almost all professional musicians have spent significant time working on managing this biochemical reaction. But I had refused the
opportunity to learn how to handle my fear, and believed it part of
who I was.

So when Molly announces the adult piano party and her expectation that I will play before a bunch of strangers, I tell her I don't think
it will be possible. "My hands will freeze, my mind will go blank. I
won't be able to do it," I tell her.

"Oh, well, then," she says, sounding unconcerned. "You certainly
don't have to play if you don't want to. But let's prepare the Mozart

anyway, and then when you are at the party, you can decide if you wish
to play or not."

Knowing I do not have to perform is reassuring. One of the benefits of taking up the piano as an adult is that practicing and performing are at our prerogative. We adult beginners have other advantages
over most children, too: we are self-motivated, we have greater intellectual powers, we are musically more sophisticated, and we are better
equipped physically to play the piano, which was designed for adult
hands and bodies, not children's. Most important, we've developed the
patience and self-discipline that effective practice requires.

Unfortunately, we also lack a child's natural confidence. We're accustomed to a certain level of competence in the world, and when it comes
to learning the piano, we must allow ourselves to be incompetent. We
climb out on an unfamiliar limb, something we may not have done
since we left school. Children compare themselves to other children.
We adults compare ourselves to Rubinstein or Horowitz and berate
ourselves accordingly. What business do we have taking up the piano
at our age? What a joke we are! To begin piano lessons as an adult is
an act of courage.

Molly has ten adult students in our small town in the sparsely pop-
ulated Northern Rockies, adults who are evidently willing to risk
humiliation by performing at a piano party. As it turns out, we are part
of a growing trend.

According to the Music Teachers National Association, the fastest-
growing group of new piano students is adults over the age of twenty-
five. Some took lessons as children, but were either pushed too hard
or lost interest. When their own children begin lessons, they return
to the piano as well. Others, like me, never did get to play the piano
as a child and always yearned to. They reach midlife, tally up what
they have accomplished and what they have left undone, and take up
the piano in pursuit of a long-deferred dream. New adult-beginner
method books, group classes, curricula, and organizations are appear-
ing. When piano teachers go to parties, they report, those they meet
invariably say, "I wish I had never given up the piano," or, "I have
always wanted to learn how to play the piano."

Adult amateurs are holding regular piano salons all over the country: There's the Adult Music Students Forum in Washington, D.C.,

the Boston Piano Amateurs, the Salon in Dallas, the Hudson Valley Piano Club, "Open Stage" in New Hampshire, and an adult piano students' group in San Francisco. Adult amateur piano competitions are gaining currency; the most famous is organized by the Van Cliburn Foundation.

I'm also not alone in my virtuoso fantasy. A cottage industry has sprung up to cater to us. "Record your own CD with a Full Orchestra" beckons the tiny ad in *The New Yorker.* "Make your dream come true." For a mere $4,595, you can record yourself playing a concerto with the Prague Radio Symphony Orchestra. The tab includes four nights in a first-class hotel in Prague, rehearsals with the orchestra, daily breakfast, daily trips to the recording studio, and the production of a master CD.

Interest in the piano is apparently undergoing more than a renaissance—it is becoming a movement.

I am surprised, because there are few activities more challenging and demanding than learning how to play the piano. So much attention must go to so many places simultaneously. It is a severe form of multitasking, where our entire beings—physical, emotional, intellectual, creative—must be fully engaged in the present moment. All at once, you are listening to the melodic line and creating the correct phrasing, listening for tone production and adjusting your touch, navigating the architecture of the keyboard by feeling for the proper intervals between notes, reading and analyzing the score and translating it instantly into physical motion, paying attention to the beat within the passage of time and the rhythm of the music, creating an artistic interpretation by understanding the music's larger structure, reading treble and bass clef simultaneously, playing two or four different parts in two hands simultaneously, operating the pedal, observing the parameters of the key signature, and paying attention to your body mechanics so they don't impede your freedom of movement.

It's a lot to ask of a brain—especially an older brain so long out of school. Especially in the context of raising a family, working at a job, having a marriage, maintaining friendships. But Molly encourages her adult students by reminding them that they are held back more by their fears and insecurities than by inability. The human brain can learn new things at any age. The difference between an intermediate player and an advanced player is primarily a matter of speed, Molly explains to me. We don't realize it, but the hands like to go fast, they prefer to go fast. They merely need to be allowed to do what they like to do, after certain patterns are learned, with slow and deliberate practice.

Under Molly's patient tutelage, my own relationship with the piano is becoming rich, complicated, and so rewarding, sometimes it feels as if it might swallow my life whole. The sensation of forging new neural pathways in my brain, of entrainment in the present moment, of the integration of my whole being from the physical to the spiritual is so consuming, so deliciously, deeply gratifying, it begins to feel like an addiction.

But attaining an "addiction" level of competence takes a lot of time and work. What does our passionate appetite for this instrument, our refusal to be daunted by it say about us? Why do we obstinately persist?

"Music teaches spirituality by showing a person a portion of himself that he would not discover otherwise," jazz pianist Bill Evans has said.

Molly puts it in more mundane terms. "It's hard to avoid yourself in the process of learning how to play the piano," she says. "You find out about your expectations, your patience, your optimism or lack of it. It's character building."

Molly's own decision to become a pianist, as a thirty-year-old returning college student, was sparked by her falling in love with Mozart, and she has very strong ideas about proper Mozart interpretation. I resist her guidance on performing the Mozart sonata at first. What I hear in this music is passion and drama. What Molly hears is delicacy and lightness. "Remember," she repeats again and again, "this music was written for the pianoforte, not the modern piano. The loudest a forte should ever be played is mezzo forte."

"But I'm playing it on a modern piano," I argue. "And I don't like delicate interpretations of Mozart." Yet I have to admit that Molly's own performance of this work, which she demonstrates for me many times, is sublime. She seems to have been born for this one composer. I have never heard Mozart played better. Perhaps I do not hear myself?

I begin tape recording my practice sessions, and immediately I do hear what my teacher hears: insensitive bombast. So I surrender to

Molly's guidance. Still, I find it difficult to make my touch light enough for this composer. I'm amazed to discover that how relaxed I am has everything to do with how I sound. Mozart never sounds right when I am tense. And performing makes me very tense. "That's why so many professional pianists avoid performing Mozart," Molly says.

A part of me wishes very much to be able to perform, and so, with the piano party looming on the horizon, I bear down on my practicing like never before, taking the sonata apart and working on individual sections, then putting them back together. First line: hands separately, then together very slow, then at speed. Second line: hands separately, then together very slow, then at speed. Then review the first line again, try to make it more musical. Work on conscious relaxation of my neck, spine, arms, wrists, hands. Envision Rubinstein's limbs falling from his straight-but-relaxed spine, his head balanced on top, his movement arising from the fulcrum of his hips, and let my body imitate him. Pick out a problem area of just a few notes and work it, slowly. Play the left hand blocked into chords, name the chords, add the right hand. Play the whole piece very slow. Then play at tempo. Check myself with the metronome and correct timing errors. Play it through without stopping, no matter how many mistakes I make. And then also I practice away from the piano—playing the music in my head as I hike in the mountains, making decisions about interpretation that I then bring back to the keyboard.

So it goes, day after day, like building a structure from blocks. Sometimes the tedium of practice feels suffocating, especially when nothing I do improves a troublesome passage. Then I take it to Molly, and together, we analyze the problem. I soon learn that encountering difficulties at the keyboard is not evidence of a lack of talent at all, but rather just ordinary and inevitable challenges to our problem-solving skills. Molly teaches me how to apply analysis and creativity to surmount every obstacle. In a few short weeks, my performance of this sonata is so greatly improved, it is hard to believe I once struggled with it to the point of nearly giving up the piano.

✦

The day of the party arrives. My husband, Oliver, no doubt imagining he'll be stuck listening to a lot of bad piano playing for hours, reluctantly agrees to come with me, for moral support. The party is at the home of Molly's student Clara Erickson and her husband, Ron. They live high on a hill, south of town. We hike up their steep driveway, a salad for the potluck supper in Oliver's arms, my music in mine. Ron takes our coats, and Sandy, the only other student I know here, jumps up and warmly embraces me. I introduce Oliver to Molly, and she introduces us both to the room full of students. They are men and women, mostly middle-aged, doctors and teachers and salesmen, housewives and retirees. Each holds a book of music anxiously on his or her lap. The spouses are immediately recognized by their relaxed affect, and their looks of bored, if affable, tolerance.

In the spacious living room we find seats arranged to face a Baldwin grand piano. The house is glassed in, with a view of the mountains all around, and the open floor plan creates an acoustically live environment, so the piano's lid is propped up on the short stick. Clara and several others are in the kitchen, arranging the food and the many bottles of wine, which the "rules" dictate we may not drink until after we have played. Others take turns trying out the piano, to prepare themselves.

I feel as well prepared with this Mozart sonata as I ever have with any piece, but I am already very nervous, and must remind myself that I don't have to play. Soon everyone takes their seats and the recital begins. Molly calls up the first student, who, she says, has only been playing for three months, and will play with only her right hand. A woman about my own age makes her way to the piano.

As she sits down, we can see her hands shaking violently. She maintains a smile that is more of a grimace, but through all her starts and stops, she keeps going. I feel her heart palpitations as my own. I wince for her. But then she finishes and stands up, flushed with pride and embarrassment. She hastily gathers her music and finds her seat again as the room explodes into applause and bravas. I join in with gusto. How brave she is!

Sandy is next, and plays a simple piece by the American composer Dennis Alexander, a mentor of Molly's. She smoothes her skirt and gives a nervous preamble about the music. She stops and starts a lot, says, "Oh, shoot!" at one point, then begins again. When she gets to the end, she grabs her music off the desk, stands up, and takes a brisk little bow. We roar our approval.

Molly calls two more students to the piano, and again, they play very simple pieces, struggle, and restart repeatedly. Their hands shake, their nervousness makes us ache for them. Each in turn gets her round of warm, enthusiastic applause. And I begin to feel foolish that I do not want to play for fear of embarrassing myself. Clearly the accomplishment here is to play at all, not to play note perfect. Furthermore, the audience is more than forgiving, it is positively supportive. We are not here to judge, as my father so often did when I played as a child, but to cheer on, to encourage. The more imperfect the performance, it seems, the louder, longer, and more sincere the applause. We are all in this together, the group's genuine smiles seem to say, helping each other conquer our fears. I need to get over myself. I cannot fail here.

"Perri, would you like to play?" Molly looks at me with her round, bright eyes, expectantly. I stride up to the piano, feeling the terror of all eyes on me, and yet feeling a bit reckless and brazen. "This is Perri. She studied some years ago in New York, and she is only just returning to the piano after many years away from it." My heart is pounding. I want to have as little expected of me as those other beginners. "Perri, tell us what you are going to play."

By now I am sitting on the bench, my music open on the desk. Molly takes a seat to my left, to turn the pages. My palms are already damp, hands shaking. I take a deep breath and exhale to release the adrenaline. Even though I am facing the small crowd, I block them out of my vision, and stare off into space when I say, "I'm going to play the first movement of Mozart's G major sonata, Köchel 283."

I play the first bars in my head, to remind myself of what I am about to do and to prepare my ear, and then I plunge in, hardly breathing. I stumble through the first page with frozen hands, but I brazen my way to the second page. Suddenly I am swimming along in the music; I don't sound too bad. This thought feels like a strong wind blowing through me, and a sense of lightness and exhilaration takes hold. In my mind, I am alone, comfortable and familiar with the piano and the music, and the audience isn't there.

When I get to the third page, I must confront some passages I haven't fully mastered, and I worry in anticipation of each. Amazingly, my hands see me through, and the thought "I'm doing it! I'm doing it!" strikes me. At that instant, I lose my place and must stop to find it again. I make some flip comment to my audience, a blurt from nerves, and then begin again where I left off.

Those derailing thoughts are what Molly calls "your own personal Greek chorus," the saboteur of many a performance. "Damn it!" I think, and start holding my breath again. Only half a page to the finish, I must power through somehow. I drop fistfuls of wrong notes, and flub the final chords, but make it to the end I do.

When my hands lift from the keyboard, there is an immense roar of applause, thundering in my ears, striking me almost blind with the shock of it. Can it be—my fellow adult amateurs are rising to their feet, giving me a standing ovation? Or is it only that somehow, in the space-time continuum, I've been transported to my opening night at Carnegie Hall?

I know their enthusiasm probably means I was the most dreadful performer yet; it is more of a newcomer's welcome than an expression of musical appreciation, but it feels good anyway. They are applauding not the perfection of my performance, but my daring to perform at all. In that grateful moment, I decide to take their measure of success for my own. I came to the party, I played, and I played my piece all the way through. It is a huge accomplishment. I am filled with happiness. Amazing myself, I think: *I want to do that again!*

As I step away from the piano, Sandy hands me a glass of red wine, which I gladly gulp. I sit back down beside Oliver, buzzing with euphoria. He puts his arm around my shoulders and squeezes. I let the wine soothe my nerves enough to focus on the playing of the next students.

It is then that I discover I have been tricked.

The next student up is Clara, and she plays a Spanish dance by Granados, a composer I am not familiar with. While her performance is a bit stilted from nervousness, she plays it all the way through without any mishaps, and finishes with a grand flourish. The students who follow her can truly be called pianists—each is better than the last. Anne plays a Bach fugue I had tried to play once and gave up on, and it sounds, if not note perfect, then very musical. Jean, who is a piano teacher herself, plays an entire Beethoven sonata, with passion and mastery. It is a beautiful and deeply enjoyable performance.

Had I known that such accomplished performers were to follow, or had these more advanced students played first, I would have doubt-less stuck to my stage fright and my chair in the audience. I would never have experienced my small triumph. Wasn't that clever of Molly. A new desire wells up: to permanently overcome my stage fright.

By now, everyone has played, and we each have our glass of wine as our reward. The room bubbles with voices as we move to the kitchen for our potluck supper. Every single person there approaches me, one after the other, to introduce themselves and to congratulate me on my playing. "You play with so much passion," says Gary, who played some jazz standards. "You did so well with Mozart, and he is so very hard to play well," says Anne. Each person finds something spe-cific to praise and remember about my Mozart sonata.

But it isn't just me they approach. All the students are roaming the room, each giving every other student a few words of praise, making specific points about what they liked. Following their example, I seek out the first player, the beginner who played with just one hand, and I tell her how she inspired me with her bravery: "I thought, 'If she can go up there after studying for only three months and risk making flubs in front of everyone . . . '"

The circulating piano students grow silent when they overhear these words. Then someone cackles: "Flubs? What flubs?" And we all break up into laughter.

5

The Search Begins

I've been practicing at the music school every evening, and most of the time I can find a decent instrument. But all music school practice room pianos suffer from infrequent maintenance and intensive use, and these pianos are no different. Sometimes all the rooms are occupied, or the building is closed, or there is no parking nearby and I must walk a long way in the dark, in bad weather, in finger-freezing cold. Still, I don't really think about buying or renting a piano to have at home; I like being surrounded by music students and the jangle of harmonious noise in the school's basement.

Not long after the piano party, a friend asks me to "babysit" her family's 1905 Steinway upright during her sabbatical year. She moves the piano into my home, and asks only that I play it and keep it in tune. I'm quickly spoiled by this windfall: The piano's case is beautiful, inlaid mahogany, and having my own instrument to play whenever I wish is a great luxury. So I decide my friend's sabbatical year will also be my timetable for buying a piano of my own.

As a modest player of modest means, my aim is to find a used upright in decent shape for about $3000. This is not to be some ultimate dream piano, but a practice tool, a workhorse.

I begin with Missoula's three piano stores. The first is on the main drag, and a grand piano beckons through the front window. Two columns of grand pianos form an avenue leading to the rear of the store, where many new uprights are clustered. I make my way to them.

I am almost to the first upright, when a very tall and imposing white-haired gentleman intercepts me. He addresses me in a harsh Dutch accent. "Do you play?" he demands.

"I am a student, a beginner," I offer. "I'm looking for a good used upright to practice on."

"Yes, well, these Samicks would be perfect for you. They were designed by my friend Klaus Fenner, a *German* piano designer. They are an excellent value." He gestures to the studio upright beside him, waving me to the bench to try it.

I sit down, and the man hovers over me. His height and his autocratic manner are intimidating, and I feel my stage fright galloping back, inducing a mild panic. I manage to play a few notes, while the man watches closely.

"No, no, no!" he interrupts. "Your technique is terrible! You should not hold your hands like that!" I freeze.

"Let her play!" A woman's voice trills sweetly, persuading. I turn to see a slender, pleasant-looking woman. Her graying hair is pulled back with a grosgrain ribbon tied in a meticulous bow, and her reading glasses are propped halfway down her nose, making her look like an old-fashioned librarian. Her voice lilts with an accent—American influenced by Dutch. She smiles at me. "Take your time."

The white-haired autocrat stalks off to the rear of the store, then disappears behind a curtain. The woman retreats to an office, so we are out of each other's sight. I recover my composure enough to play Bach's first prelude from *The Well-Tempered Clavier.*

I dislike the Samick at once. The tone is annoying, brittle. The keyboard is unresponsive. I wander from upright to upright, lifting fallboards and playing a few notes, sometimes sitting down long enough to play a few bars. They are all new Samicks. They all sound and play exactly alike.

The man reappears, towering over me again. "So, how do you like them?"

"I'm afraid I don't," I say. "What else do you have?"

"You don't like them?" he exclaims, incredulous. "Klaus Fenner is a great friend of mine, and he is a top German designer. These are the best value you will find in any upright, anywhere." The words seem to click out of his mouth, they are spoken with such clear enunciation.

"I'm sorry, they are not to my taste."

"That is perfectly all right." It is the woman again. She is at my shoulder. "Why don't we have a look at the older uprights, shall we?" And she leads me to the farthest reaches of the showroom, where a row of very tall antique American uprights, mostly in oak and mahogany, stand along the rear wall. "Try these," she says, with a gracious sweep of her hand. "They are very nice."

The autocrat, still spluttering about the Samicks, retreats to a workshop, which I can now see beyond a parted black curtain. A young man is in there, too, his face illumined by a work lamp; he's gluing parts onto a mysterious-looking contraption that must be a piano action.

I like these old uprights better; they remind me of the piano I grew up with. They have a better tone than the Samicks. But every one of them needs work. One makes lots of annoying mechanical noises. Another has keys that don't work. The woman, who has rejoined me, says not to worry; all of these uprights will be refurbished by the shop's owner, the white-haired gentleman, and they will be perfect when they are done. "I can call you when one of them is ready, and you can come in and play it," she says, very sweetly. "Here, take my card. Call me in about a month. We should have something for you to try by then."

On my way out, I allow myself the indulgence of playing a few bars on each of the grand pianos that form the aisle to the door. There are two Steinways, a Kawai, a Baldwin, and a Yamaha, all of them used. The last piano is an older grand in a beautiful, high-polish mahogany case—the piano in the window. I lift the fallboard. "Schimmel," it says, a make I have never heard of. I touch a few keys and feel stung by the beauty of the tone. I sit down to play, and my hands feel carried away by the perfection of the touch, as if the piano is playing me. I sigh. A grand piano is simply not in the cards. Too expensive. Yet this one is so beautiful. It is meant for a real artist, not a beginning adult student like me.

✦

Next I visit the local Yamaha dealer, who also sells new Baldwin verticals. This store is brightly lit, situated on an avenue of strip malls, and is owned and managed by jazz pianists. They sell band instruments and sheet music, too. Up on a mezzanine is a new Schimmel upright with a futuristic white fiberglass case. I play a few bars of the Mozart sonata on it, and it seems a perfect Mozart piano, refined and delicate. It has a lovely action, but is too expensive, and even the salesman jokes about the space-age case. There is also a new model, the Yamaha S4 grand. It aspires to the same performance level as a European or American instrument, the salesman says. It is nice—but not $64,000-worth of nice. I don't care for any of the Baldwin or Yamaha verticals I play. The Baldwins seem a bit lifeless. And the Yamaha tone is too bright and piercing.

I'm hoping to find a used instrument, and this store doesn't have them, so I move on to Missoula's third and least-illustrious piano store. The owner is an old tuner gone deaf. He and his son run the place. The "showroom" is a dim, mildewed, dusty warehouse, with upright pianos packed together so tightly it is hard to squeeze in behind the keyboards to play them. Most of the inventory is old, broken-down spinets, the smallest-size vertical piano made. I lift a few dusty fall-boards and strike many sour or dead notes. Most of these pianos are just about unplayable.

But there is a shiny, new-looking Yamaha vertical here, the model U3 in a high-polish ebony finish. I can rent it for $35 a month, with payments going toward the purchase price of $3,500. The Yamaha sounds nice, especially compared to the broken-down spinets, but the bass has a loud buzz, and it is out of tune; still, the price is right. The son says the piano is five years old, and the buzz will be fixed and the piano tuned before delivery. I ask him to put the Yamaha on hold. When I get home, I call the manufacturer and ask their opinion about fixing the buzz in the bass. I don't want to buy the instrument if this defect could return.

When I give Yamaha's U.S. representative the piano's serial number, he informs me it was built in 1964 for the more humid Japanese market, and is not designed for an arid climate. These pianos are known as "gray market," he explains. I call the store and cancel the rental. Piano shopping is turning out to be more complicated than I expected.

Remembering the promise of the first shop's manager, I call to ask if any of the antique pianos are ready. "Yes, we do have an old American upright ready for you to try." She sounds excited to hear from me. "Can you come in tomorrow?"

The piano is a seventy-five-year-old Kurtzmann, a respected American brand established early in the nineteenth century. It has a nice tone, a decent action, a beautiful oak case, and it is only $1,300.

But the Yamaha experience has taught me caution. I decide to research Kurtzmann, so as not to make any unpleasant future discoveries.

I turn to the Internet, which has only recently become a habit. A cursory online search of "Kurtzmann piano" turns up a post on a newsgroup called rec.musicmakers.piano, otherwise known as "rmmp." Someone named Rosemarie posted the year before that she had acquired an old Kurtzmann, and did anyone know anything about its quality as an instrument? There are no replies to her post, but the author's e-mail address is listed. I write to her, asking how she likes her Kurtzmann now, and what can she tell me about it.

I receive a reply back almost immediately.

"Don't do it! I paid $300 for mine, and while the bass sound is lovely, it's not a great piano otherwise. Generally it's good only for a 'beater.' A piano deteriorates with time, unlike a fine violin. Unless a piano technician is world renowned, he probably can't revive it.

Then she gives me my first valuable piano shopping advice:

The newer you can get the better. $1,300 should buy you a twenty-year-old Kawai in better shape! Look around patiently—you don't want to waste your money or be frustrated at not getting the sound you want.

We exchange e-mails in a flurry. I have so many questions, and Rosemarie, a piano teacher in Seattle who is often hired to advise on piano purchases, seems to have the answers.

Go to the best shops you can find. Play their high-end pianos a few times at least, and find out the sound you like. PLAY the Bösendorfers and Steinways—you want to know what quality sounds like. THEN choose. It's a little like decorating your house after years of reading Architectural Digest rather than Woman's Day. HA! You have a totally different look, although you may spend the same $$$ at garage sales.

Before you buy a thing, listen, listen, listen. Why not make a trip to Seattle? More pianos to hear.

◆

A month later, I am on a plane to Seattle, to commence research for a long-term project. I have a modest hotel room within walking distance of downtown, and the use of a rental car. For a week I conduct interviews from Olympia to Sedro-Woolley and points between. In whatever spare moments I can find, I pore over the local yellow pages under "Pianos," and telephone as many shops as I can. There is no time to meet Rosemarie, but we do speak by telephone, and she recommends piano stores with the best inventory. She also gives me the name of her technician, Steve Brady of the University of Washington, in case I need someone to inspect a used piano for me.

By now, on Rosemarie's advice, I have bought *The Piano Book: Buying & Owning a New or Used Piano* by Larry Fine. This is the bible of piano shoppers everywhere, and I carry it with me into every showroom. Larry Fine is a Boston-area piano technician who hired top technicians from around the country to evaluate all the piano makes available in the United States. The chief advantage of taking the book with me is if I encounter a piano I've never heard of before, I can open the book and read what piano technicians have to say about it.

And I do discover many brands I have never heard of before. Among them are Petrofs from the Czech Republic, Blüthners from Leipzig, Prambergers from Korea, and Charles Walters from Indiana.

I play new Steinways, Kawais, Yamahas, and Bösendorfers as well, and I find an immense variety of "stencil" models from Korea and China. These pianos have the names of famous and now defunct American makes on their fallboards—Knabe, Weber, Chickering—but the name is all they have in common with these venerable brands.

My goal at this stage is not to buy, but to follow Rosemarie's advice and find "my" sound. I play a Steinway "D," the concert grand, expecting to love it, but I do not—I find it unsubtle and difficult to control. I expect to be smitten by the Bösendorfer, Rosemarie's dream piano, but I am not. To my ear, it's a huge piano with a very small, inexpressive tone. The Blüthners are too saccharine, with a sweet, uncomplicated tone. The Chinese pianos' actions are difficult to control, and their tone is brash. The tone of the Kawais is subtle, but the feel of the keyboard is too stiff.

I play every piano on the floor of every showroom I visit, both grands and uprights. In downtown Seattle, I don't find many pianos within my budget, except the Chinese instruments. The dealer who sells Bösendorfer also sells Charles Walter uprights, a very good value. The *Piano Book* gives them high marks, but they leave me uninspired.

I began shopping thinking that it doesn't matter what piano you buy, so long as all the keys work and it holds a tune. So why don't I just choose something, anything? I can't bring myself to do it.

On my way to the airport to return home, I have just enough time to duck into one more store. I decide I will buy a piano now. When might I be in Seattle again? There's nothing I like and can afford in Missoula, and Seattle, nearly five hundred miles to the west, is the nearest major city.

I exit the interstate at Federal Way and follow the directions the store's manager gave me over the phone. The showroom is small, and the pianos are very tightly crammed together. There are lots of uprights, not very many grands. When I walk in, a piano technician is at work, tuning a grand in a corner. The manager greets me and I explain my time is limited, that I have to catch a plane, but I want to play everything on the floor.

"Please make yourself at home and play whatever you like," the manager says.

"Won't I disturb your tuner?"

"He's used to it. Don't worry about him."

The setup is perfect for maximum efficiency. Nearly a dozen Charles Walter uprights are laid out in a row, so I can slide myself before each keyboard, one after the other. Several new Schimmel uprights are also displayed shoulder to shoulder. In one corner is a beautiful six-foot grand piano in cherry wood. I do not even lift the fallboard. The price tag says $23,000, and I need to stay on task.

By now I have had lots of practice trying out pianos, and I only need to play a few notes on each to know if I am interested. Once again, the Walter verticals are nice, serviceable student pianos, but none of them inspire me.

I move on to the Schimmels. Remembering the old Schimmel grand I played in Missoula, I am hopeful I will like these. But they sound nothing like the grand or the futuristic vertical I played. They are very bright. They sound more like the new Yamahas. I ask the manager, "Did they change these pianos? I played a Schimmel before and it didn't sound like these."

Yes, he confirms my suspicions, this piano was recently redesigned. The new Schimmel grands here are also very bright, with a light, quick action I find appealing. The manager excuses himself to go out for lunch. I look at my watch. I have a little more time.

"Have you been looking for very long?" says a voice. It is the piano technician, who has raised his head up from beneath the grand piano.

"Just started, really."

"Well, you play beautifully!"

"And you are a very good salesman!"

"No, I mean it. When you get your piano, I have just the technician for you. He tunes the way you play. He does work for the Seattle Opera."

Tunes the way I play? Now I am thoroughly confused. What does that mean?

"You should try that one, over there," says the tuner, nodding toward the cherry-wood grand as he begins packing up his tools.

I approach the instrument. The polished cherry wood gleams. The case's Chippendale style is elegant and graceful. I lift the fallboard: Charles Walter.

"I didn't know they made grands," I say, mostly to myself. I sit down and play Mendelssohn's first of the *Songs Without Words,* just a few bars, and stop abruptly, moved by the liquid beauty of the tone. I play through all of my limited repertoire. I even pull out some music I am only just learning, to have something more to play on this piano. It has a gorgeous, great big, open, sunny American sound. Lots of complexity and depth in the tone, but warm and good-natured, kind of like the girl next door. The dynamic range is wonderful, the action easy to control, and the pianissimos are perfect. I like it much better than even the Steinway and the Bösendorfer grands I've played, pianos that sell for $60,000 to $125,000. That makes this piano, at $23,000, a steal. If only I had room for a grand piano!

"That's a very special piano, for a lot of reasons," says the technician, who now stands beside me.

"But I don't have room for a grand. I'm looking for a five-thousand-dollar upright!" My budget has increased, for realism's sake, over my week in Seattle.

The tech must hear the grief in my voice over the prospect of not having the Charles Walter, for he takes a small white card from the manager's desk and begins writing on the back of it.

"Here's the name of someone who can help you. He's a piano designer and rebuilder." He pauses as if to consider. "He also has a brother who is a piano inventor and rebuilder. One's the good brother and the other is the bad brother." He winks as he hands me the card. "I'll leave you to figure out who is which."

I look at the block letters on the back of the card:

DEL FANDRICH

DARRELL FANDRICH

"One of them should be able to help you find an upright that will satisfy you," the tech says, pointing the tip of his pen at the card as I clutch it. "Good luck."

"Thank you!" I say, and shake his hand. Then I hastily jam the card into my blazer's breast pocket, gather up my raincoat and briefcase, and dash out to catch my plane.

✦

Who is the good brother and who is the bad brother? When I get home, I look up the Fandrichs online. Del, I learn, designed the Charles Walter grand I am smitten with, and remanufactures grand and upright pianos for individual clients from his workshop in Hoquiam, Washington, on the Olympic coast. Darrell, Del's older brother, invented an upright piano action that plays like a grand piano's, and is installing it in Czech uprights and calling them Fandrich & Sons pianos. His workshop is about an hour north of Seattle, in Stanwood, Washington. Both brothers seem promising sources for a good upright, and I write to them both.

Del Fandrich's reply:

> Sorry, no, we have don't have any uprights for sale. The condition of the piano market is such that it is not economically viable for us to reman- ufacture upright pianos for resale. . . . We can only get about 25% of the price for an upright that we can get for a grand. Often that is less than we have in the piano.

From Heather Fandrich, Darrell's wife and business partner, I receive this answer:

> *Let me know when you will be in Seattle and we'd be happy to show you our pianos. We like showing them to people just to spread the word. Please bring your music and plan to spend as long as you like playing them.*

But, unfortunately, there are no more plans for reporting trips to Seattle. It will be more than a year before I can return to the area. I try to figure out how I can get that Charles Walter grand after all. Redesign the living room? Move to a new house? These questions simmer in the back of my mind as I continue to search for an upright.

Over the next year, I travel a great deal for work. In May, I attend a conference at Yale and grab a quick look at pianos in New Haven. In December, I go to Boston for another conference and take the train to New York, where I have two days to look at pianos before visiting family on Long Island. In February, my work takes me to San Francisco, and I visit two piano dealers there before catching my flight home. Then in June, I attend another conference in Banff, Alberta, and manage to haunt the piano stores of Calgary for a couple of hours.

Though my schedule is very full, including early-morning and evening interviews, I soon devise an efficient piano search strategy: I begin my arrival at each hotel with a look at the Yellow Pages and calls to as many local stores as possible. I then visit only those dealers who have the most interesting selection on their floor and who are also convenient to my hotel or an interview.

On the way home from Calgary, I arrange for a five-hour layover in Salt Lake City so I can play two makes of upright pianos I have not yet been able to find: Schulze Pollmann, made in Italy, and Astin-Weight, a local, family-owned company.

The SPs have exquisite cases—my favorite is the peacock mahogany—but every one of the four models I play has a problem with the bass/tenor break. At the point inside the piano where the copper-wound bass strings change to plain steel wire, the piano's voice changes, and the left side of the keyboard—the bass side—has a dif-

ferent tonal quality than the right side. This is a common design problem, I later learn.

The Astin-Weights have a handsome open-pore oak finish, and
they are well made, but the tone booms uncontrollably, and the action
is sloppy. These would be excellent pianos for a church or a school,
where loudness and durability are important. But the company's
advertised promise that they play like a grand piano is only true in
terms of the volume of sound, not the touch.

After playing these uprights, plus Mason & Hamlin, Petrof, Kawai,
Yamaha, Baldwin, Blüthner, Boston, Steinway, Haessler, Irmler, Charles
Walter, Samick, Young Chang, and many others, I have played perhaps
hundreds of instruments, and I am running out of available makes.

By now I have increased my budget to $8000, and there are plenty
of nice, new instruments available for that kind of money. I remind
myself that I am an adult student, still learning the basics. Why not get
any serviceable, well-made upright and be done with it? At Banff, I
practiced for a week on the Yamaha U1 studio uprights in the Banff
Centre practice rooms and was perfectly happy with them. So why
can't I bring myself to end my search with such a piano?

It's not because I enjoy piano shopping; actually, I hate it. I hate the
obsequious salesmen who won't leave me alone, I hate playing in front
of them and the other customers. I'm annoyed by out-of-tune instruments, the inconvenience of finding a store in a strange city, the added
pressures the search puts on my already overscheduled time. And yet,
I won't settle. I don't understand myself at all.

And then, I discover Piano World.

6

Piano World

*" 'What is it that's so fascinating about pianos?' I don't
have the heart to answer that it's not the pianos . . . it's
the people who love them that are fascinating."*

—POSTED BY MATT G. ON PIANO WORLD

Only a few years earlier, my piano shopping experience would
have been entirely different. Like previous generations of
beginning piano students, I would have settled for a "good enough"
local piano, and carried on with my studies. I might have bought a console at a garage sale, or an old upright abandoned when its owners
moved, or even the gray-market Yamaha with the bad bass bridge from
the secondhand shop. And, just a few years earlier, Molly's studio would
have been the only place to meet other late-blooming pianophiles.

But by the second year of my piano search, the Internet and its
online communities have become pervasive, and are the avenue of first
resort when trying to find or learn about just about anything. With a
purchase as expensive and complicated as a piano, it is only natural for
piano students—or their parents—to turn to the World Wide Web. I
quickly and easily find online many other piano shoppers in my situation, coming together to share information. One of them directs me
to a website called Piano World.

This is the best piano forum on the Net, writes a man named Mark,
from Massachusetts, whom I "meet" on an online bulletin board
known as Mr. Land's Board, a crossroads for piano shoppers, dealers,
and technicians. Mark wants to know what I think of the Astin-
Weight I played in Salt Lake City, and in exchange for my impressions,

he shares with me links to several online piano communities. Mark's endorsement of Piano World in particular spurs me to click on that link immediately: *I learned more from the "regulars" on this board than from all my reading and visiting of piano dealers.*

Those words launch an association that soon becomes essential both to my piano search and to my life as an adult beginner. Piano World is where I catch an incurable fever—a fascination with the world's finest pianos—and find kindred spirits who suffer from the same affliction.

On the day I first visit Piano World, its members are celebrating the end of "Penny's" piano search, a search they participated in for many months, some virtually, others in person. Reading back through the discussions, I learn that Penny is a wife and mother in California who is particular about decorating and is determined to have a red grand piano as a dramatic foil for her living room's yellow walls. She and her husband and their two boys are all beginning piano students. Penny chose a Schulze Pollmann model 190 grand in mahogany briar. Penny has just signed the purchase agreement, and after accepting everyone's congratulations, begins plotting with other forum members on how to surprise her husband with it on his birthday.

I explore the site a bit more. In a thread called "Piano Withdrawal," "Derick," an inventor at IBM, writes that he's had to go for two months without a piano and it is almost like trying to quit smoking. He ends up buying a Bösendorfer Imperial, a nine-foot concert grand, and putting it in his condominium apartment.

In a discussion on how to start a local piano club, "Nina" writes about her group's roving monthly meetings, which allow members to play many different pianos. Their most recent meeting was in a trailer park, near her home in Phoenix, Arizona. Inside the trailer was a Yamaha C5 concert grand, previously used by the Metropolitan Opera. *This was one great piano,* she writes. *I had to appreciate their priorities.*

A thread on buyer's remorse doesn't find much of it. "Thomas," of Sausalito, California, writes that he cannot believe he has bought a new grand piano when he is driving a car with 530,000 miles on it and living in a condominium of only nine hundred square feet. *Yet my Bechstein still qualifies as the smartest purchase I ever made, sounds better every day, and is an indispensable part of my life.*

The confounding seductiveness of pianos is a frequent topic. "Ted," a composer in New Zealand, starts a thread called "Why this wooden box with bits of wire?" and encourages us to try to explain our fascination. "Jeanne W" comes up with the idea of piano trading cards. *What is wrong with me?* she writes after posting her proposal. *See what playing all those great pianos does to your mind?* Others seem alarmed by the intensity of their fascination. *Why must new pianos look so seductive?* wails "Allazart." *Musical sirens they are, drawing hapless musicians to financial shipwreck. I must resist!*

When I arrive, Frank Baxter, the site's owner, has only just re-created Piano World after flame wars shut down its previous incarnation, and there are only a hundred or so members. Quickly membership swells into the tens of thousands, and the site becomes a busy crossroads for an international subculture of piano devotees, a unique collection of personalities marked by intelligence, wit, and—not infrequently—combativeness.

In time, Frank adds more forums to cope with the burgeoning interests of Piano World's members: a composer's forum, a jazz forum, a digital forum, an adult beginner's forum. There's even a forum to talk about everything *except* pianos and music, the Coffee Room. But initially, when I arrive, there are only three: the main Piano Forum, the Pianist Corner, and the Piano Tuner–Technician's Forum. Members cross back and forth between the three venues, but each has a core membership and enjoys its own particular culture.

The main Piano Forum is where we talk about piano shopping. The personalities of the "regulars" are soon as clear and recognizable to me through their online "voices" as if I have actually spoken with them. We get to know one another well, as members reveal things about themselves online that one wouldn't know on casual, in-person acquaintance.

The first forum member I "meet" is "Larry," a piano dealer, pianist, and technician in Atlanta. Actually, Mark of Massachusetts introduced me to Larry before I ever arrived at Piano World. When I e-mailed Larry, at Mark's suggestion, he recommended piano makes and dealers in my region. He seemed to know just about everyone involved with pianos. As he is three thousand miles away from me and we are unlikely to ever meet, Larry could only be motivated by a desire to help. Now here he is on Piano World, holding court, a primary resource for every newbie.

Larry soon becomes a pivotal—and controversial—figure on the forums. Abrasive and loving by turns, pugnacious, childish, hard-nosed, mean-spirited, magnanimous, and caring, his self-appointed mission is to rescue piano buyers in distress from unscrupulous dealers. His tagline is "I don't brake for sales weasels," and he is quick to recite, chapter and verse, the various tricks buyers have to watch for. When I report that one dealer told me he sells only the Charles Walter grand pianos built by Charles Walter himself, Larry wrote: *That one made me drop my baloney sandwich. Charles Walter is in his 70s, and is not building any pianos himself.*

To read Larry, one could quickly conclude that the piano business has about as much integrity as the used car business, if not less. Should a piano salesman show up on the forums and start touting a particular brand, he can expect a swift rebuke from Larry. Larry is legendary for his persistence in battle: get on his wrong side, and he will shout you down and run you off the forums, and he is not at all above junior high school–style mockery. Some newcomers make the mistake of trying to insult him back, but he is inexhaustible in his capacity to beat others down.

While Larry makes plenty of enemies, he also has his loyal following. They especially warm to his homespun stories about the customers in his Atlanta showroom, like the time he sold the parents of a little girl a Chinese grand piano for less than his cost, because he was so moved by how hard she fell for it. Clearly, to her, that Pearl River baby grand was the most beautiful piano in the world. To the shock of the parents, Larry made the purchase possible.

Another prolific poster is "Jolly." Jolly works in a hospital somewhere in Louisiana. With the help of Piano World members, he found a grand piano his family could afford, a Nordiska, made in China. He stayed on and became a daily community presence—even a twenty-four-hour-a-day presence. Jolly ends up making ten thousand posts on Piano World long before most of us make even a thousand. His family is in car sales, and, like Larry, he is sharp about the business side of things. But he also has a flair for the down-to-earth turn of phrase: *Quit acting like a bunch of whiny old women, laboring through Menopause*

Valley. Doggerel, ma'am. Papersack doggerel. Let 'er rip, tater chip. These are known as "Jollyisms."

Like the majority of forum members, I keep my identity and my e-mail address hidden. I show up strictly to get useful information, and I keep my posts infrequent, on topic, and impersonal. But in time, I see that Piano World is evolving into something much more than just an information resource; it is becoming a real-life community. Screen names are soon full-dimensional people to me, so much so, I even dream about them.

Norbert Marten, a German immigrant with a piano shop in Vancouver, British Columbia, soon becomes one of my favorite dealer participants. A Papageno-like character, full of twinkly mischief and humor, Norbert often makes some of the forum's most bizarre and inscrutable posts.

A newcomer asks:

If a piano "sounds great" to the customer, does that mean that whatever might be wrong with it can't be TOO badly wrong?

Norbert replies:

That's a highly intelligent but truly tricky question. Let's face it: there *are* tons of older pianos that sound *great* [of course always asking: in comparison to 'what' . . .] but when the tech comes, it goes . . . "Ach Du lieber" . . .

And then there are these technically *perfect* pianos [women-men, too! 😁] which . . . er . . . mean precious little to anyone but . . . well you tell me . . . ANYBODY?? . . . 😬

Soul-over-mind-over-heart-over-pocketbook type of scenario.

Oh I forgot over *tech* 😵

Don't forget the man.

Just make sure—he *knows* what he's doing to your soulful little heart aching for this particular piano you just found. . . .

But have mercy on the man: he may not even play the damn thing. 😫

And perhaps not *understand* completely. 😵

And you never know if he even has a heart himself. . . . 😌

So—who is the rightful *judge* here in this nice little quagmire?

*Your guess is as good as mine. [Hope you like my occasional style
of old European mysticism. . . . ☺]*

In the Pianist Corner, habitués are a bit younger, many of them are
in high school, college, or studying at conservatories. A few composers
and professional pianists hang out here as well. They post about their
recitals, their auditions, their trials with their teachers, and their posts
are often infused with a hormone-fueled anguish. This is where young
people applying to famous conservatories get advice on their audition
programs. Adult beginners get fingering advice for difficult passages.
Parents get tips on finding a good teacher for their child. Older students
embarking on a professional career get critiques of their sound clips.
Seasoned concert artists share their tips for overcoming stage fright.

For me, the Pianist Corner is like reliving my first summer at Red
Fox Music Camp, back in the late 1960s, in the Berkshires. It takes me
back to those starry nights we'd lie in the blueberry meadows and
debate if there was a god, and what was reality. It reminds me of how
we would sit, in a peaceable camaraderie, on the roof of the girls'
house each evening to watch the sun set over the hills. In my mind the
Pianist Corner has practice cabins out in the trees, and during the discussions of Horowitz versus Rubinstein, of the supremacy or the shal-
lowness of Mozart, the sound of students practicing can be heard as if
from afar in the woods, a backdrop for tears over a flubbed recital, the
triumph of a conservatory acceptance. The orchestra rehearsing in the
old dairy barn plays battle chords of melodrama, and the strings sigh
with the forum denizens as they discuss their favorite recordings.

It's exhilarating to be around musicians again, hanging out with
people who know far more about music and the piano than I do. Even
if I never see their faces or know their real names, I learn so much. I
buy the books, music, videos, and recordings they recommend; I print
out their suggestions for how to play three beats against two, and how
to improve one's sight reading. I don't post very often, I have so little
to contribute, but I savor their company.

At the Piano Tuner–Technician's Forum, pianists ask technicians
about the science and technology of pianos, and technicians discuss
how to handle troublesome clients or solve unfamiliar problems.
Though I don't yet have a piano of my own, I am keenly interested in

the engineering and maintenance of pianos. Most of the discussions are highly technical, but there is the occasional lively debate about topics like whether or not to install a humidity control system on the piano itself—techs from humid climates tend to endorse it, and techs from drier regions tend to reject it as potentially dangerous.

Sometimes the conversation becomes fervent when the community's techs leap to the assistance of some innocent new piano owner whose dream piano disappoints them. They dissect the performance of the local technician or dealer, and what he may or may not have done to cause or fail to alleviate the problem. They jockey with one another to come up with the right solution. Techs seem to love the role of hero, and the technician's forum gives them an opportunity to flex their professional muscle: most of the consumers who wander into this quarter are in profound distress and in need of rescue.

In fact, it is a cry for help from one such consumer that leads me to make my first post. A woman in New York asks for a referral to a good technician. The action of her new Petrof vertical—just purchased in Manhattan—is so stiff, it is making her hands and arms sore. I played a Petrof vertical I liked in Manhattan the previous December, and I plan to look at this make again soon, when Oliver and I head East for a family reunion.

My first post:

The Petrof 131 is the only upright I've played that I've really liked. The one I played in New York was already sold, and I am considering asking the dealer to order and prep one for me. Please tell me anything you know about this New York dealer, and about Petrof.

But no one answers my appeal. Instead, I receive a private message from "Meg B," the owner of the Petrof. She tells me her dealer is the very same one I visited, and he hasn't returned her calls. Is Meg's experience with this dealer typical? I begin my first discussion thread, to find out. One forum member, David Burton, raves about the Petrofs and this dealer. But when I ask him if he has bought a piano from them himself, the answer is no.

David Burton is one of the most impassioned and knowledgeable of Piano World's piano fanatics. If anyone asks about some obscure piano make and its history, David knows the years the piano was made, the location of the factory, who owned it, and any special character-istics of that make. He is the forum encyclopedia. He and I are usu-ally at odds politically, but we are musical soul mates in our shared reverence for the experience of being at the piano. He proclaims that his religion is *pianism*.

David often writes about his dream of returning America to the days when families gathered around the piano for entertainment, of trans-forming our culture and society through the sharing of classical music. One day I tease David about his avowed scorn for political idealists, and ask him how he squares that with his musical idealism. His reply to me:

> *When one sits down at one's piano and begins to play as only you or I can, there is no idealism to be reached for, the experience is THERE, right now, instantaneous and totally REAL. When one is able to real-ize with clarity the breathtaking achievements of some great master, to the point that one is almost not conscious of playing as being played by transcendent forces, or even transcendent beings, one is not trying for some ideal, one has achieved a state of being that exists in few other human experiences.*
>
> *. . . That to me seems the point behind all this fuss about pianos: the MUSIC they make and we, with our own two hands, can become at least for a few moments, immortal. For you see, all the shouting over political and religious issues will never accomplish what a single, simple piece of exquisite piano music will accomplish. Music can melt the cold-est heart, can cause grown men to cry openly, can move women to faint-ing, can stop wars! It can, it still can.*

David has his own website extolling all things piano, describing his piano shopping trips, but also introducing himself to the world as a potential partner for some lucky woman. On the site, he calls himself "The Polar Bear," a nickname that suits him, as he is an albino. As is common with albinism he is also legally blind. How he managed to learn to play the piano with this handicap is its own story.

David says he began to play the piano as soon as he was able to crawl up onto the bench. His family had a 1923 Kranich & Bach baby grand his grandparents had bought new, and his mother, an amateur violinist and music appreciation teacher, was his first piano teacher. He studied with a real piano teacher when he got a bit older, but the only way he could learn a work was to hold the sheet music up to his nose, where he was able to make out the notes with the assistance of very thick glasses. While holding the music with one hand, he would play it with the other until that part was memorized, then switch hands. When each hand knew its part, he would put them together. Now in his fifties, he has an enormous repertoire committed to memory, which he plays at home on his Belarus-made Schubert vertical piano.

David's mother lives in Washington State, and when he visits her from his home in Coxsackie, New York, he also likes to visit Darrell and Heather Fandrich up in Stanwood. He raves about their instruments on the forum; they are his favorites. He writes that when he plays a Fandrich grand piano, he feels what he calls "the ache" so strongly, *I want to bite my arm off.*

David takes a keen interest in my own piano search. I've recounted my shopping experiences in the Piano Forum, describing what I've liked (the Petrof 131 in New York, the Charles Walter grand in Federal Way) and what I haven't. David suggests that since I am in Montana, why not head west a bit and visit Fandrich & Sons, where he played a six-foot grand piano remanufactured by Darrell Fandrich, that David feels outplays a Hamburg Steinway model O in the same room.

I've failed to find a good excuse to return to Seattle since hearing from Heather Fandrich more than a year earlier, but David's suggestion prods me to create one.

"Oliver, let's go have a romantic weekend in Seattle soon, what do you think?" I propose to my husband that evening. "We could visit Mikey and his family, too." Mikey, whom Oliver followed to the Pacific Northwest twenty-five years ago, lives just north of Seattle, not far from the Fandrichs. Oliver hasn't seen his old climbing buddy for years. He readily agrees, and doesn't even balk when I suggest I could squeeze in some piano hunting while he and Mikey reminisce about old times.

◆

In Seattle, we splurge on two nights in a downtown hotel where the rooms are decorated in wine colors and our Mastiff, Tucker, is treated to his own special pillows and snacks. Oliver reads a book while I play pianos, then we walk along the wharf and ride the ferry out to Bainbridge Island and back. We visit Pike Place Market and buy clams and a whole salmon to share with Mikey and his family. That night, Mikey's two little boys devour the clams with the practiced avidity of the seacoast born and bred. In the morning, my mountaineering husband and his old partner are glad for the chance to rekindle their friendship alone.

◆

The road to Stanwood is leafy, and travels through meadows where horses graze. Hedgerows of wild blackberries clamber over fallow fields. I have Heather's careful instructions, written on the back of an envelope, pressed against the steering wheel of Oliver's Jeep Cherokee. Through the open car window wafts the pungent aroma of dairy farms.

The Fandrichs' two-story rustic home is in a clearing in the woods, screened from its neighbors by towering Douglas fir. When I pull into the drive, a pack of dogs runs out to greet me—a black lab, a yellow lab, a chocolate lab, and a Boxer pup on a restraining line. A woman with a gray pageboy, wire-rimmed glasses, dressed in jeans and a sweatshirt appears on the front porch.

"They're okay, they won't bother you!" She calls to the dogs and they swarm onto the porch steps, at her feet, a sea of wriggles. "The showroom is right over there." Heather points to a log building to my left, as she heads there herself. "Have any trouble finding us?"

The showroom, formerly a three-car garage, houses three grand pianos: a Fandrich & Sons seven-foot, a six-foot, and an old August Förster grand, there on consignment. Against the peeled log walls are three vertical pianos. They are Czech-made Klimas with the Fandrich vertical action installed at the factory, Heather explains. The action is built by the Renner Company in Germany. After the pianos arrive in Stanwood, the family does all the fine regulation work. Heather shows me a tabletop model of Darrell's patented vertical piano action and explains how it works.

Inside a grand piano, the hammers lie horizontally under the strings. Outside a grand piano, when you press a key, it acts as a seesaw; the felt hammer at the other end rises up and strikes the strings above to generate tone. Because the movement of the hammers is up and down, gravity returns them to their resting places. This means the hammers are instantly available for the pianist's next keystroke. The key and the hammer are continuously connected opposing forces.

In a vertical piano, the hammers stand upright, so their motion to strike the strings and return is forward and back. Gravity is therefore of no use in returning vertical hammers quickly to their resting places, and so they must be assisted by springs and leather-tipped straps called bridle straps. Without gravity's assistance, there is a pause in the return of a vertical hammer, and the pianist must wait longer before he can repeat a note. This pause also makes the touch of the keys feel sloppy, less in control.

In the early 1980s, Darrell Fandrich, a concert technician, engineer, and violinist who had tuned pianos since his teenage years in North Dakota, decided to throw all his spare time and energy into inventing an upright action that would play like a grand's. Many a piano inventor had failed in the attempt over the previous 150 years.

A night owl by nature, Fandrich spent some seven years burning the midnight oil in his Pioneer Square loft in Seattle while he tried to work out a solution. His son Brent was a teenager at the time, and remembers waking up in the middle of the night and hearing the *plink, plink* sound of the action model in the next room. To him it was the sound of his father, and reassured him that his father was there, and so all was right with his world. Working on the model was all that his father did when he wasn't out tuning pianos. "He was obsessed," Brent would tell me later.

The eventual solution, which Fandrich patented in 1990, replicates the grand piano action's continuously connected opposing forces. In other words, just as in a grand piano, the hammer inside and the key outside the vertical piano are in constant relative motion, without any pause. This Fandrich achieved by weighting the keys with leads at the near end, like a grand, installing springs that return the hammers almost as quickly as gravity, and installing repetition springs that instantly force the jacks back under the knuckles of the hammer shanks. With this system, hammers can rest on the jacks instead of on a rail, bridle straps are no longer needed, and the action's movement is smooth and efficient, with no lost motion.

While the average pianist may not understand the engineering, what he experiences is the ability to rapidly repeat notes, and the capacity to control the volume and quality of the tone. I play each of the uprights in turn, and they simply feel more responsive. Perhaps not exactly like a grand piano, but I can produce a graduated pianissimo, making the tone as delicate as I desire. That is not at all like how an upright piano usually plays.

"Go ahead and play all you want," says Heather, when I take out my music. Then she leaves.

I've found on all my shopping excursions that I need to be alone with an instrument to decide what I hear and feel. Say you go on a first date set up by a matchmaker—you don't want the matchmaker hovering over the two of you, running a narrative while you try to find out who your date is. Piano salespeople like to hover; they tell you all about the piano's designer, where the parts come from, and why the competition is no good. They seem to think that by keeping up a barrage of facts and figures they can distract you from how badly the piano plays. I was forced at times to say to overzealous salespeople: "You know, none of that makes any difference if I don't like the piano. Do you mind if I just play it?" It is a relief that with Heather, I don't need to ask.

Once I have the showroom to myself, I notice right away that these uprights have a very bright sound. It is hard to tell if this is the inherent nature of the pianos, or if it is the room. Though the old garage has carpeting on the floor, it is still a very lively acoustic environment. The action, however, is the best vertical action I have played, very responsive, with good repetition and plenty of control, and that feeling of "after touch" that all grands have.

I methodically play the uprights from left to right, giving each a fair trial. I really want to fall in love with these pianos, but I simply do not like the tone. I play them several times, just to make sure, to sort out what the problem is. They really are too bright, I decide. They have a brassy, echoing sound. And the control of the pianissimo, while easier to achieve than on the average vertical, is still not all that I desire. I know I won't get that quality unless I buy a grand. I'm still hoping to stay within my new budget of $10,000, and I can't buy a grand I will like for so little. I pause, disappointed, now certain these are not right for me. Heather must have seen me collect my music through the showroom's plateglass window, because she lets herself back in.

"What do you think?"

"Oh, the action is wonderful, definitely the best I have played on an upright, but, honestly," and I wince, "I don't care for the tone."

At that moment, Darrell Fandrich himself enters the showroom. He's a slightly stooped, gray-haired man of sixty, wearing a cardigan sweater, and his very dark, expressive eyes suggest gentleness and complexity. He carries himself with the world-weary air of a foreign correspondent who has been through too many wars. "She doesn't care for the tone," Heather repeats to him without any preamble. "It's too bright."

"Oh, well," says Darrell, his voice raspy from cigarettes. "We have to voice them bright because that is what most people want. It's what they are used to hearing. Brighter and louder. I like a mellower tone myself. Let me voice it for you and we'll see how you like it tomorrow. Can you come back then?"

The next day Oliver and the dog return with me, our last stop before we head home. Heather tells me Darrell was up all night voicing one of the uprights and she thinks I'll like it better now. I sit down before the piano, while Darrell and Heather wait expectantly. The piano's tone is much softer, but I can still hear the same basic personality of the sound, and it leaves me unmoved. I don't know how to describe it, but it seems to me it lacks dimension. And yet, I'm not even sure what that means.

I like these people so much, their originality, their passion for what they do, and their showroom in the woods. Half of buying the right piano is finding the right dealer. I want Darrell and Heather to be my dealer. But I shake my head no.

"I'm really sorry," I say. "This just isn't the sort of tone I'm looking for." Darrell and Heather look at each other. Years later, when we meet again, Darrell explains to me his theory of "the one percent," that is, only one percent of people shopping for a piano are attuned to tone, really care about and appreciate tone. "If only I'd known you were one of those, I would have voiced that piano differently," he would later lament. But at the moment, neither Darrell nor I know this about me. And I'm left mystified, yet again, by why I like so few pianos.

So, I try the grands. These pianos are Chinese, from the Dongbei company, and Darrell has remanufactured them to his own specifications. He chose them, he explains, because they are based on his favorite piano scale design, the Ibach, a German make, and because

Dongbei doesn't care what he does with them or what name he puts on them, they just want to sell pianos.

Darrell replaces the bass strings, reshapes the soundboard to make it thinner and more flexible, replaces the Chinese action and hammers with German parts, and employs several of his own inventions to fine-tune the instrument's responsiveness, such as "riblets," smaller ribs that are placed between the existing soundboard ribs to make the tone more uniform. In developing this design, Darrell experimented on forty grand pianos before getting a consistent result. He puts one hundred hours of labor into each one.

The seven-foot Fandrich & Sons is the one I like best. This is the piano that David Burton is in love with, and I can see why. It is sonorous, expressive, and responsive. The price is a third of that for a comparable American or European grand. But I don't have room for a seven-foot grand piano.

Darrell asks me if I'd like to see the shop where they tear the Chinese pianos apart and put them back together. I see Oliver sleeping in the driver's seat of the Jeep when we step outside, so I steal a few moments to follow Darrell to the old converted barn. He carries a cup of coffee as he walks, with an ambling sort of shuffle that makes him seem frail.

"This shop at midnight is an introvert's paradise," says Darrell, taking in the dim room with a proprietary sweep of his arm. A grand piano, an old Steinway awaiting rebuilding for a client, stands on scroll-work legs in the middle of the floor, lidless, its ancient action covered in a heavy film of dust. Off to the side are newly arrived Klima uprights; some have shiny-bright, custom-wood finishes. A long workbench holds a piano action, and Heather is drilling keys to put the lead weights in them. She proudly shows me her new precision power drill, a birthday present from Darrell. It has thirty-eight clutch settings.

Tools and materials are everywhere, painstakingly organized: leather and felt in plastic bins; center pin reamers, gram weights, heat gun tips, hammer shanks, and other small piano parts and tools in carefully labeled, clear drawers. There are shelves storing only exotic glues, an entire rack of various types of pliers, and a clear bin of stray piano hammers, which Darrell keeps on hand for voicing experiments—shaping and needling the hammers' felt to change a piano's tone.

Each of the workstations has a project in progress: the pedal trap-work of a grand piano is dissembled on one table, a row of hammers in a long wooden vise stands on another, a naked key frame with half its red felt bushings in place on yet another.

Darrell's grandfather was a woodworker, and he says he must have that in his blood, that love of tools. Darrell eagerly shows me tools he invented and manufactured himself: miniature beds of nails for mas-saging hammer felt, hooked wires on dowels for pulling and leveling strings; a long brass rod with tiny needles on one end, like the teeth of a baby piranha, also for voicing. I feel a buzz just from looking at these strange objects, as if I've been exposed to the bug that infects their cre-ator. I touch the string leveler tentatively.

"Voicing is my favorite part," Darrell says. "It's the beauty of the sound I am after, not the beauty of logic and design." He looks at me in a pregnant way, as if he thinks I might understand this quest. And in his liquid gaze, filled with emotion, I imagine I do. He is in search of the soul of an instrument through its mechanism, through how it is made. The shop is his laboratory for bringing the souls of instru-ments to life, and he infuses them with all his passion, all his obsession for their elusive perfection.

◆

I return home from Seattle to a message from my friend that she wants her Steinway upright back that week. Just as well, I think. After play-ing so many new pianos, the Steinway has become less appealing. And Molly has been complaining that the worn-out action is harming my hands. It is time to get serious about finding a piano.

I report in to Piano World:

I didn't find my piano. I'm heading to New York next, and have lined up some Petrof 131s to play. I liked this instrument a lot, and I hope this will work out.

Immediately Norbert posts his regrets that I did not make it to his Vancouver, B.C., store: *You could have tried the magnificent and acoustically incredible 51" Sauter uprights we bring in from Germany!* he laments.

Rich D., an administrator with the Immigration and Naturalization Service in Washington, D.C., was just in New York, and he advises me to visit Beethoven Pianos, where he played a Sauter vertical only three weeks before. *They had an old August Förster upright that I really thought sounded the best.*

Of course, David Burton wants to know how I liked the Fandrich pianos. I tell him:

I liked the 7-foot Fandrich grand very much, but it is too large for my living room. I did play the smaller Fandrich grand and felt it was too bright. The tone of the verticals is not what I am looking for.

David is very forgiving, considering how passionately people on the forums usually defend their own preferences:

OK, so they weren't the sound you were looking for. You seem to be looking for a darker sound. You said you liked the 7' Fandrich grand a lot, which is the darkest sounding of Fandrich's grands. It may be that Darrell's showroom is to blame. They did sound less bright when they were in his shop. I think it would surprise you how they would perform in a different space.

But anyway, you seem to be headed in a different direction and I wonder if you have played any August Förster uprights? One of these might be your piano. Possibly seek out an older Bechstein upright and consider replacing the hammers to get the tone you want. Fandrich may not be for everybody. You have to follow your instincts for the right tone. You will.

By now my feeling about the whole piano search, and David's words especially, is bafflement. Why am I unsatisfied with these many very different makes of pianos? What does David mean by "instincts for the right tone?" Why is Darrell Fandrich's workshop so seductive? What is this all about, anyway? Is it about learning how to play the piano? I could have settled for any number of modest instruments by now to accomplish that aim. Or is it about something else? If so, what could that be? What am I seeking?

I have no idea. I just know I'll know it when I play it.

7

Piano Row

I arrive in New York on a Saturday night and take a taxi from the airport into the city. Familiar landmarks and swarming traffic surround the cab. The city's skyline looms ahead, growing ever larger, its lights sparkling like rhinestones on an enormous black cloak that will soon envelop me. In New York, where my mother and grandmother were born and raised, where I lived and worked for more than a decade, I always snap-lock into the matrix of concrete, sirens, subterranean rumblings, exhaust, putrefaction, surging crowds, and bleating horns with a sense of belonging that is visceral, as if the city is a molecule on the spiral of my DNA.

The cab pulls up to my best friend's building. Kim is in Amagansett for the month of August, and Primo, the elevator man, hands me her key. "How is Montana?" he asks, Italian accent jovial; then he pulls closed the iron gate and launches us upward. The burnished wood paneling gleams in the dim light. I let myself into Kim's apartment and fling open the living room's casement windows to the breeze off Gramercy Park. It is good to be back. In the morning I will go to my appointments on Piano Row.

New York has a diamond district, a millinery district, a street for photographic supplies, a street of Indian restaurants, another for saris, yet another for Ukrainian Easter egg tools. It's a place of specialties, an endless wonder of them, with too many choices, too much to take in. Piano Row, strictly speaking, is Fifty-eighth Street, between Broadway and Seventh Avenue, where there are three stores, but several more piano shops are scattered through the neighborhood. There is Steinway Hall on Fifty-seventh Street, Frank & Camille's in Macy's on

Thirty-fourth Street, the Petrof dealer on Fifty-fifth Street, and various rebuilders, used shops, and by-appointment-only dealers who do
not have showrooms, all in Midtown West.

I've planned this trip like a military campaign. After more than a
year and a half of piano shopping, in San Francisco, Calgary, Seattle
(twice), Salt Lake City, and New York (previously), as well as at home,
I want to wrap it up. Twenty-four city hours are mine before Kim
expects me at the beach, and then Oliver meets me at his family
reunion in Oyster Bay. Knowing I will have to make the most of my
time, I called ahead to all the piano dealers, asked about their current
inventory, and made appointments with those who do not have regular Sunday hours.

The Petrof dealer has courted me since my visit last December with
greeting cards, personal notes, and postcards announcing "Warehouse
Sale—78% Off!" "Drastic Year End Clearance," and, most recently,
"Drastic July Clearance, Greatest Sale in Our History!" The manager
promised they would have two Petrof 131s prepared for me to choose
from by today. Faust Harrison faxed me their complete inventory list,
including prices, with asterisks next to the vertical pianos that fit my
budget, and the saleswoman who took my call arranged to meet me at
the store. Beethoven Pianos said they are always open on Sundays.
Altenburg Piano House, in nearby Elizabeth, New Jersey, is also open
on Sundays, and confirmed they have new Pleyel and Förster uprights
for me to try.

In addition to the calls, I purchased the online edition of the
annual price supplement to Larry Fine's *The Piano Book* and printed
out the pages of the makes and models that interest me. I even ripped
the piano section out of my old copy of the Manhattan Yellow Pages
and stapled it together. All these pages and telephone notes are now in
a file folder in my suitcase. No more casual "look-see" for this girl. *I
am going to buy a piano.* Any salesman who sees me coming, determined
look in my eye and decisiveness in my carriage, should be delighted.

New York is a most fitting stopping place for my piano search.
Pianos were one of the city's top industries in the late nineteenth
century—piano building was then as synonymous with New York as
the stock market, publishing, and Broadway theater are today. In fact,
before the advent of commercial radio, piano making was the largest

entertainment industry in the United States, with New York its hub. There were 171 different piano manufacturers here, many of them in the Mott Haven section of the Bronx. In addition to the ubiquitous Steinway, now in Astoria, Queens, and the only local survivor of the era, there were many other grand old American makes: Aeolian, Sohmer, Weber, Steck, Decker & Son, Hardman Peck, Krakauer, Kroeger, and on and on. So powerful an economic engine was the piano in the early twentieth century, the needs of piano makers drove the markets for wool felt, fine wood, and steel wire.

Today, New York is a center of piano *re*-building—old pianos are taken apart and re-created with new materials, but rebuilders have a tough time finding the quality and type of materials they need. The piano industry commands the markets for raw materials no longer. Nationally, sales of grand pianos are in a renaissance, but the numbers sold do not even begin to approach the peak year of 1923. At that time there were many hundreds of American piano makers. Today, there are only five American makes still in production: Astin-Weight, Baldwin, Charles Walter, Mason & Hamlin, and Steinway. Only Steinway is in New York.

Sunday dawns hot and sultry, the streets steaming from the previous night's rain. With eagerness I pass through the door of the Petrof dealer's showroom, into its cool sanctuary. To prolong my anticipation, I slowly play my way to the back room, where the vertical pianos are, working my way first through the grands. At last I arrive at the room with the verticals. I walk up and down the aisles, but find only one Petrof 131, in walnut polish, standing in the corner where a cherry version of the same piano stood the previous December. The fallboard is closed, and on the music desk is a large sign: SOLD.

How can this be? I turn around and look over all the uprights again. No other Petrof 131s. I lift the fallboard of the walnut Petrof and play the first of Schumann's *Scenes from Childhood*. The piano is exquisite. I like it even better than the one I played last winter, which was also already sold. My heart sinks. I am here for only a day.

"We can get you another one just like it."

I whirl around. It's the store manager. I introduce myself as the customer from Montana he spoke with only last week.

"You promised you would have two Petrof 131s ready for me here today. I cannot find them. Are they here somewhere?"

The manager looks flustered. "Oh, yes. While I was out this week, another salesman sold them both. He is new, and he did not know they were spoken for. I'm sorry, but they are gone. Of course, we will be happy to order you one just like this one."

"How soon can you get them in? I am leaving the city tonight, but I could come back in a week if I have to."

"I will have to check, but I don't know that we can get them in that soon." He bounces a bit off his toes, forming his fingers in a steeple before his chest. "We can order you one today, if you like."

This manager, who repeatedly promised these pianos would be here today, doesn't really seem the least bit sorry. Something funny is going on. How is it that their 131s are always sold? Is this some kind of a ploy to sell pianos without properly preparing them? I remember "Meg B" from Piano World and her despair over her new Petrof, bought at this very store. How the action hurt her hands, how the dealer didn't return her calls. Did Meg buy the piano she played? Or was she subjected to a bait and switch?

The Petrof verticals in Seattle and Calgary don't play like this one. They don't have the sensitive touch, the gossamer tone. How much does it cost the store to prepare these pianos to such a high level of performance? How many technician hours are involved? And how much more profitable might these pianos be if the store doesn't have to prepare every one?

"Come over to my desk," entreats the manager, turning to the main showroom floor. "We'll draw up the paperwork, and then we'll place the order."

"You want me to buy the piano before I have played it?"

"Just a deposit. That is the only way we can order it for you."

"And what if I don't like the piano?"

He points to a small sign posted on the wall. NO REFUNDS.

The feeling in my gut is growing into a certainty. I don't know of any piano dealers who keep deposits. Why would they want an unhappy customer?

"I don't buy pianos sight unseen," I say. "And I won't make a non-refundable deposit on a piano I have never played."

"Call us tomorrow. We'll see how soon we can get in another 131. Perhaps our distributor has some in stock." Then he returns to his desk, where he absorbs himself in paperwork.

I stand where he left me, burning with disappointment and frustration. I had looked forward to playing these pianos for months! But there is nothing more to say. I head out, into the heat, for Piano Row.

✦

At Faust Harrison, Tien-Ni Chen is waiting for me at the appointed hour. A reedlike woman, she seems to move with a breeze as she comes to the door to let me in. Her straight black hair swings about her eager face. Her limbs are exquisitely small and delicate, and her fingers hang gently in the air, expressive and floating as she talks. Her smile is radiant, welcoming, as I enter the cool of the elegantly appointed showroom.

Faust Harrison caters to a certain type of clientele—well heeled, well bred, and secure in the refinements of their taste. The owners are professional pianists, as are the employees. Each piano is impeccably prepared and displayed in beautiful, calm surroundings, with Persian rugs and tasteful lighting. It's a Park Avenue sensibility, a stark contrast to the Petrof dealer's showroom, which exudes the hurly-burly bustle of the garment district.

Tien-Ni and I are alone in the store, and she is ready with a list of upright pianos that Michael Harrison, one of the store's owners, recommends for me. Of course, I also want to try the grand pianos, and Tien-Ni encourages me. There are several new Mason & Hamlin model As on the floor, and I play three of them. They have a rather cold tone, but Tien-Ni says there are warmer-sounding model As at a warehouse upstate, if I am interested. There are also a number of rebuilt Steinway grands, some in carved art cases. I especially admire the lovely case of a tiger mahogany model A in the window.

As it happens, upright pianos are not this store's primary inventory. There are only three makes on hand: a new Mason, made in Massachusetts, a new Schulze Pollmann from Italy, and a five-year-old Steinway model K in a handsome inlaid case. The Mason interests me most, as I haven't played a new Mason upright yet. It has a powerful tone, and a nice, even action. But it is very loud. Tien-Ni tries tacking a heavy curtain behind the Mason, to dampen some of the sound. But the piano still booms.

"This room echoes," she explains. "I'm sure it would not be so loud in a quieter room."

The Schulze Pollmann uprights here, just like the ones I played in Salt Lake City, have a bad break between the tenor and bass sections, and a weak treble, so I quickly move on to the Steinway K.

This piano has delicate inlay work running across the face of the mahogany cabinet. Such a beautiful piece of furniture, I hope, will also be a piano I can love. I sit down on the bench and begin to play my shopping repertoire. From the first notes, I notice that this instrument also has a bad bass-tenor break. It is divided against itself: full, warm, rich tones in the bass on one end of the keyboard, then a thin, shrill, brittle treble on the other. But I gamely continue playing. It is the last upright in the store, and I so want it to be "the one."

I work my way through the Mozart G major sonata. Then the Schumann *Kinderszenen*. Then Mendelssohn's first of the *Songs Without Words*. Yes, the problems are real. I shake my head with disappointment as I get up.

Tien-Ni asks if she can play the Steinway for me. Her performance of a Schubert impromptu is brilliant, but the break is plain to me even though she does her best to disguise it with her playing. The tone of the treble is intolerable, too. Too bright.

"If you think you might really want it, we can voice it for you," she says, turning on the bench to face me. "I can ask Michael Harrison. But I don't know how soon our tech can do it. Can you come back?"

Here is a second piano dealer who might have what I want if only I will return. I give Kim's telephone number in Amagansett to Tien-Ni, and ask her to let me know if voicing will be possible. "Maybe I can come back in a week, just before I return home, if that works with your tech's schedule," I say. I don't have great hopes for this piano improving enough, but it is so very pretty. Why not try?

Quickly I have come to the end of a store visit that had seemed so promising. For lack of any other verticals to play, I look wistfully at the grands. "Which of these pianos is your favorite?" I ask Tien-Ni. I want to know what a professional pianist would choose, play it, see what it feels and sounds like.

Tien-Ni's face shines with pleasure. "Oh, this one," she answers without hesitation, striding over to the tiger mahogany Steinway model A in the window. She caresses the piano's arms affectionately as she sits down on the bench and launches into the same Schubert impromptu. It sounds warm and lovely, with a treble that peals like gently ringing bells. I have never heard such a distinctive tone from a piano before.

"That is beautiful. Thank you so much," I say, after she finishes.

"Would you like to try it?" Tien-Ni offers me the bench.

I sit tentatively before the old instrument, a model no longer made. It was built in the 1920s, then rebuilt in the store's workshop, given new life, with nothing of the old piano retained except the case and the cast-iron harp.

I place my hands gently on the ivory keys and play just a few notes. The tone is sweet, singing, lovely. I try the Schumann, and the piano responds in a way I can only describe as warmhearted, giving, not particularly powerful, but full of a kind of heartfelt joy and quiet beauty. I have never before heard a piano with such individuality, such sonority, such delicacy and color. When I play the Mendelssohn, I feel tenderness in it. This is an instrument of great refinement.

"Oh, what a sweet piano," I sigh. "I can see why you love it."

Tien-Ni's eyes grow bigger and brighter. Does she think I might buy this piano? I am certain it is far beyond my means. But I ask her the price, to be polite. When she says it is $45,000, I close the fallboard, smile, and shake my head. "Let me know what happens with the upright," I say as I head toward the door.

✦

Back on the scorching sidewalk, I look up and down Piano Row to get my bearings. Beethoven Pianos is across Fifty-eighth Street and a bit west. I step eagerly to the other side of the street, anticipating the many unusual pianos Rich D. and David Burton have told me to expect at this store. But when I get to the tall, glassed-in façade, the interior is dark and the door is locked. I press my face up against the heavy glass, peering past an old, scuffed-up Bechstein grand in the display window. I see such promise inside. In the gloom of the darkened store is an art deco upright in blond wood with two swinging candelabras framing its music desk. A flame mahogany grand stands just

beyond the entry. A beautiful burled walnut vertical is pressed against
a wall behind the Bechstein. The depths of the store seem to beckon,
mysterious and intriguing, with densely packed pianos of all vintages,
sizes, and colors.

I bang on the door as hard as I can. Surely someone must be inside.
The lettering on the door clearly says the store is open from two to six
on Sundays. I look at my watch. It is nearly three p.m., and I still need
to get to Altenburg's in Elizabeth, then catch the train out to Long
Island.

I look up and down the street, hoping a likely someone will appear
on the sidewalk, perhaps carrying a big ring of keys, smiling and has-
tening their step when they see me waiting. But I can't quite conjure
them. Directly opposite the store is a small hotel with a bright green
awning. Perhaps someone there knows when Beethoven's is open, or
knows if they will soon be back. I leap up the steps into the lobby and
walk over to the desk clerk.

"I don't know why they are closed," says the young man behind
the counter. He shrugs and smiles pleasantly. "The lights are usually
on over there until quite late into the evening."

There is nothing left to do but head to Pennsylvania Station.

✦

At the station, before I get on the train to Elizabeth, I telephone Altenburg Piano House for directions. A man with a heavy accent, George
Hovsepian, explains which train to take for the twenty-minute ride,
and how to walk the one and a half blocks from the train station to
the showroom. Altenburg owns whole warehouses of pianos and has
a vast inventory to select from on its five showroom floors, so I feel
certain this trip will be worth the small detour.

Finding the store is easy, but I pause before entering to admire an
enormous satin mahogany grand piano in the window. The meticulous
attention to detail in the finish of the case is obvious and seductive; this
is fine furniture making at its perfectionistic best. Then I pull my eyes
away— such a piano could never be mine—and enter the showroom.

There are no other customers, and George greets me effusively. He's
a dapper man—short, but well turned out, his hair carefully combed
and his clothes immaculate. He's at least in his sixties, and judging by

his winks, not above a bit of harmless flirting. He takes my hand as if I am a European countess, bows deeply, and flashes a brilliant smile, as if we are in an old black-and-white Hollywood movie. His extroverted enthusiasm whisks me into its vortex like a small cyclone.

I tell George I am here to play the uprights. He sweeps us past a horde of them—Samicks mostly—on the first floor, dismissing them as not worth my time, and leads the way up the steep stairs to the second floor, where the European pianos are displayed.

Against the back wall is a glossy black upright, the August Förster. "Here you are!" says George, bouncing a bit on his toes and gesturing to the piano. "Now *this* is a very special piano. I think you'll like it."

I sit down and begin to play, but there is George, still standing to my right, still rocking jauntily on his feet, hands clasped behind his back, grinning at me. How am I supposed to get a sense of the piano with him watching my every move?

"Would you mind very much leaving me alone with the instrument?" I ask as nicely as I can. "I need a chance to play and listen."

"Oh, of course! Here let me just show you where the other pianos are. Here is the Pleyel," and he pats the lid of another tall, glossy black upright. "And these other pianos, we have just uncrated them. They are August Förster grands. You really should try them too. I'll be downstairs if you need anything." And down he goes, briskly humming.

I pull some music from my bag and begin again to play the Förster upright. Immediately the tone impresses me as too brilliant and cold, not unlike the Mason I played earlier in the day. So I move on to the Pleyel. A few more bars of music and I know this is not my piano, either. It also is a bit too cool and bright for my taste, though the tone is quite pure and clear. I move on to the grands, since I have come all this way. They are much sweeter in tone than the uprights, and have a very light, fluid action. Their sticker price startles me: $23,000 for a six-foot grand from Europe. How can they do that? I look up and find George beside me again.

"So? How do you like the uprights?"

"Oh, I'm afraid they aren't what I am looking for. But thank you so much." I gather my music and put it away in my bag.

"I am so sorry to hear that." And he looks genuinely disappointed.

George follows me down the stairs. On my way out the front door,

I pause again before the gorgeous mahogany grand piano in the window. George notices my admiring look.

"We only just got it this week! A Sauter Omega 220 in pyramid mahogany, an exquisite piano. Notice the perfection with which they matched the veneer? The grain matches perfectly." He runs a finger along the near-invisible veneer line. "Nobody makes furniture like Sauter. It is perfect! Perfect! Perfect! Look at the beautiful matching bench with the music rack in the base. Here, please." He pulls the bench away from the keyboard as if turning down a bed in an exclusive hotel. "You must try it."

"Oh, no." I shake my head. "I don't think so. What is the point? I don't have room for a piano like this, I can't afford it."

"Please," he repeats, gesturing toward the bench. "You must try it."

So I sit before the stunning instrument with its beautifully crafted finish, its graceful form, and lift the fallboard. The keys seem bigger than on other pianos. I touch them gingerly. George stands right beside the music desk, his arms crossed, grinning and winking. I press down a few of the long keys and the piano sings out in sonorous, clear tones. I play the Mendelssohn, and the bass rings dark, warm, heartbreakingly sweet. Clearly this is a great piano, a piano with musical possibilities not found in other pianos.

"I wish you had an upright that plays like this piano," I say, trying to gracefully end this folly. But as I start to get up, George breaks into an even bigger grin and holds an index finger before my nose, as if to stop me where I am.

"Just for you!" he exclaims, and marches over to a large desk at the far end of the showroom. "You must not tell anyone." He writes something on a piece of paper, marches back to me with it, and holds the paper before my face. On it he has written: "$27,500."

I gasp. How can such an exquisite instrument, such a work of art, a seven-foot-long grand piano, be priced so cheaply? It isn't possible. "How can you do that?" I ask.

"Just for you. You see, we got a special price, this is our first one from the company. You must keep it between you and me." Then he marches back to the desk and begins drawing up the paperwork.

"Congratulations!" he shouts as he writes. "It includes the bench, a cover, two free tunings, and free delivery."

"But I live in Montana."

"That doesn't matter, we deliver all over the world. Now, I just need your deposit until we can arrange delivery. Is one thousand dollars acceptable?"

After another fifteen minutes of discussion about how my living room is too small, how I do not have $27,500, how I am not sure, and how I must be able to get my deposit back, I finally write the check. George writes at the top of the contract in big block letters: DEPOSIT REFUNDABLE IF ORDER CANCELED. His face is wreathed in smiles. I am stunned. I need time to think. The piano is beautiful. It is an incredible price, but . . .

It's already closing time. George rides back into the city with me on the train. I have my written contract and an application for financing tucked into an envelope in my bag. I say nothing, letting the silence between us widen, and look down at my hands. I notice George's hands are covered in gold rings. He asks me why I don't look happier. I say I am not sure this is the right thing. He says, "You think too much."

◆

"You are *crazy*," says Kim, looking up at me with a skeptical, arched eye as exotic and imperious as Cleopatra's. Her inky curls, still dripping from her swim, tumble in tight ringlets to her shoulders. "You have lost your mind, spending that kind of money on a piano!" We sit in her kitchen, chopping tomatoes, parsley, and scallions for our evening meal.

"I know," I sigh. "But you should see it, and hear it. It is so beautiful. It is such an incredible price."

"I don't care," Kim says crisply, as if trying to snap me out of an infatuation with a married man. "You can't tell me a piano is worth that kind of money to you. Really!"

"Yes, I guess I have lost my mind." I smile to myself. My piano obsession has not stopped even long enough to enjoy my closest friend and the beach. I have been on the phone to the city ever since I arrived, talking to other dealers, talking with Michael Harrison about voicing the Steinway upright, calling Beethoven Pianos to set a definite appointment to come in the following Monday, just before I take my flight home to Montana, talking to the Petrof dealer about getting in another model 131.

"The soonest we can get one is forty-five days," the manager claims. "They are out of stock all over the country. Our distributor says none of his customers have them."

Bullshit. Bullshitter. I saw several Petrof 131s at Macy's just before I grabbed the train out to Long Island. They don't play like the ones at the Petrof dealer, but they are there. I even call Larry Fine, the author of *The Piano Book,* for a consultation. He says I should buy the Petrof at Macy's. But I can't imagine buying a piano that I don't love just the way it is. What if I can't find a tech who can bring out its potential? Fine also says the price on the Sauter Omega is impossible: "That is probably below dealer cost." I call the Sauter distributor and they confirm the price is, indeed, below dealer cost, but Altenburg buys direct from the factory in Germany.

Finally, Kim loses patience with me for being on the phone all the time, and we have a rip-roaring fight, the kind of searing squabble married couples have. But I can't stop myself. I will have only one more day in the city, and I must find my piano. Now.

8

Meeting Marlene

At eight o'clock on Monday morning, Tien-Ni and I meet on Piano Row and open Faust Harrison Pianos together. She has brought bagels and coffee, and we sit on opposite sides of the big sales desk, sharing breakfast and chatting. Over the weekend, Michael Harrison had his technician voice the Steinway upright for me, so I returned to the city for just a few hours today, before catching my flight home to Montana. I will have enough time to play the Sauter Omega at Altenburg's again, and I also have an appointment at Beethoven Pianos, just across the street from Faust Harrison. These are my last piano shopping cards to play.

Tien-Ni tells me she just received her doctorate from Juilliard, and feels lucky to have a job selling pianos while she establishes her performance career. I sip my coffee and muse that this is the piano business at its most-refined best—customer and salesperson talking about music like old friends.

"Our technician spent as much time as he could on the Steinway K." Tien-Ni smiles nervously. "But he says he did not have enough time, he really needs to come back to do all he could. We will see what you think, yes?"

I sit again before the Steinway K. Tien-Ni seems anxious: she stands off to one side, her arms folded across her willowy frame, her posture erect with attention, her eyes bright.

As soon as I begin playing, I hear the bass-tenor break is still there, the treble is still harsh. I stop and sigh.

"Let me play for you." Tien-Ni takes my place before the keyboard, and launches into the Schubert impromptu, but her virtuosity only underscores the piano's defects. In fact, the piano is unbearable to listen to.

"Stop! Stop! Please!" I hold out one hand. "It sounds even worse. What did the technician say?"

Tien-Ni turns on the bench to face me. "He said you are right, there is a bad break, and this piano wants to be a bright piano. He thought if he had more time he could make it better, but he agrees with you about the piano."

I am taken aback that she shares this with me. Most piano sales-people try to convince me to distrust my own perceptions, try to per-suade me that I do not hear what I know I hear. I am very sorry to disappoint Tien-Ni, and just as sorry for myself. It is only eight thirty a.m., too early for my eleven o'clock appointment at Beethoven Pianos, and I want to make the most of my few remaining hours in the city. Tien-Ni and I review the store's inventory, but there is noth-ing here I both want and can afford.

I give her my card. "Do let me know if anything comes in you think I would like. I visit New York just about every year." We say an affectionate good-bye, and then I walk to Pennsylvania Station to catch the train to Elizabeth.

◆

I arrive at Altenburg's at nine thirty. George has just opened the doors, and is busy organizing his desk for the day when I walk in. He snaps to attention when he sees me.

"You are back."

"Yes, I am here to play the Sauter again."

"Please." With a little bow, he gestures to the piano still sitting in the window.

I compose myself at the keyboard, and bring all my attention to bear on the task at hand. Larry Fine advised me, "Buy the one you fall in love with." Am I "in love" with the Sauter? I don't know. I didn't play it long enough. I put a deposit on an unbelievable deal. In the surprise of it all, I did not ask myself, am I in love with the piano? No matter how good the deal, I am throwing away $27,500 if I am not in love. I pull my music out of my bag and set to work on a serious eval-uation, beginning with scales and arpeggios, and then my entire minuscule repertoire. A convocation of young boys gathers outside the showroom window behind me, listening.

Funny how it isn't really necessary to play all that long to evaluate a piano. I can hear and feel its qualities right away. The tone is warm, singing, and complex, with a robust bass, very beautiful and unusual, and I like it very much. But the action. The action is firm, and difficult for me to control. I try producing a variety of volumes and colors, and I simply do not have the skill to get what I want out of this piano. I feel like a beginning rider astride a racehorse, fumbling with the reins, then thrown. This isn't love.

I pause before the keyboard and carefully consider. This piano, as a piece of furniture, is to die for—extraordinary design, finish work, and joinery. But at seven feet long, it is too big for my living room. I could buy it anyway, take a chance, but if it doesn't work out, it will be difficult to resell because it is an unknown brand. Furthermore, the loan that Altenburg offers requires monthly payments at a high rate of interest. I do not want to take on debt to get a piano.

I walk over to George, still busying himself at his desk.

"George."

He looks up. His face says he knows what is coming, his expression is distant.

"George, the Sauter is not my piano. It is an extraordinary deal, one that is very tempting, but I am not in love with it. May I have my deposit back?"

"Of course." He pulls out the file with my paperwork and extracts the check.

I leave the building feeling much lighter. I made the right decision. I head back to the station to wait for the next train into the city. On the ride back, I peruse my piano search folder, go over my lists, my decision diagram, and my notes on what I have played so far.

Beethoven Pianos will be my last stop.

✦

This time, when I try Beethoven's glass door, it swings open. I look eagerly at the wealth of instruments before me—mahogany, ebony, and walnut grands—pushed together case to case on the polished wide-plank floors. The store was a carriage factory in the nineteenth century; now the brick interior walls are decorated with fine art posters, and chandeliers hang from the high ceiling. The room has a disheveled, comfortable elegance.

There are Bechsteins, Feurichs, Masons, Sauters, Steinways, and a number of makes I have never seen or played before, most of them used or rebuilt. There seems hardly enough room for them all in the narrow quarters. I inhale the cloistered air they inhabit, and feel a rush of excitement at the prospect of trying out such an esoteric collection.

Within moments I am accosted by a young man of astonishing intensity. He projects a barely contained, potentially explosive energy when he demands to know if he can help me. His inky, penetrating eyes dart restlessly from within his pale, fleshy face, capped by a short mat of ebony curls. His accent is thick and Israeli.

I tell the young man I am looking for a vertical. He leads me down a steep staircase to the basement, where easily one hundred vertical pianos stand, from one end of the room to the other, packed so tightly together it is difficult to walk between them. In the center of the room they stand back to back, keyboard facing keyboard, so that in the aisles they make, you can sit on a bench to play one piano, then spin about to play the one behind you.

"Here's a good one," says the salesman, and pats the lid of a well-worn Mason & Hamlin upright. In their heyday, before the Great Depression, Masons were on par with Steinway, and if in good condition, the old ones are still fine instruments. I lift the fallboard and play a few notes. It has a rinky-tink tone, and is out of tune. I ask the young man to let me explore on my own, and he returns upstairs.

This is the largest selection of vertical pianos I've seen in one place, and while mindful that I have to catch a plane, I am determined to try them all. Over the next hour I make quick work of them—playing just a few notes to eliminate those that are out of tune, have a loose action, or sound tinny. On those pianos that pass this initial test, I play the music I have brought with me: a Mozart sonata, Mendelssohn's first of the *Songs Without Words,* Schumann's first of the *Scenes from Childhood,* a Bach prelude, and a Chopin prelude.

Some pianos are warm and lyrical, and thus well suited to Chopin and Mendelssohn, but do not sound right with Bach or Mozart. Others have the sparkling clarity Bach and Mozart require, but lack

the lushness that Romantic works need. Finding a piano that has a ver-
satile, flexible tone, and also a responsive touch is the trick. This is a lot
to ask of an upright, which has shorter strings and a smaller soundboard than a grand, and a far less efficient action.

I notice a blond pear-wood upright against the far wall, a Sauter,
with a case as impeccable as the Omega's at Altenburg's. It has candelabras mounted on either side of the music desk; they fold in and out.
The case has clean Scandinavian lines, and would look fine amid modern, sophisticated furniture. But I find the tone disappointing; it is clear
and singing, but lacks complexity.

In the center of the room are a score of new East German pianos
I've never heard of before. They have exquisite inlay work in many
different finishes, but I am undecided on them as musical instruments.
I am playing them, one at a time, when the salesman returns. I ask him
about the pianos, which are called Rönisch. He says he doesn't know
anything about them, but asks how I like them.

"Well, they seem nice enough for my abilities, but what about later
on, if I want to play Liszt or Rachmaninoff, what would that sound
like on these pianos?"

Without a word, the salesman sits down at a Rönisch upright and
unleashes his intensity upon the keyboard, playing a late Romantic work
I don't recognize. It sounds like Liszt. His thunderous playing is almost
unbearable in the low-ceilinged room, and I involuntarily put my hands
over my ears. The tone is distorted, the sound too big for the piano's
case; clearly this piano wasn't built for concert-artist-level playing.

And make no mistake, the young man is a concert artist. This is
evident even on the little Rönisch upright.

"Where did you learn to play like that?" I ask with frank admiration.

"I just graduated from Juilliard," he says. "Here is my card." I read:
ASAF BLASBERG, CONCERT PIANIST.

"Well, you certainly play like one. Are you pursuing a concert
career in New York?"

"Yes, I am."

"What kind of piano do you have?"

"A nine-foot Yamaha. But unfortunately I cannot afford to have it
moved here from California, so it is in storage there. What are you
looking for?" Asaf asks.

"I want a newer piano, and I'm having trouble finding an upright that satisfies me," I answer. "Which of these pianos do you like best?"

Asaf shrugs as he looks dubiously around the basement. Clearly he doesn't think much of what is down here. "Why don't we go upstairs?" he suggests.

The main floor showroom, with its chandeliers and Oriental carpets, is a welcome change from the windowless claustrophobia of the basement. I walk slowly among the grands, raising fallboards, taking note of the makes, playing a key here and there. None of *these* pianos sound tinny or out of tune. I feel like a stowaway on a luxury liner—I don't belong here because I cannot pay the fare, but until I am found out I will steal some time with these instruments.

Among the vintage Mason & Hamlins, Bechsteins, and Steinways, there are three pianos called Grotrian-Steinweg: a five-foot-eight baby grand, a six-foot-three Cabinet grand, and a seven-footer. I saw a Grotrian concert grand in a hall at the Banff Centre in Canada back in May, but I have never played or heard one. With eager curiosity I sit down at the baby grand. A card in a gilt frame on the music desk says this piano was once owned by Imelda Marcos. It has an art case, with "ice cream cone" legs and a delicate open cutwork music desk. The action is nice and light, but the treble is a bit too harsh. I move quickly on to the model 220—the seven-footer. The bass on this piano is thrilling—warm and dark and colorful, but it has such colossal power it overwhelms the weaker treble. Again I quickly move on, mindful of the time and my plane to catch.

Finally, I sit before the model 192, the Cabinet grand. It stands beside a black Bösendorfer grand. Asaf pats the lid of the Bösendorfer. "This is my favorite piano here, you must try this one."

Of course, it is merely an inexplicable matter of personal taste, but I don't want to tell Asaf that I have never yet liked a Bösendorfer. To please him, as I am starting to like this fierce young man, I slide over to the Bösendorfer's bench. I play my Schumann piece, then the Chopin, then the Mendelssohn. The piano lacks the lush tone those works need. The Mozart and the Bach sound perfect on it.

"I don't think so," I say, and smile at Asaf.

"Really? I can't believe you don't love it! Listen to this!" And he takes over the bench and plays very lyrically the same Liszt work that he played downstairs, clearly overcome with passion for the piano and the music. When he stops, his face is flushed with pleasure. "Oh, I love this piano!"

"I think I'll try this one," I say, sliding back over to the Grotrian Cabinet grand. I begin with the Mendelssohn, the first of the *Songs Without Words.* The work begins deep in the bass, and at the touch of the keys, I am swept away by powerful waves of sound—rich, dark, and warm, with singing overtones. The middle section is smoky and mysterious, as if rising from the larynx of a great contralto. The treble is bell-like and sparkling; it hangs in the air, full of color, a shimmering northern lights. I am amazed at the intense pleasure I feel at the responsiveness of the keys, as if an unseen hand lay under them, guiding me to music. A soul seems to reside in the belly of this piano, and it reaches out to touch mine, igniting a spark of desire within me that quickly catches fire. This disembodied being is sultry and seductive, as if Marlene Dietrich reincarnated as the soul of this piano, and is using my hands to belt out a torch song. If only I could play this piano every day, I think, I could be the pianist I have always dreamed of becoming.

"How do you like it?" says Asaf.

"Oh, I love it!" I cry. I turn back to the piano and play more. And then I look at the sticker price: $32,000. I have no doubt this is a very reasonable price, though I have no idea what Grotrians sell for, but it is completely and utterly beyond my means.

And then I look at my watch. It is already one p.m. I tell Asaf I have only a half hour left to shop, and then I must return home.

"Well, you can always come back tomorrow," he says.

But, I explain, I live in Montana. He does not know where that is. A long way away, I say. "What else would you show me?"

"How much are you willing to spend?" he asks.

Asaf takes me to the upstairs showroom, where the less expensive grands are. There is an old Knabe that needs restoration, a Blüthner that is probably the best of the lot. An old Chickering. None of these pianos have been rebuilt, and they need it. And then there are some new Estonia baby grands in exotic finishes like bubinga, a whorled wood, resembling burled walnut, but reddish in color. I sit down to play the three Estonias, which have been universally praised by my friends at Piano World. But after having just played the Grotrian, they seem weak and insubstantial. They lack the Grotrian's power and richness. We go back downstairs, and I return to the Grotrian to play it again.

"This would make a wonderful piano for Schubert," I tell Asaf, who has returned to my side.

"Here, let's find out if you are right," he says, and sits down at the Grotrian. He then plays the third Schubert impromptu of Opus 90, one of my favorites, and I hear at once that my assessment is correct: the melody peals in pearly, liquid tones—they dance through the air in richly saturated color, with great depth and dimension. The sound is heartrending: I resonate to this piano down to my core. She is a heartbreaker, this Marlene.

Then another customer comes into the store, and Asaf excuses himself. I return to the Grotrian and play and play. I finish with the Schumann, and I feel the piano is simply perfect. The treble is just glorious. I take out my little pocket notebook and write down the information from the price card on the music desk: "New Grotrian-Steinweg 6'3" Cabinet Grand Model 192, Serial No. 154393, ten-year warranty, $32,000." Then I add: "Gorgeous treble."

I wander about the showroom for my final five minutes before I must leave, and play a few notes of the Feurich and the Bechstein, but of all the pianos I play that day, or have ever played, none match the Grotrian. I am in love. And it is to be unrequited love, for my purse is too small.

I head for the door, back out into the heat of the August day, but Asaf catches me just as I am opening it.

"Wait!" he cries. "You have my card, right?" Yes. "You will call me, yes?" No. "Why not?"

"Well, I haven't seen anything here I can afford, and I live twenty-five hundred miles away."

"Perhaps I may call you then?"

"Yes, of course." I give Asaf my business card. And then I swing out into the brilliant sunshine, into the mugginess of late August in New York, and hail a cab for the first leg of my journey home.

I know I will never own the Grotrian, and I accept that. I am, after all, a very practical person. But as Beethoven Pianos, then Piano Row, then Manhattan itself fade away in the cab's rearview mirror, I am surprised by a bitter pang of loss, as if every passing mile widens a gulf between my soul and its one true desire.

9

The Sale

I've only been home for one day when the telephone rings.

"Hello, Ms. Knize?"

"Yes? Who is calling?"

"Ms. Knize, it's Asaf at Beethoven Pianos in New York. You were in our store yesterday?"

"Oh, yes. How are you? I enjoyed your playing so much."

"Ms. Knize. I saw the look on your face when you played that piano. That is *your* piano!"

I laugh. What chutzpah. I love it.

"Well, yes, Asaf. You are absolutely right. That is *my* piano. But it makes no difference, because I cannot afford it."

"What is the most you could pay?"

I laugh again. Unbelievable. I know his type, I knew lots of them when I lived in New York. They live by the city's code of success— never give up, never say die, keep going after what you want against all odds. Achieve the impossible through sheer persistence. I've been guilty of it myself. He is young, he believes completely in this code, and his obvious devotion to it fills me with nostalgia. I've been young and hungry too. People helped me. But I must firmly discourage Asaf or I'm not playing fair.

"Asaf, it is not worth discussing. I am looking for a ten-thousand-dollar upright."

I can almost hear his face fall. "Oh, I see. We could never let it go for so little."

"Well, of course not. So you see, you are wasting your time."

"Then you should consider one of the Estonia grands you played. We are much more flexible on those prices."

"But I didn't care for the Estonias."

"I see. Okay. Well." I can hear he's scrambling for his next move. I wince for him, but then he finds his footing: "Do you mind if I call you from time to time, just to see how your piano search is going? And maybe something will come in you would be interested in?"

I pause. Normally I despise hearing from any sort of salesman. But there is something about Asaf, a purity of intention, if you will, even if it is pure hunger, that moves me.

"Sure," I say. "Call any time."

"Thank you," he says. And I think I detect a note of triumph in his voice just before I replace the receiver.

✦

I report in at Piano World, as several forum members have taken a vicarious interest in my search. I list on the Piano Forum all the pianos I played in New York, and my impressions. Of course I tell them about the Grotrian.

You found it! Penny wrote. *My perfect piano!!! Isn't it great?*

Grotrian-Steinweg was FOR YEARS my ideal of the perfect piano, wrote David Burton. *Side-by-side comparisons of Grotrians with other pianos have conclusively demonstrated TO ME that they are closest to Hamburg Steinways, as well they might be. For those that may not know, Grotrian and Steinway were partners.*

But Norbert takes umbrage at my posting of the price of the Sauter Omega grand, a piano he sells in Vancouver, B.C. *Impossible!* he wrote. Then he accuses me of being a competitor in disguise, trying to hurt his business by posting phony prices. I posted the price so that someone else could take advantage of it; after all, if George was willing to give me that price, he surely would give it to some other buyer for the same piano. Norbert's challenge pushes me to go further: I offer to scan and post the sales agreement. That silences him.

Penny advises me that Beethoven Pianos is not an authorized dealer of Grotrians, and this would void the factory warranty. A discussion ensues on the ethics and hazards of buying a "bootleg" piano. Larry says I should not trust such a dealer, but others insist there is no problem, if it is the piano I want and the price is right. I can have a technician inspect it, just as I would with a used piano from a private seller.

Beethoven's dealer status is not my concern, however, since I am now thinking I will get a used grand piano that I can afford. On the plane ride home, I drew a sketch of my living room, rearranging the furniture to accommodate a six-foot grand. If I block one of the doors to my office, it can be done. At my next piano lesson, I ask Molly for her opinion.

"I'd rather see you get a cheap Asian grand than the finest European upright," she says. "A grand action is very important for a student. I've had some grand pianos in some pretty tiny spaces." She seems to read my thoughts about the size of my living room. Then she tells me that one of her students, Anne, is going to trade in her ten-year-old Kawai parlor grand for a Steinway B. Maybe that would be a good piano for me? But when I call Anne, the deal has already transpired and her Kawai is at Sherman Clay in Seattle.

◆

The following week, Asaf calls again. This time I recognize his voice right away.

"Hello, Asaf! How are you? How is your concert career coming along?"

"Oh, very well," he replies. "Thank you for asking. Listen, Ms. Knize—"

"Please—call me Perri."

"Yes. Perri. I have a plan for you, how you can buy the Grotrian."

"Please, Asaf. You don't understand. I don't have that kind of money."

"But you see, we have this program called Keynotes. One year, same as cash. You pay nothing until the end of the first year."

"And how do I pay for it after the one year is up?"

"Let me send you the agreement, may I?"

I sigh.

"May I?" he repeats.

"Okay, send it. But you are wasting your time."

"Thank you. You will see, this is a good program for you."

✦

I receive a Piano World "private message" from "Rich D." He knows of two used Grotrian 192 Cabinet grands for sale in Seattle. Rich volunteers for a nonprofit piano-finding service that benefits a children's music program in Washington, D.C., and so he keeps a close eye on the used piano market. He's also a self-described Grotrian fanatic—he once owned a seven-foot Grotrian, one of several grand pianos he has owned, and he says he has always regretted selling it. Soon we are exchanging a flurry of e-mails. Rich played Marlene only two months before I did, and while he agrees it is a gorgeous piano, he feels it is a typical Grotrian. I seize on this information—perhaps I could love another Grotrian—a used one—just as much as I love Marlene? I have a conference planned in Portland next month; perhaps I can expand the trip to include Seattle?

✦

The phone rings.

"Hello, Perri. Did you receive the paperwork I sent you?" It is Asaf again. "What did you think of the Keynotes plan?"

"Well, as I told you before, I cannot afford the piano."

"It is a beautiful piano."

"Oh, yes, it is."

"It is the perfect piano for you. I have already put your name on it with a 'Sold' sign."

I roll my eyes. Unbelievable. How far will he go?

"Listen to me, Asaf, even with the loan, I have to be able to make the payments. How would I do this?"

"So what is the most you could pay for the piano?"

"I told you before, ten thousand dollars."

"I spoke to the owner, he said he can offer it to you for twenty-eight thousand dollars, shipping included."

"Asaf, that is an incredible deal, I wish I could take you up on it, but I can't."

"Here, Carl is right here, the owner. I'll put him on the phone. You explain to him."

This is ridiculous. Then I realize: Asaf thinks I am trying to talk him down still further. I will set the owner straight and put an end to these calls.

"Hello?" says a quiet, gentle, bemused-sounding voice on the other end of the line. The contrast to Asaf's passionate intensity is striking. Carl Demler sounds almost indifferent. He has an aristocratic German accent.

"Hello, Carl. I really appreciate the very good price you are offering me. I understand this is a great bargain on that piano. I want you to understand that I am not trying to talk you down to an even lower price. I am turning down the offer because I do not have the money."

"I understand," Carl says. There is no hint in his voice of even the slightest desire to change my mind. We say good-bye.

Well, that, I think as I hang up the phone, is that. Asaf continues to leave voice messages: "I have a price for you, call my cell phone." And: "The piano is still on hold for you. I just wanted to find out about your decision." But I don't return his calls or pick up the phone anymore.

✦

Though I'm rid of the Grotrian salesman, the sound of Marlene plays on in my mind, haunting me. Now that my friend's Steinway upright is out of my house, I am back to practicing in the basement of the music school. Playing the old, broken-down grands and uprights there presents a stark contrast to the sonorous, warm, dark voice of the Grotrian. I yearn for that piano; like a young man who has glimpsed a stunning, unobtainable woman from across a room, I cannot forget her.

I decide to pursue the used Grotrians in Seattle that Rich D. told me about. I arrange project interviews there for the following month, along with plans for the Portland conference. This will be a last-gasp trip both for my reporting, and for the piano hunt. I will play all the used Grotrians, Anne's Kawai at Sherman Clay, all the Petrofs, the Baldwins, Steinways, Kawais, Yamahas, Charles Walters, Mason & Hamlins—every used and rebuilt instrument I can find in Portland and in the Puget Sound area. When I'm not in a meeting or conducting an interview, I'll be in a piano showroom or looking at a private sale in someone's home. I start up my military campaign again, printing out the Yellow Pages listings for Seattle and Portland, calling ahead, searching online for private sales, arranging for the services of a tech-

nician to check out the used instruments, and planning my itinerary
with the help of local Piano World forum members. This will be my
most carefully mapped and strategic piano search yet.

And then, the whole world shatters.

◆

Early on a brilliant September day, while sipping hot tea and checking my e-mail and the weather report, a message from Oliver appears
on my computer screen:

Charles is safe. He made it to the midtown office OK.

What is he talking about? His brother Charles in New York?

I click on the *New York Times* link and the AP wire services report.
The World Trade Center was attacked. Charles works in the World
Financial Center across the street. Kim is usually at her health club
next door this time of day. I jump up and switch on the television in
the bedroom. The sound of the news coming on so early in the morning is strange and jarring; we almost never turn on the TV except to
watch a video or a ball game.

Peter Jennings is on the screen, a live videocast of a smoking World
Trade Center behind him. Footage of the second jetliner plunging
into the side of the second tower, from different angles, replays over
and over. Jennings explains that when the first plane struck it was
thought an accident, and now they are certain it was not. And then,
before the eyes of the world, one of the smoking towers simply disin-
tegrates, as if an invisible eraser rubs it out of the sky, as if the smoke
is actually steam, and the building evaporates. Gone.

I burst into tears and hear myself cry out, "The people! There are
people in there!" And then the second tower vanishes as well.

I sit alone in front of the television for a very long time, in a state
of shock, tears streaming down my face. I feel mortally wounded in
the part of me that belongs to New York. Why am I not there? How
could I have escaped this? What about my friends? I try to call Kim,
but her line is a fast busy. The circuits must be jammed. Then I call
Oliver at work, sobbing. "Turn it off, Perri," he says. "You'll make
yourself sick. Turn it off."

The remainder of the week drifts by in a sort of floating paralysis. News from friends and family trickles in. Oliver's mother on Long Island is safe. An associate of my brother's was a co-pilot of the plane that crashed into the Pentagon. Oliver's brother was evacuated from the World Financial Center when the first plane hit, in time to run for his life away from the burning towers, but not before seeing scores of people leap to their deaths.

I finally reach Kim by e-mail. She was not at her health club that morning. She is staying with a friend uptown, and is heading upstate to get out of the city altogether for a while. Despite Oliver's pleading, I can't tear myself away from the television. The scenes of lower Manhattan are devastating—a vision of nuclear winter.

I announce to my research team that the first deadline for our project will be a month later. Now is not the right time to talk to newspaper executives about their environmental coverage. And we all seem to need time to collect ourselves, to find our bearings in a new media landscape. In time, I return to Piano World to see what my online friends are talking about.

Certainly not pianos. Instead, the forums have become an emotional and political refugee camp, a place to gather amid the debris of American life and sort out what happened. I'm shocked that so many forum members are calling for war and vengeance. They seem to be in the majority. Politics was almost never discussed here before, but now it is clear that many Piano World members voted for George Bush and are very conservative. After all, these are business owners, many of them, and they ardently oppose government regulation. I reflect that many forum members are not professional musicians, but rather people wealthy enough to own fine grand pianos. Or sell them.

A cultural divide and political rift suddenly splits our little community wide open. Hostilities mount. Frank, the site's owner, creates a separate forum just to discuss the events of September 11, to keep the combat out of the areas meant for piano discussion. But the rift widens until it threatens to subsume all of Piano World. Frank creates another forum called "The Coffee Room," for discussing all nonpiano topics. The Coffee Room soon becomes a microcosm of the nation, with red and blue states at war. Piano World's friendly, peaceable early days are over.

I practice daily at the music school, but everything I play sounds like a dirge. Even though I have no immediate personal connection to the deaths of September 11, I realize I am grieving. So, with intention, I set the Chopin B minor prelude on the music desk and play it with great longing and sorrow, as slowly as the music will permit, allowing all my grief to pour through my fingers in a private tribute to the victims. In these solitary hours, the piano is my consolation.

The end of September draws near, and I am setting up interviews for Portland and Seattle when the phone rings.

"Ms. Knize?"

"Asaf! Are you okay? Is your family all right?" I feel a pang of guilt. How could I have forgotten about Asaf and his epic endeavor to twist my arm until I fall into a pit of debt?

"Yes, we are okay. The store is far enough uptown that we are not too affected by the debris."

"Oh, that is good to hear."

"But it is completely dead around here."

I don't think I quite understand him. Dead?

"*Nobody* is buying pianos." There is an edge of desperation in his voice; he is pleading with me. He emphasizes each of his next words fiercely: *"What is the most you can pay for that piano?"*

10

Delivery

"I found my piano."

Oliver has just come home from a job interview. He's wearing a navy wool sport coat, and a red rep tie hangs slack around his dress shirt's open collar. At my news he drops his briefcase, leans with one broad hand into the living room doorsill, and lowers his head to listen.

I watch my husband's rugged face closely as I describe the Grotrian, how I fell in love with it, what a great deal I have been offered for it. I admire how his dress clothes, which he rarely wears, show off his ski mountaineer's physique, still powerful at age fifty-three. He gave up ski guiding not long after we met, and rather than return to his earlier career in financial services, he reinvented himself as a computer network specialist. Though he has a good job, he pays what we hereabouts call the "scenery tax"—the price of living in a beautiful place without many professional jobs. Today's job interview might lead to a livable salary. But for now, with my journalism project's foundation grants, I am our household's primary breadwinner.

I watch closely for a reaction in my husband's face because Oliver does not hear well. Neither of us realized the extent of his deafness until the day, four or five years into our marriage, he nearly drove us into the path of a speeding police car. Oliver was at the wheel as we approached a familiar intersection in our neighborhood, and when a police siren shattered the air, Oliver just kept going. I screamed for him to stop, but he just kept going. I grabbed the steering wheel as we entered the intersection and, in what seemed an eternity, he finally slammed on the brakes and yelled at me in annoyance, "What? What?" In that moment, the police car streaked across our path, its brilliant lights spinning, siren shrieking. At the speed it was traveling, had it plowed into us it would have made a ghastly crash. The shock that registered on Oliver's face said it all—he hadn't heard the siren.

The test results at the audiologist's shocked me further—Oliver has moderate to profound hearing loss. Frequencies above 750 hertz, in the fifth octave, or midtreble range on a piano, sound progressively weaker to him, until he cannot hear them at all. We outfitted him with the best digital hearing aids available, but his disability can never be corrected, only mitigated.

Nevertheless, Oliver is a great lover of music; his favorite instrument is the cello, and I suspect that is because most of its tones fall within his range of hearing. But he listens to all kinds of music. In fact, I was drawn to him the day we met because he was whistling opera arias. We were part of a group climbing into the Eagle Cap Wilderness on skis, he as a guide, me as a reporter, and I thought to myself, *at last, an outdoorsman who knows good music.* Here was someone with whom I could reconcile the athletic and the aesthetic, satisfy my inner mountaineer *and* my inner sophisticate. Oliver told me he has trouble hearing, but because he is skilled at reading lips and guessing meaning from context, his disability seemed minor.

Now, as I explain to Oliver how I fell for Marlene, my excitement is tempered with sadness: falling in love with the magic of a piano is an experience my husband is unlikely to ever have, or understand.

When I finish, Oliver looks at me patiently, as if bestowing tolerance on a capricious child and her folly.

"Do you want the Grotrian?" he asks, one eyebrow raised. "Or do you want a bigger house?" We've been looking for something a bit more comfortable than our two-bedroom, one-bath, 950-square-foot bungalow on the working-class side of the tracks. Things always get cramped in the summer, when Oliver's eleven-year-old son, Charles, comes to stay. Oliver smiles at me indulgently, as if confident of my answer.

"That's easy!" I exclaim.

Oliver's face turns white. "You are scaring me."

Then I explain to him how I can do it. If I refinance our home, which I bought myself before the current real estate boom, I can take out enough cash to buy the piano and remodel the living room, and this will increase our monthly house payment by only $50. The difference in the interest rates, now far lower than on the original loan, will just about pay for the piano. The loan officer at our credit union explained the whole thing to me, after dissuading me from enrolling in the Keynotes program. Even after talking to our accountant, I can't find a downside. Besides, we can fix up this house ourselves, slowly, as we can afford to, or go back to house hunting after Oliver's job prospects or seniority improve. I can ride a bicycle when my twenty-year-old Toyota station wagon finally dies. But we can't build a Grotrian piano; there is only one way to get a Grotrian, and that is to buy it. And the price Carl has given me is so good, even if I need the money back, I can always sell it for what I paid for it. How can I go wrong?

Oliver does not even bother to counter these arguments. He sees I am a goner; there is no use in protesting. And getting the refinance loan, it turns out, is easy—I have a lot of equity. When Oliver looks over the numbers, he says, "They'd give you this loan even if you were dead."

For days I wander around in a liminal state, as if floating about on a cloud. Something in me I am unfamiliar with, some part that knows no limits, takes over and goes on autopilot. I proceed with an almost frightening degree of certainty. What has come over me? I'm not a pianist, and never will be. This piano is a highly refined, terribly elaborate tool that I do not need. My need is for a suitable, ordinary instrument to learn on. What possesses me?

Before I say yes to Asaf, I consult with my new piano friend, Rich D. He knows exactly what I experienced with Marlene, and he urges me to go for it. "Every time I bought a piano that I thought was nice but wasn't really what I wanted, I regretted it," Rich says. "I have to have the one I really want or I will be thinking of it all the time, how I could have had that piano."

That piano, specifically *this* piano, this piano with its golden voice, "like diamonds on velvet," as David Burton described it, has created a mystifying compulsion in me. *What is buying this piano all about?* I write to myself one morning. *I don't know, but my soul cries out for it.*

I suspect that on some level, I believe that owning this piano will turn me into a great pianist. I know I'm being irrational, but for some reason I can't not pursue the dream. Though two months have passed,

I remember Marlene's bell-like voice, the feeling of sureness in the keys so clearly. I am hooked on something. But what is it?

That Carl is not an authorized Grotrian dealer does concern me. I telephone Norbert Marten, the Vancouver dealer from Piano World, thinking that since he is also from Germany and in the business, he might know Carl.

"You don't need a warranty on this piano," Norbert admonishes in his rapid-fire accent. "If it is a new Grotrian, you can't go wrong. You can't buy a lemon from Germany."

But if there *were* a problem, I pose tentatively, if there *were,* I would only have Carl's warranty. Can I trust him?

"Carl is a good guy," Norbert assures me. "He won't cheat you. You can trust him."

The sale is contingent on an inspection by a piano technician. Rich's own technician once sold Grotrians, and he refers me to Evan Giller in New York, who used to work for a Grotrian dealer back in the 1970s.

"I *love* Grotrians!" Evan crows when we speak on the phone. He finds a spare hour to go over to Beethoven's and then calls me with a clean bill of health for Marlene. "It sounds wonderful! It has great sustain. But," and here he sounds a bit cautious, as if he is not certain this is what I want, "it's a little mellow compared to most other Grotrians. I asked Carl about it, and he said they ask for them to be voiced as mellow as possible."

"Yes, I thought the tone was very beautiful," I reply. I'm not sure what Evan means by "mellow," but it certainly sounds positive. Why does he have that edge in his voice? "So the piano passes?"

"Yes, it is perfect. The only thing I would caution you is if you ever want to sell it, they are hard to sell, because nobody knows what they are."

That I might ever want to sell this magic piano is, at the moment, utterly unthinkable. But Evan's voice is so kind and warm, I find the courage to ask him the question that has most plagued me from the moment I touched Marlene's keys: Never before have I allowed myself anything so beautiful and so rare. Am I worthy of this instrument?

"Evan, does it make any sense for an adult intermediate to buy such a fine piano when I will probably never play all that well? Shouldn't I be buying a 'good enough' upright instead?"

"*Don't* say that! *Never* say that!" Evan is almost fierce. "Buy the best piano you can hear. Your technique will catch up, and your hearing will only get better."

Dwight, the carpenter I hire to remodel the living room, doesn't seem to think it strange at all that I am putting a fine German grand piano in a modest working-class bungalow. I think it is rather like garaging a Rolls-Royce in a shack, but to Dwight, it seems a cause for celebration. A music lover himself, who plays classical music at his work sites, he's enthusiastic about creating a setting for a new grand piano. He even makes the new shelves for my stereo speakers in the shape of grand pianos.

Dwight and his crew use the two weeks I am in Portland and Seattle to rip out the fake wood paneling, the low acoustic-tile ceiling, the recessed fluorescent shop light that lit the living room. He covers the old fiberboard walls with something called "foam coat," which his workers sculpt to look like plaster. He mills crown molding, doorsills, and baseboard to match the original. New oak laminate flooring is laid down over the ugly old brown linoleum. The solid front door is replaced by a full-glass, insulated one that lets in abundant south light. The finishing touch is overhead track lighting with one light trained on the spot where the piano's music desk will soon be. The room is transformed, beautiful with its rich wheat-colored walls and glossy white trim. One corner sits empty, waiting for its new occupant. There, on the floor, lies a piece of white butcher paper, cut in the size and shape of a Grotrian 192.

I dream of the piano at night, and every evening I feel increasingly frustrated about practicing at the music school. During the month of waiting, as dark arrives earlier and nights get colder, I only become more impatient to have my own piano, a wonderful piano, in my own home.

Carl accepts a ten percent deposit and agrees to wait until the house closing to get the balance. In the meantime, he wants to ship the piano as soon as possible. It is already early November, and in Montana the weather will soon be severe. Carl warns that cold is dangerous for pianos. One piano he shipped to Massachusetts in winter arrived with a cracked finish because of the cold. When I point out that it is much colder in Montana than in New York, he says he will ship the piano immediately.

Two weeks later, I call Carl to find out when the piano will arrive. To my consternation, he says they just that day ordered new wood to build the crate, it will arrive in a few days, and then it will take a week to build the crate, and another week for the piano to arrive in Montana. He wants new wood, he explains, so the crate will be strong, since the piano is traveling as freight. The freight company will come pick up the piano just as soon as he calls. I ask for the name of the freight company, and Carl reluctantly gives it.

I telephone the freight company at once. Are the trucks heated? No. How many times will the crated piano change trucks? Four times, which means time sitting on loading docks. The piano will take about a week to arrive in Missoula, and then a local mover will have to bring it to my home and set it up. Six trucks in all. Thanksgiving is coming. What if the piano is shipped just before the holidays? No freight will travel over the holidays.

Why did Carl delay shipping for two weeks? I wonder. He has cashed my check. Is this normal? What is the usual procedure for shipping a piano? I don't want to make a fuss and be seen as an unreasonable customer. I want to educate myself first.

So I call Norbert again, and ask his advice. After all, it was his endorsement of Carl that sealed my decision to buy the Grotrian. As it turns out, Norbert has heard a lot about Beethoven Pianos from an employee who once worked there.

"Carl is a strange guy. Nobody can really figure him out," Norbert says. "He's not a typical German. He is known as a *schlamper.* In German that means 'an unorganized type of guy.' Maybe he doesn't have his shit together, but he is not a crook. He won't cheat you.

"I've heard some unbelievable stories, that he's sold a piano one day, and then the next he has no idea of the customer's name. Apparently he is never sure of who is working for him at any given time, who is on the payroll. And yet he is a good businessman. He is a lot of contradictory things. Carl will come through for you in the end," Norbert soothes. "Ask him, what day is the piano shipping? What day will it be here? Tell him how excited you are about the piano coming, and that is why you are so impatient."

I don't like the sound of this at all, but I don't want to pull out of the deal. I love the memory of playing that piano too much. Every night, when I practice at the music school, all I can think of is how much better the Mendelssohn will sound on the Grotrian. I cannot get that sound out of my mind. And Oliver says he misses my practicing at home.

I try to reach Carl several times, but he is never in when I call. Finally I tell the salesman who answers the phone why I am calling. "He probably forgot to ship it," the salesman says, sounding nonchalant, as if this is quite ordinary. What a strange place this store is.

I e-mail Asaf. Winter is already arriving where I live. Will he please talk to Carl? But Asaf writes back to say that he also can't reach Carl. Asaf works only on Sundays now, when Carl is not there. *I am also frustrated and concerned,* he writes.

This only alarms me more. I call Asaf and ask him to please stay on top of things. Then there is nothing more I can do.

Thanksgiving comes and goes. On the Sunday after, Asaf calls and says he has spoken to his "other boss," a woman. She has taken things in hand and will make certain that everything happens right away. He puts her on the phone. Her name is Kaoru, and she is Carl's wife. Apparently, she knew nothing about the sale. Instantly everything changes.

"The piano was crated today, and it is scheduled to be picked up by the freight company tomorrow, and you will have it a week later, guaranteed," says Kaoru, with an accent I later learn is Japanese. "When is payment going to arrive?"

I explain I am paying with cash from a home refinance, and closing is not until the end of the year. "Usually we do not ship without payment in full, but since this is the arrangement you have with Carl, no problem," Kaoru says.

The next day I receive a call from the store that the freight company is picking up the piano that afternoon. "We guarantee it arrives in perfect condition," says Linda, the delivery manager. At the end of the day, she faxes me the tracking number. Then Carl calls to ask if he may send me a new Steinway tufted leather concert artist bench, which has legs that will not match the piano's legs, but it is glossy black, and is the best bench he has. Will that be acceptable? If I want a Grotrian bench, he will have to order it from Europe. I am overjoyed to have the concert bench. Carl will send it UPS. For the remainder of the week,

I hear from someone at the store every single day, reassuring me that all is well.

My anxiety quickly turns to excitement, which turns to worry again when I see the weather report. The day after the piano ships, a Pacific storm front moves in and blizzards rage over the Rockies, spill into the Dakotas, and drop record-breaking snowfall. Interstate 80 shuts down for 140 miles. Temperatures drop to sixteen below zero in Utah, and winds clock at forty miles per hour. Heavy snow falls in Missoula as well. Weather forecasters say the storm came "out of nowhere." The piano has already left New York, and according to the Yellow Freight online tracker, it is somewhere in Pennsylvania. It is headed for Salt Lake City, right into the path of the storm.

Missoula turns bitter cold. One night I can't find parking near the music school, and fierce winds smack me in the face and stiffen my fingers on the long walk in the dark to the practice rooms. When I arrive, I find my favorite piano is taken, and the only available piano is in a room with a saxophone wailing through one wall and an electric bass with the volume turned up booming through the other. I can hardly hear myself play. What has always been for me a joyful aural camaraderie of fellow musicians practicing has become unbearable.

When I get home, I log in my tracking number on the Yellow Freight website. The piano has not moved! It is still in Lancaster, Pennsylvania. Then next morning I get an e-mail from Rich D.: *Hey, I see your piano is in Chicago now.* He was so eager to see the piano's progress, I gave him the tracking number so he could follow it himself. I telephone the freight company. "The highways are closed," a woman named Shelly explains. "We had to take your shipment to Chicago. We'll be putting your piano on a rail car. The roads are too dangerous for our drivers."

By now, despite a schedule packed with meetings with my fellow project reporters and dozens of telephone interviews every day, I am in a minor frenzy about the piano. I check the weather and the Yellow Freight website several times a day. The deadline for our first round of reporting is at the end of the month, our reporting files must be delivered, and the refinance closing is scheduled for then as well. The stress of so much anticipation and uncertainty takes a toll, and my back begins to spasm, making it even harder to work.

But each evening I go to the music school to practice, through bitter cold and driving snow, and sit at the broken-down grand in my favorite practice room, and imagine that I'm playing Bach on the Grotrian. When my practicing doesn't go well, I feel mortified, thinking I do not play well enough to own my new piano. Each night, during the week of the long wait, I dream about the piano arriving.

The piano template I cut out of white butcher paper remains in place on the new living room floor. Once I found the exact location I wanted, I left it there for Oliver and me to practice walking around. The template seems a ghost of its future self. I gaze at it, trying to imagine the three-dimensional black behemoth that soon will stand in its stead. The paper will lie in place until the movers arrive, so they can see exactly where I want the piano. Placement must be exact in our limited quarters.

The weekend before the piano arrives, the weather shifts abruptly back to normal. The snow melts. I go out at night wearing only a light jacket.

On the promised day, December 3, at the promised time, five p.m., the local moving company telephones. "Your piano is here!" says the warehouse manager. He sounds kind and enthusiastic. By now we've talked on the phone several times, and he seems to enjoy my childlike anticipation. Unfortunately, he tells me, when he examined the crate for damage, he found a corner was crushed; but, he says, it is in an area of the crate where the piano isn't, and so it is unlikely there is any harm done. However, clearly the crate was dropped. Because I don't want to hear this, I choose to believe this is a minor thing.

"It's too late to deliver it today," says the manager. "So we will bring it by on the first load out in the morning."

That night, I dream that Vladimir Horowitz personally delivers my piano.

✦

The next day is overcast and balmy, and it seems as if the terrible storms that raged all the previous week never happened. At nine a.m., I hear the truck pull into the alley, and I run out to greet the movers. They back the van up to our gate, lift the heavy door of the cargo area, and there it is.

Of course, what I see is not a piano, but a tall and narrow wooden crate, made of thick new plywood. Detailed instructions are written all over it: FRONT. HEAVY SIDE. HANDLE WITH CARE. LIGHT SIDE. OPEN FROM THE OTHER SIDE. OPEN THIS SIDE (TOP FIRST). All in big block letters. Someone also playfully drew the black silhouette of a grand piano on the box.

I dissolve into a feeling of wild anticipation, like a child about to open her first truly important toy. Perhaps for a five-year-old, the toy is a shiny, new red bicycle. My eagerness is for the dream I encountered in the showroom. I am going to possess that magical tone all the rest of my life.

The movers are four big, burly men—Dublin, Charlie, Doug, and Joe. Dublin and Charlie look like loggers in their plaid wool jackets, Doug and Joe look like ranch hands in their Carhartts and denim. They have big handlebar mustaches, the kind cowboys and forest rangers wear, and they move with a lumbering, inelegant grace.

They place the crate on a dolly and, with three of them holding on, run it down a ramp onto a series of boards they place on the grass, throwing plywood sheets across the lawn, leapfrog fashion, before their tottering charge, while I skip alongside, taking photographs. They regard me with patient smiles. I'm too excited to be embarrassed. Besides, I tell myself, they're piano movers—they've seen grown women behave like this before.

Doug measures the height of the front door with a tape, and announces it is not quite tall enough to admit the crate. Grand pianos are stored and shipped lying on their sides, with their legs removed and tucked into the crate beside them, and this makes them as tall while in transit as they are wide when they are set up to play. So there on the front walk, the movers unscrew the top lid of the crate, creating just enough clearance to get into the house; this provides me with my first glimpse of her. I stand on the top porch step to peer inside. Marlene is draped in black felt that looks as soft as velvet, and bound in clear plastic. Mint, I think. A virgin instrument.

They roll the crate up a ramp over the steps, onto the front porch, through the front door, and across the protective pad on the newly shampooed rug, to the piano's corner at the far end of the living room. They put the crate to rest just to one side of the butcher paper template.

"That's how you want it?" says Doug, tilting his head at the template. I nod back, almost unable to speak from excitement, and I clear the template away.

This is a waking dream, this uncrating. The edges of reality seem indistinct, time slows, movements blur. Doug unscrews one side of the crate with an electric drill. When the box stands open, we see the blond underside of the piano, its braces facing us. The men remove the crate entirely and tear away the plastic film enveloping her.

They unbundle the piano's three legs, wrapped in black felt. The men are curious about them. With the piano still on its side, they examine the legs closely, as if they have never seen piano legs like these before. "What kind of piano is this?" asks Charlie. When I tell him, he says, "Never heard of it."

"It's from Germany," I explain.

"I wish they were all designed this way. Look at how the legs attach," he says to the other movers, and they all crowd in to see. "Look, you just place them in, lock in the bolt and it's done. Those Germans!"

The piano is still on its side, two of its three legs splayed out into the room. The movers together lift her off her palette, up to her rightful position, and then one of the men lies on his back on the floor to install the third leg, while another holds her rim up in the air on his bent-over back. They peel away all the tape holding the black felt in place, and the fabric falls to the floor, revealing her shapely, shiny black silhouette. She is gorgeous.

All four men carefully lift her up by her rim, and arrange her in her corner. The butcher paper ghost, the phantom that haunted this corner for a month, leaps into three dimensions. My dream is made manifest.

Dublin lifts the Grotrian's wing and places it on the longest prop stick. Charlie unwraps the music desk and slides it into place above the keyboard. Then he lifts the fallboard to see the piano's name. The men stand around, grinning. Joe extends one arm toward the keyboard, as if he were a maitre d' at a fancy restaurant ushering me inside, inviting me to play. They seem to enjoy sharing in my happy delirium. Play in front of these men? Sure, why not.

I come forward to touch the keyboard, and press down a note, but nothing happens. The keyboard is locked to keep the keys from moving during travel. The movers do not know how to release them. I will have to call a technician.

I thank each man, pressing a large bill into his hand with my handshake, and this makes their grins of pleasure much broader. And then they leave me alone with her.

At once I telephone the local technician I have been planning to use, and he very kindly agrees to come by this afternoon, between clients. Only later do I learn how punishing his schedule is, maintaining pianos for the university, all the public schools, and most of Missoula's piano teachers as well. While I wait for him, the UPS truck pulls up with my beautiful new artist's bench, and I assemble it. Then Carl calls.

"Is it there?" His whispery, German-accented voice twinkles with pleasure. "Are you happy?" he asks sweetly.

Happy? I am beside myself with happiness. I explain about the locked keys. Carl sounds disappointed that the movers didn't know what to do. He wants to hear my wildly delirious joy at how great the piano sounds in my home. He will have to wait.

Releasing the piano's keys, it turns out, is a simple affair. The tuner pulls the action out of the piano and removes a retaining rod that is wired to the action rail, and the piano is ready to play.

I sit down before my new piano, my new tuner waiting to one side. I eagerly place my hands on the keys, remembering so clearly and anticipating the tone and touch that have haunted me since August.

But as I play the first bars of Mendelssohn, I freeze. Something is wrong. I can't believe it at first. I switch to Schumann, to hear that gorgeous treble voice, but it is not there. The voice I fell for in the showroom is not there. The bass and tenor are recognizable—sweet, dark, and singing. But the treble is dead. I don't recognize it at all. And all of the piano sounds subtly out of whack, in a way I can't quite put my finger on. It sounds weird and echoey. It's uneven. The action makes too much noise.

"Something is wrong," I say to the tuner.

He is an organist, and he sits down to play some Bach, but since he never played this piano when it was in the showroom, he says, he doesn't know how it is different now. "I'm afraid I can't be of much help."

This is a bitter disappointment. I had imagined how impressed he would be with my piano, and now there is nothing like admiration in his reaction. I want to protest: "But it was wonderful! It *was*! I swear it was the most magical, special piano you ever heard!" Of course I don't say anything of the kind.

"I'm sorry, I have to get back to my appointments now," the tuner says. I understand. He's been kind to come on such short notice. I see him out.

I sit down again before the gorgeous black being in my new living room, its one wing raised to the new ceiling, this time with trepidation. I play some Mozart. Treble definitely dead. The "melody section," the fifth and sixth octaves, sound like the hammers are hitting wood, a pocking sound. The tone is too soft. It lacks vibrancy. Playing harder makes little difference. The tremendous sustain I remember, the wash of tone over tone that merges into a shimmering caress of the air—it isn't there.

I check the serial number against the one on the sales agreement, which I had already checked against the one written in my shopping notes. It is the same. But if this piano is my piano, my Marlene, if it *is* her, then something has gone terribly wrong. In place of the glorious, pure, pealing clarity and sonority that possessed my memory for the past three months is a hoarse, broken voice. Marlene is gone.

11

The Inspection

"Those are the strangest-looking hammers I have ever seen," Jeff Stickney says. "Look at the bumps on the ends." Jeff, my new piano technician, has come back the next day to tune the piano and see if he can figure out what is wrong with it. Now the Grotrian's action is out of the case and on his lap.

I look at the tops of the felt hammers. They seem to have growths, or swellings on them, as if they are suffering from bee stings.

"Are you sure these are Renner hammers?" asks Jeff. "I've never seen anything like *this* before." Evan Giller, the New York tech, told me that Renner manufactures Grotrian hammers.

"Maybe that shape is what makes the sound so special?" I venture weakly. I am at a loss.

"I'm sorry. I have no experience with hammers like that. I don't think I can help you."

I feel crushed at these words. Jeff was supposed to be my technician. Now what will I do? He puts the action back into the piano, packs up his tools, and tells me that unless he knows how the piano sounded in the showroom, he would be shooting in the dark if he tried to fix the problem. And then he leaves.

How it sounded in the showroom. Who knows how it sounded before? I call Evan Giller.

"I did find it a bit more mellow than is typical for a Grotrian." There's a warning tone in Evan's voice. "But the piano was in perfect condition. I went over it quite thoroughly. There was plenty of crown in the soundboard, I measured it. Plenty of sustain. All was excellent.

"You need to have someone look at it. Call Rick Baldassin, in Salt Lake City. He's the nearest technician to you that I know of who has the expertise to work on your piano."

I immediately dial the number Evan gave me. Rick listens to my description of how the piano plays, but as I explain the situation, I feel certain he will dismiss what I say and tell me the problem is room acoustics, or that I am hearing things. When I finish, he speaks without hesitation.

"Something happened to the piano," he says, surprising me. "That's what my gut tells me. Why do some parts of the piano sound good and some don't? The plate could have shifted. The strike point could be out of alignment. Did something happen to the rim when it was dropped? Maybe the soundboard collapsed—that can happen with extreme temperature changes. That was a very severe cold spell. How many days did it sit out in the cold on a loading dock? It could have been knocked over by a forklift, and nobody would ever know. Call the dealer and tell him something is wrong, and what does he propose? Don't be panicked. Express concern."

I feel sick. Why didn't Carl ship the piano in a heated truck? Why did it go by freight? Indeed, what could have happened? And how will it get taken care of? Suddenly, Missoula seems so terribly far away from anywhere.

"Will you come look at it?" I ask Rick. His reply is a short laugh.

"I'm having a hard time right now even getting to customers in Provo. I run a retail store here. I can't get away. But I can recommend a good technician. If it seems like it will be major work, you can bring it to Salt Lake City. Let me know what happens."

✦

"Yes! Hello!" Carl's sprightly voice, gentle and warm and kind, greets me over the phone. "How do you like your new piano?"

All I know of Carl so far is this telephone voice, his broken, raspy whisper, almost a phantasm of a voice. When I talk to him on the phone it seems like I have to shout, as if trying to pierce a veil of consciousness.

We are now embarking on the first test of our dealer-customer relationship, but we have never even met each other; will he believe me? Or will he insist the problems with the Grotrian are all in my imagination? How do these things work, long distance, anyway?

"Carl, something happened to the piano."

"No. That can't be. We use these shippers all the time. They always do a great job. It must have been your local movers."

"I watched their every move, Carl. They did a terrific job. All I know is something is wrong." I describe for him the weak treble, the noisy action, the unevenness of the tone, the echoing. "It is not the piano I played in the showroom."

"But what could have happened? The piano was perfect when it left here. Your technician inspected it and said so."

"Maybe it was the weather?"

"But it was in the seventies when the piano left New York."

"And it was sixteen below on the Great Plains, Carl. The highways were closed. Yellow Freight had to detour to Chicago and put the piano on a rail car."

"Oh-h-h!! No!"

"Yes. A freak storm. No one predicted it."

"It is probably just cold. Do you have down comforters?"

"I have sleeping bags."

"Perfect. Cover it up with the sleeping bags and let it warm up gradually. That is what they do in Germany. Leave them on for a couple of days, then try playing again."

So I cover the piano with every sleeping bag we own. For a pair of lifelong backpackers and winter ski mountaineers who hang on to all their old gear, that is a lot of sleeping bags. Big ribbed, blue, green, and black nylon cocoons smother the glossy black case. I leave them on for three days.

While I wait, I consult with my friends at Piano World on what could have happened. Maybe the room acoustics are to blame? But no, the tenor section of the piano sounds as lovely as I remember it. The acoustics wouldn't be wrong for one part of the keyboard and not another. The technicians say the wood must have contracted from the cold, and as the piano warms up, it will go back to the way it was in the showroom. I will be happy in the end.

Rich, especially, works hard to reassure me. We talk on the phone often now, since he is the only other person I know besides Evan who played my piano in the showroom. He says he played another Grotrian 192 in Boston about the same time he played mine, and both were equally beautiful. He thinks mine sounded like a typical Grotrian.

As we know this piano played "perfectly" to our ears in NYC and was examined and praised by the Grotrian tech you brought in, Rich e-mailed me. *There should be nothing wrong with the piano that a good tech cannot correct. Don't let this piano stuff get you down. It's going to work out well in the end! Chin up.*

But when I finally remove the sleeping bags and play it again, a few days later, there is no improvement. I crawl underneath the piano, draw a length of thread along the grain of the soundboard, and find that the soundboard has plenty of "crown," the convex shape that puts it under tension. The board has not collapsed, as Rick Baldassin postulated. There is a nice, healthy gap between the midsection of the thread and the soundboard.

I research "dead treble" on the Piano Technicians Guild discussion archives online, and find out about something called the "killer octave," a problem of the treble section, caused by improper design and poor impedance of the soundboard.

I e-mail Larry Fine and tell him what happened. Does he think I have a "killer octave" problem? He writes back to suggest I try the "pluck" test. Step on the sustain pedal to hold the dampers off the strings, then pluck a string with your fingernail instead of striking it with the hammer. Then count to see how long the tone lasts. In the treble, it should be over ten seconds. Also, listen to hear if the tone is different when plucked than when struck by a hammer.

The tone is fine when plucked—beautiful, with a long sustain, well over twelve seconds. But the same notes are dead when struck by a hammer. I start to write Larry Fine back, only to find he has written again to say that if the piano *ever* sounded good, it does not have a killer octave problem. Then the problem is the hammers. They need voicing.

✦

"How do you like your piano now?" Carl sounds genuinely hopeful when he hears my voice.

"Something is still not right."

"Okay, we need an inspection. Is there a technician there that you trust?"

I ask Rick Baldassin for a referral, but he has not personally worked with anyone in Missoula except Jeff, who has already thrown up his hands. I start calling around town. There is a guitar and violin repair shop in town. Perhaps they know of someone.

Only the haughty Dutch owner of the local piano store, the one who sells the Samicks, they say, is experienced enough for the job. "There is no one else."

✦

Lucien Hut is not just the owner of a piano shop, as it turns out. He taught piano at the music school for many years, performs locally on the harpsichord with an early music group, is a recording artist, a rebuilder, technician, and a piano design consultant with an international reputation. Despite his sterling credentials, I feel some trepidation because I am a customer who got away. For two years, Katherine, his store manager, called me regularly to tell me about new pianos arriving, and I visited the shop several times. Now I have no choice but to ask him to inspect a piano he didn't sell me. Will he be gracious about it? Will he tell me the truth?

Since the Grotrian arrived, it has snowed every day, deep winter blanketing the valley at last. Lucien and Katherine dust off their coats and stomp their boots clean on my front porch as I open the door. Katherine extends her hand. "Congratulations on your new piano!" she crows, and her eyes say she means it sincerely.

But Lucien barrels into the room without so much as a greeting.

"This room is too small! You need a bigger house! No wonder the piano doesn't sound right!"

"Lucien!" Katherine protests, and looks at me apologetically.

"Actually," I say evenly, "the problem is that the piano is too quiet sounding, so the room being small is not a factor."

Lucien raises the wing to its full height and I set up the longest prop stick. He raps on the soundboard in several places around the plate. "Dead!" he proclaims. "Hear that?" He raps again. "The soundboard is thuddy. It should have a drumlike sound.

"And look at this!" This time he raps his knuckle on the bronze-colored iron plate. "It's a vacuum-cast plate." He clicks his tongue dis-approvingly. I let this roll off me. I know that Grotrian plates are made with the preferred wet-sand cast method.

Then he lets the pneumatic fallboard drop slowly over the keys. "That's a Schimmel design," he declares. "This piano was built by Schimmel!"

He plucks the strings in front of the agraffes on the treble side with his long fingernails, scraping them back and forth. "The inharmonic-ity is intolerable!" he booms. "It's not possible to tune it. Steinway does this much better!"

"I liked this piano much better than any Steinway I've played."

Lucien ignores me and gets out a screwdriver from his black tool case. He pulls the action out and begins tightening screws. "Every sin-gle screw and bolt is loose," he exclaims. "The piano is dried out from traveling. It is a German piano, you have to maintain the humidity between forty-five and fifty-five percent. It is all dried out."

Katherine and I look at the digital hygrometer that has stood sen-try by the piano since the day it arrived. The relative humidity is 45 percent. I explain I have kept the room at that level consistently, but he ignores me.

"Lucien," protests Katherine. "Shouldn't she let the piano adapt to this climate instead of trying to create a German climate in her room?" Lucien ignores her as well. Then he crawls under the piano with a socket wrench.

"All the bolts are loose!" Lucien exclaims from under the piano. "The plate is loose!" The socket wrench clacks and grinds under his brisk ministrations. I shudder.

"Please! Just look at the piano," I protest. I am in a panic—he could compromise my warranty. I try to sound firm. "Please just write up a report. That is all I need. The dealer will arrange for any work to be done." But Lucien keeps right on tightening bolts, lying on his back under the piano's belly.

The phone rings. It is Carl.

"Is he there?" he asks, without any preamble. I hand the phone to Lucien, and Katherine takes his hand to help him out and up from under the piano.

"There is nothing wrong with the piano," Lucien booms into the phone. His long white hair is askew, his glasses foggy, and his face is nearly crimson with the effort of getting back on his feet.

"He has a heart condition," Katherine whispers to me. "Now that he is over seventy, he really should not be crawling under pianos."

"Every screw and bolt is loose," Lucien continues into the phone. "The piano is completely dried out. It is too dry here for it."

I open my mouth, but then close it. Lucien hands the phone back to me. "I will call you back in a little while," I tell Carl.

When I hang up, Katherine and Lucien are already putting on their coats. Actually, Katherine, a tiny, birdlike woman, holds Lucien's coat for him to climb into, while he, towering nearly to the ceiling, heaves it over his broad shoulders.

"You need eight to twelve hours' worth of work on preparation," Lucien says. "Set the strings to the bridge, install a Dampp-Chaser, put a rug under it, voice the hammers, re-regulate the entire action and the dampers, measure the crown." He rambles off his to-do list rapid-fire, spluttering with emphasis, and counting each item on his fingers. I can't understand half of what he is saying, and I quit taking notes to look up at him, bewildered.

"We'll write up a report and mail it to you," says Katherine as Lucien gathers up his tools and heads for the door. From the front porch, with Lucien almost out to the street, she looks back across the threshold at me and says kindly, "You got yourself a very nice piano. One of the best."

And then they are gone.

✦

"Carl, there is nothing wrong with the humidity here. It is at forty-five percent at all times in my living room." I called him back immediately, quite worried about the impression Lucien made.

"Yes, that is fine, I'm sure it is fine." Carl sounds distracted, as if is thinking.

"Lucien did tighten all the plate bolts and it seems to have helped." I sat down to play as soon as the inspection was over, and at once noticed that the strange echo was gone. It was as if a vibrating double image had suddenly registered and clicked into one. "At least now the piano's voice is recognizable to me. But the treble is still dead. This is still not at all the piano I played in the showroom. It says right in my notes, 'gorgeous treble.' "

I begin making my case, expecting Carl to argue with me. I expect him to say it is the fault of the movers and he isn't responsible, I'll have to take it up with insurance. I expect him to repeat that Evan said there was nothing wrong with it, and now Lucien says there is nothing wrong with it.

But *I* know something is wrong. And I am powerless. I am twenty-five hundred miles away from my dealer, I do not live near a world-class piano technician—hadn't the Sauter distributor said that should be my first concern?—and I have hocked my house for a dream that is vanishing before my ears, shattering before my eyes.

But miraculously, Carl takes me at my word.

"Don't worry," Carl says. His voice is soothing, gentle, very calm. "Don't worry. I know a *wonderful* voicer. He has a co-op in Montana."

"A co-op? Carl, I think you must mean a cabin."

"Yes, yes," he says a bit impatiently, "I am sure it is a cabin. Anyway, he has a co-op there and he visits Montana twice a year. He is the most knowledgeable person I know of to voice. There is only one other person in his league. He is a magician. I will have him give you a call, and we'll take it from there."

12

The Voicer

*"The most expert and rapid tuners are possessed of a
highly excitable, nervous, and emotional temperament,
verging on the border of insanity at times."*

—DANIEL SPILLANE, *THE PIANO*

"I t doesn't surprise me to hear that the voicing is out of balance,"
Carl's voicer says over the telephone, after listening to my story.
"It is common for it to become dull. When I voiced your piano, I
used natural lacquer to enhance the tone, and lacquer breaks down
and loses its effect. If that happens before the hammer has hardened,
weakness develops."

I do not have a clue what he is talking about, but then, he asks the
only question that matters to me now.

"I created the piano personality that you fell in love with. What if
I make it your dream piano again?" he asks. "I don't want to come all
the way out there unless I am sure I can make you happy. If I come
out there and re-create what you heard in the showroom, will you be
happy?"

Of course, I tell him. What a question. If he does that in my own
living room, then I will know for certain my piano is not a lemon. I
will not have to send it back.

But what does he mean, he created the personality of my piano?
Is such a thing possible? Isn't my piano's sound the sound of a Grotrian? After all, Rich told me it sounded like a typical Grotrian to him.

"You need the right person to come and make it what it was," the
voicer continues. "You can tighten all the screws you want, it won't fix

115

your voicing problem. I know what I did, and I know exactly what to do. Anyone else would be guessing."

As for his Montana "co-op," the voicer only recently moved back to New York after living in Montana for four years. How strange a coincidence is that? Until just last year, he was in Montana four times a year, but now he is selling his condominium in Bozeman, and will make the trip to see me also a trip to wrap up his affairs, and see some old clients. Their payments will cover his expenses. He won't charge me or Carl for his time. He just wants us both to be happy, he says.

But his visit will have to wait until March. "My life is totally *crazy*, like never before," he explains, his voice almost a squeal. It sounds like he is driving somewhere in a car while he's talking. A horn honks in the background. "I have my full-time job as head of piano technology at the Manhattan School of Music, plus a full roster of clients. I'm squeezing this in. I really have no business going out there."

Still, we make a date, and I feel a rush of relief and hope. I give him the code for an airline discount I've been saving, to help with the costs.

"I know what you are going through," he soothes. "We'll work together until I've exhausted all the possibilities."

The months pass, and winter beds us down deeply in cold and snow. I practice daily on the Grotrian, but the piano does not improve on its own. I try to be patient, all the while holding in my clear and vital memory how the piano played in the showroom. What I experienced then so deeply resonated in me, I am certain I will know that voice again, if ever I hear it, as plainly as I know my mother's.

During the months of waiting, I often replay in my mind the conversation with the voicer. What are the odds that the one piano I fall in love with in all of North America, after a two-year search, is a piano voiced by someone from my own backyard? Does that mean anything? To me it suggests the possibility that Carl's voicer might share my contradictory affinities for living near remote, wild mountains on the one hand, and owning a rare, handmade piano requiring urban technical expertise on the other. I'm eager to learn if this is so, for until now, I've been a tribe of one.

◆

Marc Wienert appears at my door at eight o'clock on a wintry March morning. He is a fine-boned man, about five foot six, with a mass of thinning, reddish curls pulled tightly back into a ponytail. His sparkly blue eyes are small and hooded, like a turtle's, and framed by thick, half-rimmed glasses. His mouth is pursed like a rosebud, his chin recedes into a short, flaccid neck. Though a blizzard is raging outside, he is dressed in only a black T-shirt, black jeans, and black leather sneakers. The clothes accentuate the pastiness of his soft, expressive face. His long, white arms hang at his sides; one pale hand grips a black faux alligator kit bag, like a doctor's bag.

"You are here so early! What time did you leave Bozeman?" I say as he stomps the snow off his sneakers and enters the house. He does not appear to be at all cold. "Can I make you some coffee?"

"I've been drinking *this* on the drive over," he says. He holds up a small Nalgene bottle, the kind you take camping, half-filled with dark liquid. Though we've only talked on the phone once, I immediately recognize the voicer's edgy tenor, suffused with emotion and manic energy. He dangles the bottle from his blue-white fingers and shakes it until it froths. "Espresso. I sip this all day every day. It's my fuel. I've been taking sips since I left Bozeman at four o'clock this morning."

I gasp. From tracking his flight I know it arrived at one o'clock this morning.

"It's okay," he says. "This is a normal workday for me. I would have been here earlier but I had to rent a car. Mine can't handle this weather." He gestures to the window, where fat snowflakes drop furiously from the sky.

This is a piano technician's visit of epic proportions. A nerdy, bantamweight superhero—I want to call him Technician Man—has just crossed my threshold, come to save my piano. The whole scenario is operatic. I look at him in wonder. Why is he making this trip? Why didn't he say he's too busy, or the drive is too dangerous?

Marc says he owes Carl a favor. Carl sent Marc's wife, Connie, to a homeopathic doctor last year and her cancer went into remission. "I wouldn't make this trip for anyone else."

I offer him breakfast, but this he also declines.

"Let's get started," he says. His tone is brash; he exudes a punishing intensity. "I have to be back in Bozeman tonight."

Marlene is wearing the garnet-colored paisley shawl Oliver's mother gave me for a piano-warming present. I uncover her, revealing the immaculate black polish finish. As I fold back the front lid, Marc peers at the brass hinge closely, then points to its tiny screws. "See that?"

I look, and see the grooves in the screw heads are very slightly bent. The damage is almost invisible. I would never have noticed it on my own.

"Whoever tightened those screws? Don't ever let them touch your piano ever again." He sounds angry.

Marc removes the music desk and sets it across the arms of an over-stuffed chair. I lift the piano's wing so it rests on the longest prop stick. Marc raises the fallboard and plays octaves, fifths, fourths, a run, and a piece I do not recognize that covers the keyboard. Then he plays some strange chords—"Tenths and seventeenths," he says. "It seems like it's in pretty good tune, for a machine tuning."

How does he know the last tuner used a machine?

"A piano tuning is a myriad of tiny little lies brought together into one great big lie of being in tune," Marc says. "I don't want to diss machine tuners, but a tuner connected to the vibrational reality of the piano who is willing to tell an artistic lie ends up with a better tuning than someone who uses a machine."

Seeing my clueless look, he moves on. "Now tell me what your problems are with the piano."

"It isn't like the piano I played in the showroom," I begin. I feel a bit desperate as I explain, like a patient being interviewed by yet another doctor, a patient who has suffered too long with mysterious symptoms a dozen experts have failed to diagnose. "The action is noisy, the treble is weak and wooden sounding. The tenor and bass have buzzing notes. The bass lacks the full, resonant power it had. The treble lacks sustain. Repetition is poor."

I give Marc the detailed notes I made on exactly which notes have problems. A3 through F#4 have a metallic buzz and a nasal tone. E♭5 has odd overtones. F5 to B♭6 are thin and weak. When I play these notes the action makes a "pocking" noise. From the fifth octave up, the piano has lost its sustaining, bell-like qualities. The sixth octave is harsh and brittle. Only the notes B5 through D5 sound good, have a clear tone and good sustain.

I also give Marc a list I compiled from talking to Rick Baldassin and Evan Giller—an inventory of all the problems a technician should check for, and what to do, in the right order, to correct them. I don't know what any of these steps actually entail, but I hope Marc will:

1. Inspect the piano to make certain there is no damage
2. Check crown and downbearing
3. Check soundboard and plate
4. Tighten all bolts and screws on the plate, case, and action to the correct degree
5. Set the strings to the bridge
6. Level the strings
7. Lightly file hammers
8. Seat key frame properly in the key bed
9. Check and correct hammer travel
10. Concert tuning
11. Voice to the room

"Uh-huh," Marc says, sitting on the concert artist's bench, turned halfway toward me, reading my notes and the list. He hands the papers back to me. "Now how would you describe what you heard in the showroom? How was it different?"

"Oh!" I exclaim, animated by the memory. "It was a warm, sweet, singing, dark, rich, resonant, complex tone," I tell him. "The action felt like it played itself. The treble was incredibly full, rich, deep, and singing. Yes, a singing tone. It had clarity, roundness, projection. It was lush and clear."

"You are describing what Carl and I call a 'rounded, creamy' tone," Marc says, with evident satisfaction. "Carl isn't like most other dealers. Most of them want you to make the piano quite bright and brash, because that gets a customer's attention. Carl and I like a creamy tone, and he doesn't tell me what to do, he just says, 'Make it as beautiful as you can possibly make it.' That's one reason I like working for Carl.

"Let's get a fresh tuning on here and then see what we have." He opens the doctor's bag and unrolls a brown canvas filled with tools. Out comes his tuning hammer, a bent metal lever with a socket on one end and a burnished cherry-wood handle on the other. I offer to leave Marc to his work, but he encourages me to stay. "I can watch TV while tuning a piano, it doesn't affect my ability to tune to have a conversation at all."

Then he proceeds to prove it by talking a blue streak for the next forty minutes, his arms and hands working swiftly and automatically all the while, as if his mouth is not even connected to the same body.

First he unrolls a length of bright red felt called a temperament strip and presses it in between the piano's strings with the end of a fine metal ruler. This isolates the strings from one another so he can set just the middle of the groups of three strings to pitch.

"I'm going to tune the piano to a higher pitch, to A4 = 443 cycles per second. That's what they tune pianos to in Europe. It's good for a new soundboard to be under a little extra tension from the tighter strings. Your tuner here probably won't want to do this, but just tell him the records you play along with are recorded at that pitch."

In America, the standard pitch for tuning pianos is set with the fourth A, or A4, vibrating at 440 cycles per second, which you can think of as a variable speed, like rpms on a turntable. A4 = 440 is a slightly slower speed than Marc's tuning, meaning it is a lower pitch. A lower pitch means there is less tension on the strings and soundboard.

Marc rests his right arm on the front edge of the piano's case, puts his tuning hammer astride the pins that hold the strings, and gives the handle swift little tugs and jabs to ease the strings into pitch. All the while his left index finger pounces into the keys, first hard, then soft, then hard. "When I strike it really hard like that? That makes the string bounce a little and evens the tension out along the string, so it will stay in tune longer. Does your tuner here do that?"

I have no idea. At the moment I don't really have a tuner. I lost Jeff, the first technician to visit, when he decided he was the wrong person to resolve the piano's problems. Another local tuner, after tuning the piano once, declined to visit again, saying he didn't want to be involved in a warranty situation. There is no one else that I know of, except an old man who once tuned my friend's Steinway upright. He was nearly deaf and asked me to tell him when the treble was in tune. Hearing loss is an occupational hazard for tuners.

Marc's tuning hammer moves rapidly, leaping on and off the tuning pins, making metallic whooping sounds. His index finger pounds up the keyboard; the volume is punishing.

Most of what is wrong with my piano, Marc asserts, is that it is out of tune. But, I protest, the piano has been tuned. "Many, many times when people think they have a voicing issue, really all it is is a tuning issue," says Marc. Voicing is manipulating the felt of the hammers. Tuning is adjusting the tension of the strings. Each affects the other.

He finishes the tuning, and I sit down to play. The tuning is nice, but I hear the same dullness in the treble. Marc decides to use chemicals on the hammers to harden them. "I really should let these chemicals set for a couple of days, and then come back to do my needling, but if I go out to lunch for a few hours and then come back, it should be good enough."

From his doctor's bag he produces a small clear plastic bottle with a syringe. He shakes it vigorously. "My chemicals," he says. "You probably don't want to be around to smell these. This is the reason piano tuners are so *crazy*." He lets out a wild cackle at his own joke. He does look a bit like a mad scientist, holding the bottle up and examining its contents.

Now he removes the fallboard, the lid that covers the keys, the cheekblocks that bracket the keyboard, and the key slip, the front cover of the keys. He reaches inside the belly of the piano with both arms, curls his fingers up under the metal action rail, and slides the action out onto his lap. I'm fascinated by the intricate mechanical contraption revealed: thousands of tiny wooden parts, all precisely calibrated to interact with one another and respond to the most subtle and demanding of touches.

The hammers are big tufts of wool felt compressed around hardwood moldings. Marc carefully places the tip of the bottle's syringe on the nose of each treble hammer and applies the clear liquid. The chemical smell delivers a kick. I step back.

When he has treated all the hammers in the melody section, he slides the action back into the piano and tells me not to play it. The solution needs time to harden first. I try to persuade Marc to stay for lunch, but he refuses, saying he'll stroll around Missoula and pick up something to eat downtown, and be back in a few hours. Besides, he says as he puts on a headset and plugs it into his cellular phone, he has calls he must make during New York business hours.

By three o'clock he is back. He pulls the piano's action onto his lap again and stabs the hardened hammers with a voicing tool, a set of four sewing needles held by a wooden handle. When he is done, he asks me to play the piano again.

It's better, I can tell, but I still do not hear the piano I fell in love with. By now, I am losing my focus. Both my ear and my attention are exhausted. With so much at stake for the piano, I've been on an emotional high wire, and I feel wrung out.

Marc lubricates the leather knuckles on the hammer shanks to reduce action noise. He levels the strings, checks hammer travel, and lubricates the key pins.

"Play it again now," Marc says.

I beg off. I need to lie down.

Marc becomes very agitated. "Listen, if I have to spend the night I will, but if I do that you will not be able to get me back again in a few days if you need me. I have clients in Bozeman I'm supposed to see first thing in the morning, and I'll have to reschedule them if I stay here."

But I no longer trust my hearing. I'll take a nap while Marc puts his finishing touches on the tuning, regulation, and voicing, and then we hope I will be rested enough to judge the piano.

"I understand," Marc finally relents. "Listening well is tiring. When I first started this work, I could only do a few tunings a day and then I would be wiped out. I have much more stamina now."

After an hour of not-quite sleep, I feel ready to listen again. When I return to the living room, Marc is still tuning and voicing, tuning and voicing. It has grown dark outside. The snow has finally stopped. I slip into the kitchen and begin preparing the antelope steak dinner Marc requested.

Oliver comes home and I introduce him to Marc. Marc seems distracted as he shakes Oliver's hand. He is immersed in the piano, and seems unable to bear breaking his attention from it.

"Now what kind of music are you going to play on this piano?" he demands.

I have to think a minute. Am I only supposed to play one type of music on a particular piano? "I think it is a perfect piano for Schubert," I say, remembering Asaf's performance of the third impromptu in the showroom.

"Schubert?" Marc says with what seems like delight in a happy coincidence. "Okay! I'm going to give you my best Schubert concert tuning."

Oliver and I lay out plates and silverware for three on the kitchen table. We keep the door to the living room closed so the steam from cooking doesn't affect the piano. Just as supper is ready, Marc opens the door and says that so is the piano. He and Oliver sit down to eat while I go back to the living room, shut the door tightly against the distraction of their conversation, and begin to play.

As soon as I touch the keys I am carried off by the sound I remember so well. Perhaps it is even *better* than I remember. A gossamer northern lights of shimmering tone, an impeccable, effortless touch that draws music out of me as if I were merely a vehicle for the composer. I stop, breathtaken. Then I start again. I play the Schumann, the Mendelssohn. The Chopin prelude. Some Mozart, the most demanding of the tone taskmasters.

She is back! Marlene is back! She is more beautiful than ever. She is dressed in a golden gossamer gown that brushes the toes of her golden silk slippers, up on a dark stage, the spotlights on her, singing "Falling in Love Again" in her smoky contralto. My heart flips over. This is the most gorgeous piano in the entire world. I am humbled to have such an instrument in my living room. I am not its owner, but a mere custodian. Such an instrument could never really be truly owned by anyone.

I've run out of my memorized repertoire, so I play some arpeggios. I dive deeply into the gorgeous, bell-like tones, the pealing treble, the sonorous, warm bass, the richly complex tonal tapestry of the tenor—all of it deeply pleasurable. The music is a shimmering phosphorescence, reverberating all around and within me, suffusing the room with a halo of light.

I get up and open the kitchen door and stand on the threshold. Marc and Oliver look up from their conversation, expectant, silent.

"Thank you!" I whisper, tears in my eyes. "Thank you for giving me my piano back!"

Before Marc leaves, he shows me how to pull the action out of the piano and onto my lap, how to "sugarcoat" the strike point of the hammers by pricking them with a voicing tool, how to lubricate something called the key bushings so the action will stay fluid. He recommends I learn the "Black Key" étude by Chopin to keep the voicing even, that I buy a brass-wire pot scrubber to keep notes from getting too harsh, that I buy a can of Elmer's Slide-All to lube the key bushings, and that I get a four-needle voicing tool. He draws pictures of exactly where to needle on the hammers to get certain effects.

"Don't train the local techs. They won't appreciate it."

"You mean other techs don't know what you showed me?"

"No, they all do it the way the hammer manufacturers have taught them, without chemicals, and too much needling that just ruins the hammers. Hammer manufacturers are ruining their product because now everyone wants a prevoiced hammer. That's why they make them so hard." He is spluttering now with agitation. Clearly we are treading into polemical territory. His voice becomes shrill. "I have to basically completely undo what the manufacturers have done to get the sound I want." His face goes dark, his jaw set. Then he brightens again.

"I can coach you over the phone, it wouldn't be the first time I've done that." He gives me his cell phone number. "That should hold you until I can come out again."

And how long will that be?

"Probably a couple of years."

By now it is eight o'clock, and very dark outside. Marc says he must be off. Oliver and I protest that we have reserved him a room in the nicest hotel in town, but Marc refuses it. He says he must go, into the night, over the wintry mountain passes, back to Bozeman.

After he is gone, I play my piano, luxuriating in its lush tone, even more beautiful than I remember. I call Carl in New York and tell him Marc has given me my piano back. When, at last, I can pull myself away from the piano to go to bed, I fall asleep feeling fulfilled and at peace.

The next morning, I go straight to the piano, eager to resume my embrace of Marlene's magic. I sit down, open the fallboard, and begin to play.

Then I stop, stunned. I can hardly believe what I hear.

The treble's tone is dull and wooden. It will not project above the bass and tenor sections. Every flaw Marc corrected is back! I try playing again, then recoil. It seems the piano's beauty and vibrancy were restored for one brief, magical evening, only to be lost with the dawn, like a glittering coach turned into a pumpkin while I slept. At once, I call Marc on his cell phone.

Marc sounds unperturbed. "I told you the shelf life of what we are doing is very short, including tuning," he says. "It's an infant piano. It's utterly volatile, and its rate of change will eclipse any changes I make. We've reached a point of diminishing returns, as far as what I can do. I have no further cards to play. The only thing I could do is replace the hammers."

"Does it need new hammers?"

"No. It is still evolving. Ninety-nine percent of what I did is tuning."

That can't be right. The piano has been tuned three times since it arrived and that didn't solve the problem.

"Play it for five hundred hours and then voice it again," Marc continues. "If you don't like how it sounds, just listen to the music, not the piano."

How can this can be—don't other people get new pianos and aren't they happy with them from the beginning, and remain happy?

"The only people who are happy from day one and remain consistently happy are those that don't really have a relationship with their piano," says Marc. "Either they don't play or they can't hear. The piano is like one of those blow-up dolls to them. Anyone who can hear will have this problem with a new piano."

So, according to Marc, my ability to hear, so carefully nurtured in me by my father, so key to my enjoyment of music, is now an affliction? My inner skeptic goes on high alert.

"Look," he says. "I'm a piano makeup artist. I simulate a seasoned concert instrument. It's all just smoke and mirrors." He laughs.

I feel a pang of horror. He can't mean this.

"You are at the beginning of a journey," he explains. "It's volatile. It's unpredictable. The piano will react to you, and your ear will adapt to it. Adapt to the piano. Engage in a dynamic communication with it. Don't come to it with a preconceived idea of what it should give you at a particular moment in time. It's growing and evolving. It's alive and living, and you have a relationship with it. You can hurt it and it can hurt you.

"You've bought a ticket for a ride. You can either take the ride or turn the ticket back in. You'll get the ride you get."

I am deeply skeptical now. How can I believe what Marc is telling me? Isn't he just trying to protect Carl? I talk to Rich about it, and he agrees that pianos are unstable when they are new, but Marc's other comments sound off base to him.

"I don't know what he could have done to only temporarily make it better," says Rich. "That's beyond my feeble brain. I've never heard such a thing from any techs I've spoken to, and I've talked to good ones. Guess you might ask that question on the forum."

The techs at Piano World say they don't understand why lacquer voicing should change so quickly. My sense of geographic isolation deepens.

Marc assured me that Carl will take the piano back in a heartbeat and refund all my money, if that is what I want. But what I want is the sound that Marc created. I want it so badly, just knowing that my piano can do that, even if only for a few hours, makes me want to not give it up. What did Marc do to create Marlene? I need to know. I need to understand.

Months pass and the piano is no better, despite all the "playing in" that everyone tells me will make all the difference. What happened to my piano? But beyond that, what has happened to me? Why am I in the thrall of a piano? What, in practical, technical terms, is the difference between the Marlene who seduced me, and the piano that leaves me cold?

In the fall, my reporting project ends. One September day, I telephone Marc. May I spend some time with him in New York, I ask, to watch him work? To my surprise, he says yes.

Just as an inner compulsion called me to the piano late in life, just as an inner vision of tone led me to Marlene, so now I am drawn to New York, to immerse myself in Marc's world, find out his secret, and bring it back.

II

13

A Piano Education

Grand Central Station is nearly deserted when I reach the ticket counter, well past the weekday morning rush. Footsteps and voices echo in the cavernous hall. I find a seat on the empty train, and enjoy the rhythmic clacking of its progress, the blur of autumn trees blazing by the windows, the familiarity of northeastern villages with their period architecture, their history, their intimacy. Gazing into their quiet streets as we stop at each station feels like putting on a very old shoe. This is the territory of my own origins, the terrain of the eastern seaboard hometown.

When I step onto the platform at Pelham, Marc is in plain view in the parking lot, waving wildly, a big, welcoming smile on his face. He flings open the passenger door from the inside. "I'm sorry about the car being such a mess."

A piano action fills the rear cargo area of his Subaru station wagon. Bottles, wrappers, and various piano parts are jumbled on the back seat and on the floor. "That action has been riding around with me for weeks, until I have some free time to put new hammers on it." He snorts at the idea of free time. "I'm the kid who's running down the street pushing the bicycle 'cause I don't have time to get on."

Our first destination is only a few blocks from the station. We pull up before a stately, early twentieth-century home buttressed by enormous oaks. Marc explains that the owner recently bought a 1909 Steinway model A-II, a piano Marc prepared for sale, and we're here to tune it.

A petite woman in her forties opens the front door. Her tousled, light-brown hair grazes high cheekbones, frames luminous blue eyes.

She and Marc embrace and greet each other in French. Then Marc introduces me to Dominique Browning, the editor of *House & Garden* magazine. Dominique leads me to her library, an alcove just off the foyer, painted in red lacquer. We sit on velvet cushions and talk while Marc begins work on the Steinway in the adjacent living room.

Marc told me Dominique has her own story of piano obsession, and evidently he revealed to her the same about me. We are soon comparing notes.

"My mother was a serious classical pianist," says Dominique. "Very demanding of me, musically. I began playing when I was four years old. I practiced six hours a day. My parents gave me a Steinway upright as a graduation present from college. But then I gave it up because I couldn't stand to play, because I couldn't play well enough.

"Finally I said, who cares?" She shrugs and runs her long fingers through her hair. "I'm not playing for anyone else. I'm not interested in how good I can be. I'm looking for something else now. I don't know what it is. At this stage of my life, at forty-seven, I've become obsessed with the *Goldberg Variations*. What is it that Bach is leading me to? I don't know."

I shiver with recognition. Here is someone else experiencing the mystery: at midlife we're called by the inexplicable. What is it that calls to us? I tell Dominique how I found Marlene, how I felt seized by a compulsion I didn't understand. She is nodding. Yes. Yes.

When Dominique was in her early twenties, she coauthored a book, *The Lives of the Piano,* a collection of essays. Hers was a profile of the famed Steinway concert tuner, Franz Mohr, who was Vladimir Horowitz's technician. Now she places her only copy of the hardcover book in my hands. "Please, take it with you. It is out of print now. You can return it whenever you wish."

Then Dominique excuses herself to look after a remodeling project, carrying on noisily in another region of the house. I drift into the living room, where Marc is ministering to her tiger mahogany grand. The piano is silhouetted by enormous windows looking out to a leafy backyard.

Marc opens the fallboard and tenderly removes the embroidered key cover that belonged to Dominique's mother. He plays a few chords.

"It's a mess," he declares at once. "I think we got ten inches of rain over the summer. It was very humid."

The slightest change in temperature or humidity affects the tone of a piano, Marc explains, as he tucks his red felt temperament strip between the strings. When the temperature rises, the steel strings go slack, and the pitch drops. When humidity rises, the wooden sound-board swells with moisture and the strings become taut, raising the pitch. The hammer felt also takes on moisture or dries out, affecting tone. The ideal temperature is 68 degrees, and the ideal humidity is 42 percent. Dominique's living room has open windows, and the climate is not controlled.

"Making a piano beautiful is a very complex puzzle," Marc says. He begins playing intervals, nudging his tuning hammer to set the temperament. "Knowing exactly what to do and in what order, and to what extent. I solved it very late in life, at forty. Then it took me from forty to nearly fifty to really understand how to bring out a piano's inherent beauty."

There is the craft of voicing, Marc explains, where you even out the tone from note to note, register to register. And then there is the art of voicing, the discovery or revealing of the ideal voice of a par-ticular piano.

"I've been on a quest for an archetypal sound. I had to learn how to make pianos ugly first. And when I had that figured out, there isn't a whole lot left to do to make them beautiful. I made millions of mistakes, I wept over pianos on my birthday. It's like making a sculpture, chipping away the useless material to reveal the figure that lies underneath."

"How do you arrive at an understanding of what the innate, ideal personality of the piano is?" I ask. "Is it purely intuitive?"

"I'm not a magician who intuits," says Marc. "I let the voicing process guide me. I try to build as rich and as full a sound as I can, until the piano sends me a message that it can't go further."

He pulls the temperament strip from the piano and begins tuning the unisons, two strings for each tenor and three strings for each tre-ble note.

"This piano has a good box. There's potential for many different personalities, characters, voices. It's got loads of sustain, loads of power, and the fortissimo is really beautiful."

He strikes the keys with his index finger, up and down the keyboard: loud, soft, loud. His tuning lever climbs the scale, leaps from pin to pin. "Very few instruments, no matter who voices them, can sound really beautiful at fortissimo playing. The belly finally turns in on itself. It just can't convert that much energy into sound, if you see what I mean."

Dominique appears just as Marc is rolling his tuning lever away in its canvas case.

"I put it at A4 = 442 to 443, and it will slide back down again," he tells her. "You will need to have it tuned again in a month or two. The rain this summer didn't do it any favors."

"I'm not too worried," says Dominique. "The piano is already old and has probably been through a lot."

"Yes," says Marc. "But remember that it has a baby soundboard."

Dominique clasps her hand over her mouth, covering her gasp as she does remember.

✦

"Dominique certainly seems to love you."

We are back in the car. Marc sighs with satisfaction at my observation. "Really?" He turns to me and beams. "She's got a wonderful piano, and I feel I am an intimate part of her piano destiny. And we both have French mothers, there is a bond there."

We pull away from the house, on our way to his next assignment, at a piano rebuilding shop in Dobbs Ferry. Marc's wearing the same uniform I remember from his Montana visit: black T-shirt, black jeans, black sneakers, and the curly auburn ponytail. But there's also a Manhattan School of Music photo ID on a lanyard around his neck, and a telephone headset that he never seems to take off.

The cell phone rings constantly, and when Marc is not on the phone—complaining to Joanne, who arranges his schedule; making a date with a client, advising his assistants at the school—he performs a rapid-fire, impassioned monologue that I can hardly follow, his ideas are so new to me, and so uniquely expressed.

"There is a relationship between the piano, the technician, and the pianist," Marc explains, expanding further on his role in the life of Dominique's piano. "It's a triangle, a ménage à trois. The content of that relationship, if you took it to a marriage counselor, would look like any other marital relationship. It's intimate. Sometimes dealing with the pianist's psychology is harder than dealing with the piano.

"The pianist is desperately trying to bond with the piano. It has to become a part of her musical soul. The technician is there to make it a healthy, functional relationship. The technician ferrets out whatever it is the pianist needs from the piano, so that the pianist can gain free passage of her soul through the instrument."

The phone rings again. From Marc's end of the conversation it sounds like a pianist is pleading with him to please drop everything and come to a recording studio *today*.

"Your phone seems terribly busy," I say when he hangs up. "Are piano technicians really in such high demand?"

"Pianos are so 'in' right now!" exclaims Marc, shaking his head as if in awe. "They are on top of the collective unconscious! Yeah! Pianos are percolating! In the Victorian era there was a big effort to put a piano in every home. But that went away. Now they are coming back! People want to experience the vibrational energy from pianos, and what it does to their souls. I'm doing well because I'm really connected to that vibrational energy, and I'm able to make it just right for people who crave what is coming from pianos."

I look at him in wonderment. Again, someone is describing my experience. "You and Dominique both talk about the piano in very esoteric terms," I begin, cautiously. "There is this mystical, spiritual, disembodied soul element to it."

"Ooooh! I get chills up my spine when you say that!" He turns to look at me, bright blue eyes squinting behind his half-rimmed glasses, beaming a crooked smile. "Vibration is the core of the universal experience! And the piano is a wonderful way to send vibrational energy out into the universe." His fingers flutter off the steering wheel, climbing into the air. "To me, it is *totally* esoteric—it's a connection to beyond the beyond."

The phone rings again. "Excuse me, I have to take this. Ça va?" He chatters away in French for several minutes.

"Your mother?" I ask, when he hangs up.

"Yes, my mother. We've never spoken anything other than French to each other."

"Was she a war bride?"

"Yeah. A prima ballerina with the Russian Ballet de Monte Carlo, in the 1940s. She's eighty-two now."

I mention to Marc that my father is also eighty-two, and by the way, he played clarinet in the orchestra pit of the Ballet Russe de Monte Carlo. But did the dates overlap? We aren't sure. "Cool!" says Marc. "Maybe she was onstage while your father was playing in the orchestra."

✦

We drop down a steep, winding drive to what once was a Navy warehouse. Inside is a room filled with grand pianos, covered with sheets and blankets, awaiting the move to the showroom. Marc weaves his way through them to a far, sunny corner, to a rebuilt Steinway model M from the 1930s.

Marc is here to give the piano its showroom sparkle. He lifts the fallboard, plays a few chords, and does not like what he hears. "I hated this piano the first time I heard it, then I thought maybe I liked it after all. Now I see I was on the right track the first time."

"What's wrong with it?"

"I can't get a broad range of color out of it. Eighty percent of pianists would love this piano just the way it is. Pianists who look for lots of color, rather than just dynamic change, are only about twenty percent of pianists. Based on my experience, that's just my opinion."

Dynamic change, he explains, is simply the range between very soft and very loud. Decibels. Color is something more subtle. It's the quantity and volume of partial tones released. Each note is actually a blend of many tones, known as overtones. With some pianos, these overtones, or partial tones, are more prominent. Partials determine the quality of the tone, its timbre, as opposed to simply its loudness or softness.

Marc plays a rapid scale, then some chords. "What do you think?" Then he stops me before I can say anything. "Wait until after I've done more work on it, then we'll see what you think."

Marc unsnaps a vinyl case containing four glass bottles. He pours a transparent fluid from one bottle into a plastic applicator with a needle syringe in its cap.

"Excuse me," he says, holding up the partially filled applicator. "I have to go add water to this."

"May I do that for you?"

"Actually, it is better if you don't. There is an exothermic reaction that happens, and it gets really hot, and it's probably better if . . ." He stops, as if considering how much to tell me. "The chemical in here is deadly."

He heads off to the washroom, and in his absence I look over the display of tools he has laid out. There are pliers, vise grips, soap, a knife, various glues, pieces of wood veneer, pieces of felt, varying grades of sandpaper, a flashlight, a Dremel sanding tool, a metal string pulling hook, a six-needle voicing tool with a fat, brass handle. I pick up this last item and feel its heft. There's also an electric drill, a tool that looks like a hole puncher, a copper wire brush, and more.

Marc returns and joins me in looking over the contents of his bag. He shows off the tools as if they are exotic butterflies he captured, or rare rocks he collected from distant shores.

"There's only four of these on earth," he says, proudly, holding up the brass voicing tool. "Another tech and I commissioned them from a machine shop."

I point to the case holding the glass bottles.

"That's my chemicals." The Snapple bottles are filled with pure lacquer, pure thinner, a mixture of both, and then, "I've got my softening chemicals in here." He lifts the unmarked bottle. "I mix them in these applicators for every job. Here."

He hands me the plastic applicator he took to the washroom. It's very hot. So hot, I'm surprised the plastic isn't melting.

"What is it?" I hand the applicator back to him.

"It's *like* alcohol and water, but one of the ingredients you can't just walk into the drugstore and buy. You have to go to a chemical supply company, and you have to write a letter saying how you are going to use it, or they won't sell it to you. A computer geek would clean the insides of a computer with the poisonous stuff that is in here."

He turns to the piano now and removes the action, pulling it half onto his lap. The wool felt hammers lie in a row, slightly tilted, like a partially fallen row of dominoes. Marc turns the plastic applicator upside down, and with the tip of the syringe barely touching the felt, he runs the clear liquid swiftly across the nose of every hammer, from the lowest bass note to the top of the treble. The chemical penetrates the wool in a controlled flood. The smell is very strong. It reminds me of benzene.

"You are really saturating those hammers."

"I'm getting them wet, but not down below, because it is good for them to be hard down there." He stops and faces me. "I wish you wouldn't talk about that to other technicians. I'm young enough that I don't need to give away all the secrets I've worked hard to discover for myself, if you see what I mean."

"How did you figure this out? Did you study chemistry?"

"I wish I were a chemist, but since I'm not, it's been total trial and error."

"You mean, you just try it and see what happens?"

"Yup. Yup." He slides the action back into the case. "Some people use fabric softener, some use Krazy Glue, some use steam, some iron them.

"I'm endeavoring to remanufacture these hammers. I'm gessoing over the painting, creating a fresh canvas. These are brand-new Steinway hammers. Softening them removes the lacquer the factory put in and adds air between the fibers of the wool. Using chemicals puts space between those fibers at a very deep level."

"Do voicers usually soften hammers with chemicals?"

"No, they do not." He packs up the bottles, then moves on to his next patient, a Steinway D in the center of the room. "Even revealing the approach that I am softening them before hardening them is giving something away. It is part of my secret that only I do. Most people only apply softener to old, dry, overused hammers to try to rejuvenate them. My opinion is that some new hammers are dead already, in the sense that they are in stasis, and won't evolve the way they should.

"Imagine how a rock bounces. It hits the ground and stays there, and makes a very sharp sound. It doesn't bounce well at all. A very hard hammer stays in contact with the string too long and brings out an ugly initial attack. What I'm doing with my chemicals is teaching these hammers how to bounce, so they will release sound instead of driving it out of the piano. They become more like tennis balls, and less like rocks. Then I can harden special spots on them to get the color, character, or overtones I want."

He pulls the action out of the D; the keyboard rests on his knees. "At the first stage I get them really wet. This does no damage to the hammers. They'll grow. They'll poof out. Air gets between the fibers and they'll expand. It's like blowing up a balloon."

Suddenly I recall the hammers in my own piano. The strange, swollen distortions on them that made Jeff, the local technician, say, "I've never seen hammers like this before."

As if reading my thoughts, Marc, his eyes still intent on his work, says, "I *think* I used this exact same protocol on your hammers, in the showroom." Then he looks up at me and smiles.

Is *that* what happened? But why was Marc brought in to voice a brand-new piano? Did it arrive in the showroom with a problem he was hired to cover up, and all he could do was a temporary fix? If so, when did this happen? Before or after I fell in love with Marlene? Which piano is she—Marc's creation? Or Grotrian's?

"When did you first voice my piano, do you think?"

"It must have been immediately after it arrived in the showroom," Marc says. He slides the action back into the D and turns to me, grinning. He is clearly pleased to think he made me fall in love with my piano. "I think Carl called me right away."

I tell him I played the piano in August, but he can't remember when he was there. More than a year has passed since then.

Marc bangs out some chords on the D. I didn't get to play this piano before he applied his chemicals, but I can hear the sound is blooming, continuing on and on for a very long time, changing dimension and shape even as it fades.

"Before the chemicals, the sound would die, because the hammers weren't bouncing off the strings effectively," he explains. "Later this week, after they are dry, I'll come back and listen again, and then I'll use hardener where I want it. This lets me achieve a balance of hardness and softness within the hammer. I'm after a tennis ball bounce, with a golf ball attack, if you see what I mean."

Marc packs up his bag and we prepare to leave. I reach to lift the bag for him, but he stops me. "A pianist should not carry this. It's bad for your hands."

I look at him quizzically. How heavy can it be? But then I realize what he is saying—*I am a pianist who must be careful of her hands!* His concern is misplaced, but the idea that anyone could even think this about me is a little bit thrilling.

✦

We're due at a recording studio in Suffern, twenty miles away, in half an hour, so I buy us takeout lunch at a Dobbs Ferry deli—hefty sandwiches on good rye. Marc revels in the food.

"Thank you so much." There is delight and gratitude in his voice after his first hungry bite. "Usually I eat whatever I can find in the car." He raises a stale, half-eaten bag of potato chips from behind the front seat to show me.

En route to the studio, Marc tells me about his music background. He was born in 1954 in Baltimore, where his father and grandfather spent most of their lives. His father's father was a pianist, and his mother's father was an architect who played piano and violin. Marc spent childhood summers with his maternal grandfather in France and weekends during the school year with his paternal grandparents near Annapolis, on the Severn River—where I grew up.

Marc began piano studies at the age of six, with the "blue-haired lady down the street. Her big thing was *portamento*," he says, waving his arms over the dash expressively in an extravagant gesture as the changing fall foliage flies by. His sandwich is in one hand, the steering wheel is missing from the other. He thrusts his head toward me, his eyes closed in memory. "You have to use your whole body.

"I never learned how to read music, because I had a reading disability growing up, but I had an incredible memory," he says, one hand back on the steering wheel now. "I memorized music immediately and played everything by ear."

Marc studied film scoring at the Berklee School of Music, but when he realized how competitive that field is, he switched to piano technology at Boston's North Bennet Street School, one of the best places in North America to learn the trade. He worked as a tuner in Boston for a couple of years, then went to Paris. There he restored the actions of historic pianos—Pleyels, Erards, and many other makes not often seen outside of Europe.

In Paris, Marc met a young American dancer and collaborated with her as a composer. When she moved to New York, he moved to

New York also, and got a job tuning pianos at Steinway Hall. Two years later, the dancer brought him to Bozeman, Montana, to visit her family.

"I took my first whiff of Montana air and I was *smitten*," he says. "For the next year and a half, I would travel there and work on people's pianos. I was the Steinway tech from New York, and I was *God*."

And then he moved there.

He thought he had established a clientele among the music faculty at Montana State University, but as soon as he came to stay, his status quickly changed.

"People who had jumped at the chance to have me work on their pianos when I was only there for ten days suddenly didn't have the money. As soon as I lived there, I was dog dirt. I went from being in tremendous demand, to being lucky to tune a Wurlitzer spinet." He spits the last word.

Curious. He moved to Montana about the same time I did. As children, we both played by the Severn River, during the same years. His mother and my father, the same age, both performed with the Ballet Russe in the 1940s. When he moved to Montana, he tells me, he fell in with mountaineers. I married one.

Do these commonalities mean anything? Is there something of the Severn River in us both, something of the Rocky Mountains in us both, something of parents in the Ballet Russe in us both? Do parallel experiences create a shared sensibility? Do they imprint on our character, create a resonance, like a frequency on a radio dial, that we both are tuned to? And then, that character, that frequency, that sensibility: Did Marc voice Marlene to it? And then I resonated to it? Was *that* what I experienced when I played Marlene for the first time?

No, I think. That's just crazy.

✦

The Suffern recording studio is an old stone-and-timber barn set in a clearing at the end of an obscure track through the woods. The studio is quite famous, Marc says. It's called BearTracks.

We head up dark, narrow stairs to a converted loft. There sits a satin black Steinway model L, framed by hovering acoustic baffles, crowded by microphones. The sound engineer, Steve, is adjusting a mic under the open wing of the piano. Without any preliminaries, he and Marc begin talking shop.

"The tenor is cloudy, no matter what mic setup we use," Steve complains. Marc plays a riff in the tenor section, then gives each note a swift strike.

"The voicing is different than it was this morning," Marc says, his ear turned to the keyboard. Marc tunes and voices this piano in the early morning, before the client records, then he returns to tune and voice again in the afternoon. The client is John Stetch, a Canadian jazz pianist.

Marc runs more riffs up and down the piano. "It was even and very effective this morning." He sounds annoyed. He opens his bag, pulls out the four-needle voicing tool, and pulls the action from the piano's case. He vigorously plunges the tool into a hammer, and its wooden tail thumps from the impact.

Steve explains that the power went out, and the climate control is not working. The room has become hot and dry.

"How can you stand it?" Marc's voice is shrill. "You need to go out and refresh your spirits now. It's a beautiful day out."

Marc asks me to play the piano. Me? In front of the sound engineer? I say a silent thank-you to Molly for working so hard with me to get the Chopin B minor waltz performance ready. It is the only piece I have memorized and polished.

The treble is glorious. I wish my piano's treble sounded like this—clear and powerful, yet sweet. Marc modified this piano for Stetch, using a Hamburg Steinway action and hammers in a New York Steinway chassis. I like it, a lot.

"So, John," Marc says evenly to a long-limbed, gaunt young man who has just entered the room. He wears huge, puffy ski gloves on his hands. I stop playing. "This is a total disaster. I'm not available on Friday."

"Can you come by at all on Friday?" says John Stetch, hopefully. The pianist has sunken eyes, hollow cheeks, and wears his hair in a buzz cut.

"Not really," says Marc. "I'm going to work at the school early, then I leave for Philadelphia."

I tell Stetch I love the piano.

"It's unrecognizable with the hammers Marc put on," he says. "It convinced me that what I like about Hamburg Steinway is the hammers."

"Yeah," Marc chimes in. "They lend themselves to the kind of sound you are looking for—a fatter, richer sound."

"Yeah, more punch," says Stetch. "You get more power out of phrases that otherwise wouldn't have it."

Marc asks Steve about the mic placements. They discuss how to compensate for the stone walls, which are less lively than expected. The three of them talk about what modifications can be made to the room, where else they might place the piano. Stetch wants the tone to be "tubbier," he says.

Suddenly the lights come on, and there's a rushing sound of equipment powering up. Stetch asks us to join him in the glassed-in control room, so we can listen to the morning's work, his riffs on Thelonious Monk. The piano sounds different on the recording. Stetch put erasers under the bass strings to make them sound like steel drums, he explains. They stop the sustain. He also played a drumstick inside the piano. Marc nods along with the beat, a beatific smile on his face. He likes it. I do, too.

✦

We emerge from the studio into a perfect autumn day. Marc looks about, admiring the stately trees and their flares of orange, crimson, yellow.

"It's so *turned* here," he says.

"It's incredible that if the temperature changes, the voicing changes," I say, mulling over the conversation in the studio.

"No. It's the tuning," Marc corrects me. There's a hundred and sixty pounds of tension in each string, on average, for a total of twenty tons of tension from all the strings. Temperature affects that tension. Warm lights will make a tuning go out immediately. In a concert hall, filling it with warm bodies will make the tuning go out.

"Voicing may change if the *humidity* changes. If the hammers dry out."

Back in the car, we wend our way to the main artery to the city, onto a highway with a view of more highways, traffic rushing, then clogging, drivers fiercely impatient, blaring their horns. I comment that I'd forgotten how people here lead lives of noisy desperation. Marc laughs. But then he turns sober again, thinking of his own obligations.

"It is utter neglect for me to run off in the middle of the day like this," he says, glancing down now and again at the screen on his cell phone to see who has called.

Sooner than I expect, we pull up to the foot of a staircase to the elevated train. It's the Riverdale station, the northernmost stop on the Number 1 subway line. I'll ride it down to Times Square, then take the R train back to Gramercy Park.

"We've reached the end of my day," says Marc. "I'll pick you up in front of your building at five o'clock tomorrow morning. Our first stop will be a recording studio in your neighborhood."

On the ride home, I recall Marc not letting me carry his bag, wanting to protect my pianist's hands, and I smile—I lugged much heavier bags than his while traveling here from Montana. But once I get home, will I change my ways? Will I give up weeding, remodeling, backpacking, correcting my 180-pound dog with a leash? Is there a line I will cross when I will avoid all activities that could hurt my hands? I decide I will get a wheeled suitcase, a concession to the piano's increasing hold on me.

◆

At 4:55 the next morning, I step outside Kim's building to find Marc already parked and waiting for me. We drive through the silent, deserted streets, not saying much. Marc still wears yesterday's uniform: the headset, the photo ID around his neck, the all-black clothes. I sip from my mug of strong Darjeeling and let the first fingerlings of caffeine start up my brain. It is two hours earlier in Montana right now, and I need to be fully awake so I don't miss any important clues to solving my piano problem.

The recording studio is at Fifth Avenue and Thirty-first Street. Inside, it is supremely silent, thoroughly soundproofed. There is a Steinway grand in each of the two rooms: a model B in the back room, a model D in the front, both black satin, both rebuilt vintage pianos.

While Marc tunes the unisons on the B, he asks me to go play the D, which he says is a very rare piano. It is a "Centennial" D, built in 1881. Centennial Ds were launched to commemorate the centennial anniversary of America's birth. This one has a continuous bent rim—the laminations are seamless. Only one hundred of these pianos were made. Marc owns two of them.

"You can't tell anyone I have two," he says. "It's a secret Steinway. I found it online, and there was a bidding war, and I don't want the person who I bid against to know where it is."

The front room is just large enough for the Centennial and three people, if they are standing. I touch a key in the midtreble, and the sound seems to carry out to beyond infinity. Is it the piano? Or is it the precious, extreme silence of the studio? I love the silence. I love the cavelike cloistering of the pianos here. And I'm astonished by the sustain of this piano.

I try another note, higher in the treble, where the tone usually will not last for long. The sound carries on and on and on, first on a rising swell that blossoms out, full and ripe, then gradually diminishing only slightly as time wears on. The bloom of tone is extraordinary.

I play the Chopin waltz. The piano is surprisingly mellow; it does not overwhelm the room. It reminds me, in fact, a bit of my Grotrian, in that I wish it were not quite so soft in the treble.

"What do you think?" Marc is already done with the B, and is standing in the doorway. He is all expectancy, his face lit up.

"The sustain is incredible."

"Isn't it? I timed it at a minute and a half."

That *is* incredible. Usually treble sustain lasts about twelve seconds.

"Gorgeous," I say. And it is. This is Marc's signature sound, a warm, rounded, "creamy" tone, as he describes it. I press a treble key again. There is a sensuality to the lingering tone, hanging and hanging on the air.

"People don't understand a mellow concert grand," he says, clearly excited that I like it. "They expect it to have the biggest sound on earth, but that costs them sustain. The brighter the piano, the shorter the sustain. The softer the tone, the longer the sustain—up to a point. It has something to do with the physics of soft, bouncy hammers, versus hard hammers with a brittle initial attack."

We trade pianos, and Marc begins tuning the D, while I play the B.

Because these rooms are so carefully climate-controlled, Marc says, his tunings can be done in five minutes or less, if they are done daily.

I play the B for a few minutes, but then Marc calls out from the front room to tell me more about the secret Centennial. "It was in Africa. It had been a symphony piano for eighty years. Every great pianist of the twentieth century played it."

The competition for a piano like this one, says Marc, is always intense. "Most of these pianos are inarticulately rebuilt by bozos. The real prize is one in original condition, with the original soundboard, that still has a voice. If I had the money, I'd scoop up every continuous bent rim Centennial D that I could get my hands on, and I'd have a *fleet* of them."

The Centennial D is different from a modern D, Marc explains, lifting its wing to show me the string scale design. There are six supplementary bass strings on the tenor bridge, an attempt to cure the tenor break, a common problem. This is the part of the piano where the strings change from copper wound to plain steel wire. These six strings are on a hooked bridge, laid out on the soundboard like a switchback, and if you play them fortissimo, says Marc, "they sound *schnarfelli*." That's a word he must have made up. "But if you play them less loud, they sound like cellos. You hear the voices of the orchestra more in the Centennial than in a modern D. It's an orchestral reproducer."

We close the piano fallboards, turn out the lights, and lock up the studio.

◆

"So, how many pianos do you have?" We're racing up the West Side Highway at dawn, to Marc's day job as head of piano technology for the Manhattan School of Music.

Marc silently counts on his fingers.

"You have to *count*?"

"I have five concert grands. An 1875 Broadwood, a Baldwin, and three Steinways, but maybe say two. One is the secret Steinway."

In addition he has a Steinway M in his apartment, and a model A at his country house in the Adirondacks. But those are his personal pianos. The concert grands are either rented out to recording studios or will be rebuilt for studio rentals. Pianos like John Stetch's customized Steinway are in great demand among certain clientele. And voicers like Marc, he himself will tell you, are few and far between. Stetch, Marc informs me, is so dependent on Marc's skills, he has telephoned him nearly every morning for the past eight years.

"The ones who need me the most are the ones who can't pay. But how can I turn them down?" His voice goes up an octave. "It's not like I can multiply myself out, leverage myself to make my business more lucrative. And there are only so many hours in a day."

"Your ear must get tired."

"My stamina has grown over the years, like any athlete's would. Five years ago, finishing a voicing job would have ended my energy level for the day. Now I can whack out four of those jobs a day and get a better result. But I'm in a unique position. I do hundreds of voicing jobs a year on brand-new sets of Steinway hammers. Very few piano tuners get to make that many mistakes."

Mistakes?

"You have to understand," Marc continues. "You're in my laboratory here. I wouldn't dare experiment on your piano the way I do on these pianos. The worst-case scenario is I glue on another set of hammers. But in your house, if I ruin your hammers, even if I offer you a new set, it will never be the set it was before. That could be a big problem for you.

"Look, it wasn't an easy road, even with all the opportunity I had to voice so many pianos. It was very difficult. No one will give you any instruction. Zero instruction. *Zero.* The only advice I got was to buy my own concert grand and use it as my laboratory."

Marc's experiments with voicing and the lessons he taught himself are what saved him when he returned home to Baltimore from Montana, broke and in debt. After four years in Bozeman, he found himself defeated, unable to survive as a piano technician. But a former client in New York welcomed his return, and lined up jobs for him.

"I was willing to work very hard for very little money. I'd work like a dog for ten days, then go back to Baltimore and do nothing, just *be.*" In a sudden burst of emotion he exclaims, "Being is the most important thing in life! And I'm just a doer now. Beingness is the birthright of all humans. We are human *beings,* not human doings!" He laughs, but the tone is dark and sad.

Marc works twelve days then takes two off. "I have probably three to five more years like this before I can slow down. I've already been at it over three years. I'm a late bloomer, a late starter in everything."

Including his personal life, which is definitely better now. In 1995, as he was getting reestablished in New York, he was preparing a piano for a music festival and fell in love with the festival director. Connie is a cellist, and Marc became her student. "I am fond of saying she abused the student-teacher relationship," he says of his wife with a grin.

We pull into the underground garage at the school and take the elevator to the technician's workshop, where Marc's three assistants are waiting for him. I find a piano stool to join them in their daily ritual—eating breakfast together in their cloakroom kitchen as they review the day's assignments.

We do not linger long. At MSM, Marc insists on tuning all the performance pianos daily, and today he is point man for the job.

We rumble down the hallways, his giant set of keys pulled out again and again to let us into the various performance spaces. Each room has its own key, and he has a key to every room with a piano. "These students are paying twenty-five thousand dollars to become the best musicians in the world, and they need the best tools. That is why we don't let the pianos go out of tune. They simply have to be in tune at all times."

When his tuning rounds are done, we take a break in the school's cafeteria, and over soup I ask Marc about his private clients.

"I'm delivering something they don't even know how to ask for," he says, looking at me plaintively. "It's toying with people's obsession, which makes my work difficult. You have to earn their confidence in your abilities, enough to admit when you are wrong."

A good voicer has to have compassion for pianists, Marc explains. A string player tunes his own instrument, which he carries around with him. A pianist is dependent on his technician for his sound, and on whatever piano happens to be in the hall.

It's a problematic relationship. Pianists can be high-strung, and so can techs. The tech is there in service to music, to beauty—and so is the pianist—but communication can be trying.

"My disdain for pianists grows year by year, as I work with them more," says Marc. "They don't do their homework. They don't understand the instrument. They don't learn the vocabulary they need to communicate with me. Of course, there are exceptions.

"But most pianists are torqued out, confused, alienated. They don't have an *inner vision* of what they are seeking in a piano. They only know they like a mythic piano that they played once. What was it that they loved about that mythic piano? They don't know." He says this in a voice dripping with disdain. "And they are looking for someone to 'fix' it for them. They've been screwed, and the next technician has to take their baggage and make it all better.

"How can I have the psychic energy to continue in such an environment? It's incredibly draining. And it seems that the better I get at what I do, my clientele gets quirkier and quirkier. It's not a friendly interchange. If I'm there, they are *desperate*."

I feel somehow reprimanded, as if I myself might be such a client. One of my biggest fears is that anyone who might be able to help Marlene might think I am too strung out or upset to deal with me. I don't want that to happen.

"So, who is your ideal piano client?"

"Someone who knows what their musical goals are. They trust that I'll transfer the information they give me to technical information that will allow them free passage of their vision through the piano, to the sound they are trying to create."

Marc must see the dismay on my face. I hardly know what it would be like to be such a client. He softens his tone.

"And then there is a second-level ideal client," he says. "They know enough about the technical aspects of the piano to use the terminology to inform me of what they want. They did the thinking and experiencing to identify their own preferences."

"What about making you meals, making you coffee?" I ask, hopefully.

"Brownies, coffee," he says with derision. "Friendship only comes from people for whom the piano is secondary in their lives. For those for whom the piano is primary in their lives, they are torqued out, totally. Sometimes for years. Social graces are the furthest thing from their minds."

"So do you have criteria for who you'll work for?"

"Nobody is excluded. But the kind of person I would avoid working for would be someone who seems to be totally wrecked by their emotional-psychological baggage on the basis of what happened between them and their past technicians. But then, I recently took on someone who hadn't had their piano worked on for forty years, because they didn't trust anyone. And all of a sudden, I'm the first person they trust. You know what kind of psychic pressure that is?"

"No."

"Well, it's like being somebody's first lover. And you're going to define lovemaking for them for the rest of their lives. You know, never touched until I came along. Literally. It's a *huge* responsibility."

✦

"So tell me again, what is it about your piano that is making you unhappy?" We're back in the Subaru, heading north to Yonkers, where Marc works with a rebuilding team called Cantabile.

I tell him again what the problem is. The treble section is too weak, though some notes are too harsh and bright.

"That's the territory of a piano that is breaking in and needs to be taken in hand again."

I feel my frustration mounting. How can it be that this piano needs so much maintenance? Why won't the sound stay in one place? I am afraid that Marc doesn't really understand the problem. And I still don't have the right words to communicate what I hear. I struggle to express myself better.

"The lower partials don't come out enough, is what I think is bothering me." I don't yet know that partials are always upper, never lower.

Marc doesn't correct me. "Oh, so it doesn't have enough body."

"Exactly. What is the solution to the treble problem I'm describing?"

"I would use lacquer and lacquer thinner, and I would mix a particular concentration after hearing your piano. But a really good tuning will take care of about eighty percent of it.

"You want to know why yours sounds unique compared to all the others?" Marc looks at me sidelong while steering the car. "It's this chemical process you see me using. I used it on your piano. I'm dead certain. I remember it now. Absolutely, absolutely, absolutely. Carl told me you bought one of the pianos I voiced. I actually think your first meeting with that piano was not long after I voiced it."

Was it? I still don't know for certain, but rather than raise this point with Marc, I say, "I must have been right on your heels, because it had that gossamer quality that you re-created in my living room. Now I know that doesn't last. So I was *tricked*."

Marc giggles. "That's what they pay me the big bucks for. I'm the guy that puts the makeup on the model, you know?" He sounds gleeful. "They thought I was a miracle worker ten years ago, but compared to what I do now?" He makes a raspberry. "It was like *nothing*."

I don't say anything. How to make sense of this? He creates an impression that doesn't last so that dealers can sell their pianos. Isn't this unethical? How can he tell me this with such forthright good humor? Is there something I don't understand about pianos, that makes what he is doing okay?

"Don't make the mistake of thinking that when you buy a piano you are getting some sort of absolute when it comes to tone," Marc continues, as if reading my mind. "The tone of any piano changes with who is playing it, what they are playing, what day it is, what key they are playing in, and how it has been prepared. These variables are so changeable that you are unlikely to feel that the piano is consistent in tone from one day to the next. This is true of any piano."

But I'm not willing to believe this. This is so contrary to my expectations. Nobody ever told me this before. Why should I believe Marc?

One thing, however, is clear: I no longer have Grotrian hammers—or at least, not the way they came from the factory.

"So, in future, should my piano's hammers be treated differently than most techs would treat them?"

"In any voicing situation, somebody who voices after someone else is at a disadvantage. They don't know the history."

"So when are you coming back to Montana?"

"My time is harder to manage than ever before, but I'd love to help you out." He smiles at me winningly. "But how will I find the time to pull this off? The last time was tremendously tiring and difficult. I didn't want to say no. Carl felt the deal would go sour. He was worried the tech there had damaged the piano."

"Did someone damage it?"

"No one damaged it. It needed basic, honest, nuts-and-bolts servicing. I told Carl *you* required more work than the piano did. If we hadn't talked at all, I would have been there only five hours."

I blush, stung. "We didn't have to talk," I protest.

"You had to understand and embrace the work I gave you. Besides," he says, softening, "I've had clients that it has taken me a *year* to understand what they want and with you it only took a few hours. We have the same taste. The problem is that what you want is something that, by its nature, is *even more ephemeral.*"

"So, what should I tell whoever works on my piano?"

"Ask for a richer, fuller sound. I tried to voice ten levels of dynamic on each note. That's easy to do on the long strings, and incredibly difficult to get right on the shorter, treble strings. I may have to harden the treble section three or four times to get the tone I want."

"Should I tell them what you did?"

"Tell them I chemically softened, then rehardened your hammers. Find a recording you like, play it for your technician, and ask him to make the piano sound like that. Tell him you want *more* in the treble. He'll know what you mean."

I can't imagine there are recordings that sound like Marlene, but maybe I will find something I like well enough. As for "more" in the treble, if it is that simple, then why have I never before heard a piano like mine?

◆

We are in the stairwell of an old industrial building, taking the steps two at a time. Marc, as usual, is in a hurry. At the top floor he pushes open a heavy metal door, and we enter a room flooded with light from clerestory windows. The walls are painted coral. Rows of grand pianos are lined up under skylights, covered in white sheets, separated by white pillars. It is a striking vision, like a scene from a Cocteau film.

While Marc tunes a Mason & Hamlin model A, I wander about the loft, which is divided into airy rooms. In one of them, a white-haired man is adjusting an action on an old grand. He looks up at me; the gold in his smile gleams. As I move through the vast space, a strong chemical smell suddenly throws me back. Marc sees me recoil and joins me.

"We huff that stuff every day of our lives," he says, then throws open the door to a spraying booth, where pianos are refinished. I cover my mouth and nose with my hand, unable to tolerate the fumes, and back away.

While Marc voices another piano, I wander off again and discover a storage area the size of a ballroom, filled to capacity with ancient uprights and solemn grands perched on their sides, lined up like wall-flowers awaiting an invitation to dance.

When I return to Marc, he is working on the Mason again, play-ing chords and arpeggios up and down the keyboard. He tells me he's rehardened the hammers with lacquer. "Hear how it has lots of sus-tain?" he says. "It has lots of 'spin,' which is the thing that makes you think it's the best piano on earth."

"I don't hear that."

He asks me to play it for myself.

"I think the treble is bright to the point of being needle-like," I say.

"They all want a bigger, brighter sound," he explains. "They want more and more."

I shrug. This sound is not for me.

"I work in a commercial environment," Marc persists. "My pianos have to sell. So I have to make a perky, bright sound. I can't make a rich, voluptuous, *liquid velvet* kind of sound, which is what I would prefer to do."

"But you did that on my piano?"

"Yes, I did. Because Carl wants me to make the piano as beautiful as I think I can, and he doesn't care if it sells or not." Marc laughs wildly, the Mad Hatter with a tuning fork.

"Carl is an idealist?"

"Yes, he is."

"When you soften hammers with chemicals instead of deep needling, does that last as long?"

"Oh, God, it lasts longer! It goes *deeper* and it's more effective and less invasive." He plays a rapid, circular riff up and down the Mason.

"So, does that mean my Grotrian's hammers were never deep needled?"

"Well, I can't say what happened at the factory." He plays some big chords.

"Can you tell by the sound?"

"No, you can actually, literally see the damage."

Damage. That's what he calls it.

"What would you look for?"

"Swelling and deformation in the shape of the hammer." Marc bangs out the chromatic scale in the treble, listening, listening. He pulls the action and lightly tufts some treble hammers with his voicing needles.

"You mean, like that egg-shaped bump on top of them? If they have that kind of poof on top. Do you remember that?"

"Yeah. Then your hammers *did* get deep-needled. They got deep needled *here*," he points to the shoulders of the hammer between his fingers. "And because of that, when I applied my chemicals, that little head grew. And now that I know that has happened, that would give more of an indication of what I need to do when I come to your place. I might have to do some careful filing."

My heart sinks. My hammers were *damaged*!

"I guess what I'm wondering is"—I try to not let my voice quaver—"does that mean that a procedure that was done twice should only have been done once? Or something?"

"Well, no matter what, they do the deep needling at the factory and it still doesn't get the job done." Then he says, sotto voce: "That's why I want to patent my voicing protocol, because I think every piano factory on earth needs it."

Then Marc packs up his tools, and before I have even a moment to absorb what he is telling me, we are flying down the stairs and out the door.

◆

"Why is your chemical protocol such a big secret?" I ask. We're back in the car, leaving Yonkers' industrial zone, entering the ramp onto the highway.

"Well, voicing is one of the big, *big* secrets because it's the top of the pyramid. And anybody who has those skills wants to protect their job."

Very few piano technicians are skilled at voicing, I've gathered by now. Most are tuners who can also regulate piano actions. Still, I am mystified by Marc's protectiveness. He could be helping so many more techs bring beauty to so many more pianists and their listeners.

"What about teaching? Wouldn't you like to teach?"

"I'd love to have an apprentice! But who wants to make their living doing this? I have no financial ease in my life. Maybe there are other techs out there who are in it for the same result I am, which is to create beauty in the world. But if you are really interested in making money, you'd avoid pianos like the *plague*."

He punctuates the end of this discourse with a wild giggle, and then his cell phone rings. I hear him promise John Stetch he will run back up to BearTracks on Friday after all.

Marc has complained a lot about how he has no life, how underpaid he is, how the demands of his private clients "rips my life into hamburger." Yet he seems to embrace this punishment, to thrive on it. If the terms of his professional life are as difficult as he claims, then why doesn't he charge more? Why doesn't he say no more often? And why is he letting me, just your ordinary, clueless piano buyer, take up his time?

"Thanks for being patient," he says, as he hangs up the cell phone and puts his eyes back on the road. "What more can I tell you?"

"I'm wondering how someone who feels that 'being' is our most important activity in life can run around as hard and as much as you do," I begin. I feel, somehow, after listening to his complaints, that Marc should explain this. I plunge on with my impertinence. "Why did you say yes to Stetch?"

"How can I say no?" Marc demands. "He depends on me, he needs me for his career." His voice rises, plaintive and insistent. "I will always want to help out people who have a recording project that may make or break their careers and they need their piano to be beautiful. I don't think I could ever turn my back on circumstances like that.

"The highest calling in life is to give back to those around you with the gifts that have been given to you freely. So, because of that, when my clients need me, whatever the personal cost may seem to be in a penny-wise world, I try to transcend.

"I mean, I just can't bear to see someone who's got a tremendous amount of talent and wants to create beauty by playing their piano, and no beauty is coming out because I want to make an extra five hundred bucks off their job. So what do you do?"

"What about your own dreams and aspirations?"

"Playing Bach on the cello. That would be it for me. That is the dream for the second half of my life." A shy smile curls up one corner of his lips. "I'd like to become the adult beginner cellist that I want to be."

So. We have the same dream. Be it the piano or the cello, it's the same dream.

"When you play the cello, what happens to you? Where do you go?"

"Well, you lose yourself to the higher calling, I guess," says Marc. "It's the opposite of virtual reality. It's the opposite of the higher and higher levels of overstimulation that our society offers. It's a way of exiting the petty self and entering the Over-soul. It's transcendental. In Eastern terms, it would be a form of meditation. But pure meditation isn't the way. The state of your heart is the way. Because it's not about doing. It's about being."

Suddenly it seems the conversation shifts, taking on a momentum, a rhythm that is almost musical. We're traveling on a verbal, vibrational confluence; our voices merge into a soliloquy, or become an opera duet. It's a very strange sensation.

"Exactly. Absolutely. It's about existing at a certain vibration."

"There you go! We're back to the word we started from."

"And I wonder if the piano—even more than the cello, when I think about it—that was my first instrument, by the way. . . ."

"Here we go again!" says Marc, with a big grin, referring to yet another coincidence.

"The direct experiences I've had with the piano are frightening to me. It is a way of taking the condition of your heart and putting it on the airwaves for others' hearts to receive. It's electrifying. Like Chopin himself is traveling through the air. It's about this experience of direct contact with the soul of the composer, and that soul is transmuted through your expression. What does it do to the very molecules of our being, to do this? It must transform them. It's almost like I can't contain it. Like it's hard to have a physical body."

We enter the dark cavern of the parking garage under the Manhattan School of Music as I say this. Marc parks the Subaru and turns off the ignition, but makes no move to get out of the car. This is the end of our time together before I return home.

"I never thought our conversations would come to this," Marc says, turning to look at me in the garage's weak light. "I don't get much of a chance to express any of this. I'm dealing with people's piano lives and what I can do to help them there. This isn't part of the conversation. So, *why you?* Now we're finding out, *Why you?*"

"What do you mean?"

"Well, this is a very big circle. You know, you to Carl, and me to Montana. But it's a very small circle now that I've gotten to know you. We have a lot of the same background. And I think the way Carl treated you was evidence of the same kind of thinking we're talking about. He wasn't going to stop you from making your dream come true in order to facilitate the cash flow of his business."

"I still haven't met Carl. I'm going to see him tomorrow."

"Well, what Jimmy Carter was to the presidency, Carl Demler is, in my mind, to the world of piano dealers. A wonderful man who somehow doesn't really belong there, but is a breath of fresh air all the same. He's too kind, too generous, too honest, too caring, too all-of-those-things to be involved in such an ugly business as the buying and selling of pianos. He wants people's dreams to come true. And in whatever measure he can participate in that, even to his own detriment, he seems to be willing to do it."

14

Beethoven's Warehouse

At eight in the morning, I'm standing on the corner of Park Avenue and Eighty-third Street, looking up and down the long rows of red brick townhouses, hoping to see the building number I've scrawled onto my pocket memo pad. Suddenly, the driver's door of a Mercedes station wagon swings open, and an arm reaches out. The hand beckons, and then the slight man attached to it emerges and waves at me. He has fine gray hair groomed back roughly from a sunken, aristocratic face, and his limber ease makes him seem ageless.

"Hello!" the man calls out in a lighthearted voice, and I recognize the whispery tenor of Carl Demler. "Shall we?" He nods to the passenger side, then dives back into the car. He clears the seat of an open briefcase so crammed with files, the lid stands perpendicular. The German accent is unmistakable. I get in.

"This is my partner's car," says Carl, as he pulls us out into traffic. "Normally I drive a van, but there aren't enough seats." He nods sideways, to the rear, and I see an elderly woman propped up on the back seat, sound asleep. She looks very frail, and in her sunken, fine-boned face, I recognize Carl's features. "My mother," he says. "We have someone at the warehouse to take care of her."

We charge north on Madison Avenue, and soon we are flying through Spanish Harlem. When I lived on East Eighty-eighth Street in the early 1980s, Spanish Harlem did not look like this. I stare out the window, amazed. "This area is in a revival," says Carl, noticing my interest in the handsomely renovated apartment buildings. "We have a storefront here we are thinking of putting our cheaper pianos in. The families up here will be interested."

I ask Carl how he got started in the piano business.

"I was a gymnast," he begins, taking the story back a bit further than I expected. "I trained with two Olympic gold medalists in Cologne." Carl was born in Munich in 1936, the son of an engineering student who died in World War II. As a young man, he wanted to travel, so he studied hotel management, first in Switzerland, then at Cornell University in New York. After jobs planning hotels in the Philippines, Singapore, Hawaii, and Boston, he arrived in New York City in 1970 to plan facilities for the Oyster Bar at the Plaza Hotel. He and a partner were going to open a fancy restaurant of their own, but the bank financing the project went bust. Carl had already signed the lease, so he tried to make a go of it alone, but when he could no longer pay the restaurant's rent, he found himself in difficult circumstances. New York was going bankrupt, people and businesses were fleeing the city. Carl had two old upright pianos someone had given him. He decided to sell them to raise some cash.

A man who came to look at the pianos told Carl they were junk, but if they were fixed up, they'd be worth something. So Carl had the pianos renovated, then sold them at a small profit. Soon he was acquiring pianos to rebuild, storing them in his ground-floor Manhattan apartment. When he had nine pianos in his apartment, including two concert grands in his living room, he decided to get a store.

The first Beethoven Pianos was on First Avenue in the East Eighties, a funky little place I used to visit when I lived in the neighborhood. This was the store where I once fell in love with a new Chickering console, but could not spare $1,200 for it. There were lots of old uprights for sale; it was a place a poor student could find a piano. This is still true at Beethoven Pianos, though the showroom is now on glitzy Piano Row.

In only fifteen minutes we are in the Mott Haven section of the Bronx. Carl navigates through construction zone barricades onto a barren bit of land surrounded by a tall chain-link fence topped with razor wire. An unobtrusive sign hangs on the gate: "Piano Sale," it says. We're in the yard of a brick edifice soaring five stories into the sky, beribboned with decorative medallions and scrollwork baked in clay.

This is the warehouse for Beethoven Pianos, a surviving relic of early New York. It was built in 1860 by the Mott family, who owned what were once surrounding apple orchards. In its day, cast-iron claw-foot bathtubs and pot-bellied Franklin stoves were made in this building. To look at it now from the outside, a stark silhouette against a backdrop of debris-covered ground, no one would guess what a hive of activity is inside, a place both fascinating and strange.

Carl moved into the warehouse ten years ago on the advice of a numerologist, he tells me. "She said it would be a good building for me. And it has been." When piano sales are slow, Carl keeps his cash flow moving by renting out billboard space on the warehouse's façade.

A young woman arrives to collect Carl's mother, and Carl grabs his overstuffed briefcase and packs it under one arm. I ask if I should lock my door, but Carl says no, he never locks doors. A new Third Avenue bridge is under construction, right outside the warehouse gate. Cranes stand over concrete pilings, moving steel beams into position over the roiling Harlem River. "This is going to be great when it's finished," Carl says, with a nod to the bridge. He seems invigorated by the progress of it. "Perhaps we'll put a restaurant down by the river." The warehouse sits on the river's bank, and from the small yard, I can see the dark, oily waters, sluggish with trash.

Carl has a reputation as a canny and adventurous businessman, but his vision for a riverside restaurant in the gutted wasteland of the South Bronx takes me by surprise. His colleagues say he's an enigma even to those who have known him a long time. "He is different from you and me," Reinhard Landskron, a decades-long associate of Carl's told me. "None of us can figure him out." One employee describes Beethoven Pianos as a pirate ship, and its crew as an "interesting crowd" drawn to the owner's quirkiness.

Carl's whimsical spirit is contained by a life of prosaic regularity: each morning at eight he drives to the warehouse, and each afternoon and evening he is in his store on West Fifty-eighth Street until late hours. My simple agenda is to inhabit a typical day of his life, but I am unprepared for the strangely compelling world within the warehouse walls.

We enter through a steel door. The light on the ground floor is dim, moving in dust-clotted beams across a sea of piano carcasses, endless rows of verticals, parts and materials for pianos scattered everywhere, with no seeming reason or organization. Metal plates lie over one another, old hammers recently excavated from some wreck are piled on sheaves of newspapers. The pianos stand end to end, keyboard to soundboard, as far as the eye can see, dusty and scraped and ready for the landfill, most of them. The high ceiling has decorative tin tiles painted white. The wood plank flooring is warped and worn; it undulates, rising and swelling like waves. "We'll pour concrete down here eventually," says Carl.

An enormous rusty fuel drum, converted into a woodstove, stands beside the south wall. A metal pipe travels from the stove into the wall, then up through the stories above to the roof. Some landfill pianos are fed to this stove in winter, heating only a fraction of the thirty-five-thousand-square-foot building so that other pianos might have a second life. Some eight hundred pianos at a time cycle the rounds of death and rebirth here. Carl buys them by the container load, often at auction. Perhaps a store went out of business, or a factory went bankrupt and creditors sold off all the inventory. Sometimes Carl sells them as is. Sometimes, though, he finds a gem in the mix and fixes it up. Usually these pianos need too much work to be profitable, but Carl says he does not want to see them to go to waste.

"Our accountant says that what we do here is of little economic value." Carl shrugs. "If we simply rented out the storefront and the warehouse and did nothing, we'd make twice as much money."

"So then why do you do it?"

"It would be such a letdown to stop."

We head up a well-worn staircase. Carl takes the steps two at a time. It's easy to see the former gymnast in his lithe, agile frame. Even in his shabby jacket and scuffed shoes, there is something elegant in his every movement. His bearing is regal, with a naturally erect carriage. In a suit and tie, I bet he could pass for a duke, albeit an unshaven one.

On the landing is an old Franklin potbellied stove that was made here when this place was an ironworks. "They had the trains come right through the building to pick up the stoves and bathtubs," says Carl. "You can still see the tracks in the floor downstairs. I'll show you before we leave."

The second floor is bright and airy, with large multipaned windows on all sides. Crystal and gilded chandeliers, covered in dust, mismatched and incongruous in this industrial setting, hang from the pressed-tin ceiling, accompanied by fluorescent shop lights and the pipe works for the sprinkler system. White Doric columns march down the aisles of grand pianos, supporting the building's central beams. The pianos' wings are open, tilted toward the light.

By one window is Carl's gray metal desk, heaped with papers, a battered office chair behind it. A bust of Beethoven sits on an old file cabinet, and in a nook behind the desk is a storage shelf filled with books reaching to the ceiling. I wedge myself into the nook, curious to see what sort of library a piano warehouse might have.

There are opera librettos, a handbook of piano tuning, John Thompson's modern course for the piano, Japanese children's books, books in German, and some rather disparate titles, including *301 Great Ideas for Using Technology, Theory and Practice of Pianoforte Building,* and *The Mystery and Romance of Astrology.*

Carl sets the overstuffed briefcase down on the desk, then takes me on a tour. "Pianos come to this floor for inspection, and to have work done. We sell some pianos from here."

He sets his hand on the lid of a beautiful Victorian upright in a light burled walnut veneer, with delicate leaf carvings and gold inlay. It is exquisite. "This one I bought on eBay, for the case. We will put a new Schimmel piano inside."

I look about the vast sea of bedraggled pianos—a hospital ward for misbegotten, mistreated instruments. Square grands have their lids missing, their actions and strings exposed, gathering dust. Piano cases emptied of their guts serve as sideboards for their action works. Sheaves of copper-wound bass strings hang from the brick walls like wire macramé. Mounds of evicted hammers cover old benches. Delicate cutwork music desks carved from maple, ebony, mahogany, and birch are displayed against the white brick walls, as if in a gallery. Some pianos are covered in clear plastic sheeting, others with movers' blankets, still others with Bubble Wrap. Dingy iron harps lean every which way, standing alongside fragments of discarded soundboards.

Carl introduces me to some of the pianos. There's an ebony Knabe concert grand that was owned by a technician who has died. A mahogany Henry F. Miller with a collapsed soundboard is here on consignment. Another Knabe with an art nouveau case needs rebuilding. A Fischer piano is painted green and wants refinishing. An Aeolian Duo-Art player piano is here because nobody likes the color. It is painted berry red.

"Here's an Erard from 1840. We just got it in to do some work on it." The piano is nine feet long. Carl tells me it was in the salon of a prominent London family, where many famous pianists played it. The owner wants $75,000 for it. "It's not as good a piano as the Pleyel. When Erard died, the heirs battled over the estate. The winner got Erard Pianos. The losers got *Michelin*." Carl tosses me an impish grin and a raised eyebrow, looking to see if I caught his irony.

Another historic piano, a Königsberg from 1848, has the initials of the maker cut into the soundboard in a scroll-like script, as if it were the case of a violin. The music desk has a lyre and leafwork motif carved out of ebony and set against rose-colored velvet. The underside of the fallboard is decorated with a highly elaborate brass-and-enamel inlay in many colors framing the maker's name. "It's also a consignment piano," says Carl. "It is nearly not saleable. It has a very primitive action." The strings and action are white with dust.

"I had a guy drive by here in a Rolls-Royce once and ask me, 'What is the best piano here?' I said, 'This one, but it's not yet finished.' He gave me a thousand dollars in cash and said, 'Call me when it is finished.' A couple of years went by. I lost his phone number. Then I get a call from someone saying, 'I'm down on my luck. I gave you a thousand dollars for a piano, can I have it back? I'll buy a piano from you when my luck gets better again.' Of course I gave him the money back."

"So, which *is* the best piano here?" I ask, looking around at the dubious candidates. There are easily a hundred grand pianos and many more uprights. Carl winnows himself through the narrow avenues made by the instruments, and I follow him. He rests his hand on the edge of an eight-foot rosewood grand. The action is missing, and a new set of bass strings hang from the plate's hitch pins, wound around each other like a copper pigtail.

"I hope this will be the best one here. It's a Steinway C. It had a new soundboard, but a pipe froze and unfroze at the wrong time, there was a flood, and it needs to be restored from the flood damage. I own it."

"When will it be done?"

"It takes six months to a year for a complete restoration. Normally it's not a priority. You do it when you feel like it, unless there is a buyer. This one has a buyer."

"What is the most beautiful piano you've ever had here?"

"The best sounding piano I remember was a Steinway A with eighty-five keys." Modern pianos have eighty-eight keys. "I was sorry to sell it. It came out absolutely magnificent, a surging sweet tone. I like the richness of sound of the American pianos, with a big bass. It's really special when the middle-upper treble matches the rest. It is really difficult to achieve that because the strings are so short in the treble. Often it is an accident if it sounds really perfect.

"But everything in a piano is temporary," Carl says, leading the way through the maze of pianos again. "A piano is perfect for only a *split second*."

"How do you judge piano tone so well? Are you also a pianist? A technician?"

Carl pauses and leans against the case of a white Yamaha baby grand. "I'm no expert. I'm not even a musician. But I hear a lot of pianos. I played piano as a kid. Now I can't. I have a condition called Dupuytren's contracture, it makes my fingers contract." He holds up one hand and shows me how a finger is forming into a claw. "At one time gymnastics was my life, and back in the 1950s, they didn't have the protective padding they do now. I may have injured my hands on the bars. But sports taught me to be very competitive."

I don't think of someone who rebuilds old pianos on a money-losing basis as competitive. How, exactly, I ask Carl, is his business competitive?

"We offer better service at a better price." He smiles, his eyes twinkle. "We say, *If nobody else can do it, come to Beethoven's.* We have two basements here loaded with parts we bought from defunct companies. When someone needs piano legs to match the old ones, we make them. I found a company that will sell us artist benches for twenty-eight dollars. I found a source of nine-hundred-dollar new uprights. You meet these suppliers at trade shows. Out back we have a fifty-six-foot trailer I bought at auction for three hundred and fifty dollars, with two levels, built for moving uprights.

"Also, our company is very international. We have a woman in our office who is from Shanghai. So we have her call China if we need something. We have someone from Thailand.

"In this business, the biggest challenge for many is to pay the rent. We own our buildings. And because we do so many things—moving, appraisals, sales, rebuilding, rentals—we are nearly recession proof. We can do many things others can't. For example, yesterday we provided a concert grand on two hours' notice. A piano teacher called looking for a Steinway for twenty thousand dollars—a good one. I can do that. I can buy a piano for seven thousand dollars, refinish it, repair the soundboard, put in some new shanks and flanges and hammers and still make a substantial profit. We've moved a concert grand up twelve flights of stairs. The owner wouldn't let it be hoisted through the window, and it wouldn't fit in the elevator. Sometimes we put pianos on top of the elevator to lift them. We build a structure to hold them."

Carl picks up a wool felt hammer from a pile that has been stripped out of some old wreck, and turns it in his crooked fingers. "The trend now is to make harder hammers because few people are good at voicing. The sheep's wool is not as good as it used to be. They bleach them to look nice and white. You know what happens to hair when you bleach it. Most are shaped in a hot press. Others they put lacquer in to harden them. Once they are a certain hardness, it is difficult to make them soft again. The wood also was better back then, not just the wool. The new pianos are not as good as the old ones. But pianos wear out, just as people do."

Then he turns about, weaving through the instruments again. We nod hello as we pass a silent giant of a man who wields the biggest screwdriver I have ever seen. He's making adjustments to a piano action. He seems not to notice us, his huge dome of a shaved head bent over his work, his gigantic black eyebrows arched like a pair of bat wings in flight. His radio softly broadcasts the news in Russian.

"That's Yuri," says Carl. We keep moving, weaving ourselves more deeply into the loft.

In a sun-filled corner, hidden behind rows of ancient uprights, is another man, listening to a radio broadcast in Ukrainian. He's rubbing out the finish on a piano bench, and is surrounded by extravagant pieces of decorative furniture—massive inlaid tables, gilt-framed mirrors. "We do furniture refinishing as a sideline," Carl explains. "I don't like to do the same thing all the time."

A call comes in on his cell phone. A woman wants to know if Carl will buy her piano. "We will charge you to take it away," he tells her. "You can get some money if you sell it yourself."

"We have to throw them away," he explains to me after he hangs up. "I've asked people if we could give them the wood to make toys. They don't want it." He shrugs.

We head back to his desk, dodging piano parts and cases strewn across our path. "There are endless details to stay on top of," Carl says. "A building like this needs a lot of work to get it back to where it should be. In December it will be paid off, and then we can refinance."

"What will you do with the money?"

"I plan to sell art case pianos in Shanghai, China. Steinways and Bösendorfers do well there. The wealth of the world is created there right now, and that type of piano is not made in China. They sell very fast when we put them in the window.

"Here in New York there's Steinway, Steinway, Steinway. Everyone wants a Steinway," Carl says. "Except for those who want Yamaha." I note that bemused look again.

"I see my business as a service. We all have to do something to contribute to life. I do a lot of things others say wouldn't make sense, businesswise. Someone needs a piano, and they are not well-to-do. I sold a young student a piano for five hundred dollars. Some years ago I donated a concert grand to the Harlem Boys' Choir. I also told a customer yesterday that I refuse to do business with him. He didn't like that.

"At one time, I was going to go out of the piano business," he says. We're back at the desk now. He sits on it, gripping the edge, his legs swinging like a schoolboy's. I take the battered chair for my seat. "Mark, my sales manager, has a yacht, a racing sailboat. We were going to sail around the world, but then I got married."

Carl's wife, Kaoru, is a Japanese lithographer who came to New York to study art, and met Carl when she rented a room in his large apartment. She now manages the store's finances and handles sales. As Carl tells me this, I remember well her dark voice from when she made sure my piano was delivered.

"Kaoru has very strong opinions. She is nearly the opposite of me.

So far, we've lasted twelve years. An astrologer said it would be a challenge." He says this lightly, as if he is making the best of it. "My wife works a lot on intuition, and is more often right than wrong. She is very good at many things—customers, a good business sense. Her family in Japan owns a car dealership, and she has a shopkeeper mentality she inherited from them. I never had that." The couple has three young children.

"In my religion," he continues, "there's a reason for everything. Whatever we do we pay for it sooner or later. This gives me incentive to see myself in the long run."

What is he referring to? I wonder. His eyes gaze off into the distance. They are a piercing blue, yet somehow elusive. A direct gaze from him is rare.

Then he does look at me with a smile of detached bemusement. "My private interest is where we come from and why are we here, and where are we going," he says. "I'm not a member of any church or organization, but I have been studying Western esoteric teachings."

Yes, Marc mentioned this to me. When I told him I found Carl confounding, he said, "You probably haven't met many anthroposophists." I'm not sure what an anthroposophist is, but since Carl seems open to talking about his inner life, perhaps he is the right person to ask about my own?

"So then, Carl, can you tell me . . ." I pause. I have to think for a moment about how to explain my question. "When you have a customer who falls in love with a piano, who responds deeply to one piano above all others, why does that happen? You have no doubt seen this many times. What happened to me when I fell for my Grotrian?"

Carl looks at me quite keenly. "Yes, of course, I have seen that happen." He clears his throat. "We all have a keynote that is different from anyone else's," he begins. "You find it here." He touches the base of his skull. "When that note sounds, you have a sympathetic vibration and you feel elated. We all react to vibrations or to tone differently. When you come across a sound that makes you feel good, that's the piano you should get.

"It's all vibration. All that is, is vibration. We've known this since Einstein: sound, energy, and mass are interchangeable. All that is, is music.

"Music is the closest link to the inner world, the higher worlds. Playing music is a self-transforming experience. The experience of being a conduit for the spirit of the composer, who is also a conduit for the divine. It's the divine that is in all of us. Music transforms. When it is played, emanations come from that music. This is the secret influence of music throughout the ages. It could have a healing effect on illnesses, illness from having the wrong vibration in your body."

I feel chills at his words, as if, like the Grotrian, I resonate to them. How eerily similar they are to the words I spoke only yesterday when I described my experiences at the piano to Marc.

Carl's soliloquy ends when a wiry man, all hardened sinew and streetwise tough, suddenly appears and announces that a piano is being delivered downstairs.

I follow Carl and "Junior," as he is introduced to me—though judging from the gray in his kinky hair, it is decades since he was a junior—down the swayed warehouse stairs to the ground floor and back out to the concrete stoop. A grand piano, swaddled in blankets, is lashed to a railing in the open cargo area of a truck. A man in a black wool overcoat, wearing leather gloves, waits by the loading dock. The man introduces himself to Carl as the owner of the piano. His accent is Russian, and as Carl and Junior climb into the back of the truck, I greet the man in his native tongue, which was also my grandfather's. His face lights up.

"This was my teacher's piano in Moscow," says the man, named Sergei, a professor of piano who arrived in New York ten years ago. "He willed it to me, and I went over there to get it. It's a 1912 Bechstein C, seven-foot-four. The movers in Russia broke the lid and damaged the case. Yuri told me to go only to Carl." He must mean the technician with the long screwdriver who was listening to Russian radio upstairs.

Sergei turns to Carl. "I was told to trust you and only you, and so I will," he says now in English. But Carl does not seem to hear him. He is helping Junior and the two movers muscle the behemoth onto a dolly.

Junior places a ramp from the tailgate of the truck to the lip of the loading dock, and together Carl and the movers wrestle it uphill. Soon they are joined by four more workers from the warehouse. Each takes charge of a section of the piano, watching carefully to keep it atop the narrow ramp. Once the piano is inside, they hoist it into an ancient freight elevator. Then Junior, Carl, Sergei, and I cram over, under, and around the piano, clinging to it for ballast as Junior pulls the heavy door closed. The platform creaks as it crawls up the floors. A window in the roof draws nearer and nearer, until it is right over our heads. Then the door clangs open with a heave of its mighty lever, and we are on the top floor of the warehouse.

Sergei and I unkink ourselves out of the elevator into a dank room filled with stored pianos. Unlike the gracious second floor, this room is lit by bare lightbulbs; their pull cords dangle from heavily stained rafters. Carl and Junior wheel the Bechstein around a corner, through a sliding metal barn door, and into the workshop of Beethoven's master piano rebuilder, Rudolf von Bartesch, known to all as Rudy.

Rudy is a great, hulking giant of a man, with massive hands and a permanent limp caused by a concert grand collapsing onto his foot. He moves with a shuffle and hunched shoulders toward the Bechstein and gestures to the men to move it over behind his electric planer, where several other pianos await his ministrations. He wears a black leather jacket over a faded plaid shirt, and his gray hair is scraped straight back from his deeply furrowed forehead. His face is set with a pair of gentle black eyes; they gleam with intelligence, and a bit of sadness. A hint of a smile twitches on the corners of his lips when Carl introduces me.

Carl and Junior unwrap the piano, while the pianist stands anxiously by, explaining to Carl and Rudy what happened to his prize inheritance. "It was loose in the box, it was broken when they opened the box."

Carl lifts the fallboard, and we can see that its decorative molding is fractured, and the ivory tops of the keys are missing.

"Where are the keytops?" I ask.

"It's a problem to bring ivory into the country if the piano is one day younger than one hundred years old," Carl says with some vehemence. "It's because of some stupid ass in Tobacco and Firearms. To bring in antique piano ivories you have to petition Washington."

Sergei removed the ivories in Moscow and sent them to New York by mail. He is standing beside me, his gloves still on, very agitated. "People who need piano don't have money," he pleads. "People who don't need piano have money. It is my own piano to practice on. I don't like shiny finish. I don't know the word in English."

"I would do as little as possible," Carl soothes. "It's a very delicate instrument. Nobody knows how to make the old soundboards properly for Bechstein." He projects calm and kindness in the face of the pianist's fears. "Yuri will come take a look at it tonight and then call you."

After Junior shows the pianist out, I hazard to play a few notes on his precious Bechstein. It is in sorry shape.

"We'll clean it up, repair the lid and the molding," says Carl. "He can't afford anything more than that."

"You don't want to rebuild a Bechstein with a new board." It is Rudy, his voice gruff. "The plates always crack." He shakes his head slowly.

"Rudy knows how to do it," amends Carl. "But it is always a risk. Besides, he"—he nods in the direction of the departed pianist—"he can't afford a rebuild. We will fix it up within his means."

Rudy has removed his leather jacket and begins arranging tools on his workbench as if setting the table for his day.

"You must see the legs Rudy makes," says Carl. From under the workbench, he hoists two massive decorative piano legs, made of new, raw wood, and brandishes them proudly. "A whole set of these legs costs three thousand dollars."

The workmanship is breathtaking. The legs are ornately carved in a Victorian style, with an encircling tulip and leaf motif, precisely repeated. Carl holds one leg out so I can run my finger over the unfinished wood, admire the delicate, uniform perfection of the carving.

"How did you do that?" I ask Rudy, who has come over to join us.

"My grandfather was a sculptor, my father was in furniture. Here," he says, turning to his workbench and beckoning me to follow. He shows me an array of carving tools in many different sizes; their heavily worn wood handles look ancient. "These were my great-grandfather's, in Germany."

"And what about the parts you didn't carve?"

"I do this." He holds a battered ebony leg, the original he copied from, up to a lathe, and shows me the jig he cut to its shape, fitting them together. He is stumped for the English words to use.

"The lathe follows your cutout?"

He nods once. "Here," he says again, and holds up two carving tools, large spatula-like blades set in heavy handles. "This one?" He waggles one of the tools. "It is fifty years old. It is in perfect condition. See this one?" He waggles the other. "Only eight years old." The younger tool is smashed up, its edges worn and twisted, nearly useless in comparison. "See how much quality has changed?"

Just past Rudy's left shoulder is a sight I can't pull my eyes from: A worktable, cut in the shape of a grand piano lid, has sprouted a small forest—more than a dozen 1x2s stand on their ends, from the tabletop all the way to the ceiling. They must be about eight feet long. They are jammed so tightly between table and ceiling, they bend from the pressure. All around the edge of the shaped table are giant clamps holding a flat piece of thin blond wood in place. It's a piano sound-board being made, Rudy explains. The table, which is a butcher-block top, is concave, its surface hollowed out like a shallow pool, and the soundboard, which arrives flat from Germany, is pressured into this hollow by the force of the standing 1x2 boards. This concave shape is the soundboard's crown, which must have a particular form if it is to properly project the piano's tone.

Carl becomes very animated when he sees my interest in the soundboard. He shows me a small closet he calls a "steam box" at one end of the workshop. Inside, flat soundboards and other precious woods are carefully stacked. The steam box maintains precise temperature and humidity levels, 88 degrees Fahrenheit and 28 percent humidity. The wood acclimates in here for about a year after it arrives from Germany or Canada.

"For the smaller pianos, the Bavarian spruce is better," Carl says. "They come from the Alps. Listen to this."

He strides over to an old grand piano case with a brand-new soundboard in it. Carl pounds a fist on the board and it booms, drum-like, the echo repeating and repeating along the length of the cavernous fifth floor, a deeply resonant heartbeat.

"The company that makes these boards is Strunz; they've been in business since 1820. I assume they own certain forests. They are very strict over there about forestry. Forestry is the most difficult school to get into. It's like Harvard."

Carl says one day the fifth floor of the warehouse will be a school for piano technicians. "The only place for a thorough technical training is in Germany. Immigration makes it very difficult to bring German technicians here. My idea is to get German techs to come for six months out of the year and teach."

His cell phone rings. "Excuse me." He takes the call, then quickly hangs up. "I must meet some workmen downstairs, I will be back in a little while." And swiftly, he vanishes, leaving me alone with the dour Rumanian and his workshop.

A radio on a shelf is tuned to the opera. A small woodstove with a glass door has a fire crackling away, fed by old, broken soundboards and wood scraps. Above Rudy's workbench are enormous multipaned factory windows looking out over the city and the river below. The room is flooded with warm late-autumn sunshine, making indigo shadows across the hard-worn plank floors. The scene could be a Renaissance painting of a master craftsman at work. Rudy turns to me, a quarter turn, and gestures to the view.

"We stood here on September eleventh and watched the World Trade Center in flames, and then vanish," he says, his doleful eyes meeting mine, his voice quiet, slow, his accent thick. I look out the window and indeed one can see all the way to the southernmost tip of Manhattan from this fifth-story aerie.

With a shuffle, Rudy moves over to the piano with the new soundboard in it. Directly above the piano's case hangs the cast-iron plate, newly repainted in a bronze lacquer finish. It is gripped by ropes and suspended from a chain-and-pulley assembly. Rudy points to the underside of the plate, showing me where the foundry man signed it in white chalk a century before: *Petterson,* it says, in a flowing script. Piano builders always signed the parts of the piano they made, Rudy explains.

He slowly lowers the plate into position in the case, his massive hands tight on the chain, the pulley clanking. Such large hands, and yet so delicately they unwind a roll of fine waxed cotton string tied to a small piece of molded brass called an agraffe. Rudy pulls the string across the topography of the plate and the bridge, following the exact same path the piano wire will travel, measuring with his eye and wood shims the angle for the strings.

This string angle measurement is called *bearing*. Without proper bearing, the piano will not speak, the tone will not bloom. Rudy says he wants a five-millimeter angle at the bridge in the treble, and four in the tenor section.

His measurements made, he pulls the chain to raise the plate again. He bends his body nearly horizontal over the piano's rim, reaching out across the soundboard with a small metal template. Rudy fits the template over one of the fluted dowels that run around the perimeter of the soundboard like studs. He cuts the dowel down to size, using a flat saw with very fine teeth. When all the dowels are cut, they will hold the plate off the soundboard at just the right height for proper bearing.

I closely watch Rudy work, trying to see all and yet not get in his way. Rudy looks at me from time to time. His dark eyes are bemused, and perhaps a bit sad.

"My children aren't interested in this," Rudy says, as if commenting on my rapt attention. "I taught my sons, but they don't want this. They want to do computers, marketing."

"Are you teaching anyone?" I think how terrible it would be if these skills were not passed on.

"Not yet. Now I must make new bridge cap."

The bridge is a long, flat arc of wood attached to the soundboard, the only point of contact between the soundboard and the strings. When the strings vibrate, the bridge carries their vibrations into the soundboard, which acts as a transducer, amplifying the vibrations until they are audible. Rudy is retaining the original bridge for this piano, but making a new cap, or top piece, for it, out of quarter-sawn rock maple.

He has already removed the original cap, and now lays the dark-brown, aged wood of the old bridge out on his worktable. It looks like an elongated cribbage board with its rows of tiny holes. The holes are from metal pins that once guided the strings across the bridge. Rudy pounds wooden shoe pegs into the holes with a ball-peen hammer, then grinds the surface smooth with a belt sander.

In less-experienced hands, a heavy belt sander would send the bridge flying or perhaps crush it. But Rudy manipulates the powerful machine freehand, as easily and lightly as if it were a hand planer.

Rudy must have once stood at least six foot four. But even stooped and round-shouldered as he is from decades of bending over his work, he has a linebacker's silhouette. When he works with wood, he also has a balletic grace—his movements are efficient, even beautiful in their deceptive simplicity.

Inside the steam box, Rudy examines several pieces of maple harvested in the Canadian Rockies, looking for the straightest grain. The bridge cap's grain density must match that of the soundboard it will rest on, he explains. He selects a one-inch-thick board and carries it back to his workbench, where he traces the old bridge onto the new wood in three sections.

He switches on a bandsaw and holds the maple board up to the running blade, cutting along the curved pencil lines. He uses no guides except his own sure hands, which steer the heavy wood without effort, cutting the lines exactly. It's a strange way to describe woodworking, but Rudy's artfulness with tools is poetic. I am fascinated.

A mustachioed man suddenly plows right past us, as if out of nowhere. "I see you have a new apprentice! You can retire next week!" the man calls out, then disappears through a door at the opposite end of the room.

"That's Mark," says Rudy, tilting his head in the direction of Carl's store manager. "Mark is all the time in a hurry."

An apprentice! I have a pleasurable moment of imagining myself on a path I know I won't take. With Rudy as my teacher, some day I too could dance with wood, bring pianos into being, possess the secrets of their magic. I remember Rudy's comment about his children not being interested.

"How many children do you have?"

"Two," says Rudy, raising his eyebrows and pursing his lips as he roughs up the old bridge and its new cap with a scraper, preparing them for glue. "One child in marketing. Other has a construction equipment rental company."

"How long have you been married?"

"Married in 1965. The government wouldn't let me follow her until 1969. She got out because she is Armenian. If you were Jewish or Armenian you could leave. But everyone wanted to leave Rumania."

Slowly, as he works, in bits and pieces, with my promptings and questions to help me understand his English, Rudy's story unfolds.

Rudolf von Bartesch came from a family of woodcarvers and piano builders, going back many generations in Leipzig, Germany.

After World War I, Rudy's grandfather was forced to leave the country. He settled in Rumania. When Rudy, who was born in Rumania, was fourteen, he went to work in the Doina piano factory. Fifty years later, he is still in the family trade. "Back in Rumania my grandfather, my father, everyone in my family played instruments after work. They had chamber music—no radio—I tried violin and piano."

Under the Ceauşescu regime, Rudy was a tuner in a conservatory in Bucharest, where he met his future wife, Seta Karakashian, a pianist of Armenian descent. After only a year at the conservatory, Seta seized on a sudden opportunity to leave Rumania. The couple rushed to marry with the consul of the American embassy as their witness. Two hours after the ceremony, Rudy's new bride was out of the country, without him.

Seta wrote to Rudy every day, 365 letters a year for five years. She also wrote to then U.S. President Richard Nixon, who visited Rumania in 1969 and negotiated for the release of certain Rumanian citizens to the United States. Because of Seta, Rudy was on the president's list. "A very strong woman. She was fighting constantly," Rudy says of his wife, who was then studying at Juilliard by day and working at a Robert Hall dress shop at night.

Rudy arrived in New York with nothing but the clothes he had on. The very next morning he began work as a technician at Juilliard. He spoke no English. When he left Juilliard for the day, he went to work at a renowned piano rebuilding shop, A&C Pianocraft, eventually becoming a partner. His workday began at seven in the morning and ended at ten at night. Five years later, he went off on his own. He has rebuilt some famous pianos, including the ornately decorated Steinway B that was owned by the Woolworth family, and a piano that once belonged to King George V.

In 1973, Rudy received his green card, and he was able to return to Rumania to see his parents. He had saved every one of his wife's letters from their five-year separation, and together, the couple climbed the top of a mountain in the Carpathians and burned them all. As soon as he became a U.S. citizen, in 1978, he brought his parents and sister to America.

Rudy lumbers over to another old grand piano, this one a scuffed mahogany 1905 Steinway model A he is rebuilding for a private customer. The action and keyboard are already removed, as are the strings. He fires up an electric saw with a long crescent-shaped blade like a scythe, and cuts out the old soundboard, breaking it into pieces and setting them by the woodstove. "I paneled the inside of my cabin with these soundboards," he says, holding up a golden, varnished shard. "I built the cabin myself. I watch the electrician, then I copy. I watch the plumber, then I copy. All pass inspection. You watch, you learn. Just like soundboards. They won't teach you anything, but I watch." He points a meaty finger to one eye, and gives a knowing look.

"So I could learn to do what you do by watching?"

"Sure!"

Rudy's cabin is in the Catskills. "I love the mountains. In the Catskills I can be all alone—no neighbors." He smiles.

Suddenly the huge barn door rolls aside on its casters again and Carl appears with Junior and Joel, a young man who looks about nineteen. They are moving with purpose across the workshop. "We are going up to the roof," Carl says to me, his hand beckoning. Reluctantly, I leave Rudy's company, his hulking silences, his terrible Rumanian-laden pronunciation, his lumbering woodcarver's grace. I hate it that I may not see him notch the bridge by hand with a chisel, or see him install the new soundboard in the model A.

The access to the roof is up a narrow wisp of a ladder, made out of steel strips, and it doesn't seem especially safe, but Carl nimbly climbs right up it after Junior and Joel, and I tentatively follow. The brilliant sunlight and blue sky startle me. The wind is brisk. Standing on the roof, I can see a vast 360-degree panorama of Manhattan to the south, and the Bronx to the north and west. Carl and his assistants are already at the far end of the enormous rooftop, looking at a major hole that drops straight down into one of the storage areas, and I join them. Carl explores the edges of the hole with the tip of one dusty black dress shoe, and seems lost in thought. The roofers are expected at any time, he says. He gives some instructions to Junior and Joel, who then disappear back down the rickety ladder. Carl turns to me and makes a sweeping gesture to the view before us.

"These warehouses you see up and down Bruckner Boulevard," he says, pointing north. "Many of them were piano factories. On the corner, right there, that was Estey Pianos. Two blocks up was Krakauer.

The Winter factory was just a bit farther up." Over the years, there have been many piano factories in this industrial neighborhood.

"We were lucky to get this building. We own this land, and this is a solid building. I want to put two more floors on top and put an herb garden on the roof." He points to the sky with a crowbar, as if using it to sketch his plans. "I've been a vegetarian for more than forty years, and I believe in the healing power of herbs. Herbs hold the secret of life."

He strides back and forth as if giving a discourse before a class-room. "Alternative medicine is a growth industry. We'll grow fresh herbs for cooking, under a big greenhouse with plastic sheeting you replace every other year."

He stops pacing, turns to me, and puts his fingers to his lips, pen-sive. "I should have been an alternative healer. I had a gift for it, but it is too late now," He shrugs. "So instead of healing people, I heal some pianos."

✦

"Yuri was here," says Rudy when we reenter the workshop. "He looked at the Bechstein. He says it needs new hammers." Rudy wants the Bechstein out of his shop. "No more room," he says with a slow shake of his head.

"We'll know more tomorrow," says Carl.

Carl heads back downstairs, but rather than follow him, I seize the opportunity to watch Rudy string a piano. Until the piano is strung, Rudy cannot know if his rebuilding job is a success. "Sometimes," he says, "it doesn't sound right and I have to take it apart, start over."

Rudy unlatches a black Samsonite briefcase filled with large pieces of felt, in red and green, a tuning hammer and various-sized sockets, scissors, steel tuning pins, a roll of white tape, a mallet, wire cutters, and an odd little elbow wrench that looks like the handle for a jack-in-the-box. This is his stringing kit.

He begins by wrapping his left thumb and index finger with the tape until they look as if they are wearing casts. Then he tapes a long piece of green felt over the front rim of the piano to protect it. With the scissors, he cuts red felt in long strips, applies rubber cement to the piano's plate, then pats the red felt strips into place. A rough wooden contraption—a horizontal wheel—is mounted on the piano's case. It's a carousel for unraveling big spools of piano wire. Rudy says he made it himself.

"You make your own tools, the rest you buy," he says, as he pulls the first length of wire from the spool. "It takes years."

The barn door slides aside again, and two men enter the workshop. One carries a propane tank, and the other pushes a roll of tar paper before him on a dolly. Rudy directs them to the roof.

He threads the wire through a tuning pin, then uses the elbow socket wrench to turn the pin twice, wrapping the wire around the pin tight. He pounds the pin into the piano's pinblock with a sledge-hammer until the blueing on the steel disappears under the plate. He clips the tail off the wire with a mighty pair of snips that bite down horizontally, like a set of teeth.

There is pounding overhead.

Rudy loops the other end of the wire around a hitch pin on the plate, pulls the wire back to the pinblock, and again threads and wraps a pin, pounds it into the pinblock. He pulls more wire, threads and winds, pounds and snips, all with a practiced uniformity. He watches his handiwork intently through half-glasses. After tightening the first section of strings with the tuning hammer, he asks me to pluck one.

This is the first sounding of the piano, its rebirth moment. I pluck a treble string with my fingernail, and it sings out cleanly, with good sustain, traveling through the air for a long time, audible even over the radio and the banging on the roof.

Now when Rudy strikes in the new pins, the tightened strings cry out in sympathetic resonance.

The pounding overhead intensifies, and suddenly dust and debris come crashing down onto the piano. A hole opens directly above us, letting in daylight. Junior's disembodied head appears, grinning at us like a jack-o'-lantern. Rudy mutters something I cannot understand. "The varnish is still fresh!" he complains. He finds a sheet of clear plastic and hastily covers the piano with it. "That's it for today," he says, reaching for his jacket.

My heart catches with disappointment. I could watch Rudy work forever.

◆

I find Carl on the fourth floor, where pianos are refinished. Workers, their heads wrapped in bandanas, rub empty grand piano cases with sandpaper blocks. Bandanas are tied over their noses, too, like they are bandits, so only their dark eyes are visible. The radio broadcast is in Spanish. The air is heavy with the smell of chemicals. In a spraying booth, pianos are coated first with a layer of polyester sealer, then nitrocellulose lacquer. A woman rubs a lacquered walnut piano case with a wad of fine steel wool, satinizing the finish.

"Everyone in our refinishing department is from Ecuador," says Carl. The workers look up and smile at me with friendly eyes. "Once I counted we had thirteen different nationalities at the warehouse. Right now, they are from Russia, Ecuador, and Germany."

At the moment there are ten workers in the warehouse, says Carl, not including Rudy, who is not an employee, but does Beethoven's rebuilding work in exchange for the use of his shop.

"We have Yuri, from Steinway. He just got a job offer from Peabody Conservatory to assist the chief of their piano technology department." Carl is counting on his fingers, thinking through his staff. "We have Simeon, a Russian from Kiev. He worked in a piano factory there. He does stringing and repinning. His brother used to work for us, too, but he had a stroke.

"Miron Bilyeski is our woodworker. He can do anything with wood. He is Polish-Russian—or at least he speaks Russian. He's an artist, a sculptor. Then we have our warehouse manager, Judy Macancela. She handles a lot of things—refinishing, she does all our keytops and rebushing, and she knows where everything is. Her sister, Rosa, is also doing refinishing. Right now she's touching up a French polish." He gestures to the woman rubbing out the lacquered walnut piano case, and she nods hello.

"Alois Kronschlager, an Austrian, from the School of Visual Arts, is an avant-garde sculptor. He's our expert on color matching and is our best polyester repair person. He charges now one hundred dollars an hour he is so good. Then we have our three full-time refinishers, all from Ecuador, as are Rosa and Judy, who have been with us many years.

"Carlos Perez, from the Dominican Republic, he has done damper work for us for about ten years."

"And then Junior and Joel?" I prompt.

"Yes. Junior has been with me for nineteen years. We've been through lots of changes. Joel just started with us. He used to work on an organic farm upstate. He will be in charge of the herb garden on the roof."

We rumble down the dim stairwell, feet clattering. Carl pauses on the landing in the near darkness, turns back to me to say something, but then his cell phone rings. The boiler man is on his way to the building in Spanish Harlem, someone is calling to say, and Carl must let him into the cellar. We have to leave.

The darkness of the ground floor embraces us again. This is indeed the warehouse's most chaotic floor, a pack rat's delight. But it is an organized chaos. Carl knows where everything is. He rests his hand on a stack of thick laminated boards, and tells me they can make three pinblocks from each.

"We are thinking of creating a really great upright. A great technician works with me, she learned from the legends in New York— she fell in love with the old Kranich & Bach uprights, the tall ones. When we get some money together, we'll cast fifty plates in China and do the frame to our specifications and come up with a vertical of no equal. But," he says with a shrug, flashing me an impish smile, "this might be pipe dreams."

Carl, I think, you must have at least a dozen pipe dreams going all at once.

◆

Carl double-parks the station wagon right in front of the Beethoven Pianos showroom on West Fifty-eighth Street. When Carl found this storefront during the real estate recession of 1991, it was a medical supplies shop, but originally the red brick building was a carriage factory, built in 1880. Through the glass doors we head directly for the rear of the showroom, where computer stations on a raised balcony face out over parallel embankments of grand pianos, in finishes plain and ornate, their wings raised in a repeated salute.

Employees in charge of sales, moving, storage, and rentals take and make calls from the balcony. Their voices clatter above the tapping of computer keyboards and the bleating of a piano being tuned. An intercom announces a call for Carl, and he excuses himself, leaving me to wander the showroom alone. I play a few notes on a Feurich, a passage on a Hamburg Steinway, some chords on a Mason.

"Can I help you?" says a woman's voice. The accent is distinctly Japanese. I look up to see a slender, self-confident woman, dressed in a black pants suit, standing immediately beside me. Her round face is framed by black hair tied up in a knot. I look into her friendly, alert eyes, and I am almost certain this is Kaoru, Carl's wife. The timbre of her voice is unmistakable.

I introduce myself as the troublesome Grotrian buyer from Montana, and she breaks into a huge smile. "Yes! I heard you were coming!" She invites me to sit with her on a divan below the balcony.

Kaoru has worked in the store for about seven years. At first it was a way for the children to have time with their father, she says. She helped with bookkeeping, avoiding the customers because of her then-poor English. But one day she sold two very expensive Steinway grands to some Japanese customers. "Carl was so happy. I said, 'See? I can do it!'" Her face is radiant, and she pumps her fist in triumph, as if the victory was only yesterday.

Now Kaoru stays on top of the cash flow. Carl, she says, is supposed to ask her if it is OK to purchase a big item. "Sometimes he doesn't ask, and he tries to hide it." She laughs.

"It is very difficult to be married and in business together. It helps that he is an optimist. He's extremely lucky, too. Every time we have an edgy situation, a miracle happens. For example, when we needed the money to buy the warehouse, or lose it, a jazz pianist came in to buy a piano stool, and ended up buying a Louis XIV Steinway grand. Carl believes something will happen and he doesn't worry.

"But Carl's not the easiest person. I have to stand over him, and he doesn't like the control.

"For example, I want to sell new pianos. They are more profitable, fewer problems, you get cash quicker. It takes a long time to rebuild, and then people are so particular when a piano is not new.

"I call the rebuilding 'Carl's hobby.' The financial planner says it isn't making us money. But Carl isn't interested in money. He wants the musician to get a better piano. An old piano, he doesn't want to waste it. He enjoys seeing someone buy it who appreciates it."

I ask her what the store's customers are like.

"Oh, they are such funny people!" She laughs with her crooked-toothed smile, her face bright with charm. "Musicians are characters. I never saw such people like this in my country. There is a great pianist who comes here. He carries a piano stool with him all the time, even when he's on a bicycle.

"We have another customer who has been looking for his dream piano for ten years. He puts the sold tag on himself. Then he comes back two days later and says, 'It's not my dream piano.' Sometimes he puts a deposit on his credit card and we end up tearing it up. Once he put the sold tag on and I didn't see it and it fell off. And I sold the piano. He was furious. After that, I asked Carl to not let him put the sold tag on anymore. But Carl likes him—'Oh, he's looking for his dream piano, let him do it.'"

Kaoru excuses herself to take a phone call, and I see that Carl is greeting a customer at the front of the store. He is now wearing a navy wool blazer over his turtleneck sweater, transformed from ware-house manager to showroom duke. The only hint of his warehouse persona is the gray stubble on his cheeks and the dust on his dress shoes.

As I draw closer, I hear the man say, "How much for an upright?"

"Fifteen hundred dollars and up," says Carl, his hands nested in each other behind his back. There is a great, solemn, friendly dignity about him.

"And how much for a grand piano?" says the man.

"The same. Fifteen hundred dollars and up," says Carl, pleasantly. The man says he'll have a look around, and Carl turns to me.

"I have something to show you." He beckons me to follow him up the stairs to the second floor.

"We just got this in. Fresh out of the crate. Nothing has been done to it." He pulls aside the bench with a flourish, inviting me to play a glossy black grand. The fallboard says *Ritmüller*. I sit down and begin the opening bars of the Chopin B minor waltz. The treble is tender, clear, sweet, delicate, and complex. The bass is warm and rich. The touch is superb. I look at the gilt-framed price sheet on the music desk.

It's a new piano, made in China, only $8000. For that kind of money, it's not believable.

"Very impressive!" I say, quite surprised.

"It's made by Pearl River in Guangzhou, China. They are now making four hundred and seventy-five pianos a *day*. They are the reason Yamaha is looking to make pianos cheaper." Carl explains that Chinese pianos are driving down new piano prices—18 percent in just the previous year—and profit margins for piano dealers are shrinking. "They have the economies of scale, they pay their workers only a dollar fifty an hour, their workers are very disciplined, they have the most modern equipment, they can buy all the piano design talent in the world. They are making hundreds of thousands of pianos, and they are creating wealth."

I play the Ritmüller some more, and I am stunned at how beautiful it is. It definitely feels and plays like a German piano. The Germans have been making, arguably, the world's finest pianos since the instrument's invention more than three hundred years ago; the Chinese entered the global market only in the past ten years. Most Chinese piano factories are less than five years old. They have learned quickly.

"That is clearly a piano that sings to you from the moment you touch it," says Carl. He says this quite matter-of-factly, as if it is an undeniable truth. He clearly believes it. After playing the piano, I do, too. Would I have fallen for this piano if I had not met Marlene first?

"I would have considered this piano very seriously, Carl."

"There are many roads to Rome. You can't take all of them," says Carl. "There will always be a market for hand-built pianos. Those who develop ears, or who were born with them, will always notice the difference and pay for it."

✦

It has grown dark outside, and cold. Rush hour is over, and fewer people pass the showroom window. Kaoru and the store's staff have all gone home. Carl and I sit on benches in the midst of the grand pianos, our backs to their keyboards, while Carl holds forth on the piano business.

"You need a lot of optimism," Carl says. "It's a declining business. We are always on the fringe, financially. There is an enormous competition for time from computers, TV, soccer, stereo. Yet at one time, it was the biggest form of entertainment at the turn of the century.

"The wood industry was scared to death when the radio came along. Piano manufacturers were their biggest customers. But, to their surprise, they sold even more wood to make radios." He chuckles. Carl likes these business ironies.

The front door swings open, and a man with a bouffant of white hair, bright-eyed, in his sixties, walks in. He carries an attaché and has a muffler about his neck. He looks familiar. Yes, I saw him at the Yonkers warehouse yesterday—he was the white-haired man at work on an action while Marc was tuning a piano. The man looks at me curiously; he recognizes me, too.

"This is Reinhard Landskron," says Carl. The man clicks his heels and bows deeply with a flourish of his arm. "He is the best action man in the city. Worked at Steinway."

Reinhard quickly pulls up a piano bench to join us, and loosens his coat and muffler. "I remember you!" he says, his smile gleaming with a bit of gold, and he reaches out his hand.

"So you know Marc, too?"

"When you are a long time in the business, everyone knows everyone else." He looks at me kindly.

Reinhard has been in the business since he was seventeen. He began his apprenticeship at the August Förster piano factory in Lobau, East Germany. In 1956, during the Hungarian Revolution, Reinhard escaped to West Berlin, where he finished his apprenticeship with Bechstein. In 1963, he arrived in New York, and immediately went to work at the Aeolian piano factory, right around the corner from Beethoven's warehouse. Then he was at Steinway for seventeen years, their top action man. Now he is on his own. Impressed by his credentials, I ask him if he has an apprentice.

"I never trained anyone," says Reinhard. "If I did, I would lose my job. In America, you teach someone you lose your job. I was with a company here for thirty years, and one day they just quit calling me for work. Why? They found someone else for ten dollars an hour."

"But what of all your skills, all your knowledge? That should be passed on."

He waves away my question. "I'm not idealistic. I learned the

American way is a fight for survival. In Germany, sure, I would teach. We Germans don't learn things for the money. We learn to do things well, to excel at it. When I was at the Steinway factory, sure I would break in people, fine. I won't lose my job. But on the outside it is different. You go to Steinway and they teach you. But in the last ten years, they don't have the old-timers there anymore. The old guys are gone. Now Yonkers is the place. Everyone is there."

He shrugs off his coat and pulls at his lamb's wool sweater, decorated with pale blue snowflakes. It is warm in here. He rests his hands on his splayed knees, his elbows akimbo. "Fifty-four years working and I am tired. I tell Carl, it has to come to an end."

"So, why not take on an apprentice now?" I persist.

"There is no one who would have the patience to stay with me for a year and learn it. And they will learn nothing in a few weeks. And not all of them are very honest. Carl can tell you so many stories." He tips his head in Carl's direction.

"There was a character who was here," Carl begins. "He wanted to buy a Grotrian. He heard German pianos are well made. We gave him a good deal. His technician wanted a commission and when we wouldn't give it, he went on Piano World and said that Grotrian is going out of business!"

"It's a terrible business!" says Reinhard, shaking his head.

"We had a gorgeous Louis XV Steinway B, and someone came in and asked for a B. We said, we have a wonderful B. He brought his wife and daughter and they loved it, too. He said, we buy it, but we want our tech to look at it first. His tech said, 'It's not for you.' He wanted to sell it to another one of his customers!"

"A terrible business!" says Reinhard again. "You find out who the good guys and bad guys are. And then, there are the movers who steal the pianos, and Carl hires them back anyway."

"Why would you hire back workers who steal from you?" I ask Carl, who is resting against a keyboard with eyes half-closed, his hands clasped about one knee.

"No one else would hire them," Carl answers, as if this is sufficient explanation. Then he sees my surprise and sits upright. "I used to hire people right from jail and had very little problem with them. When I first came here, I had a few hundred dollars. When I was a student, I had just enough for my first year of college. I had a job, but never an inheritance. Money makes monsters. Adversity makes men. The real advantage of having money is to give it away."

A bell announces the opening of the front door again, a customer. Carl stands to see if he is needed, and then excuses himself, leaving Reinhard to his indiscretions.

"He treats money like he doesn't care," says Reinhard, sotto voce. "He forgets to bill people. He doesn't know if he has paid people. There is no time clock at the warehouse. How does he know how long they work? He doesn't! There is no payroll department. Every Friday, they say, 'Carl, you owe me.' Without Judy and Rosa, the warehouse would not function.

"That is Carl," says Reinhard, tipping his head to his old friend, who is speaking with the visitor. "He has one foot on earth, and the other one is in outer space!"

15

The Piano Crawl

At the front of the store, Carl is speaking with a man I recognize. I would know him anywhere, with his dense mat of white, white hair, and his florid complexion, and his eyeglasses thick as Coke bottle bottoms. He is David Burton from Piano World. I've seen his picture on his website, where he calls himself "The Polar Bear," and describes his visits to piano showrooms. I move in closer, hoping to join their conversation.

"We're going through a period of materialistic, intellectual dependency," Carl is saying. "Though in the long run, I don't see a decline. Music is such an essential part of human development and evolution."

"We are at a critical point in human history," replies David. "We have to decide what it means to live a life well, and what does it mean for a society to live well. We should start piano clubs where people play for each other monthly. Piano as hearth."

"We could have amateurs come here to the store and do that," says Carl.

"Hi, David," I interject, and wave to him shyly. I have a soft spot in my heart for David, who once told me that the piano is his consolation in a life that has been marred by tragedy. He clasps my hand.

"You *do* know me," I say.

"Of course I do."

"Are you in town for the Piano World party?"

"Yes, indeed, I would not miss it. But please, can we not call it a *Piano Crawl*? It sounds like a pub crawl. So demeaning."

I just laugh. How like David. Actually, it was me who named the gathering, thinking it sounded catchy. A whole bunch of us have been organizing the event online for months.

I put out the word at Piano World last August: I'll be in New York in October, would anyone like to meet? Bernard immediately responded with an offer to host a party at his apartment in Brooklyn. Then members from as far away as Pennsylvania, Kansas, Bucharest, and New Hampshire said they'd make the trip to New York for a gathering, and we decided to do something grander than have a mere party: we'd have a Piano Crawl. Since on Piano World we talk about our impressions of various piano makes, we decided to tour Piano Row's showrooms together and show one another what we mean when we say a piano's tone is "bright" or "mellow," "dark," or "sweet."

The online planning became feverish, extending over several pages. We contacted all the piano shop owners and made appointment times for our group. Faust Harrison announced they would host a concert and lecture by the owner of Estonia Pianos, virtuoso pianist Indrek Laul, the night before our gathering, and we were all invited. Once we had a head count, someone made reservations at Bangkok Cuisine on Eighth Avenue for dinner.

By now, Piano World has become a daily habit for most of us, and our friendships have deepened. The bulletin board has also become an increasingly complicated place since the attacks of September 11, with membership now at over seventeen thousand highly opinionated people.

A core group rages at each other over politics and pianos, hurts each other over shifted alliances, storms out and comes back, confesses their sins and apologizes, conspires privately, shares their triumphs publicly. And with it all, despite it all, over time, we've become a close-knit community, bonded in our shared and inexplicable piano addiction. This is where I found support all through my search for my piano, my piano studies, and my journey to find a solution for Marlene's lost voice. This is where my passion is understood. Not to mention, it can be a very entertaining place, a veritable daytime soap opera: *As the Piano World Turns,* as one waggish forum member quipped. Several group projects were born, including a fund-raiser to give a needy child a piano, and a compact disc of recordings by members playing their own pianos to raise money for the website.

An in-person gathering is a momentous event for us, and playing for one another is a big part of such a gathering. That I have worked so hard to memorize and refine the Chopin B minor waltz is no accident. This will be my New York debut, performed before a bunch of old friends I have yet to meet.

✦

On Friday night, Kim joins me for the opening event—the private concert at Faust Harrison. We take our seats on folding chairs set up in the middle of the showroom floor, and I look around to see who I might recognize. David Burton is here, dressed in a jacket and tie. I also see Bernard, and Topeka Bob, who has just disembarked from his train from Kansas. But there is little opportunity to talk. We have only enough time to wave to one another before the performance begins.

We face an Estonia concert grand, placed before us at the front of the showroom, its wing raised. A shaggy-haired, long-legged young man bounds across the improvised stage as if he is on springs, halts before the piano, then takes a deep bow. Dr. Indrek Laul, a pianist from Talinn, Estonia, begins by telling us the history of the Estonia Piano Company, and explains the many improvements he has made to the piano since he acquired the company in the mid-1990s.

And then he launches into a raw, uninhibited, totally uncontrived performance of George Gershwin's *Rhapsody in Blue*. He sways his long trunk, attacks the keyboard with loose, vigorous limbs, shakes his shaggy head, closes his eyes as if transported, and stomps on the floor. I'm startled by the vigor of the performance, and my first instinct is to dismiss Laul as just another virtuoso showoff, a practitioner of a marketing tradition that goes all the way back to Liszt.

But soon I change my mind. I sense in this performance something different, and quite rare. The theatrics are not for show, but are rather a man's inner soul revealed, utterly on display, with a sincerity that is transporting, if a bit terrifying.

Indrek Laul is performing naked. By that I don't mean he isn't wearing clothes, but that he holds nothing back. His heart is fully open and unguarded. He allows us to see the Indrek who is a big, goofy kid having a blast, full of rhythm, passionately in love. When I think of what it might feel like to play this way in front of an audience, I am both thrilled and horrified. How revealing, and how embarrassing. Laul is as fully exposed as if he were making love onstage. His energy electrifies the room, overcomes our cynicism, turns us into believers, carries us off into his palpable world of sound.

I am so moved, and in fact feel so connected to the pianist through his music making, I actually walk up to him afterward and ask, "What does it feel like to perform like that?"

Laul is standing with a small cadre of admirers, nursing a glass of wine. He looks at me blankly at first, as if he doesn't quite comprehend what I am asking. So I persist: "I would be afraid to play like that in front of other people. Don't you feel exposed?"

"Yes, I do," he replies, with a very direct gaze. If he is startled to be asked such an impertinent question by a stranger, he does not show it. "My teacher always said, 'Better ten concerts a year than two hundred.' Then you can burn onstage. You're burning the candle."

He must mean burning the candle at both ends.

"When you let yourself go like that, you become vulnerable," he continues. "You concentrate on the sound. You start hearing the vibrations and you mentally take people's concentration with you into that vibrational sound world, gracefully so. The composer is speaking through you. While you are playing, that hits you hard. And then, a day or two later, it hits you even stronger. You feel this shocking effect. It's a lasting, powerful thing."

His words remind me of an evening I played a Chopin prelude for some friends at my home, on the Grotrian, and it seemed as if arcs of electricity were traveling through the air, from me and the piano to them, binding us together through the soul of the composer. It was thrilling and unnerving. I could *feel* my audience having the same experience. Afterward, my friend Dan came up to me, reverently touched a key of the Grotrian, and asked, "Is this some kind of special piano?"

"What creates this experience?" I ask Indrek.

"This is something the ancient Greeks knew about," he says, leaning in close so as to speak beneath the hubbub of the gathering. "Later, we will know more, when research on the brain has reached a higher level. Then we'll understand the importance of music, and by that I mean *natural* music, music you hear without an electronic intermediary, when you have direct contact with the sound waves."

✦

The day of the Piano Crawl is crisp and sparkling, a perfect October Saturday. I catch up with the group at Carl's store. When I pass
through the now familiar glass doors, I see most of us are already
here, and deeply engaged with the riches of the showroom. I wave
to Rich D., visiting from Virginia, whom I recognize from his photograph, and he comes over and gives me a hug. I also wave to David
Burton, down from the Hudson River Valley; he waves back, then
returns to an intense conversation with Carl. Carl looks quite distinguished in a navy double-breasted jacket and tie, and he has even
shaved.

The showroom is alive with the sound of a half dozen pianos
being played at once. Schubert floats out from one corner, then is
overwhelmed by Rachmaninoff, which gives way to Liszt. Liszt dies
away and I hear some lilting Mozart, then overtaken by Scarlatti. The
cacophony reminds me of a music school hallway with all the practice
rooms in use. Like excited children, the forum members roam from
piano to piano, listening and comparing.

"Don't you just love it? Don't you?" exclaims Calin, a darkly handsome young man who is visiting from Bucharest. Calin is a diplomat
at the Romanian Ministry of Foreign Affairs, here on a delegation to
the United Nations. He began his piano studies in college, he says,
only four years ago. He has just played Mozart's D minor fantasy on a
vintage Bechstein, and he leans back from the keyboard and sighs.
Then he plunges back into the piano, avid for it.

"May I try it?" Axtremus asks. Ax is a tall weed, all bones and
angles. He is new to Piano World, and the rest of us do not know
much about him except that he made the trip down from his home in
New Hampshire to join us. The music he plays begins mysteriously,
and soon all other playing stops. I can tell by looking at the rapt and
curious faces around the room that none of us recognize the strange
work; we're all trying to figure out what it is.

"Did you write that yourself?" asks David, when Ax lifts his hands
from the keyboard and leans back. The rest of us are silent, still absorb-
ing the impression the music made on us.

"Yes, I did," says Ax. The group murmurs in appreciation and praise. "Very impressive." "I really liked that." "Wonderful!" Then they return to the pianos, and the happy cacophony resumes.

"Take a look at these babies," says Rich, touching my arm. He leads me to two Steinways in the window, a B and a D, both vintage and restored. The D is a dark rosewood, heavily carved, with a decorative music desk. "Let's see which one you like better."

How strange. Though this is our first meeting, I feel as if I've spent years in Rich's company, so very familiar have we become to each other through e-mails, long telephone conversations, and exchanging pictures of ourselves with our dogs. I've even already heard him play the piano over the telephone.

Last summer, I was driving home, listening to the radio, and suddenly the most exquisite piano music came on the air. It was rapturous, inspiring, and I immediately decided I would learn how to play it, whatever it was. The announcer said it was a love song by Robert Schumann, arranged for the piano by Liszt. I hastily wrote a rough approximation of the melody on a scrap of paper, then called Rich as soon as I got home. I knew he played a lot of Liszt.

"Is it this one?" Rich asked, and then I heard him play his piano. His Steinway A sounded wonderful. No, it wasn't that one. "How about this one, then?" and he launched into yet another richly tapestried work. My friend not only had studied these lovely yet challenging pieces, he had them memorized. I didn't think I knew any other adult amateurs who played so well. It wasn't the second song, either. "Ah, then it must be this one," he said, and played the work I had heard on the radio. "That's a really beautiful one, my favorite." Then he gave me the name of it, so I could order the sheet music: "Widmung," or "Dedication," by Schumann.

Now here we are, playing pianos for each other in person. Rich's friendly, sweet-natured face has a bottle-brush mustache, and his wavy, graying hair lends him a distinguished air. He's about my height, with a runner's slender build, dressed casually in a chocolate-colored leather jacket over faded blue jeans. He's limping from recent knee surgery, and I offer him the bench in front of the D.

"You first," I say with a grin. We've already discussed who has the worse stage fright. Rich seems to be fine as long as the rest of the group isn't paying attention to him.

Though I already know Rich is a very advanced player—his teacher told him he could have been a professional pianist—I'm not prepared for what one forum member later described as his "soulful and transporting passion" in playing the middle section of Rachmaninoff's G minor prelude. I am wowed. Then he switches to the B.

When it is my turn, I play just a bit of the Chopin waltz on each and decide I liked the B best. Rich asks me to play the whole thing, but when I sit down to give him a private recital, suddenly all the other music and discussion stops. I'd suggested, online, that the least experienced piano students play first, so as to avoid becoming too intimidated to play, and I guess my friends are accommodating me. No question, I am the least advanced pianist here. But the hush is a little unnerving. Still, Molly taught me performance self-talk, and I try to put it into practice. Listen to the piece in my head. Take a deep breath. Take another one. Place my hands on the keys. Remember to keep the exposition at a steady tempo the first time out.

I begin to play, but only two bars into the music, David Burton interrupts me in the tone of a benevolent pedagogue: "Not so fast! Take a slower tempo! Here, listen."

I turn and look. David sings the opening bars, one pink hand describing the shape of the melody in the air, the other patting out the beat on his dress slacks. I nod and turn back to the piano. He is right. It's a common mistake to begin too fast, especially when you are nervous.

I regain my composure, and this time listen to David's slower beat in my head. I know what he wants: the melody should be sweet, mournful, and singing. Chopin wrote this waltz, "L'Adieu," when he heard his best friend had died in a war his own parents had sent him to Paris to avoid. Though it is a waltz, which we think of as being happy and graceful, this one is quite slow and heartfelt, more of a dirge than a dance. I put my soul into it, and let my hands do what they know how to do.

First, there is the opening theme. Chopin has learned his closest childhood friend is dead. It is repeated, this time with more rubato—not quite so strictly in tempo. Then the second theme begins, a cry of protest and sadness as he expresses his pain in recalling their love for each other, and what great friends they were. Then, there is a lighter, sweeter middle section, where perhaps he recalls their happy times, how innocent and carefree they were in the past. But then, the realization of death returns, and the painful opening theme, which is repeated twice, closes the work with a slow sigh.

As I draw my hands from the keys and sit back, I am gratified at how little they shook, and how well my internal dialogue spared me the usual panic and musical amnesia. I stand up, flushed with adrenaline, and from the sincere applause.

My performance opens the door to the concert portion of our showroom visit, and David asks for volunteers. One of the fun aspects of the crawl is we can each choose the piano we wish to perform on, as it suits our tastes, and the piece.

Topeka Bob walks over to an especially sonorous Bösendorfer we have all admired, and sits down before it. Clearly he is nervous: sweat saturates his windowpane plaid dress shirt, his face is pink and perspiring above his full beard, and he starts and stops a couple of times, excusing himself with a quip to make us all laugh and release his own tension. Yet he performs a beautifully realized prelude from Bach's *The Well-Tempered Clavier*. The Bosie is perfect for it.

Each in turn finds their way to a piano they especially admire, and plays for us.

I catch a glimpse of Carl in the back of the room, quietly observing with a pleased smile on his face. He looks like a very satisfied impresario to have so many lively pianophiles descend on his eclectic collection.

◆

The atmosphere is quite different across the street at Faust Harrison, where we arrive in time for our 3:30 appointment. Michael and Marina Harrison are waiting for us, and have a presentation all planned. We stand solemnly, respectfully, listening as they explain to us their rebuilding methods, and describe the types of pianos they carry. Their stock-in-trade is rebuilt Steinways, especially art case pianos, and new Masons and Estonias. Each and every instrument in the showroom is impeccably prepared and displayed, spotlighted to its best advantage. The funky disorder of Beethoven's could never gain a foothold here.

But I am restless to play the instruments, and look around to see if anyone else is chafing. In addition to Calin, Rich, David Burton, Axtremus, and Topeka Bob, we have with us Frank Baxter, Bernard, and RealPlayer, whom I have yet to meet. Bernard and I know each other from a previous meeting, and now we exchange smiles. He is dressed in a black dress shirt and slacks, his dark hair is cropped closely, and his sincere, expressive eyes could be those of a basset hound. Bernard is a very sensitive pianist, and I am eager to hear him play.

Frank Baxter and I have already met for drinks and dinner, earlier in the week. Over his vodka tonic and my hot tea, we dished about the forums and Frank's lifelong fascination with the piano. It all began when he was ten years old and he took his family's old upright apart, then had to figure out how to put it back together. There was always piano music in the Baxter household—Frank's father, an ironworker, could play anything from ragtime to popular to classical, and his older sister took lessons.

"As a little boy, I danced around the house as my father played the 'Poet and Peasant Overture,'" Frank recalled. As a teen in Massachusetts in the 1960s, he began piano lessons, played keyboard in a garage band, and told his father he wanted a career in pianos. His father said, "This will pass."

"It hasn't yet," said Frank as we sat in the lounge of his hotel. "The piano is the perfect marriage between art and technology. It still fascinates me. For instance," he said, turning around in his chair, "I have a hard time not getting up and going over to look at that piano over there." I followed his gaze to a white baby grand piano near the bar. I knew just what he meant. I'd been fighting the same urge myself. "I just want to lift the fallboard and play a few notes."

Frank got his first job in a music store, became a store manager, and then a piano shop owner. But his lack of business acumen doomed the store; it went bust after only three years. "Unfortunately, my talents were in sales and tuning." Feeling he'd let down his customers, he exiled himself to northern Connecticut and ran piano stores for someone else. Then he discovered the World Wide Web and started tinkering with HTML.

In 1995, he read an article on Prodigy about how to build a website. His first site was called "All About Pianos," and used the browser Mosaic. The bulletin board opened in 1999, and Frank says many current Piano World members have been with him since that original board's inception.

"It's surprising how much it has fanned into people's lives," Frank said to me as we walked through Times Square on our way to a Chinese restaurant. "There are some people who practically live on that forum. They are logged on all time." We laughed. We both know who he means.

I'm hoping to hear Frank play his pop standards, but for now, nobody is playing piano. We are listening to the Faust Harrison presentation. My attention wanders to the center of the showroom, where a magnificently restored Centennial D in an art case is on display. Does it have the kind of sustain that Marc's Centennial does? I want to steal over and see. What else is on display? The inventory is about the same as I remember from my piano shopping days more than two years before. There is even another tiger mahogany Steinway A in the front window. Will it be my favorite piano in this store, like last time?

Later, I play a few notes on the A and recognize Marc's signature immediately—a sweet, dark, creamy, rounded tone. His voicing has a very particular quality, as distinctive as the one he speaks with.

Michael Harrison is standing by and smiles when I play the A. He tells me about the case, which is carved, a gorgeous piece of furniture in a satin finish.

"Who voiced this piano?" I ask, eager to discover if my ear deceives me, or if I can hear what I think I hear.

But it seems the strangeness of my question throws Michael a bit. How many customers ask who the voicer is, after all? He hesitates, and looks at me uncertainly.

"Marc Wienert," he says at last. "He voices most of our pianos."

"I knew it!" I exclaim like a kid who has just guessed the number of jellybeans in the jar at the neighborhood carnival. And the prize? I *can* trust my ear. I *do* know what I am hearing. I turn to Michael. "His voicing has a very distinctive sound, don't you think?"

"Marc voices *to* the piano," Michael protests. "He brings out the personality of the individual instrument. He doesn't impose his taste on it."

To this I have no reply. I just smile. I recognize the voicer in the piano.

"Do you like this piano?" Michael asks. "We have a very good price on it."

Yes, I tell him, I like it very much. Yes, it is a beautiful piano. But I already have a piano. Marlene. And she has a beautiful voice, too. At least, when she is in the mood. Which hasn't been since Marc visited her. Nevertheless, I am in love with my own piano. Or rather, I am in love with who she is when she's wearing her makeup, has done up her hair, and is wearing her gold lamé evening gown. Which hasn't been for a while.

But I don't say any of this to Michael. Not only am I afraid he might tell me I got a lemon, but I myself do not yet fully understand the single most important secret that every piano shopper should know: buying a piano is like dating, and owning one is like marriage.

After perhaps months or even years of trying out many new and used pianos—the courtship—you finally find "the one," your perfect piano. You buy her—a pretty voice, with just the right sort of musical intelligence—and you have her delivered—the wedding.

After a brief honeymoon, you find that your piano is far from perfect. She has bad hair and bad breath days. She has mornings when her voice is shrill and cutting, and evenings when she hisses, "Not tonight, dear." Her unisons are out. Her hammers are dry. You wonder whatever happened to the beautiful bride you brought home, the dream you fell for and believed you would possess forever.

Fine pianos are tender, temperamental creatures, and the more beautiful their voices, the more high-strung and demanding they are: they need exacting conditions and regular maintenance or they throw tremendous temper tantrums.

No one tells piano buyers about this. They are led to believe that the piano they play in the showroom is the piano they will have forever. But the truth is, pianos change constantly. At least, this is what I am to understand from talking to Marc and Carl. But I am still the skeptic. I am not yet entirely convinced. I still want to believe in the perfect piano.

The voicing of this Steinway A is impeccable. But will it stay that way?

"May I?"

It is Bernard, who has gently arrived by my side.

"Oh, please!" I say, ceding the A to him. Bernard's touch should be a perfect fit with this glorious instrument, and this I want to hear. He sits down, pauses a moment, then plays the second movement of Ravel's Sonatine. The sound is so warm and evocative, several of our revelers stop what they are doing to listen.

It's already 4:30, and time to go to our last appointment of the day. We thank Michael and Marina for their hospitality and head just a few doors west, to Klavierhaus.

I am most interested in this shop, because on my last two visits to New York it was closed for remodeling, and I have no idea what they carry. A number of other forum members have said they are eager to see a new make of piano at Klavierhaus: the Fazioli from Italy.

We are greeted at the door by an imposing man dressed all in black, with a pastel plaid tie. His beefy face has heavy jowls, a bristly mustache, and small, deep-set eyes. His welcome is austere and formal. Klavierhaus carries the most expensive pianos on Piano Row—Hamburg Steinways from Germany, restored art-case European instruments, and the most exotic and rare of them all: the Fazioli, a piano only recently in production from Sacile, Italy, and reputed to be the most perfect—and most expensive—piano ever built.

The man takes us on a tour of the premises, including a basement restoration workshop, a quite narrow and cramped space we can barely all fit into. From the rear of the procession I am unable to hear the demonstration, so I look over the inventory hemming us in. Rare, decorative pianos are crammed together and against the walls, fascinating in their variety.

My eye is drawn immediately to a very old Gaveau, a French piano no longer made, a square grand with eighty-five keys. It is painted oxblood red, and a collection of white muses and angels parade across its fallboard, framed by bouquets of flowers and candles in scroll-work sconces. It looks so frail, I do not dare touch the keys without permission.

We traipse back up the steep, narrow stairs, then through the main showroom, past the inviting arms of vintage grands with decorative cases fit for a palace, through a door in the back wall to a hidden concert hall. Chairs are already arranged in neat rows for our gathering.

They face two glossy black pianos parked side by side under spotlights, like a pair of waiting limousines: a Hamburg Steinway D, and a Fazioli, both concert grands.

A collective gasp of pleasure goes up at the sight of the pianos, two of the most incomparable and rare of all the brands made today, awaiting our comparison. Klavierhaus could not have offered this group a more exciting prospect unless the shop booked us each a date to perform at Carnegie Hall.

"This is like having too much candy in one day!" Bernard exclaims. We all take seats, except David, whose excitement so animates him, his arms bounce up and down in anticipation. He seizes the privilege of playing first, and launches into the Brahms Intermezzo Opus 118, no. 2, on the Steinway. The tone is brilliant, overpowering. Then he moves on to the Fazioli and plays Beethoven's "Pathétique" Sonata, and the tone is even *more* brilliant, more powerful. Is it David's playing? Or is it the pianos? Rich and I, sitting together and comparing notes, aren't sure.

We don't remain a concert audience for long. Everyone wants to play these two pianos, and the many rare, art-case pianos in the front showroom. Seeing the small crowd waiting to get their turn on the concert grands, I migrate to the showroom.

And there I find the piano I love best of all those we encounter today.

It is not a piano case I would want in my house. Gold leaf is painted over its entirety, serving as one large canvas for ornate pastoral scenes in oils under the lid and on the sides. There is a matching bench, also gold, with scrolled legs and a floral tapestry cushion. She looks like nothing so much as an old lady in a powdered wig, wearing too much pancake makeup and too much perfume. The carved music desk spells out the make's logo: Pleyel. A gilded Louis XVI Pleyel.

From the Pleyel, I do not expect anything exceptional. I have a prejudice against garish art-case pianos. I presume they were built to be furniture, not musical instruments. But at my first touch, the Pleyel amazes me. It is exquisitely sensitive. The tone is warm, round, complicated, full of subtlety and color. The Chopin waltz and this piano seem to fall in love with each other right away, they waltz together beautifully, they are made for one another. Perhaps Chopin wrote this work on just such a Pleyel. That's my impression. Chopin could not have sounded more like Chopin on any other instrument. I can't resist playing the piece through twice. This piano is the composer's perfect other half, and it is the best I have ever played the waltz. I hope whoever buys it is a musician.

"Phlebas," standing beside me, observes my infatuation and asks to try the Pleyel. Phlebas, who named himself after a character in a T. S. Eliot poem, is also known as Mike, and is a research librarian for a New York financial concern. Our e-mail correspondence began when he asked to read some of my magazine articles, and we have talked on the phone a few times. Like me, he's the offspring of a professional musician, a composer and conductor, and he rebelled unsuccessfully against his father's legacy.

"Music is so compelling, if you love it, it just beats you over the head, you can't deny it," Phlebas once said to me, explaining how he'd wound up at a conservatory studying piano, though he later quit. When his daughter began lessons, he returned to playing himself, and he joined the forums to learn more about pianos so he could buy one. "Now it's an addiction," he says of Piano World. "I go there for the same reason you go to the coffeehouse instead of brewing it in your own house. It's for the community. The piano is a big part of my life, and at work there's nobody I can talk to about the piano. On the forum, I can talk to people from all over the world about it."

Phlebas is still wearing his dark wool topcoat, his blondish-white hair is neatly trimmed, and his doughy, pale face is punctuated by equally pale, shrewd, and intelligent eyes. He sits a bit awkwardly on the pincushion bench, but his hands move deftly across the Pleyel's keyboard. He likes it too. "Very nice! Have you tried the Faziolis yet?"

We drift over to a smaller Fazioli in the main showroom. Calin is playing it. "I love it!" he exclaims. "This one and the Bechstein are the best. Try it!"

As soon as I've played just a few bars on the Fazioli, I know this is not the right piano for me. It is hard to pinpoint why at first, because the Fazioli seems so, so *perfect*. The touch is perfectly even. I have never played an action that has better control. The tone is brilliant and rich from the lowest note to the very top. So what is wrong with it?

"It has a stark quality, doesn't it?" says Phlebas.

Yes, I think. It's cold. Coming directly from the vintage Pleyel is perhaps a mistake. The Pleyel is a Victorian drawing room, overstuffed velvet sofas, looking glasses, topiary, aviaries, heavy brocade. The Fazioli is a cool, modernistic glass tower, imperious and impervious. Glass and steel. Shattering in its brilliance. A piano is of course a machine, but usually it has a soul. This one has no soul. It possesses more power, volume, and brilliance than I would ever wish for in a musical partner. I almost recoil.

Back in the little concert hall, "RealPlayer" is at the long Fazioli, mixing it up with some stride piano, then some ragtime. His shaggy head hangs horizontally over the keys, long auburn hair in his eyes, his lips pursed in concentration inside his several days' growth of reddish beard. His real name is Joseph Kubera, and he's a well-known performer on the New York contemporary music scene.

Joe plays a 1928 Mason CC concert grand at home, a piano he found after an eight-year search, he tells me later over dinner. He had the good fortune to study classical piano at SUNY-Buffalo in the late 1960s, when the resident Center for the Creative and Performing Arts held regular concerts of what was then called "avant garde" music. This was a time of fervent experimentation in musical composition and performance, and those concerts shaped Joe's impressionable eighteen-year-old ear and his career as a pianist. Now he works directly with composers on their music, and many of them have dedicated their works to him. I will be curious about *his* impressions of the Fazioli. Next to it, the Hamburg Steinway sounds mellow.

We gradually file out of the showroom and into the oncoming dusk of Fifty-eighth Street, and head toward Eighth Avenue and the restaurant. At Bangkok Cuisine, we're spread out among three tables in our own little corner, close enough to converse with just about everyone, and eavesdrop on the more distant conversations. It takes the waitress three tries to get our orders because we're too busy comparing opinions of the day's pianos to concentrate on our menus. Plus, more forum members have joined us. Soon I can no longer follow all the conversations, and they start to merge like a fugue, the effect further enhanced with the lubrication of some red wine, which someone already ordered for our table.

"Which piano did you like best?"

"I loved that model A-III at Faust Harrison."

"The Bosie at Beethoven's was my favorite."

"Didn't you just love the Bechstein?"

"Not my taste. Too bright."

"Loved Bernard's Ravel."

The dinner is over all too soon. Frank is taking the train back up to Connecticut. Phlebas needs to spend some time with his family in Queens. I have a plane to catch in the morning. And a piano riddle yet to solve.

16

Tom

As I fly home, leaving my new piano compatriots behind, I catalogue what I have learned so far. I now know that my piano's hammers were chemically softened and rehardened. I know that Marc can bring Marlene back to life in one day, however fleetingly. Furthermore, all of the pianos he voiced, when I played them in New York, were exquisite, beautiful, among the best I have ever heard. Marc's work, however unconventional, creates a sound I love. If only it would last! Then the solution would be easy. Why doesn't it?

The technicians on Piano World say the strike point could be out of line, the bridge height could be wrong, the strings might not be level, the soundboard might lack impedance, the front duplex might leak. I print out all of their hypotheses, but I don't really understand them. Despite my intense determination to be the master of my piano fate, I am still, technically speaking, in over my head.

At least I have found a technician. His name is Tom Kuntz, and he hails from Coeur d'Alene, Idaho, three hours to the west of me. Rick Baldassin, the Salt Lake City piano dealer and U.S. representative for Renner hammers, who so generously advised me over the telephone when Marlene first arrived, referred me to Tom, one of his voicing students. Tom, Rick assured me, has plenty of experience voicing Renners. These are the hammers everyone says are in my Grotrian. In a week, Tom is coming for his first visit.

I prepare for Tom by following Marc's suggestion to find a recorded piano tone I like. First I listen to Rubinstein playing the Chopin waltzes, the celebrated recording that inspired me to return to the piano. Rubinstein made this recording in Rome in 1963, in a single night. He used a Hamburg Steinway prepared for him by a local technician. Though I love Rubinstein's playing, the tone of the piano is more brilliant than I like. I set it aside.

Next I try another favorite recording, that of Christoph Eschenbach playing the Mozart piano sonatas, on the Deutsche Grammophon label. This piano has a thin tone, without harmonics. I want a richer tone.

I try a recording of Indrek Laul, a gift from the pianist, performing the Grieg piano concerto. It is too harsh and brilliant, and I suspect this performance is on a Steinway, not an Estonia.

Finally, I put on a 1965 recording of Ivan Moravec playing Chopin nocturnes. This is the sound I want, or as close as I am likely to find. It's warm and rich, but with enough sparkle in the treble to give glittering highlights to the music without becoming harsh. Could the piano even be a Grotrian? The liner notes do not say.

Moravec, I learn later from a concert technician who has worked with him, is famous for his particularity about piano tone. He even brings his own voicing tools with him, and has been known to take over the job himself, if the technician on hand cannot satisfy him. His wife carries the tools in her purse.

◆

Tom Kuntz arrives on a bright December morning. He's lean, tall, and angular, dressed in jeans and a blue denim work shirt, and carries his tools in an attaché case. Shaggy eyebrows overhang small but inquisitive blue eyes, and a hawklike nose presides over a bristling, gray-flecked mustache. Bemused is his default expression. I show him to the Grotrian.

By now, the prospect of anyone working on my piano is freighted with my considerable anxiety—not a happy situation for a technician. Lucky for me, Tom is patient and curious, eager to learn new things, even after thirty years as a tuner. I tell Tom the story of how I fell in love with Marlene, and how the piano arrived with a dead treble, and he seems to want to get to the bottom of the problem almost as much as I do. We sit at the piano together, and he plays a few riffs in the treble, his head cocked to one side, listening, listening.

"Doesn't that sound dead to you?" I say.

"Well, I dunno. I didn't hear it in the showroom. Let's take a look inside." He pulls the action out onto his lap.

"Whoa."

"What is it?"

"I've never seen hammers shaped like *that* before. These are Renners?"

"I think so."

I tell him about Marc, and how he voiced the piano with some secret chemical.

"Usually you don't use chemicals on Renner hammers," Tom says. "So you say Marc made it sound beautiful again when he was here? Do you know what he did?"

"He lacquered the hammers."

"Usually you don't lacquer Renner hammers. And then if you do use lacquer, it lasts. It shouldn't be different the next day. If anything, they should just get brighter." Tom has put a straight edge on top of the strings, and then across a section of hammers, checking their evenness.

"He said he lacquered them very lightly, and it breaks down."

"Hm. So what was the tone like, when you liked it?" Tom shoves the action back into the piano, lifts a hammer up to meet the strings and then plucks the strings with his fingernail to see if each is in full contact with the hammer.

I describe Marlene's sound, the sound I fell for. Then I show him. "It matched the tenor section, here." I play a few chords in the middle of the piano. "Marc said to tell you I want *more* in the treble. That you would know what that means."

"*More,* eh?" He slides the action slowly in and out of the piano, strikes a key when it is in, then moves the action and strikes a key again. He's checking the strike point.

I show him the CD of Moravec playing the Chopin nocturnes. "Do you think it would help if I played this for you? It isn't what my piano sounded like before, but it is closer to it than what I have now."

"Sure. I always like to have music when I work. I'm going to start out by doing a basic setup prep for a new piano. It looks to me like you need some standard regulation work done here."

For the next few hours, Tom sets the strings tight against the bridge pins, levels the strings, mates the hammers to the strings, finds the strike point and marks the edge of the action on the keybed, and mates the action to the keybed. All throughout he explains to me what he is doing and why, and how it is done. I'm terribly excited to learn these things, but I worry that I am making a pest of myself.

"Are you sure this is okay?" I ask. "I can disappear if that is better for you. I don't want to be a difficult customer."

"You are not a difficult customer," says Tom as he pulls a string level, using a wire hook. "Now someone who works behind a cash register in a store, *they* have to deal with difficult customers. I've got it *easy* compared to them." Actually, Tom seems to genuinely enjoy explaining and demonstrating his work, tools, and materials.

He asks me for a piece of newspaper. I hand him today's front page.

"Watch this, this is really cool." He lays the newspaper across the keybed, the plain wooden base the piano's action rests on. Then he puts the action back on top of it, leaving just a corner of the newspaper sticking out. Tom pulls the paper from between the action and the keybed and it slides free smoothly, like a scarf pulled out of a magician's sleeve. "See? That's how you know you've got the action properly settled in the case. You want just a *little* bit of pull on it. But it comes out all in one piece."

We've been listening to my piano recordings on the CD changer, discussing the tone we hear. Now the Moravec nocturnes come on.

"Very nice!" says Tom. "Listen to that pedaling—so clean! Let me see the jewel case."

"It doesn't say what kind of piano it is."

"It almost never does. Doncha just hate that? I want to see who the sound engineer is. It's very hard to make a piano sound that good on a recording."

"Can you make my treble sound like that?"

"I dunno." He pulls the action out onto his lap again and lifts a few of the treble hammers with his long, meticulous fingers, examining them, pinching them. "Feel this. See how soft they are? That's not normal."

I pinch them, but I can't tell anything. What are they supposed to feel like?

"So you want *more*. Heh, heh," he chuckles as he pulls a thin strip of fine sandpaper over the surface of the hammers, back to front,

front to back, as if he's shining the toes of a pair of shoes. "She wants *More*-avec!"

We both laugh at his pun. "*More*-avec!" we crow in unison, cracking up. His good humor certainly helps take the edge off my anxiety.

Tom decides he's going to take a conservative approach for his first visit. He shapes the hammers with sandpaper, but he doesn't lacquer them. I play the piano while he's packing up his tools, and I don't hear much difference in the tone, though the action does feel even more wonderful than before, if such a thing is possible, and the tone is cleaner.

"Next time I may try a little lacquer," says Tom as he pulls on his jacket. "See how the shaping alone does. That may be what it needs. Play that in, and we'll see where it goes."

◆

So now I have a technician. He's kind and patient, and he even seems to like my piano. But the treble doesn't get better. It doesn't bloom into the full, rich sound I remember. Where is the piano I fell for? When I can't stand the dead treble anymore, I call Tom and ask him to come back. "Can we try the next step now? It's still dead."

I make detailed notes on everything I don't like about the piano, determined to get this right on the next visit. I don't yet understand that voicing is an unfolding process over many visits, never really finished, not a feat accomplished in a day.

A month later, Tom returns, this time with a white cardboard box the size and shape of a pizza box. He sets it down on my coffee table and opens it. It's full of hammers of different shapes and types.

"Here, feel this," he says, handing me a hammer with a red inner felt. He shows me how to pinch it between my fingers. Then he hands me another, with blue inner felt. "See how different they are from each other?"

But I don't. They all feel hard as rocks to me.

"What are they for?"

"We're going to put them on A5 in your piano and see which one sounds best."

He pulls the Grotrian's action out, removes the original hammer and shank assembly for note A5, and sets it aside. He fits a Renner Blue hammer on the end of a new shank, cuts the shank to length, and screws the flange onto the action rail. Then he puts the action back into the piano and strikes A5. It sounds strident. My hammers are better than that. "That one was never needled, just shaped," he says.

Next he puts a Schaff hammer into the piano. This one sounds muffled; it's too soft. So he replaces it with an Isaac hammer. "This one is a little harder," Tom says, "but not as hard as the Renner." It is really brilliant. I don't like it. Then he puts on a Tokiwa, a Japanese hammer. "This is a very hard hammer, it has reinforcement on the lowest part of the shoulders."

The sound is suddenly blooming. It is a marked improvement. "I like this one!" I say.

"Okay!" says Tom. He removes the hammer from the action, and pinches and feels it.

"Are you going to put Tokiwa hammers on my piano?"

"No, I'm going to feel and analyze the way this hammer was voiced, so that I can decide how to voice your hammers. I can tell where it's hard, and where it's soft, just by touching it, and I can make your hammers hard and soft in the same places."

He goes back out to his car and returns with a small blue-and-white Igloo cooler. This holds his bottles of chemicals, or "juice," as he calls it. He tells me he uses a one-to-one solution of sanding sealer and acetone. "It's softer than lacquer, so it's more forgiving if you make a mistake."

He pulls the action out again, touches a bit of the sanding sealer solution to the hammer shoulders, then slides the action back in and plays some more notes, deciding which need juice and which do not.

When he is done juicing the hammers, they need time to dry, so we go out to lunch at Tom's favorite Missoula restaurant, the Hob Nob. Last time Tom was here, he had lunch with his son, Mason—named for his favorite piano—who is in his freshman year at the university, but Mason is busy today, so I'm his stand-in.

I ask Tom how he got involved with pianos. He tells me about growing up the fifth of ten children of a sewer department supervisor in Mandan, North Dakota.

"It was tough. We were very, very poor." Tom was drafted into the army right out of high school and went to Vietnam. After his discharge from the service, he went to college for a while and studied music. He became interested in piano technology because he couldn't stand the pianos in the practice rooms at school. They were always out of tune. He learned tuning as a way to defend himself from his overly sensitive ears. Soon he was in Minneapolis, studying piano technology as a career. Now he is much in demand at universities in Washington and Idaho, and he plays string bass in a jazz trio that performs in Coeur d'Alene on Friday nights.

When we return to my house, Tom plays some jazz riffs on the piano. The treble has a voice! He spends two more hours, needling each hammer individually, pulling the action, then putting it back in to listen to the results, over and over again.

"Pretty nice!" he says. "Pretty nice piano you have here, Perri Nye." He always calls me Perri Nye. I don't know if it is a misunderstanding or just his own private joke. With Tom, it is hard to tell. "Why don't you try it?" He settles himself on the sofa to listen.

I'm truly pleased with the improvement in the treble. It doesn't sound like the tone Marc created, but I no longer have to hurt my right hand to bring out the melody in a piece. Still, I want to hear more partials, more harmonics. The fundamental tone is too prominent.

"I know what you want," Tom says, when I ask if he can make a more rounded tone.

"It's not about bright or dark," I try to explain. "It's about color."

"That's what everyone wants."

"Can you do it?"

"I dunno. . . . I can try." He's packing up his case. He's done for the day. It's time to meet Mason for supper. "That's trial and error, and many, many hours. It would be great if the piano was in my shop, but that's not the situation. I'd do what I do on my own piano—give it a little more juice, then a little more needle, then a little more juice. . . . Tweak it up, tweak it down, back and forth, and sometimes, all the notes just fall into line. It's beautiful when they all just come together."

Hearing this could not be more frustrating. But I'm not going to move the piano to Tom's shop in Coeur d'Alene. At least the piano's treble finally has a voice.

"Your piano is beautiful," Tom says as he heads for the door. "Do you realize how special it is? Most people have never even played a piano like this. I bet it is the most beautiful piano in all of Montana."

If the piano is not Marlene as I knew her in the showroom, or under Marc's ministrations, at least it is now a serviceable practice instrument, with a well-balanced voice across the scale. My technique quickly adapts, and I regain my light touch on the treble. I do wish I had Marlene back, but I am willing to let the voicing evolve and give Tom a chance to work with it over time. And all perhaps would have been well, if not for a phone call I receive a month or so after Tom's second visit.

✦

I have been reporting my piano tribulations on Piano World, of course, and the technicians there have taken an interest and are advising me. One day I receive a telephone call from a salesman at a shop interested in representing the Grotrian line.

"I know what is wrong with your piano," the salesman announces. "And we're about to become Grotrian dealers, so we can take care of it for you—as a warranty repair."

"What is wrong with my piano?" I ask cautiously. Why is this salesman so interested in helping me, I wonder? He is not in my area, and I already have my own dealer.

"Any type of chemical at all on your piano is not appropriate. You should be using only needles and sandpaper. No chemicals, ever, at any time. My recommendation is you put on a new set of Renner hammers. The original compression structure has been compromised. If it works out for us to represent Grotrian, one option is I'll cover you with my warranty."

"But if I have a warranty issue, it is covered by my own dealer."

Immediately his tone changes. "Of course, call Carl. Ask him what he will do for you. But don't put a Steinway or a Mason guy on it. He will kill it. Lots of American techs do not understand the Grotrian scale design."

These words send me into a panic. I felt I was making progress with Tom, but maybe we never would get back to the sound I'd fallen for without a new set of hammers? Maybe, since Tom is an American tech, even he is not right for my piano? Do I have to import a technician from Germany?

"Are you a technician? Why would you be interested in my piano?"

"I'm a piano geek of the first order. I read your posts. I know what is wrong. When I play a good scale, I tear up. It's a sacred thing for me. Your piano would be an exciting challenge. It's a unique instrument of exceptional qualities. Grotrian pianos have no deficiencies."

I still don't get it. But then, silver tongues have always put me on my guard.

"Go to Beethoven," the salesman glibly continues. "Tell Carl the piano's hammers were compromised because of chemicals. The fact is, the piano has never been right. The hammers are past the point of reclamation. Have him send you a new set of hammers. Tell him you've never been satisfied—he guarantees your satisfaction, right? Have your tech write a Carl a letter. Tell him you've been through enough. He should make it right. Two years is too long. You don't have to serve that much time for some class three felonies. And don't let a Steinway tech touch it—they'll try to Steinwayize it. You don't get a sushi chef to make a soufflé. Get someone with Grotrian training."

I hang up the phone. This is a shock to the system. Why is this person insinuating himself into my situation? Where does he think I will find a Grotrian technician in Montana? Only later does it occur to me: if his store does begin representing Grotrian, Carl will be his direct competitor. Is he trying to make Carl, who by now is an authorized Grotrian dealer, look bad to the factory by undercutting his warranty service? Carl's prices on Grotrian are the cheapest in the country; perhaps this dealer can't make a go of selling Grotrians unless Carl is out of the way?

Norbert, the piano dealer from Vancouver who provided me with so much support when I was shopping, warned me about the seamy underside of the piano business, about the dangers lurking at Piano World, with dealers trying to hurt one another through unwitting consumers. Am I being used as a pawn?

I haven't yet posted online about the improvements Tom made to the Grotrian. The fact is, even though I don't have the sound of Marlene, I am much happier with the piano now than I've been for two years. Should I enjoy what I have, or pursue that showroom sound? I know that quite possibly what the salesman told me is true. Marc tried to make the Grotrian sound like a Steinway because that is what sells in New York. Though Marc re-created in my living room the sound

I fell in love with, I'm still confused: I don't know if I played the piano in the showroom before or after Marc chemically softened the hammers. Maybe I do need a new set of hammers.

Tentative and unsure, I telephone Tom.

"Tom, do you think I need new hammers?"

"If you can get a new set, do it! Those hammers didn't come from the factory like that. They've never been right."

I start to write a detailed letter to Carl, explaining everything, documenting the investment I've made in solving the problem. But then I stop myself. Carl is not just my piano dealer—he has become my friend. I pick up the phone. Carl answers on the first ring. When he hears my voice, he is effusive and warm and kind.

"How are you liking your piano these days?" he says.

"Carl," I say simply, feeling apologetic. "My piano still does not sound like it did in the showroom. I am afraid it has never been right."

"We'll get you a new set of hammers," he says without a moment's hesitation. "I'll order them today."

"Thank you, Carl!" I feel elated and grateful. But what I should feel is trepidation. Because now my piano troubles are only just beginning.

17

Hammers

"Is that a piano?"

The Federal Express delivery man cranes his neck to look around me, through the front door and into the late-afternoon gloom of the living room. I'd been practicing when I heard his knock, and the piano's wing is up. I have my hands out to take my package, but now I turn in the direction of the man's gaze, and see the Grotrian does cut a striking figure in the rear corner. A huge glossy black piano is not what one expects to see in a tiny 1930s bungalow. It's like discovering a new Rolls-Royce stashed in a barn.

"Do you play?" I ask.

He freezes for a second. "Uh, not really. But we have a piano at home. I fool around on it."

"Would you like to try this one?" I stand aside, opening a path to the piano.

He hesitates. Then he charges past me, eager, carrying his clipboard and my box, making a beeline for the Grotrian.

"Wow. This is the most beautiful piano I have ever seen. Is it new?" He stands six feet away from the instrument, admiring it, unconsciously clutching my package.

I pull out the bench for him. "Please, be my guest."

"I'm pretty shy about playing in front of people."

"Me, too. Here, I'll go in the kitchen and close the door, and you play whatever you want. Is this package for me?"

"Oh, yeah! Here you go. Can I have your signature?"

I sign for the box, hand him back his clipboard, and take the package into the kitchen. It's from Beethoven Pianos. I slice the packing tape with a knife, eager to get inside. Folded up in plain brown wrapping paper, in four neat rows, is a complete set of wool felt piano hammers, prevoiced and shaped, their tails prebored, and arranged in strict order from the bottommost bass to the topmost treble.

A Beatles song, "And I Love Her," drifts faintly through the closed living room door. First just the melody, then he adds the accompaniment. He sounds like he's having a good time. But long before the end of the song, he stops.

I open the door just wide enough to poke my head through. He's sitting at the piano, a sandy, curly-haired man with bright blue eyes in his navy FedEx uniform, just looking at the keyboard.

"Please don't stop playing, you sound great."

"Really? This is a great piano. I've never heard of this make before. I wish my piano played like this."

"What kind of piano do you have?"

"A Steinway. It was my mother's. It needs a lot of work. This is just *beautiful!*"

"Please play some more."

He starts the Beatles ballad again. It's actually a sonata, I remember from a Leonard Bernstein lecture long ago, one of the most musically sophisticated of their songs. I start to sing along, quietly at first, and then the FedEx guy joins in. I ease myself back into the living room to stand beside the piano's open wing, and together we sing the chorus:

*A love like ours
Could never die . . .*

At the end of the song, he sighs, reluctant to leave the keyboard. He lingers over it, running his fingers across the white keys, noodling a few notes. He seems to have lost himself in some private reverie.

"You can come back and play it any time. Really."

He jumps up and grabs his clipboard. "Well, I better be going."

He hurries out, and we wave good-bye, he from his big white delivery truck, and me from my doorway. Then, when the door is closed again, I can't help it, I crack up laughing. The FedEx guy! Who knew? It's a beautiful thing when you can share your love of the piano with your FedEx delivery guy.

I call Carl to tell him the hammers are here, in good condition, and to thank him again.

"They are in exactly the right order," he advises.

"I see that."

"When is your technician coming?"

"He will be here tomorrow."

✦

Tom arrives early the next morning. It's late April, and the trees are budding up. I already have the hammers laid out neatly on their brown paper wrapping on the coffee table, and he examines them closely.

"These look perfect," he says. "No little bumps on top. But are they Renners?"

I do not know. Carl did not know. Certainly Tom should know before he voices? We can't find a label anywhere on the hammers or in the box.

"I'll ask Grotrian," I say, wishing I had thought of this before. I look at the time—Germany is eight hours ahead of us, I should still be able to reach them today. I'll send an e-mail. I may as well ask their advice for how to voice, while I am at it.

> *Dear Grotrian,*
> *I have just received the hammers my dealer, Mr. Carl Demler, recently picked up for me at your factory. My technician is preparing to install them now. We would like to know if they are Renner hammers. Also, please, if you have any recommendations for him on voicing these hammers, could you please advise us this morning?*

I send off the e-mail, then rejoin Tom. "Let's just put on the treble section, so we can see how you like it," he suggests. "Then if you want the rest of the hammers, we can do that later."

Tom has carefully laid the new treble-section hammers in numerical order on the music desk of the piano, with the faint dot-matrix numbers on their tails faceup. He's pulled the action from the piano and turned it around, so the keys are inside the case and the hammers face out, with the treble now on the left and the bass on the right. He's using the keybed as his workbench.

With a tall screwdriver, Tom unscrews every other flange from the treble section. The alternating gaps in the hammer row look like missing teeth. The hammers left behind will serve as guides for installing the new ones.

Now the old hammers must be removed from their shanks. Tom uses a shiny, chrome tool that looks like a giant hole puncher. He slips a hammer into the maw of the extractor and presses the punch head down onto the tip of the shank, forcing it out of the hole in the hammer's wooden tail. The extractor has no springs to help, and the shank must be removed with sheer brute force. Tom's face screws up with the effort, grimacing, turning deep red. His powerful hands shake with exertion.

"I need to cut these off with a knife," he says, shaking his head. "Look how hard they are to pop off."

I try to cool my surging panic, and keep my voice calm. Tom knows I want to save the original hammers, if at all possible. Just in case.

"Please, would you try it just a bit more?" I coax. "Maybe they won't all be that hard?"

But they are. Tom grunts and groans and his arms tremble with every single hammer removed. He curses and complains. Soon he has an open blister where the tool cut into his hand. I run and get a bandage and blister dressing from my first-aid kit and doctor his hand. He's rapidly losing his good humor, but he finishes removing the hammers, and numbers forty-nine through seventy-two are lined up on the edge of the coffee table. Fifty-two's tail is split open.

"Sorry," says Tom. "It couldn't be avoided. That one was just too hard to get off."

Tom screws the now hammerless shanks and flanges back onto the action rail, and begins the tedious process of gluing the new hammers onto the old shanks. Each hammer must be positioned precisely in correct relationship to the strings, the keys, and the adjacent hammers.

Tom dresses the tip of the first shank with glue, then quickly slips the new hammer on upside down, and with a swift turn to right side up, he creates a "glue collar" at the base of the hammer tail, securing it in place. I pick up the bottle of glue, curious. It's a rubbery sort of glue, Tom explains. It stays soft—an *aliphatic* glue, he calls it, "It's like a white glue." Moving left to right, he soon has all the new hammers glued on and lined up with the old hammers.

Once the hammers are square with the strings and level, Tom heats the shanks with a small pocket torch. This warms the moisture in the wood, allowing him to bend the shanks until they are straight.

Now he repeats the whole procedure, this time replacing the hammers he left in as guides. When all the new treble hammers are installed and regulated, Tom pulls the action out, turns it around on his lap, and replaces it in the piano, keys facing out again. It's time to voice.

I run to my computer to see if Grotrian has written back with voicing instructions.

Dear Mr. Knize,

Your Cabinet Grand was fitted with Abel hammers. The hammers you've got from Mr. Demler are also Abel hammers. There is no identifying label on the hammers because we take away the labeled ones. The reason is that we build GROTRIAN pianos and not Abel pianos.

The hammers you've got are prevoiced in the factory so that the result should be quite good. The only advice we can give you is never to needle right on the top of the hammer and to try very carefully and try . . . and try . . . and try again . . .

We needle only the side area up to nearly 2-3 mm before the top of the hammer (in the bass area even 4-5 mm). But generally not more and nearer than necessary. By the way: these instruments are not built to sound very mellow! This is against the basic character and cannot lead to a good sound result.

We hope for a good result and remain in the meantime with kind regards,

Burkhard Kaemmerling

I print out the e-mail and show it to Tom.

"Try and try again, eh?" he says. Tom plays the piano for a bit.

The treble speaks! It projects, with good sustain, and lots of color. The roundness I was seeking, that Tom had not yet achieved on the old hammers, is there. I tell Tom I don't want to compromise that roundness, to please be very conservative.

"We'll do just a *little* voicing," he says. "Then you can play it tonight and see if you want me to do the rest."

He shapes the hammers with a three-eighth-inch wide, 220-grit sandpaper strip. Then, using a voicing tool with three needles, Tom pokes the shoulders of the hammers four times on each side, in the two to three o'clock position, then again in the nine to ten o'clock position—just a little. He peppers the top just slightly with shallow pokes—called "sugarcoating."

"Try it," he says.

He packs up his tools while I play. He's off to North Dakota to see his father, who has just had heart surgery, and so he won't be able to complete the job for a month.

"I really like it," I tell him. In fact, I do not need a month for my assessment. The treble is quite beautiful now. But the scale sounds as if it is divided between two pianos—the dark, mellow tenor and bass that Marc voiced, and the new, brighter, lovely treble of the fresh hammers. The new hammers make the old ones sound much duller than they did before. I quickly decide I would like the piano to speak with all one personality—that of the new hammers.

◆

A month later, Tom returns. Hanging the rest of the new hammers takes two days, and this visit might go down in the annals of piano ménage à trois history as one of the most difficult and painful ever experienced between a pianist, her piano, and her technician. Tom arrives early one morning at the end of May, expecting to have a very full, very demanding day. He gets right to work.

Again he asks me if I'll permit him to split the tails on the old hammers to get them off the shanks more easily. Again I plead and persuade that he should try to save them if at all possible. Once they are split, the hammers can never be used again.

So Tom, trying to preserve the old hammers, struggles for hours, punching them off the shanks with his shiny metal hand tool. I heavily pad the joint between his right thumb and index finger with foam and moleskin, so he won't get another blister. But by the time he gets to the bass section, he has had enough. There's a black cloud over his head. More than once he has muttered how difficult it is to do this job in someone's home, away from the familiarity and convenience of his workshop. I go into my office to give him some space, to avoid doing or saying anything that will push him too far. When I return to the living room, he's gluing on the last of the hammers. There, on the coffee table, lies the old set, lined up in a row. The tails of all the bass hammers are split. I just look at them and say nothing; it's too late to make any difference now. If I am not happy with the new hammers, there can be no going back.

Tom doesn't even turn around. He knows what I am looking at. "That's the way it had to be, sorry. They were too hard to get off without splitting them."

What's done is done, but since I love the treble with the new hammers, I'm not too worried. For the past month, except for the few hours after Marc's visit of more than a year ago, I have been fully enjoying the piano for the first time since it arrived. I join Tom at the keyboard. He's heating the shanks with his little blowtorch and straightening them. It's been a very long day.

Finally, Tom turns the action around so the keys are facing out of the piano again. "Ready?" he says. And I sit down to play.

What happens next is in some ways too painful to describe. Something is dreadfully wrong with the piano. It sounds horrible. Strident. Harsh. Too much sound pouring from the belly, sound that clashes against itself until it turns into a storm of dissonance that whips itself into a furious tornado of ringing tones that actually hurt my ears. I put my hands over them. Whatever suggestion of Marlene's personality still lurked in the piano is now completely gone. In her stead is an ugly witch.

"There's some kind of high-frequency thing going on," I say. "It's like a dog whistle. I think it will make me go deaf."

"I don't hear that."

"It's a very high frequency. It's like the vibrations are all clanging against each other."

Tom tries some judicious voicing, but the first note he tries to soften dies, just like a balloon that has been popped with a pin. All the roundness, the complex harmonics are gone when I play just that one note. He replaces it with one of the extra hammers that came with the new set.

For the first time, the thought occurs to me that maybe Tom, in his early fifties, after thirty some years of piano tuning, has lost his capacity to hear high frequencies. It's very common in piano tuners, and some studies have suggested that women hear higher frequencies than men do, to begin with. Maybe the harmonic ringing that is sending me into torment really is like a dog whistle.

After his voicing touch-ups, I try playing the piano again, but the ringing tones continue. They are intolerable. And Tom cannot voice away that which he cannot hear. Besides, there is nothing more he can do today. It's been a long month for Tom, and he's tired. He doesn't know how to solve the problem. About that, he is utterly frank.

"Do you have any kind of cloth ribbon?" he asks.

I go into our linen closet, where I keep our gift wrapping materials. I find some white cotton grosgrain ribbon and bring it out in a large clump.

Tom takes the ribbon and weaves it through the rear duplexes of the piano, poking it under and over the strings with a screwdriver.

"What is that for?"

"I'm damping down the ringing tones."

"Will that solve the problem?"

"It's the best I can do for now."

It's time for him to return to Coeur d'Alene. He packs up his tools and leaves me alone to face what was my piano.

I approach the keyboard again with caution, as if the piano is a snarling, cornered animal. I close the wing to make the sound as quiet as possible, and I try playing again.

The ribbon damping has reduced the harmonic ringing, but it is still there. It still hurts my ears. Now I fold the music desk flat and lower the lid as well, so the belly is totally enclosed. It still sounds horrible. The tone is harsh, wiry, edgy. Like someone is turning a drill into my ear.

This can't be happening. The new hammers were supposed to solve the problem! I cover the piano with a heavy quilt, hoping to soothe its savage voice. I play the piano again. The animal is wounded, dangerous. I can't bear to touch it anymore. I want to cry. The telephone rings.

"How do you like your piano?" It is Carl, sounding gay and expectant.

I close my eyes and hold my breath. When I finally speak, my voice sounds as if it is coming from someone else—weak and heartbroken. But despite the depth of my disappointment, I don't tell Carl how I feel. I try to make it okay for both of us. Perhaps I'm not able to do anything else just now, because if I tell Carl that Marlene is gone, my dream might be lost forever.

"I think it may need a voicer," I tell Carl, trying to sound reasonable and calm, though in that moment my heart feels rent, as if the piano is an extension of my body, as if this wound to her is my own physical injury. "I think the hammers must be too hard. It's setting off some harmonic ringing that is very unpleasant."

"Well, what do you want to do?"

"Can you help me find someone?"

"I can try."

◆

Why did I—an amateur adult pianist, not a technician, not a dealer—decide for myself that the piano just needs voicing? Why didn't I just tell Carl what happened and see what he offered me as a solution? To this day, I do not know. Perhaps he would have told me to send the piano back. In fact, several of the experts I consult—and some of my Piano World friends—urge me to do just that. "Just exchange it for another one," Derick says, when I tell him what happened over the phone. "Carl can still make money on the deal. You've been through enough."

But I have never played another new Grotrian, so I don't know if that would solve my problem. I still don't know if it is the Grotrian I fell for or Marc's voicing. I only know that the voice I fell in love with was so unique and special, I doubt I can find it in any other instrument, even the same make and model. The sound of that voice is emblazoned even now on my memory; it calls to me. I'm not ready to give it up.

Marc's warning about how the pursuit of perfection can destroy beautiful things returns now to haunt me. His stories of pianists so "torqued out" about their pianos, in such terrible distress about their pianos that they no longer trust anyone and no tech wants to work with them, reverberate in my thoughts. Now I know their poignant agony for myself. I fear becoming one of them.

When Oliver gets home from work, I seek his arms as a salve for my despair. There is nothing he can say; he can tell the piano is different somehow, but his hearing loss in the upper frequencies is profound, and he can only hold me while I cry. Not for the first or the last time, I marvel at his willingness to offer empathy and comfort for the loss of something he has never experienced and cannot understand.

"What should I do?" I feel helpless enough in the moment to ask him, and the question no doubt makes him feel equally helpless.

"Take up skeet shooting and don't use hearing protection," he says. "Become a logger and forget to wear your ear cuffs."

"You mean, damage my hearing?"

"I don't know what else to tell you."

It becomes difficult to pursue my piano studies. I can only stand to play the piano if I wear earplugs, and my practicing suffers. I find solace in long hikes in the mountains. Summer is here, and as I roam the hills surrounding Missoula, I find myself involuntarily fantasizing about selling the piano and finding a replacement. I replay in my mind the most memorable pianos I tried during my two years of piano shopping. Surely one of them would have worked out just fine for me, better than Marlene had?

After all, I think to myself during these sojourns in which sanity temporarily returns, Marlene turned out to be a dream, an unattainable fantasy. Surely I can find happiness with some other piano, one less fickle and difficult? The bottom line is, I would never have bought this piano as it is now. I even consider giving up piano lessons. Perri, you will only hurt yourself with this obsession, I tell myself. You have to wake up from this dream.

And then I come down from the mountains and resume my search for a voicer. Try as I might to be practical, I don't call Carl and tell him to take the piano back. Instead, I launch a campaign to find a hero, a prince who will awaken Marlene from her slumber. For I know she is still there, if asleep, in that black, shiny case, if only the right rescuer can be found. If I can't or won't wake up from my dream of the perfect piano, then Marlene must be revived.

✦

My first call is to the salesman who so persuasively advised me to replace the hammers. He sure sounded like he knew what he was talking about. And he'd even offered to work on my piano. Maybe he will come to Montana and make it right. He was so eager to solve my problem, won't he feel as if he has a stake in how this turns out?

I decide to write him a note.

Well, it is regulated to perfection. I have phenomenal control over the key-board. The tone is relatively even, I begin, wanting to first acknowledge the positive.

But the more brilliant tone has created sympathetic ringing, coincident harmonics, which my tech had to damp down with ribbon. That helped somewhat. Of course, the voicing is very different from what I am used to . . .

I break off for a moment, thinking how to frame my request.

I know this piano could be so much more than it is at the moment—I need to find a really talented voicer, someone who has both the ear and the technique to bring this piano to its full potential. Any ideas for me?

The salesman's reply has a very different tone than his initial phone call, when he urged me to change the hammers. Gone is his eagerness to help:

Your decision to live in the outer reaches of the known universe has severely limited your options.

He advises me to check that the strings are level and asks if the hammers are prebored, or did my tech bore them?

Anyhoo I hope it goes well.

Unwisely, I pick up the phone and dial his number at the store.

"I was hoping you could refer me to a voicer, or possibly, since you have taken such an interest in the piano, you would be able to work on it yourself?"

"*Me?*" he says, and lets out a derisive little laugh. "Oh, heavens, no! I am much too busy. I could never get over there. No, I don't know who you could find anywhere near you."

"You don't know *anyone* in the inland Northwest?" I persist.

"I don't. One of our distributors might."

"Where is he?" I've written the name down as fast as he said it. "What is his number?"

"Oh, his number? Oh, I don't have his number. I've got to run. There's a customer."

Click.

The man is his distributor and he doesn't have a number for him? This doesn't sound right. I track down the distributor without too much trouble. He turns out to be a wonderful man, very sympathetic and happy to help. He gives me the names and telephone numbers of perhaps a dozen technicians, and some background on each of them, from Los Angeles to Chicago and on to New York. "Tell them I sent you," he says. "And please call back and let me know how it goes."

Then Carl calls.

"I've got a voicer for you. Call this number. She is a top voicer in New York, a genius. I have already spoken to her about you."

I take the number and dial it at once. There is no answer, and no outgoing message, just the sound of tinkling music. I think I must have the wrong number, so I dial it again. Again, the only sound on the other end of the line is a strange, tinkling medley, so I leave a message.

Meanwhile I e-mail Grotrian in Germany for a referral, and they send me to their other dealers. I call those dealers and get more referrals. I soon have the names of technicians in Oakland, Mill Valley, Los Angeles, Chicago, Denver, Virginia, and even a couple of techs in Montana, more techs in New York, more from Los Angeles, Seattle, San Francisco, and on. Everyone seems very interested in my piano troubles, and they each offer their own hypothesis about what is wrong and what to do about it. They are all quite definite in their opinions, which, by the end of the week, have become a nearly deafening static of contradictions:

"The ringing harmonics will come out with deep needling."

"I'm personally against needling. Use steam, it's much more pleasant sounding and it lasts longer."

"Steam is a good way to experiment with a temporary effect."

"You don't want to experiment with these pianos."

"Run a paper file on them, that will bring them up."

When I mention to the U.S. Abel hammer distributor that I am getting so much conflicting information, he says, "Good voicers always have very strong opinions."

Names that are recommended three times go on my short list. But many of them don't return my calls, despite my repeated attempts to contact them. And Carl's technician hasn't called me back. I try her again. This time the tinkling music is interrupted when she picks up the phone.

"I did get your message," she says in a throaty contralto. "At the moment my life is so full of many things." She has two elderly cats, she explains, and she's afraid if she travels they will die while she's gone. One of them is sick. As an animal lover myself, I empathize with her.

"One day I would love to come to Montana. In the meantime, I can get your piano to New York for quite a little money. I have a deal with a piano mover, and if it was in my studio, I could tend to it here. That way I could work on it at my leisure."

"But wouldn't you need me there to tell you what I want?"

"Oh, I can't have you here looking over my shoulder. I go with my feeling for the instrument. If I have you telling me what you want, I'll just end up handing you the lacquer and the needles and telling you to do it yourself. What kind of hammers does it have on it?"

"Abels."

"I'm used to Steinway hammers. I might be tempted to take the Abels off and put Steinway hammers on. Or I'll proceed as if they are Steinway hammers."

"Have you ever worked on Grotrians before?"

"I owned a seven-foot-four Grotrian once, an old one. All the European pianos have the same sound—really bright."

That isn't my experience, but I don't contradict her.

"Send it back to me," she continues. "Or send it to Carl's warehouse and I'll look at it there. That way you could fly in and see if you still want the piano after I voice it, and if not, it's already at Carl's and he can send you another one. Or, if this has been going on and on and on—and it sounds as if it has—just have the piano exchanged now."

After we hang up, I call Carl. "She says I would have to ship the piano to her."

"Well, that won't work. We'll have to figure out something else. There's a tech in Los Angeles. He dresses up like Elvis. He's very, very good. I'll have to try to find his name. I only know him as Elvis."

Elvis! Carl has said he will pay for the voicing, but as far as finding the right tech, it looks like I am on my own.

18

The Voicers

Three years since I found the Grotrian, two months after Tom installed the new hammers, my marriage to my piano is in serious trouble. Not only is the harmonic ringing intolerable, but some treble notes have gone weak again after Tom needled them, trying to calm down the tone. The piano is now the worst of everything, a strident disaster, a shrill crone, and I feel nothing for her. I don't care to run the humidifier for her, to protect her with her red shawl. I don't want to touch her. I am bereft.

"You are like someone who buys a Lamborghini and then complains when the local mechanic screws it up," says Oliver, who has heard enough about the piano by now to last a lifetime. "What did you expect?"

I get more sympathy from my Piano World friends. Rich and Derick help me evaluate who, among the many technicians I've talked to, I should hire. Rich has a Grotrian technician he promises to send me to—once the man returns from South America.

"I don't think you should sell it," says Rich. "You'll always regret it. Once you've been to the top of the mountain, there's no going back."

Yes, I think, I know. But I'm nowhere near the mountaintop now.

I supported Derick through his own piano agony with his Falcone grand last year. He ended up selling it, and now he also is looking for a voicer for his new Bösendorfer Imperial concert grand. Derick is far more demanding than I am—fanatical about each and every note being perfect at all times.

"It sounds like a banjo!" I wail to Derick over the phone.

"Send it back, Perri," he says. "Think through the worst-case scenarios."

I have a terrible headache from thinking them through, and wracking my brain about who should work on the piano. I worry about what one technician said to me: "It sounds like you've already been through too much, and pretty soon, no tech is going to want to work with you."

I telephone Wally Brooks, the U.S. distributor for Abel hammers. Surely he knows who should voice my piano's Abels?

"Nobody in this country knows how to voice those hammers," says Wally. "They are much harder than the Abels I sell. They are more like a Bösendorfer hammer. Look for a Bosie voicer."

I spend an hour on the phone with a technician from Bösendorfer in New York. He admits he has never played a Grotrian. He's done voicing for Carl, though, so I ask Carl about him.

"You don't want him," says Carl. "He'll make your piano sound like a Bösendorfer!"

I will tell Derick about the Bösendorfer guy; he will be thrilled.

"Why not have Marc come out again?" says Carl.

"I love Marc's work, Carl, but it doesn't last," I say. "I live so far away, I need voicing that is stable."

A Grotrian dealer who posts on Piano World offers me his top technician at the exorbitant rate of $1000 a day, three days minimum, plus all travel expenses and meals. I take that offer as sour grapes that I did not buy my piano from him.

I remember that Darrell and Heather Fandrich, the owners of Fandrich & Sons pianos, in Stanwood, Washington, come through Missoula every summer on their way to visit family in North Dakota. When I call, Heather says Darrell can certainly help; she'll call me when they know their schedule. But other people in the piano business, probably confusing Darrell with his younger brother Del, say Darrell will only tell me my piano needs to be redesigned. "You don't need that," says one advisor. When I don't hear from Heather again, I don't pursue him further.

I hear about a Los Angeles technician, one of the best voicers in the country, I'm told; he vacations in Montana every summer. Very excited that this might be the one, I leave several messages for him on his answering machine. One day I arrive home to find a return message:

"I vacation on the Yellowstone?" he says, Valley style, as if it's a question. "I would never come to Missoula in *a thousand years.*"

Gee, thanks for letting me know.

In the course of a month, I speak to more than thirty technicians from all over the country. Nearly all of them are confident they can solve my problem, but how will I know who is the right one? Even if someone has a sterling reputation, does that mean he likes what I like? Does that mean he loves and understands the sound I hear in my head? I can't travel to listen to their work, and this is a one-shot deal. Too much is at stake. I have to go with the surest bet.

✦

He stands by the curb in front of the baggage claim exit: a tall whip of a man, pale and bookish in his wire-rimmed glasses, red-rimmed eyes set deep in a narrow face, a shock of mouse-brown hair falling awkwardly over one brow. His goatee makes him look stern, even scholarly, until he smiles at the sight of my station wagon and waves. He loads his gray Rollaboard, heavy with tools, onto the back seat.

We've met before, during one of my piano shopping trips to Seattle, in the store he once co-owned. He's been the head piano technician at the University of Washington, the editor of the *Piano Technicians Journal,* has trained countless young technicians to tune and regulate, and he conducted the technical review process for Larry Fine's *The Piano Book.* He's prepared pianos for Ivan Moravec and Murray Perahia and the notoriously finicky Alfred Brendel for their Meany Hall concerts. And he is a pianist himself, married to a concert pianist; together they teach technicians how to communicate with their clients. Of all the technicians I considered, this man is the only one not a single person in the industry bad-mouthed, the only one who was universally praised. In the often cutthroat business of pianos, and among the petty jealousies and egotism of high-end piano technicians, that is a singular achievement. He is as near a sure bet as I can find, and he has agreed to come to Missoula at a price Carl and I can afford.

"Thank you for coming!" I call out over the roar of airplane engines from the tarmac.

"You are very welcome," says Steve Brady as he climbs in beside me. And the clock begins ticking. We have ten working hours.

✦

Before Steve can do anything, we must talk. "We need to define our terms," he says, as we sit together before the piano. "We use the same words, but we all have different ideas about what they mean."

I describe to Steve, as best I can, what Marlene was like, the sound I fell in love with.

"What you are asking for is what I call *head room*," Steve says. "Like in a car." He raps an imaginary car ceiling over his head with a knuckle. "Head room means a broad dynamic and color range to the tone."

First, he announces, he will check all the bolts and the screws in the piano. When he sees that they are good and snug, and that all the strings are well set against the bridge pins, he puts a black work apron on over his teal dress shirt and white khakis and unscrews the cheek-blocks with an electric drill, swift and efficient.

"Let's find a couple of really, really bad notes and see what we can do with them."

He plays a Chopin nocturne, then a Brahms intermezzo. His touch is sensitive, very musical. I hope he voices half as well as he plays. He pulls the cotton ribbon Tom installed out from the strings and hands it to me in a wad. Then he plays the piano again.

"It does seem to be a matter primarily of finishing the voicing they began at the factory. That A5 is *really* nasty sounding." He plays it a few times. He checks to see that all the strings are level, and then he pulls the action onto his lap, entirely out of the piano, and sets it on the coffee table. He kneels before the piano and peers into the farthest recesses of the case. I get down on my knees, too, and peer in there with him. I've never looked inside a piano that far, all the way back behind the action. There's some strange contraption back there. What is that back there?

"That's the damper action," Steve says, looking at me with surprise. I suppose he thought I should have known that, but my piano knowledge is not very broad.

"That's so cool!" I exclaim, with sincere appreciation for the mechanical complexity of the instrument. A damper action—another universe to explore.

Steve lets out a gentle laugh and pats me on the back. He must sense the power of my curiosity, because at once we move on to a different footing—master and protégée.

"There are three components to piano tone," Steve explains, plucking a bass string from behind the dampers and looking at me intently, as if commanding me to listen closely. "There's the *boom,* or fundamental. That defines the note."

He plucks the string again, this time from in front of the dampers. "There's the *clang.* That increases the note's definition and power."

He plucks the same string all the way in the front, just before the agraffe. "And there's the *sizzle,* the color. That adds brilliance. We're aiming for a proper balance of the three. Your piano has plenty of clang and sizzle, and not enough boom. Low, vertical needling increases boom. We'll stick with A5 until we're happy with it."

Steve decides to go after the "sizzle" first. "Let's get rid of that nastiness." He sugarcoats—shallow needling on the surface of the wool— very close to the strike point. "We're only going one millimeter deep. Just scratching the surface. It's a signal-to-noise ratio. We want more signal and less noise."

He slides the action back in and tries the note, pressing it down a dozen times, increasingly louder. "How many gradations of volume can I get? At least ten or eleven is what I want. Let's try another note and do something different, and see what happens."

This time he takes the edge off a D-flat. He stabs the shoulders deeply, trying for what he calls a "fatter" sound. As he did with the A, he resets the felt by pounding it with the butt of his voicing tool. Then he plays the note again.

"It's diamondlike," he says, stroking the key as we listen together. "We want pearl-like." He fits a curved piece of wood faced with 400-grit sandpaper over the hammer and polishes the felt. Then he slides the action in and strikes the key again. "Hear the boom?"

Steve expands on the concept of a piano tone lexicon later that night over dinner at a local restaurant. A wine connoisseur, he selects a Pinot Noir he especially wishes to share with me. On my first taste, he asks me to describe it.

"Dark, warm, complex . . ." I begin.

"Sounds like you are profiling a piano tone," says Steve. "Every wine has a taste profile, and so does a piano."

"Yes!" I laugh in recognition, and try the wine again. "Yes, I see that it is exactly the same idea!"

"Good! This will help us communicate better about your piano. Take another sip."

I do so, rolling it on my tongue.

"There's the attack at the beginning, right?" Steve coaxes, while I mull over the flavors. "That's the top note. Then notice the middle: Does it swell? Or does it rapidly decline? Then the finish on the wine— that's comparable to the long decay of the tone."

I confess to Steve that I am starting to toy with the idea of becoming a voicer myself, since I live so far away from one. What does he think?

"Tuning is much harder to learn than voicing, and it takes a long time," Steve replies. I have heard that learning to tune the piano is no less difficult than learning to play the piano. One tech told me he tuned a thousand pianos before he was competent. "A large part of voicing is a good tuning," Steve continues, "so you have to be a complete technician before you can even approach voicing. Otherwise, you won't have good judgment about what to do."

Steve himself became a technician after becoming a pianist. "I am uniquely suited to what I do," he says. "I have a lot of mechanical aptitude. A really good sense of pitch. And there's my love of music, my obsession with pianos. I can't imagine doing anything else and doing it as well."

After I drop Steve at his hotel, I sit before the piano again. Steve is only partway through the voicing, but since he has a plane to catch at 3:30 tomorrow afternoon, time will be of the essence. I spend an hour analyzing the tone and making notes.

The treble is kind of harsh—too extroverted—it needs more dimension and subtlety. The bass has a lot of bad noise, twangy, mechanical noises from the action. I want a darker, moodier, bell-like, sweet, warm tone. Hard to get enough pianissimo. Initial attack is too steely, penetrating, needs a rounder tone . . .

In the morning, Steve looks at my notes and shakes his head. "You really should take up a loud sport, because you can hear every little thing," he says. He plays the piano again, to reacquaint himself with the sound; more Chopin and Brahms. Listening to him play is heaven.

Already it is ten o'clock. Steve needed to borrow some tools, and fortunately, Jeff Stickney, the tuner who set up my piano when it first arrived, was happy to loan them and was available for breakfast. Now we are under the gun, driven by the merciless ticking of the clock.

Steve stabs his needles into the hammers with aggressive authority. Then he pounds the wool fibers smooth with the butt of his voicing tool. The hammers must have been really hard, I think, to require so much needling.

Steve's focus is intense, and I am terribly anxious. We can't afford the time to chat and discuss. My anxiety becomes overwhelming—so much is at stake, and the clock is moving relentlessly forward. I feel like my feet hardly touch the floor, like I am moving through some sort of viscous fluid that distorts everything I hear and see. So I remove myself. I pace around the backyard, prune roses, pull weeds. I read on the patio for a while. I try to be available, but not in the way.

"You want to come take a look at it now?" Steve's head is out the back door. We exchange places, and Steve relaxes in the July sunshine, eats the sandwich I made for him, while I return to the piano to play.

Now I can pick out the notes that are clean, and those that still sound dirty. The bass and tenor still buzz. I write down what I hear. Steve comes back in and plays rapidly up and down the chromatic scale, finds the notes that jump out, don't fit, and pounces on them with the needles. He plays it some more. I play it. He voices some more. He heats the hammer shanks to straighten them, mates the hammers to the strings, checks over all the other regulation steps that could impact the tone. The hands on the clock keep moving. I begin to announce how much time is left before we have to leave for the airport.

Steve asks me to play the piano again. The tenor and the bass are simply not yielding to the needles. The ugliness persists. I start to fear he'll leave without solving the ringing problem. Steve takes out a pliers with the ridges ground off its maw. "This is kind of controversial, but I learned this from Wally Brooks." He takes the hammers by their midsection and, one by one, squeezes them between the jaws of the modified pliers. "This will make the sound bloom."

He shoves the action back in, I quickly run through the scale, and at last, the ringing harmonics are gone. The piano is playable once again. "You did it! Thank you!" I lean into the keyboard, and play my Chopin waltz. It's not Marlene, but it's a nice piano.

"You have a taste for an exceptionally dark, warm sound," says Steve when he sees how I respond to the new sound. "I want to see the hammers Tom took off your piano. The original hammers. You said you have them, right?"

I bring him the cardboard box with Marlene's hammers carefully wrapped in brown paper. Steve takes a few of the treble hammers out, and squeezes them thoughtfully between his fingers. Then he squeezes a few of the hammers from the tenor section.

"This is really odd—they are soft on top, and hard on the shoulders."

"Tom treated them with sanding sealer."

"Sanding sealer is good," he says, examining a few more. Then he puts them down and turns to me. "But I'm sorry to say, I could have voiced these for you to get you what you want, and you could have kept your original piano."

"What's done is done." I shrug. "I can't go back to that now." But I feel a terrible pang of grief. What if I had ignored the interference of the salesman who said to get new hammers? Tom had been making steady, conservative progress. Now I feel anger and regret.

"You have the makings of a tech, Perri. You have the ear for it," Steve says. "People like you and I are hardwired for growth, complexity, and challenge. I know I am and I can see you are. The more you satisfy that urge, the happier you will be."

"I'd love to become a voicer," I say. "But by the time I've spent twenty years learning how to tune to concert level, I won't have my hearing anymore!"

We laugh. Then, mindful of the time, I ask my most urgent question.

"Steve, the piano is lovely, it's a huge improvement. But—it still isn't the piano I fell in love with. Will I ever get that piano back?"

Steve starts to speak, then catches himself, and bows his head a moment in thought. He answers very slowly.

"What's best is to remind yourself that there are things you really like about this piano that are still there."

"Should I sell it and find another piano?"

"You will have this problem with any piano. That is, unless you happen to fall in love with a piano while it is in its basic state, as it is without refined voicing. In your case, the exact sound you responded to is the result of some pretty unusual treatment to the hammers. That tone had everything to do with the way these hammers were processed. You fell in love with an illusion."

Steve looks at me to gauge my reaction to these words, then he amends them. "But I do think it is possible to get closer to what you want, I really do. It's just, I take these things gradually because there is a middle ground that most people agree is a nice piano sound, and we're there."

"What more can be done?"

"We don't want to do much more to the treble. You could pursue the bass and tenor to what they were before. Every set of hammers is slightly different, so there is no guarantee. An experienced voicer, given enough time, can do it.

"I can hear the sound you are looking for and imagine it. Two pianos I've worked on in the past had exactly that sound, and one was a Grotrian. A lot of power, but a complete absence of harshness."

We have to leave for the airport. Steve packs up his rolling tool kit, and we wheel it out to the car. On the way to meet his return flight, Steve talks of having me come to Seattle and experimenting with voicing his wife's Falcone grand piano, so he can understand better what to aim for next time he comes to Montana.

"Wouldn't it upset your wife to have the voicing changed on her piano?"

"Amateur pianists are often more passionate about things like voicing than professionals are," says Steve. We're parked before the departures entrance at the airport now. "Most concert pianists are easy to please. They've logged in countless hours in piano practice rooms, so their expectations are lower. My wife just got back from a concert tour in Europe and she said the pianos were atrocious. But she played them. You play whatever piece of wood they put in front of you."

I mull this over. It is an idea I suspect I will consider again in coming days.

✦

The phone is ringing when I get home. I fumble with the back-door
key and race to catch the call before the machine picks up.

"Well?" It is Rich, his voice jaunty and expectant, anxious to hear
how it went.

"Well . . . I can stop wearing earplugs now." I laugh, a little breath-
less. "He put in the foundation voicing, and got rid of the ringing."

"Ex-cellent!"

"But Rich, I would never have bought this piano. I didn't refinance
my house to get this piano. It's a nice piano, but it isn't the piano I fell
in love with."

"Give yourself a month of playing it before you decide."

"That's what I plan to do."

"But let me know if you decide to sell it. I might be very interested."

"You're in the market for a piano *again*?"

✦

Several of the technicians I've consulted over the previous month call
to see how it's going. To one of them I complain that the Grotrian is
not what it was.

"That's not possible," says Dave Lovos, who apprenticed at
Bösendorfer in Vienna, but now builds guitars. He is quite matter-of-
fact. "Even if it is the same make and model of hammer, to the same
specifications, it's different wool from a different sheep, made by a different press operator. Of course, they have very stringent standards, but
it can't be the same."

"It's no longer the same piano then?"

"It *is* the same piano," Dave insists. "It *is* the same. My wife was in
a car accident and now she can't walk. She can't hike anymore. Does
that make her not the same person?"

He doesn't wait for my answer. I am nonplussed by his personal
revelation.

"The important question is, the experience you had at this piano, do you ever have it away from the piano? Or is it dependent on something outside of you?"

The question takes me aback. But when I recall the compelling, exalted feeling the piano gave me, the sense of contact with another spirit, suddenly I realize that, yes, I have known this experience away from the piano. When I've been alone in the mountains, when I've made love, when I have remembered who I really am in the world. The piano connects me to this experience, but Dave is right, *it is not the experience itself. The experience is in me.*

I now have a more tolerable mental framework to go along with the more tolerable piano tone. The marriage metaphor seems more apt all the time: I commit to trying to find the best in the piano, and appreciate it for how it is in the moment. I may still sell it, or ask Carl to exchange it, but at last I am able to turn my attention back to learning how to play.

And then, one day, I get a call I am not expecting.

✦

"Hi, Perri, it's Heather Fandrich. We're going to be in Missoula tomorrow afternoon and can stop by and look at the piano. Darrell has brought his tools with him."

The Fandrichs are on their way home from their annual vacation to North Dakota. I had completely forgotten about this. I vaguely remember that someone—I can't remember who—said not to let Darrell voice my piano.

"Oh, hi! You know, when I didn't hear back from you, I went ahead and had Steve Brady come voice the piano. He was just here two weeks ago."

"Well, then, Darrell can even out the voicing."

"It's very even right now."

"We'll call you when we get to town."

After we hang up, I send a panicked SOS e-mail to Steve:

How do I handle this? Would you like to know what Darrell thinks? Or should I just disappear tomorrow?

Luckily, Steve writes right back:

Darrell is an expert voicer. I'd be interested in his input. Get his insights as to how to recapture the sound you want, but explain that you don't want any work done just now.

Little do we realize, that is easier said than done.

✦

"Please, where is the piano?" demands Darrell Fandrich, a tone of desperation cutting through the pleasantries of my greeting, his eyes only for the Grotrian sitting at the back of the room. He almost lunges through my front door. "I haven't touched a new Grotrian in twenty-five years!"

Before I can say anything more, he is sitting before the instrument; he lifts the fallboard with trembling hands.

I quickly explain to Darrell that the piano was just voiced and tuned, but he seems not to hear me: all his attention is focused on the Grotrian. He plays a dreamy, slightly jazzy version of "Somewhere Over the Rainbow," and then he turns to me.

"Well, I can see why you are unhappy with it."

"Yes, listen to that 'wolf howl' in there," says Heather, who has followed us into the house. "That's what I call that twangy sound."

Darrell picks up the tan, hard-sided suitcase he has brought and opens it. It is packed with voicing tools. He holds out a brass instrument with a handle of polished mahogany for my inspection. It is the most beautiful needle holder I have ever seen. "I got this in Germany. And look at this one, I made this one myself."

This next tool, with workmanship almost as fine as the German one, has a circular cap of tiny needles on it, packed together like the hairs of a toothbrush. The handle is brass with a flat bottom. "I use the needle end to gently massage the strike point, and the butt end to pound the hammer felt down." He holds out several more. All are Darrell's inventions, and some he sells to other voicers.

"I guess they don't manufacture all the tools voicers need for all the techniques they use," I say.

"You got it!" Darrell says, and turns back to the piano, playing each note individually now and listening. "I think this is a bad one!" he says when he gets to the B-flat in the tenor that has bothered me the most.

Without another word, he unscrews the fallboard and cheekblocks and removes them, pulls off the keyslip, and draws the action out of the piano's case and onto his lap.

"The piano is very even right now," I tell him nervously. "I don't want to lose that evenness."

"I won't leave here until the piano is perfectly even," Darrell says. "Let's see what we can do about that twanginess. You know, I used to sell Grotrians, years ago when I had a piano store. They were always the piano in my home. There is nothing like them. They are so ethereal, magical, and yet so powerful and singing."

"Yes! Well, that is what this piano used to be like," I say sadly, very surprised to learn that Darrell knows and understands Grotrians. "Do you think it will ever be that way again?"

"Oh, yes. I think so. It can't not be. It is the nature of this piano. Every Grotrian I have ever played is like that. You see, no one in this country can replicate the kind of voicing they do at the Grotrian factory. They are masters at it, and they know precisely what needs to be done, and they do it quickly. They have tools for it that no one in this country has.

"But, you see, that factory voicing wears off in about fifty to one hundred hours of playing, and then you are left with the situation that you are in right now."

First he takes the German voicing tool and plunges the needles deep into the lowest part of the hammer's shoulders. Then he takes out a long strip of emery paper and chafes a layer of felt off the top of the hammer. He slides the action back into the piano and plays the note again. The twang is gone, and the note is round and full.

"Yes! That's it!" I cry. "Hear that roundness? It should be a round, full, deep, powerful tone, but clear. Right now the tone of the bass is too shallow and dirty."

"That's right!" says Darrell. He plays the note again and then those around it. He plays three adjacent notes and asks me to tell him what I hear. "Are these alike?"

"The C is dirty. The D is brighter, clearer. The E is softer," I tell him.

"That's right!" he says. "She can hear!" he says to Heather.

I tell them how my father taught me to listen from the time I was a toddler. How he quizzed me when we listened to the radio.

"I wish someone had trained my ear like that at such a young age," Darrell says, with what sounds like genuine envy.

Darrell plays the note he corrected, to remind himself of the tone, then he voices the three adjacent notes to match it. Of the four corrected notes, one has the sound I remember from Marlene—that deep, rich, glorious, mysterious sound. "That one!" I almost shout. "That's the sound! Make them all like that one!" I am pleading.

"You got it!" says the voicer, and pulls the action back out onto his lap. He sets to work with needles, sandpaper, and files, slipping the action in and out of the piano with expert rapidity to test the notes as he goes. His gray hair hangs over his work, and his thick glasses gleam with the reflection of the piano's white keys. His hands and tools deftly coax the hammers.

When he tries the notes again, the bass has a rounded tone, if not exactly like I remember, then at least with the clear potential to arrive there.

"What do you think?" Darrell asks, playing a scale as he looks up at me from his work. I am leaning on the rim of the piano, gripping it.

"Well, the buzz is gone, but I wonder if you can make it have the depth and power it once had. It had so much warmth and mystery."

"You have an internal, auditory vision of the tone you want," Darrell says. "That is very good, that's half the battle. Now you stick to that, and don't let anybody tell you to settle for less, and you will get it."

Stunned by this affirmation, this recognition, this *validation* of my musical vision, I join Heather on the sofa, trying to stay inside my skin. No one has ever said such a thing to me before. They have always told me I hear things nobody else cares about or hears, so I should settle for less.

Fate synchronized this afternoon's events with an almost ferocious serendipity—the call, out of the blue, from Heather the day before we were to leave for our vacation, her refusal to be deterred when I told her Steve had already voiced the piano, Darrell's evident passion for Grotrians—"It is so important," he says pointedly, "that whoever voices your piano loves that piano and understands its soul." And then the almost miraculous discovery that Darrell and I hear alike, we don't

need to define our terms. "It cuts both ways," he says when I thank
him for appreciating my ear. "You can hear what I'm doing. Usually
I'm working in a vacuum."

Heather is talking to me about something—their shop? Their customers?—but there is so much static building in my head, I can't hear
her. It's a buzz of recognition that, just maybe, the universe has dealt
me a winning hand: Darrell is my voicer. I won't have to sell my piano.
The nearly three years of grief over Marlene are finally over. Dare I
hope for that? I feel hot tears of relief and gratitude surge to my eyes,
but I stop myself, embarrassed.

Darrell gets up and reassembles the piano. "My ears need a rest
now. You play it for a while and tell me what you think."

I take the Fandrichs to my backyard garden and bring them ice
water and fruit to refresh them in the hot evening air, and then I return
to the piano.

I begin with *Songs Without Words,* a good piece for testing the bass.
The ringing is all gone now, and so is most of the twanging, but the bass
is now muddy and the treble is much too bright for it. They no longer
match. Some of the tenor notes have lost their power as well. I decide
I want to leave the treble as it is for now. I don't want it brought down
to the bass's level, but the bass brought back up. Can Darrell achieve this?

I go out to the garden and report this to Darrell, who has hardly
had time to get comfortable.

"I'm your voicing tool," he says, as I follow him back into the
house. "Just use me as a voicing tool."

Another half hour or so of reshaping the bass hammers and sanding the tenor brings the power back up, along with the twang. "It's a
tightrope you have to walk," says Darrell. "That twang is the longitu-
dinal motion of the strings. It will go away after a while as the piano
becomes more stable. If I remove it completely, you will lose power."

He plays the piano again, and we pick out a few notes that are
"nasty," as Darrell calls them. "This one's crusty," he says, taking the
needles to it. "This one is crusty and weak, so we have to break down
the outer skin, but also needle the lower shoulders."

Finally, after more sanding and shaping and needling and squeezing, he pronounces it good. "Play it as much as you can," he says as he
packs up his tools and snaps the suitcase shut. "It will go through ugly

stages. Ignore them, keep playing right through them, and we'll begin to develop a base of stability. I'll be coming through again next summer, and then I will take it to the next level."

"Don't you think she would have been better off if someone had explained to her the whole process of how a piano evolves in the first place?" says Heather.

"No," Darrell says. "She wouldn't have believed them. You didn't believe them, did you?"

I don't have to consider his question long. "I think I am still in the process of understanding," I reply.

"I had to go through the same thing," he says.

And then they leave.

I return to the piano, tentative, hoping against hope that I will love what I hear. At the first touch of the keys, playing *Songs Without Words,* I am stunned to find that I am carried away by the piano's deep, round, lush tone. Marlene is in there, I can hear her, though what Darrell created is not quite Marlene. I am overcome with restless excitement. I play through every work I know. The treble peals with tones of silver; the bass is warm, dark, with a touch of mystery. I play through the adagio of a Mozart sonata, and the piano takes me by the hand, shows me how to evoke the most exquisite music possible from its keys. This piano voice is so seductive, I can't pull myself away from it. I begin to shake with emotion. I will not have to sell my piano. I lay my head against the music desk and cry wracking sobs of relief for a very long time.

❖

This should be the end of my story. But just as Darrell promised, the piano gets ugly again. I try to ride it out, but as time goes on, the idea of waiting an entire year to take the piano to "the next level," and having no guarantee of it being reclaimed, becomes harder to accept. Next summer seems a long way off. For one thing, the harmonic ringing comes back. The piano reverts to a wild, unmanageable state. I am worn out, tired of wrestling with it.

One day an advertisement in the local paper catches my eye: a Mason & Hamlin dealer from Billings is in town with several grand pianos on display in the lobby of the Missoula Children's Theatre. I've heard good things about the Mason's newest model, the AA, a six-foot grand. I call for an appointment, and head downtown.

The pianos are arranged around the circumference of the lobby, a playful, multicolored space with active mobiles dangling from its soaring cathedral ceiling. The dealer is Greg Depner, who is also a concert technician and rebuilder who apprenticed at Bechstein in Berlin, Germany, and he is expecting me.

I make swift work of playing the floor models. The prices, I note, are very reasonable. Greg explains that there is a flaw in the finishes, and so they are all on clearance.

I like a Monticello style A, the five-foot-eight grand, in mahogany, but the bass lacks power. One model BB, the seven-foot grand, has a warm, round, singing tone, but the tonal color is not as broad a palette as the Grotrian. There is no AA, Greg apologizes; he was unable to get one, as only ten have been manufactured so far. None of these pianos have an action that can match my piano's for control and subtlety.

I am just picking up my jacket and expressing my thanks to Greg, when Jeff Stickney walks in. He heard some of my Grotrian saga from Steve and asks how my piano is doing now. I thank him for his help during Steve's visit, and tell him my story, all in a rush, oblivious to the eavesdropping dealer.

When I get to the part about how horrible the hammers were after Tom installed them, Greg cannot hold himself back.

"Why didn't they send you the hammers on the shanks?" he demands. "That is what I have done when some tech tries to turn a customer's Bechstein into a Steinway. It comes out perfect. The hammers have to be voiced in a piano at the factory. That is the only way they will ever be right."

I look at him, stunned, not quite taking in what he's saying. "Hammers on the shanks? What do you mean?"

"Have the factory send you the whole assembly. They voice the hammers in a piano, just like they would for the showroom. Then they send them to you glued on the shanks, with the flanges. That way, all your tech has to do is unscrew the flanges on one set and screw in the new set. And you have the old hammers intact, you can put them back in if it doesn't work out. I have done this many times for my customers. It would have avoided your entire mess!"

If this is such a good idea, I wonder, then why did nobody ever suggest it? Not Tom, not Carl, nor any of the dozens of technicians I consulted with on the phone. I may have to take this up with Carl.

"Don't let too much time pass," Greg warns as I leave the theater.

❖

The more I think about Greg Depner's advice, the more unsettled I feel. I telephone Darrell Fandrich.

"Darrell, what do you think about having the factory send me a new set of hammers on the shanks, voiced in a piano there?"

"Hell, yes!" he replies immediately. "That is what they should have done in the first place!"

In the meantime, Rich has just returned home from piano shopping in New York, and he writes to tell me that Carl now has three new Grotrian Cabinet grands in his showroom. And they are beautiful.

This news opens before me a whole new landscape of brilliant possibilities. If Marlene was an illusion, then what is real? I've never played a Grotrian just as it comes from the factory. If I play a factory-prepped Grotrian, I'll know if another set of hammers or an exchange of pianos will solve my problem. And if it won't, if it can't—if Marlene was entirely Marc's creation—then I need to understand, at last, why I have been so powerfully affected by this sound, and why I can't give it up.

It seems insane, but three years later, that sound still resonates in me, unforgettable, and I must pursue it. I'm as helpless as Emil Jannings in the film *The Blue Angel,* when Marlene Dietrich sings "Falling in Love Again": *What am I to do?* goes the refrain. *I can't help it.*

III

19

The Grotrians

Carl is not in when I arrive at Beethoven's Fifty-eighth Street showroom on a dusky November afternoon. Linda, the delivery manager, is talking into her headset up on the balcony; she peeks over the top of the ledge to see who has come in, and I wave hello. I set my coat on the lower office divan and proceed to the sales floor.

There are several Masons and Steinways, a Bösendorfer, two Yamahas—all grands. Among them I find—as Rich promised—three brand-new Grotrian Cabinet grands.

The first Grotrian I play has a plain black-polish case, like mine. It is bright, powerful, ringing—it doesn't sound anything like Marlene at all! The second Grotrian is the Clara Schumann model with a decorative case, ice-cream-cone legs, and an open-cutwork music desk. I like this one a little better, but the tone is both cooler and more brilliant than Marlene's.

The third Grotrian has a high-polish walnut case. Mozart is luminous, transparent on this piano. The tone is clear, refined, brilliant without any harshness. I am not smitten on first touch, as I was with Marlene. I am not instantly mesmerized, passionately in love. But perhaps I could be passionately *in like*. The walnut Grotrian is warmer than the other two, with a singing treble, very seductive and sweet. The tenor has complexity, a hint of darkness brought out by Chopin. I try some Bach, then a page from Schumann's *Kinderszenen*. The Schumann is especially lovely and mysterious on this piano—it gives me chills.

I play a few more pianos. A Hamburg Steinway sounds the most like Marlene, with a throaty, dark complexity. The treble is less brilliant than the Grotrians, more subdued and warm, with a lush tenor and rich bass section. Is this the nicest piano in the room?

I return to the walnut Grotrian. The tone is rounded, pealing— shooting stars of sound streaking through a velvet darkness. And like all the Grotrians, the touch is amazingly responsive. The walnut Grotrian is growing on me. I wish my piano had this tone. It isn't Marlene, but it is an immensely beautiful and satisfying sound. This might be the best piano in the showroom.

Now I have played four new Grotrian Cabinet grands—these three, and Marlene. What do they have in common? How do they differ?

All have sparkling trebles with complex, colorful overtones, but then their personalities diverge. Marlene was warmer, sweeter, much darker than any of these pianos. I hear a family resemblance, as if they are siblings; but they are also individuals. Clearly, a new set of Grotrian hammers will not guarantee a particular tonal personality. Each piano is unique.

Perhaps if Marlene was a doomed love match, the walnut Grotrian could be a successful arranged marriage? What would Carl say? I feel nervous about asking him, despite everyone's urging that I exchange my piano. I believe that Marlene's soul must still live in the belly of the instrument that sits in my living room. If I return her, I will have forever lost the chance to revive her.

"Well, hello!"

Carl's greeting jolts me from my ruminations. We embrace.

"Did you see that we have three Cabinet grands now? And Grotrian is going to send us a concert grand!"

"That's wonderful! So you are doing well with them?"

"Yes. Quite well."

"I think this is my favorite one." I touch the keys of the walnut Grotrian. "Has anyone voiced it?"

"No, no! It came in just like that. We want to keep this one just the way it is."

"And the other two?"

"Maybe a little voicing was done on them."

My mind, bent on efficient calculation, files this information away. I like the factory voicing.

✦

Carl's Grotrians are not the only Grotrians I am in New York to see. I've been corresponding for several months with Jerry Korten, a biomedical engineer who bought his Grotrian-Steinweg Cabinet grand in Germany last winter. Jerry wrote to me after reading about my piano troubles on Piano World; he wanted a referral to a technician experienced with German hammers, as he also had to damp the duplexes on his new piano because of harmonic ringing. On his own, he found a local voicer who solved the problem. I am very eager to hear his technician's work and learn what was done.

Jerry and his family live on Central Park West in a modern brick apartment complex that commands two city blocks. The night is very dark, and the address is confusing, but at last I find the right entrance. Jerry opens his apartment door with a cordless phone against his ear—he's ordering in Chinese food for all of us, including his two young sons, Lex and Oliver, who are engrossed in creating fantastic structures with their Legos in an adjacent room.

The Grotrian's keyboard faces me directly as I enter the apartment, and I gravitate to it, as if unconsciously pulled by the force of its magnetism. It is my piano, exactly, in size and finish, with the Grotrian-Steinweg logo delicately etched in gold on the fallboard, reflecting on the white keys in the living room's moody lighting. Jerry has raised the piano's wing, and almost before I know what I am doing, I am on the bench, touching the keys.

But before I can play, the piano's owner is off the phone.

We take each other's measure, as if we are long-lost siblings—after all, we both fell hard for the same obscure make of piano. Jerry carries himself with an insouciant angularity: he's square-jawed, square-shouldered, linear in motion. His blondish hair is cut short and stands on end, forming a chevron over his brow. He's a modernist, a gadget geek. This is obvious from the stereo speakers flanking the Grotrian like airport control towers: they are Magnepan MG 3As, six feet tall and an inch deep.

"The philosophy is that if you move a lot of air just a little bit, you get less distortion," says Jerry, noticing my interest in the speakers. My father, an audio systems builder, might have explained the design in just this way. On the wall opposite the speakers is Jerry's eclectic LP record collection, filling an entire floor-to-ceiling bookcase. I pore over the titles, seeing many of my own obscure favorites. Jerry practically ignites when he sees my interest in his albums and puts on a space-age pop version of the "Hawaiian War Chant" by the Ray Charles Singers so he can demonstrate the sound system for me. Only a few bars into the music, we excitedly discuss the nuances of the speakers' performance. I comment on the vast superiority of analog recording over digital. Jerry agrees, there is no need for debate. Not everyone can hear the difference.

"You're like me," he says. "Sound is everything." He holds out his wrist and then entirely encircles it with the thumb and forefinger of his other hand. "My theory is that women and small-boned men have better high-frequency hearing. It's probably related to the size of the eardrum." I hold out my own wrist and encircle it. I suddenly realize that Marc Wienert could probably do the same thing.

The Chinese food will be here any minute, and I have yet to play the piano. Playing Jerry's Grotrian will give me one more example of the make's sound character. I sit down with the music for the Andante from Mozart's Sonata K. 330, my latest performance-ready piece, and I also play the Chopin waltz.

This Grotrian is the best I've played on this trip. Its voice is warm and singing, with a wonderful balance of darkness and shimmer, full of mystery, a woman seductively caressing the pianist with her sparkling veil. I'm starting to recognize that sparkle as a signature Grotrian trait, along with lots of complexity and color in the overtones and a powerful, chocolaty bass. All the new Grotrians have these qualities, though some are cooler or warmer, brighter or darker. I ache with wishing I had a technician at home who could make my piano sound like Jerry's. And yet, it does not move me like Marlene did.

Jerry is listening thoughtfully, intently, from the sofa, his head bowed. As soon as I've finished playing and complimented the beauty of the piano, he wants to show me what the instrument can do. My repertoire is too puny to truly demonstrate the piano's range, so Jerry knocks off some difficult Ravel and Brahms with fluid, effortless ease and sensitivity.

"Grotrian has worked out the geometry of the action—the weight of the hammers, the length of the shank, the rate of acceleration, how far back the hammer falls—so perfectly," Jerry enthuses, turning to me on the bench. His is an engineer's perspective. "It's an über piano. It does just what you want. There is nothing you can't play on this piano."

Then the buzzer rings. Dinner's here.

We set out the food and dishes on the dining room table, looking out over the darkness of Central Park. Lex and Oliver, towheads ages ten and six, leap to attention and help distribute egg rolls and hot and sour soup. Lex is studying the piano, his father informs me, and specializes in jazz—Duke Ellington and Thelonious Monk—though he is barred from demonstrating for me until dinner is over.

Jerry and I *do* have a lot in common, we soon discover: born in New York in the same year, the children of musicians—Jerry's father played violin—and students at the University of Michigan in the mid-1970s, where we were both habitués of Liberty Music, a legendary record store that catered to audiophiles. We could easily have been in adjacent listening booths back in those days. At the time, Jerry's primary instrument was the clarinet; he played in the Michigan Symphony Band. Later, in New York, he was an amateur orchestra regular.

Jerry dabbled in piano growing up, but when he and his wife, Carol, moved from Ann Arbor to New York so she could dance with Merce Cunningham, the piano became his primary instrument.

"The clarinet is very demanding," Jerry explains. "You have to practice every day, long tones, tongue exercises, breathing exercises. You miss a day and everything goes nuts." When Jerry took a job as the CEO of a biomedical company and began traveling, he couldn't maintain a regular clarinet practice schedule anymore. So he bought a vintage Steinway M, a small grand, and resumed his piano studies. Soon he was making so much progress, he felt the ageing M was holding him back.

"September eleventh gave me the feeling that you'd better live fully each day, you might not be here tomorrow, so why not buy a nice piano? That's when I started piano shopping."

Like me, he traveled all over the country, playing pianos everywhere he went. He thought he'd buy a larger Steinway. After all, it was the sound he'd learned to think of as the sound of a piano, and his mother-in-law—a pianist who studied with the legendary Cortot—

owned a Steinway B, the seven-foot grand, which she considered to be the ultimate piano. But then Jerry happened by Beethoven Pianos and played a Grotrian model 220, the next size up from the Cabinet grand.

"This was a whole order of magnitude beyond any piano I had ever played before," Jerry says of the Grotrian. "It was incredibly beautiful. I could control the dynamics in the softest passages, and yet it has incredible power, all the way up the scale, like a concert grand. That's very compelling."

But the model 220 was too large to be moved into Jerry's apartment. So he began looking for a smaller model during business trips to Germany, ultimately finding a model 192 Cabinet grand in Düsseldorf that he felt was "terrific."

"All my life I believed it was Steinway, Steinway, Steinway. You get so indoctrinated in the United States about Steinway. Because of this, I was looking for validation of my choice of the Grotrian. That's how I found Piano World. Piano World was really important to me, because I needed to feel okay about dropping so much money on a piano I'd never heard of. Still, to this day, my mother-in-law doesn't say anything about it. It's understood that it's not a Steinway."

"What is it you think we are responding to in the piano?" I mean the Grotrian in particular, but Jerry answers as if I am asking about all pianos.

"You have everything in one instrument: all the harmony, the melody, the accompaniment—it's all there," he begins, taking the broadest possible tack on my question. "That's so much more satisfying than playing the clarinet, where you have to have others to play with to make real music. Then, with a piano longer than six feet, you have this tremendous, awesome sound, a bass that kicks ass. It's like having your own orchestra right there in your house.

"When I play, I become so totally focused, all the stress of the day is put aside, and I'm in my own world of joy, harmony, rhythm, melody. Music transports you to a timeless place. And it's so rewarding physically—your fingers are making it happen. You re-create these awesome people when you play—Bartók, Ravel, Brahms—it's like you are channeling them, they are hovering in the air."

Jerry's technician voiced the Grotrian using needles only, he says.

But then, to my surprise, Jerry reveals that he has also tuned and voiced the piano himself. And he does all the piano's regulation work, unafraid to experiment in ways I would not dare. In his apartment workshop, he can adjust the action on a bench. He also makes clarinet mouthpieces and sells them. Clearly he's a natural technician.

I get to see the workshop on a later visit when I meet Carol, Jerry's wife, at a piano party the couple hosts. Carol pulls me away from the other guests, curling her finger in a beckoning motion.

"How many people do you know who have a garage in their New York apartment?" Her tone is sardonic. She leads me to what was the kitchen of the second apartment they added to their first. There is a huge workbench in the windowless room, a table saw, routers, a lathe, sawdust on the floor.

"When Jerry gets into something, he has to do it all the way. He can't just get a piano. He has to do the three different hygrometers, the Dampp-Chaser, the cloth under the piano. I just say 'whatever.' That's part of being with Jerry. You'd think maybe the boys could have separate bedrooms, but no, Jerry needs to have a garage."

Carol, now the faculty head at the Merce Cunningham Dance Studio, is petite, elegant, and ironic. I like her at once. Jerry has already told me she is jealous of the Grotrian. "She says all it needs is a vagina, and then I won't need her anymore."

When they planned the piano party, Carol asked Jerry if he was going to provide "fainting chairs" for the guests, who presumably would swoon when they played the Grotrian. "He's in love with the piano," she tells me pointedly, with a raised eyebrow. "He *pets* it."

I take this as hyperbole, until I actually see Jerry do it.

Jerry asks me who else I'm going to see while I'm in town, and I tell him about Marc Wienert. Of course I called Marc and told him I am in the city. He has become more than just the guy who voiced my piano—he's inextricably bound up in my piano fate. Marc and I haven't talked at all over these past months, during the disaster with the new hammers. Even though I picked the brains of dozens of technicians, I didn't call Marc.

Other technicians insisted that putting any kind of chemicals on German Abel hammers is wrong. One tech even called it "barbaric." I'm reserving judgment on that. By now I have talked to enough technicians to know that they often disagree with each other. One tech's barbaric is another's genius. Marc's brand of genius achieved a small miracle right in my own living room, as fleeting as it was. I haven't forgotten that. But in replacing the original hammers, I rejected Marc's work. He is sure to feel that keenly.

I tell Jerry I am not sure what more I hope to learn from Marc when I see him tomorrow. I only know that beyond the strange karmic connection the voicer and I seem to share, he is the keeper of Marlene's secret, and if I let him go, I may never regain her.

20

Szott's Secret

At 4:55 a.m., Marc is already parked at the curb, waiting for me in front of Kim's building, just like last year. I get in, and I'm surprised to find I feel a bit giddy at our reunion. I can tell Marc feels it, too—we both light up at the sight of each other. "It's great to see you," we say in unison, and embrace. And then we are off on the day's adventure, which soon becomes a wild ride.

First Marc takes me to the nearby recording studio to play the Centennial D again, since he has put new hammers on it. "What do you think?" he asks, after I have tried it out. I have to tell him honestly, the tone isn't my taste. It's too muffled.

"Really?" exclaims Marc. "Because this is my ideal sound, or as close to it as I've been able to get so far. This is very satisfying for me, this sound. It is what I'm aiming for."

"I guess in every piano I play, I am still looking for the personality I fell in love with in my own piano." I say this almost as an apology— *it isn't your piano, it's me.*

"And what was *that,* exactly?" says Marc, still incredulous at my rejection of his Centennial. "Was it the hammers? Is it the belly? Could another piano move you the way that one did?"

"I don't know." And I don't. There's no point in being dishonest with him. "I shopped for two years for my piano. It was the only one I played that sounded like that."

Back in the car, on the West Side Highway, Marc grills me on what Tom, Steve, and Darrell did to try to solve my hammer problem. He weighs every little piece of information, even though I tell him repeatedly that I may not understand what I saw or what I was told, or may not be describing it accurately.

"It's such a shame, you know," he finally relents, as we pull into the underground garage at the Manhattan School of Music. "What they did should have been enough to fix the problem."

"Well, it is vastly improved. Really not bad at all. The thing is, I fell in love with a sort of magical, extra-dimensional quality to the sound, and when I asked Darrell for that, he said, 'It's just not going to happen in one visit.'"

"Right. That's what I've been telling you."

"But the thing is, Marc, it's becoming unplayable again. It's all uneven, and very twangy."

We take the elevator to the fifth floor, Marc holding his enormous hoop of keys in his right hand, his tool bag in his left. The halls are alive with the sound of students playing their instruments. He opens the door to the first practice room.

"I want you to chase me down the hall. I'll tune, then you play, while I move down to the next room and tune the next one. It'll be like a relay."

Why does he want me to play every piano? I have no idea, but every time I catch up to him, he asks my opinion of the piano I just played. When we have worked our way down all the floors, when we have been through every room and performance space with a piano in it, I find Marc at the end of the last corridor.

"Did I take you to 130 already?"

"I don't know. Which piano is that?"

"It's the best piano in the school."

We head back down to the technicians workshop to get the key to room 130.

"So you've never heard another piano like yours?" Marc says as we trip down the stairs.

"Last night I heard a sound similar to what I remember from my piano in my friend Jerry's piano. He has the same make and model."

"Exact same piano?"

"Exactly."

"Okay. So you really like that particular scale design. That goes against the conventional wisdom of most of the world regarding who's got the best scale design. Like Fazioli."

"I don't care for Faziolis."

"Bösendorfer."

"I've yet to play a Bösendorfer I like."

"Steinway."

"I've played some really lovely Steinways, but none of them ever made me weak in the knees the way the Grotrian did. So."

"So, what is it? Is it the sustain? Is it responsiveness? Is it power? Is it character? Is it color? Is it—"

"Tremendous color."

"So—none of the pianos you played today have this extraordinary amount of color that you're talking about?" His voice rises, unbelieving. That would include his cherished Centennial D.

"No. No."

"Not even the B you liked in the small recital hall here?"

"There were other qualities I liked in that piano."

"But still yours is the one you like the best."

"Yes."

"Okay. We'll get the key for 130. If this piano doesn't rock your world, then I give up!"

Room 130 is a small room off the school's main concert hall stage. There stands a black Steinway B. Marc tells me this is the favorite piano of Dr. Silverman, the chairman of the piano department. He stands back a bit, expectantly. I feel foolish. I have neither the repertoire nor the expertise to properly evaluate a piano. All I know is what I like, what I hear, what I respond to. Why should Marc care about that?

The 130 is quite lovely, with a soaring treble, a grumbling bass, and a very responsive touch.

"Well?" says Marc, with a look of expectant triumph on his lips.

"It's a very nice piano, but it's not my sound."

Marc looks stunned. "You haven't given it enough of a chance. There's more to discover there. Play it some more."

I play some more. I play Chopin, Schumann, pieces that bring out the colors of the Grotrian best. But what I listen for in a piano isn't here. I don't need to play more than a few notes to hear that. I shake my head.

"Just a minute." Marc pulls out his cell phone. "Joanne? Marc. I've got Perri Knize with me." It's his scheduling assistant, who lives up in Westchester. "I was wondering if it would be okay if I could show her the two pianos in your living room. So, we'll come over, we'll be there by ten ten–ish. Okay?"

He puts the phone back in its holster and motions for me to follow him at warp speed down the hall. "Come on, we need to do this quick."

"We're going up to Westchester? But why?"

"I have to find out what it is you are talking about. There has to be another piano that will do it for you. Then we can figure out what creates this experience for you." In less than two minutes we are back in the Subaru and heading north into the countryside.

What has electrified Marc with this sudden determination to have me play and compare every piano within his reach to the piano personality that I lost? Is it ego, that he wants to prove that I love what he loves, that he can make me fall in love, as he did once before? Is it his own unending, insatiable curiosity about the source of our piano desire? Or does he feel some sort of responsibility for my piano happiness, as he often does for his clients, and this quest is his way of finding a means of reuniting me with "my" sound?

We soon pull into a circular drive up to a house so new the lawn is not yet planted. The entrance is still decorated for Halloween. Joanne—petite, chestnut-haired, cheerful—greets us at the door, then runs back into the kitchen, where she is helping her son's Cub Scout troop make muffins.

In a long room furnished with only two enormous concert grands, Marc and I hover over an ancient Broadwood he intends to rebuild. I play it, and it sounds like a ghost from the past, a very different sound than the modern piano, a whisper of the powerful instrument we play today. I am not sure how I will get any clues about the Grotrian from playing this. The other piano is a Baldwin he has great plans for. This is a modern instrument, with a fat, rich tone. I hear the potential in it, but it doesn't bear any relationship to the Grotrian. Perhaps Marc just wants to assess my ear, test my taste against his own? This seems like grasping at straws.

"I've got another piano for you to play!" he exclaims when I shake my head no, yet again. "At home. A Steinway M. It's Connie's to rehearse with. I keep it in top condition for her."

We say a hasty good-bye to Joanne and get back into the Subaru. Marc looks at his watch and seems to be making some mental calculations. Then we spin out onto the highway again, heading for his condo, and his own personal piano.

"Marc, what is it we are learning here?"

"We're learning if you could get what you had with your piano with some other piano. When you buy a piano, you don't know what you are buying. You only know what someone *did to it*."

"So once that wears off, then what?"

"Then, then—it's like, *the honeymoon is OVER, baby*!" he laughs, really a wild giggle.

"Marc, that is a very evil laugh."

"Well, I laugh because people think the honeymoon is forever, you know. *Aaah! I finally found my perfect piano!* Well, you better not play it. You better put it in a museum-quality controlled room so it never changes! And then you can look at it."

"So how do you find the person who can bring it back?"

"I don't know. Dating services are easier than that!" He laughs wildly again. "As horrible as that sounds. Either look for somebody who will actually interact with the reality of your circumstances, or find somebody who voices your way even though they don't know who you are or anything about what you like. That's like winning the lotto."

We pull up before Marc's apartment building. It's a two-story, with perhaps ten units, in a vaguely Tudor style, a bit down at the heels. Marc lets me into his apartment, which is a manic mingling of chaotic disorder—quite wildly unkempt. Directly opposite the entrance is a cello on a stand, its bow resting expectantly on a chair beside it. Behind the cello is a grand piano, silhouetted by the full glass patio doors beyond.

"Hi, sweetheart!" Marc calls out, and a tall, imposing woman appears in the kitchen doorway. "This is Perri, who I've told you so much about."

"Hi, Connie! It's very nice to finally meet you!"

Connie smiles down at me pleasantly. She must be a half a foot taller than I, or more. Her face is round and a bit florid, her sandy hair is neatly wrapped in a chignon at her neck. If Marc had not told me about her recent history, I would never guess she is ill.

"You're here to see the piano?"

"Yes, we'll only be here a minute," says Marc. "I'll be back with groceries later. What would you like?"

The treble of Connie's M is beautiful; I can hear how carefully Marc has maintained it to have just the right sparkle. This is the nicest piano I have played today.

"Really? That is high praise," says Marc when I tell him. "But does it do for you what the Grotrian did?"

"It's a superb piano. I'd be privileged to own it. But to answer your question . . . There's an extra-dimensional magic in the Grotrian that I'm not hearing in the Steinway. I don't know what it is."

"Yeah. I'm dying to know what it is." He ponders a moment, chin in hand. "It could be that your piano's the only piano on earth that does this, okay? Maybe, as with everyone, you're more sensitive to particular frequencies, and your piano is replete with those frequencies. But just like in all the universe, there has to be another planet that supports life as we know it, there has to be another piano that can do what you love. That's what I'm thinking."

We're both silent, thoughtful on the drive out to the highway. Marc's comments have sent me back through the past three years, to the experience I had with Marlene in the showroom, the dead-on-arrival treble, the twelve glorious hours she was resurrected after Marc's visit a few months later. I hear an echo of what Marc said to me at the time—*Ninety-nine percent of what I did was tuning.*

"Marc," I say suddenly, turning to him. He seems deep in his own exploratory rumination, hands on the wheel, eyes looking off into some middle distance down the highway. "Marc. What is the Schubert concert tuning?"

"What?"

"You said you tuned my piano with your 'best Schubert concert tuning.' What is that? How is it different from a Bach tuning or a Brahms tuning?"

"It's just something I developed through working with clients who had a particular taste in tuning. It's an interpretation of what Schubert's music needs. It's a very clean tuning, a very demure tuning. It has a certain refinement, a certain repose. It's not a busy, jingly, jangly, you know, 'say as much as it possibly could say' tuning."

"But what is it that you're actually doing that's different?"

"Oh! I guess it could be simplified down to just 'less stretch.' If you wanted to boil it down to some really low, low common denominator."

"Less stretch between? The octaves? The fifths?"

"Just less stretch in general. I'm definitely going to be tuning a narrow fifth. But not overly narrow. Just narrow enough to, you know, kind of create a richness without creating any busyness.

"A pure fifth is just mmmmmmm. Whereas a narrower fifth kind of has a b-i-i-i-i-g roll to it." He illustrates with his hand through the air in front of the windshield. "That roll is like a motor that sends out billowing partials, a combination of notes that are ringing together. The fifth is a really critical interval for the kind of color you are going to get out of the piano. It's very sensitive."

"Would you do a Schubert concert tuning for me?"

"What, today? I don't know if it's going to work today. It could have easily worked if I had known you wanted to do that earlier."

"I understand. But I didn't think of it before. So, if I were to say to your average Joe piano tuner, 'Make me a narrow tuning,' would he have any idea of what I was talking about?"

"Yeah, he probably would, but you wouldn't get what you wanted. Because he would just apply that narrowness to the octaves. And you would end up with a dull tuning that's turned in on itself, that doesn't have a spatial quality. And I think you like a spatial quality. You like it to open up, but only as much as it needs to be open."

The more Marc describes the Schubert concert tuning, the more I realize I need to hear it again. But once Marc explains his schedule for the rest of the day—he has to voice a piano at the Dobbs Ferry shop, then take Connie to the doctor—I resign myself to not hearing the tuning. We won't have another opportunity before I leave New York.

Then suddenly, Marc accelerates the car.

"What's going on?"

"We're going to do the tuning. I can do it on the piano I have to work on anyway. I'll make it happen."

"You're willing to do that for me?" I grab hold of the little handle above the passenger side door. Fast driving makes me nervous.

"Yeah, why not? But it's not how I usually tune pianos that are getting prepped for sale."

"It might be the first one to fly out the showroom door."

"Maybe. I think the majority of the people who buy pianos, their tastes aren't as refined as yours."

We enter the warehouse.

"Goddam it!"

I look to see what Marc is swearing at. He's already stomped off to the workshop in the back. I can hear him yelling, "Where's the action for that B?" His voice is shrill.

I see that the piano he was standing before a minute ago is just an empty case. The action is gone. While Marc exclaims furiously to someone back in the workshop, I wander about the room, looking at the pianos. Under a high window sits a beautiful satin-mahogany Steinway. The furniture refinishing work is gorgeous. This is the case I would have loved to have had on my own piano. It's a model L. I sit down and play the Mozart K. 330 Andante. Marc voiced this piano, I can tell. It has a family resemblance to the tone of all the other pianos I played today, but the treble is quite dull, like Marlene's when she first arrived in Montana.

Marc comes storming back and stands among the quilt-covered instruments, his fists on his hips, fuming. "Well, we are *screwed*! They've taken the action out of the piano I was supposed to voice. I don't know what to tell you." He sounds very apologetic.

"How about putting the tuning on this one?" I say, stroking the keys of the L. "It's a beautiful piano."

"That piano's just been tuned, it's on its way to the showroom." He pauses. "Well, I guess I could tune it even faster than the B, since it's already in tune. Sure, why not."

Already he has his tools out and the tuning lever is unrolled. I let him have the bench. His rubber mute is between the strings, he's playing double octaves, tenths, and seventeenths, quickly setting the temperament. The sound fills the cavernous space, as does the metallic slip and sliding of the tuning lever off and on and off and on the pins. Quickly, quickly.

"That piano is leaving here in two hours." It's the shop manager, a woman I've never seen before. The sound of Marc tuning brought her out to investigate.

"Okay, no problem," says Marc, his head down. Tuning, tuning.

"Oh, my God, the tuning is changing the voicing," says Marc. "I can hear it changing the treble."

"Really? Why would it do that?"

"Because it is changing the tension on the strings, so the hammers bounce differently."

Marc is tuning the fastest I have ever seen him tune, the lever flying along the pins, the rubber mute leaping up the scale, his left hand climbing up the keys in chords—fourths, fifths, octaves, tenths, seventeenths.

"I'm nearly there."

Suddenly the outside door swings open and in walks Indrek Laul, dressed in a heavy topcoat. A very tall, white-haired gentleman is with him. Indrek and I are stunned to see each other. We embrace. "What are you doing here?" we both say at once.

"I'm here to show my father the warehouse." He introduces me to Venno Laul, the distinguished Estonian conductor. "And you?"

"I'm here with Marc." Marc looks up with a wan smile, waves a small wave to Indrek, and returns to his tuning.

Indrek and his father excuse themselves to wander among the pianos. I realize this means the owners of the workshop will be here at any minute. What would they say if they saw Marc tuning an already tuned piano with the delivery truck on its way here to collect it?

"It was so very nice to see you again," says Indrek. Then he and his father head for the workshop in the rear of the building.

"Marc, that piano is *going.*" It's the shop manager again, bustling about us, curious about what we are doing. Two men come in the door. Movers? My adrenaline races. But they are dressed in suits. They play a few notes on a few pianos and then leave.

"Okay, *now!*" says Marc. "I really should do it a few more times for you to get the full effect, but try it."

Quickly, before there are any more interruptions, while we have the room to ourselves, I sit down at the L. I set the music for the

Mozart K. 330 Andante on the music desk, the exact same piece I played before Marc changed the tuning. This piece is a good test of a piano's treble because it demands clarity and sustain. Otherwise, the melody will not sing. Marc packs up his tools, then stands beside me, expectant. This is the last piano we will test together.

I play the opening bars of the music, and instantly I hear that this piano is no longer same instrument it was just ten short minutes ago. The treble soars and shimmers, like moonlight on water. My heart seems to burst open at the wash of sound. It's almost painful. I have played only the first line of the Andante when I have to break off. I collapse over double on the bench.

"That's it! That's it!" I cry out like I have been struck. "That's the sound!"

"You're kidding!" exclaims Marc.

I right myself, tears in my eyes. We have only minutes before we must leave, and I don't want to leave this piano. I begin the Mozart again. The same northern-lights quality I remember from Marlene hangs in the air, seductive, enveloping, moving me outside of any sense of time and place. I play as long as I dare to, letting the tones carry me off. Perfection. I try the Chopin. It sizzles under my fingers, the throaty contralto voice full of depth, warmth, complexity. This is the sound I fell for. I know it on the instant, it is so branded in my memory, so unforgettable.

"It was the tuning!" I whisper. I have to stop again. I put a hand over my heart. It actually hurts.

"We have to go," says Marc, gently. "I'll take you to the Riverdale station."

It all makes sense now. A voicing lasts for at least a few weeks, even months. A tuning lasts only a few hours. That tuning is the siren that called to me in the showroom. When Marlene arrived in Montana, she had lost her voice because the tuning had worn off. As soon as Marc replaced the tuning, she came back.

But why *this* tuning? It casts a spell over me. My heart still res-onates, bursts with it. It's physical. How can just a tuning do that?

"What is that tuning?" I ask Marc as soon as we are back in the car. Marc waves to the occupants of another car coasting down the steep drive as we head up it. The owners of the workshop. That was close.

"That's a life-changing story for me," says Marc. "I learned that tuning from a Polish tuner at Steinway who is now dead."

"How did he die?"

"He had an accident in the subway. He never recovered. His name was Szott."

"Just Szott?"

"That's the only name I knew him by. We were friendly spirits at Steinway."

Marc remembers Szott as a slight man, hunched over, balding, blue-eyed, with a thick accent, who moved about on crutches. He had poor circulation and was often in pain. "He was always quietly in a corner," Marc recalls. "Old before his time. I was young and over-whelmed in my first full-time job. He was a fatherly figure. He emanated kindness and humanity."

"It's from Szott that I got this tuning. His tunings were the sweet-est, most shimmering . . . like moonlight on water."

Like moonlight on water. I turn and stare at Marc, at my own impres-sion coming out of his mouth.

"It was the first time I was moved by a piano tuning. I knew it was the most beautiful thing I'd ever heard." He sighs. "I realized then that . . . my tunings did not sound like that. I figured it out, how to get that sound. He didn't have the words to explain it."

"You just figured it out by listening?"

"That tuning keyed me in to a different way of approaching the work. I was thirty-two. It had been six or seven years since I left piano tuning school. I had a hotshot tuning. I had had my temperament sequence verified by Franz Mohr, the head of Steinway's Concert Artists department. I was doing zinging, spinning, woowoowoo tun-ings. But I had a healthy dose of reverence for what Szott could achieve with this tuning—like mists floating along the river in an early autumn. His sound would float in the air, just float. . . . Emanate and hover and . . ."

Marc's voice trails off, his right hand floating in the air to describe the sound. Then he turns to me.

"He created only one tuning, just this one. That's like saying I only carved one statue and it was the Venus di Milo."

We've pulled up to the curb at the bottom of the stairs to the elevated train that will take me back to the city. I reach for the car's door handle, but Marc turns to me, agitated.

"Well, I'm deeply concerned now because I just realized something myself—when I tune the same piano over and over again when it is already in tune, something happens. Between a 99.3 and 99.9 percent level of accuracy, something fucking happens." He is almost yelling.

"What happens?"

"I don't know, maybe it's this matrix world that Michael Harrison talks about. Maybe it's just that the crystallizing structure goes up higher or is better organized or I don't know what. It's the difference between a quartz and a diamond. Who knows what it is. But something happens! *Something happens.*"

"You've experienced that." It's not a question. I think I know what Marc is describing.

"I've experienced that. But for me it's not a particular tuning. For me it's just any highly organized structure that becomes more organized and more structured and more and more refined in a beautiful way—and then you cross over into something."

"So you think that maybe it's just any tuning that has been highly refined?"

"That's really, really, really in tune, yeah, really voiced, really tuned." Marc says this quite passionately. He's gripping the steering wheel, even though the car is parked.

The force of his words strike me hard. I think I know exactly what he is talking about. It's the sound of Marlene, the last time I heard her.

"The more you refine it, the more powerful it is?"

"Yeah, like that."

"My God, I'm not crazy."

"Yeah, no." That wild laugh again. "You *are* crazy and you just joined this nice little band of crazies."

21

The Anthroposophist

So, now I know. The experience of Marlene, or, shall I say, the Marlene Experience, is even more fleeting and elusive than I or any of the technicians I've consulted could have ever imagined. Who falls in love with a tuning? But now, the more pressing question is, what can I do about it? Where does this leave me on my piano journey?

I have to give up on Marlene and do something else. Marc's voicing without Marc's tuning clearly doesn't work for me; our wild goose chase around the music school and Westchester County proved this. And I can't fly Marc out to Montana twice a month to tune the piano. The most practical move is to go for the Grotrian factory sound. Just as soon as I arrive in midtown, I walk over to Beethoven Pianos, hoping to find Carl. But he isn't there. I play the walnut Grotrian again and it is just as beautiful as I remember it from earlier in the week. Now I know for certain what I must do. But it will have to wait until I can speak to Carl.

I'm putting on my coat and gathering up my music, preparing to leave the store, when its impresario enters through the glass doors carrying a plastic shopping bag. He looks delighted to see me.

"I have something for you," Carl says, sounding excited, and he presents me with the shopping bag. Inside are several books. "Keep them for as long as you like."

I slip the books out of the bag and sit down on a piano bench to look them over while Carl goes up to the balcony to make some phone calls. The books are well worn and are obviously from Carl's personal library.

The first one is *Music Forms* by Geoffrey Hodson. A fleur-de-lis sketched in colored pencils decorates the torn dust jacket. On the fly-

leaf is written "Theosophical Publishing House of Madras, India."
Inside are color photographs of strange organisms. They look like
puckered mollusks or the mouths of sea urchins, unidentified matter
in bizarre formations. I read a caption:

> These shapes, leaping and gyrating like dancers in a frenzied ballet, are
> some of the dynamic "sculptures" created during a series of experiments
> that demonstrate the amazingly diverse effects produced by vibration.

I open the next book, *Healing and Regeneration Through Music,* to
these words:

> The human organism is a sounding board. The physical body of man is
> a musical instrument that is either in tune with celestial harmonies or in
> dissonance with them according to the degree of health, well-being, and
> advancement of the individual.

In *Clairvoyant Investigations,* a Theosophical Society paperback, I
open to this page:

> While performing, every true musician is brought into relationship with
> the Ghandarvas, or archangels of creative sound, and can become a chan-
> nel for their uplifting influences. Musicians are thus presumed to be
> effective agents for creative energy, which, particularly if it is of a more
> spiritual nature, is poured forth into the world and into people's lives.

There are several more books in the same vein.

"Thank you very much. I look forward to reading these," I say to
Carl, when he comes back down the stairs. The books seem incom-
prehensible, but perhaps they will help me better understand Carl
Demler, who, as I get to know him, only becomes more inexplicable.
These books must be a part of Carl's "religion" of which he spoke to
me last year.

"How did you become interested in these subjects, Carl?"

Carl takes a seat on the piano bench opposite mine and clasps a
knee with both hands. His face looks surprisingly haggard, but his eyes
shine as he answers my question.

"Before I was in hotel school, I was working as a chef in a restaurant in Geneva, and there I had a French teacher, Madame Appia, who introduced me to the philosophy of Rudolf Steiner and the idea that there is a world beyond the one that we see."

"Can you see it?"

"I can't, but I know people who can. My own answer for myself is that we are divine sparks, here to gain experience in the physical world, on the way to becoming creative intelligences.

"I'm not much of a philosopher. I'm also not much of a mystic. But if I lose something I have, I shrug it off. I can't take it with me anyway. It makes it easier to deal with irate customers, for instance. Sometimes they think they were wronged. My job is to help them, to bend over backward—more than others would."

Then Carl says something that surprises me.

"Sometimes, I would love to be rid of the business. I'm more interested in seeing if we can start a piano technician's school. And I'm most interested in opening a healing center."

"These books seem to say that music heals. Don't you already have a healing center, then, in a sense?"

"Yes. Music is a good part of healing," says Carl thoughtfully. Then he pauses a moment. "Would you like to join me for dinner?"

✦

"This place has healthy food, and it's very reasonable," Carl says as we head up the street from Beethoven's, to a restaurant on the corner of Fifty-eighth and Seventh Avenue.

At the counter, we both order soup and bread to knock off the chill of the raw November evening, and settle in at one of the long farmhouse-style dining tables in a corner window.

Carl tells me about his recent trip to Germany. He visited a healing center on Lake Constance that follows the teachings of Hildegard von Bingen, a medieval composer, abbess, and visionary. "I have a bad knee. But I am using the therapy they gave me, and next year, for my seventieth birthday, I hope to run the New York Marathon."

"That would be wonderful! What did they say is wrong with your knee?"

"Stress!" says Carl. "There is too much stress in my life."

That seems a strange diagnosis for a knee, but a reasonable one for Carl's appearance. His thin, angular face is sunken and gray. He seems even slighter than I recall, frail and fragile; I imagine I could scoop him up with one arm, as if he were an injured bird, and carry him.

"When you go to Germany, you should visit the center on Lake Constance," he says. "It is beautiful."

When I go to Germany?

"And when you go to the Grotrian factory, there is a museum you must see in Braunschweig. They have Clara Schumann's Grotrian there."

"Yes," I say uncertainly. "I would like that."

"So," he says, changing the subject. "How is your trip going so far?"

"Very well. I am learning so much." I break open the loaf of French bread we are sharing and put it back down before him.

"That is wonderful. When you stop learning, you are as good as dead."

I tell Carl about the Schubert concert tuning, how this is the sound I fell for, how this is why the piano did not retain Marc's voicing when he came to Montana.

"The right tuning can do wonders," says Carl. "It's a matter of which type of tuning fits your psyche best."

"Is this common, for your customers to fall in love with a tuning?"

"Most people have lost contact with vibration because we're too enmeshed in the material part of our existence," Carl says. "Music is the essence of everything there is in existence."

"It's a real problem, living where I live, I don't think there is anyone who can do this tuning. I suppose I will just have to settle for getting the best tone I can."

"How *is* your piano?" he asks gently. He looks down, buttering some bread.

Here is my opening. The words I've been rehearsing in my mind for weeks come rushing to my lips.

"Carl, I don't know what to do about my piano. I've had it for nearly three years, and in all that time it has been a pleasure to play for perhaps a month. I've talked to many technicians about the new hammers. Some say I may have simply gotten a bad set. I've also been told the hammers should have been sent to me prevoiced on the shanks, so that we could simply swap them out."

"I should have thought of that," Carl says quietly.

"Well, you are not a technician." For some reason, I don't want it to be Carl's fault.

"No, but I handle these things all the time." He pauses, thoughtful. "Grotrians are so consistent, they are manufactured to such tight tolerances, I bet it would work!" He takes a spoonful of soup, and thinks some more. Then he says, "We'll see if Grotrian will do this. We'll have them put the hammers in a piano at the factory, voice them there, and then take them out and send them to you. Remind me when we get back to the store, and I will make a note to telephone them in the morning."

"That is wonderful! Thank you so much! Perhaps the new hammers on shanks will be the end of the saga."

"With pianos it is never the end of the saga," says Carl, grinning, his eyebrows arched with bemusement. "Unless you get used to the sound and you learn to fall in love with it all the time." Then he seems to have another thought. "Did you like the new Grotrians in the showroom?"

"Oh, very much! Especially the walnut Grotrian, I would be very happy if my piano sounded like that."

"And are you happy with the touch of your piano, the action?"

"Oh, yes! I have never played a better piano for touch."

"Well, then, why don't we take the hammers out of the walnut Grotrian and send them to you? Then you know you will have a voicing you like. Of course, I can't do it until I have a new set from Grotrian. I don't know if they will agree to it. We'll put the ones from the factory in the walnut Grotrian, and then I'll have a technician come and see how she would voice them."

I am blown away by this offer. How can he do such a thing? And how remarkable that he sees this as an opportunity to try something new with the pianos. I feel a sudden surge of excitement mixed with doubt.

"But are you sure? What if that doesn't work?"

"We'll try it. It will be an experiment. And if it doesn't work, we'll try something else."

"What if someone arrives in the meantime who wants to buy the walnut Grotrian?"

"Well, we'll hold them off. We'll stall them."

"That's crazy."

"No, it's perfect. It's done!"

22

Revelation

*"Many say that life entered the human body by the help of
music, but the truth is that life itself is music."*

—INAYAT KHAN, SUFI MASTER

It's quite cold and dark outside by the time we leave the restaurant. I walk with Carl to his store, thank him again, and then make my way back along Piano Row to the subway. There's a new Kawai dealer across the street. The shop is closed, but spotlights in the window shine on a Pleyel in an exotic wood case. The next shop to the east is Faust Harrison. Through the plate glass, I see Michael Harrison talking on the phone, and behind him I see a satin mahogany piano. It looks just like the Steinway L that Marc put the Schubert concert tuning on earlier today. I ring the doorbell, and Michael buzzes me in.

"We're having an Indian raga singing class here in a few minutes," Michael says. "You're welcome to join us."

Decorative wool pillows, seats for the soon-to-arrive singers, are strewn about on a Persian rug in the center of the room. A tamboura, a sitarlike instrument with a long neck and a body made from a giant gourd, is propped up on its own cushion. Then my eyes are drawn again to the satin mahogany piano.

"We just got that piano in this afternoon," says Michael, following my gaze. "I haven't had a chance to play it myself. Would you like to?"

I lift the fallboard. It is a Steinway. I play just a few bars of the Mozart and recognize the tuning immediately. The Schubert concert tuning held up on the move from Dobbs Ferry. I tell Michael I would indeed like to stay for his raga singing class.

✦

Nine of us sit on dhurrie pillows, and Michael sits before us with the tamboura on his lap, gently strumming the strings with his long fingers, his forehead pressed against the back of the instrument's neck. The strings vibrate in a soft drone, and Michael matches his voice to them. He pauses after each note, and we call the note back to him, tossing the sound between us. He sings unfamiliar syllables, moving around in the exotic scale of North Indian classical music. We match his pitch, varying our intonation, and together we make strange and moving harmonies.

✦

"Tuning is everything," says Michael, curling up in a big armchair in the music studio of his Yonkers home. The composer-pianist is rail-thin, with long, delicate fingers, and a scholarly look suggested by his owlish wire-rimmed glasses. His long legs fold over each other like stalks. I've taken the train up to meet him, because after experiencing the intonation of raga singing last night, and our conversation afterward, I know that if anyone can explain to me what the Schubert concert tuning is, and why it has the effect on me that it does, it must be Michael.

"It's resonance," he says. His eager, reassuring manner suggests that I am being admitted to a brotherhood, a tribe. We sit to either side of a small table that holds our cups of tea. Along the wall behind us stand what look like enormous, towering stereo speakers, but are actually acoustic "tube traps," Michael explains, designed to absorb and balance sound. Opposite are two grand pianos, seven feet long each, fitted together rim to rim like the polarities of the Yin-Yang symbol. "Everything is resonance, vibration," Michael says. "You are resonating to those frequencies."

Last night, after I explained my interest in the Steinway L, Michael gave me some concrete examples of how sympathetic frequencies operate in the world. In a room filled with pianos, if you play just one note on one piano, all the other pianos in the room will also play that note if their dampers are raised. If you fill a room with grandfather clocks, pendulums swinging in their own, individual rhythms, then leave them closed up together overnight, in the morning the pendulums will all be swinging together, in sync.

"It's physics," he explained. "The airwaves want to be efficient. There's less resistance in the airwaves if they are operating in harmony with each other. This happens between people, too. For example, when women live or work together, they menstruate together."

Michael also gave me a history of tuning to read, *Temperament: The Idea That Solved Music's Greatest Riddle* by Stuart Isacoff, and a compact disc of his own performance of his composition *Revelation: Music in Pure Intonation,* which he says uses a special tuning he designed himself. And then he invited me to visit him at his home so I can hear for myself what a piano tuned in pure intonation sounds like.

Michael Harrison grew up in Eugene, Oregon, the son of a famous mathematician, in a family of scientists. He became fascinated with pianos at a young age, and admits to spending most of his adolescence sneaking onto the stages of darkened concert halls so that he could play a properly prepared and tuned piano. He recalls being so desperate to own a grand piano, when a keyboard magazine offered one as a prize and allowed unlimited entries, Michael spent more than $700 on postage to enter the contest multiple times, an endeavor that proved futile.

In his early twenties, he was drawn to Sufism, an eastern philosophy that uses music as a vehicle of enlightenment, and studied under a famous raga singer. A year of singing Indian ragas, which use a different tuning system than is used in the West, left him fascinated with tunings—and dissatisfied with the tuning on his piano. He began experimenting.

"Part of the special appeal of the piano is that the strings create overtones," Michael says. "There's a composite tonal quality that's richer than what you hear in a guitar. A flute is limited to low overtones. An oboe has high overtones. But with the piano, there is a rich, complex overtone structure with each note—it's a whole orchestra in one instrument. A piano is the most sympathetically resonating instrument in the world."

Last night I told Michael about the Schubert concert tuning and my response to it. Now I tell him my story of how I came to own

Marlene, and my quest to restore her voice. I hope that if I recount my tale, Michael might offer some insight as to what I experienced.

"But *why* do I resonate to these particular frequencies?" I ask. "Why was this piano so compelling that I made sacrifices I would never have considered before to get it? What is it I am seeking in this instrument? It just all seems so unreal and crazy."

Michael smiles. "Let me answer by telling you a Sufi fable that I think will resonate with you.

"Before the human soul incarnated, God was trying to get the soul to go into the human body. But the soul didn't want to go into the body because the soul was in this infinite realm of joy and bliss beyond limitation. Why would it want to go into this human form where it would experience disease and be limited in time and space? So the only way God could get the soul to incarnate was he got the angels to play music. And the soul was so intoxicated by the music that it wanted to hear the music better. And it could only hear the music better by listening with the ears of the human body. And so that's how God tricked the soul into incarnating into a human form."

We both laugh out loud. But midlaugh I burst into tears. They stream down my face.

"That's incredible. I don't know why I'm crying. It just feels so real to me."

"I thought you would resonate with that story. Do you want a Kleenex?"

"Thanks. I think I have some in my pocket." I reach for them and wipe my eyes. "I seem to be doing a lot of crying on this trip. Yesterday, when I heard Marc's tuning. Now, this story. What am I resonating to?"

"I think in this chapter of your life, you're very finely tuned on some vibrational level. Like you could say on an angelic level. So what happens is, when you hear something, like these pianos that you had these experiences with, they're on a certain level of vibration—it triggers a state of remembrance for you. Of some other realm that your soul has experienced. It's a kind of alchemy—the vibrations of the tones trigger a memory of this nostalgic, beautiful place.

"And so that's what this is all about for you. It's finding out where did you come from? What is it that will bring you back there? The piano is a microcosm of universal truth. The sacredness of perfect mathematical proportions heals the soul, literally, absolutely, and they also heal the human body."

It did seem that when I was embraced by the shimmering beauty of Marlene, I was taken to a place of inner truth, or at least transcendence. When I was not near that, I yearned for it, for something half remembered.

"That's pretty intense. And what is it about for you?"

"My life has been this search. The bottom line is that I have experienced what you're talking about. In 1979, I came to New York, and the composer La Monte Young invited me to his loft in Tribeca to hear a recording of a performance he'd done the year before of his work *The Well-Tuned Piano*.

"At that point, the *Well-Tuned Piano* was four and a half hours long. Now it's six and a half hours long. So I sat in this loft, with these huge speakers about five feet high, and listened to this four-and-a-half-hour-long performance. And listening to that music had the same effect of what you're talking about with these pianos. I heard the music I'd always somehow dreamed of but didn't even know was possible. And it just changed my life on the spot.

"I had no idea how he was creating that extraordinary, angelic, beautiful music that was beyond anything I'd heard ever in my life before. And so I immediately told him I wanted to be his student, to learn from him. And that was the beginning of a huge odyssey for me, the way your experience is the beginning of an odyssey for you."

Michael became Young's personal tuner, working on his customized Bösendorfer for all of his concerts and recordings. It was a form of discipleship, as Young would not teach him composition until Michael had mastered his tuning.

"To La Monte, the most sacred and important task was the tuning," Michael continues. "La Monte has a theory that I believe is correct. That tuning is a function of time. He's like a philosopher: I think of him as a modern-day Pythagoras."

Pythagoras, the Greek mathematician and philosopher, discovered the natural laws that govern music quite by accident. Legend has it that one day in Croton, around 530 BC, Pythagoras was passing by a blacksmith's shop and was arrested by the sound of hammers hitting anvils.

Sometimes the sound was grating, ugly, and dissonant. But sometimes the hammer sounds blended into an exquisite, transcendent harmony. Pythagoras entered the shop to investigate why. It turned out that hammers of different weights produced different tones, and whenever the relative weights of the hammers formed certain mathematical ratios, say 2:1 or 3:2 or 4:3, the notes they struck simultaneously created beautiful harmonies.

Pythagoras seized on this finding as a sign of a natural order in the universe. By experimenting with the sounds made by a taut string when it was subdivided according to these ratios, he established the foundation for how keyboard instruments are tuned.

"Astronomers have known for centuries that the more time you have to observe a planet in motion, the more you can predict its orbit," says Michael, to offer an analogy. "The larger cross-section of this orbit that you see, the more information you have.

"Now, tones are exactly the same thing. They're like orbits. For example, when you're tuning two notes, let's say you're tuning a perfect fifth, they're in a relationship. And what happens is that if they're a little out of tune they're creating acoustical beats where they vibrate against each other. And as the fifth gets more in tune, those beats slow down until they start to become in sync. Well, how in sync are they going to be? Are they going to be beating once every two seconds? Once every five seconds? Once every ten seconds? The longer you listen, the more precisely you can tune those intervals to lock in perfect sync. So tuning is a function of time.

"So therefore, I spent a lot of time tuning La Monte's piano. In fact, I was down there for hours and hours, every day, for weeks at a time, perfecting this tuning, in a near-perfect temperature- and humidity-controlled environment. For his work. Because his work is also very different from how you would tune a normal piano. Basically, the way the piano is normally tuned creates nonperiodic waveforms. Which means that the waveforms in the air don't repeat themselves. And in just intonation, the intervals create periodic, composite waveforms. Which means the waveforms *do* repeat themselves."

Just intonation, I learned from reading the Isacoff book Michael gave me, is a method of tuning so that all the intervals—the spaces between the notes—are in their natural proportion to each other.

They follow the harmonic ratios Pythagoras found in nature, also known as the overtone series.

Each individual note is made up of many tones; they comprise a kind of a tonal envelope. These are the overtones, or harmonics, or *partials* excited when the fundamental tone is struck. They follow a predictable mathematical pattern made up of whole numbers. The fundamental tone is the first partial. The second partial is heard an octave above the fundamental. If the fundamental tone vibrates at a frequency of 100 cycles per second, since the second partial is always a doubling of that frequency, it would vibrate at 200 cycles per second, for a ratio of 2:1. Octaves are always a doubling of the frequency, so the next octave would vibrate at 400 cycles per second.

The third partial is always a fifth above the second partial, and it is always a multiple of three, so it is 300 cycles per second, for a ratio of 3:2. From here the partials continue to climb up the scale, and the intervals— the distances between them—get narrower and narrower. As they narrow, they become more discordant. The simplest ratios create the most harmonious or consonant tones, and are therefore the most pleasing. These tones are all heard simultaneously when just one note is played.

The overtone series is a universal, natural phenomenon; it is the very foundation of harmony. "Just like the rainbow in the sky," says Michael. "The colors always occur in exactly the same sequence." He plays a C on his Schimmel piano. "Hear how the C also contains within it the C an octave above, then the G, or fifth, above that? And then can you hear the third above that?"

When tuning a keyboard in just intonation, the type of tuning Michael uses, the intervals between individual notes are tuned pure, that is, they are made to match the frequencies of the natural overtone series. But there is a problem, which Isacoff describes so fluently in his book: if each note within an octave is given the appropriate frequency for the overtone series, they will not fit within the container of a pure octave. When Pythagoras and his followers discovered this, they kept it a secret, believing that the uninitiated would misunderstand it as a flaw in the universal order.

This was the beginning of the riddle of tuning. How to fit all the notes within the octave? No matter what method the tuner uses to make all the intervals pure, somewhere there will be one or more that are impure. The whole number ratios don't add up. Fifths, with their 3:2 ratio, and thirds, with their 5:4 ratio, can never arrive at the same place. For example, in just intonation, in the key of C major, the A that is a third above F cannot be the same A that is a fifth above D. The difference between those two As is called the comma. Most keyboard music composed before the invention of equal temperament was designed to avoid it.

Equal temperament is the modern solution to the comma. The twelve semitones of the chromatic scale are divided up equally within a pure octave, so that each note is 1/12th of a semitone flat, not really enough for most people to notice. Michael gives me a great metaphor to help me understand this concept better: lunar months and solar years do not fit together. As with the octave, we adhere to the dictates of the solar year, because that determines our seasons. We stretch the length of a month—the notes—from twenty-eight to thirty or thirty-one days to make the months fit within a year. Similarly, the frequencies of notes are made slower, or flat, so they will fit within an octave.

"Many intervals in equal temperament are actually hideously out of tune," says Michael. "The thirds are as much as fourteen percent of a semitone sharp." The ratios, rather than being consonant whole numbers, become dissonant irrational numbers. The ear may be deceived, but some other part of us is not. When a barbershop quartet sings, they naturally sing in just intonation. When a great, old-school string quartet plays, they naturally tend to play in just intonation. We don't need to be taught to recognize this type of tuning; it's already a part of us. And because we have a natural responsiveness, because we naturally resonate to pure intervals, a beatless tuning—one with periodic or repeating waveforms—is an entirely different aesthetic experience than a tempered tuning.

So this is what Marc meant when he told me that a tuning is a bunch of tiny little lies that add up to one big lie of being in tune! The truth has a very different feeling to it than a lie.

A pianist does not have the freedom to intonate at will the way a singer, a string player, or even a wind player does. When you play a piano, you can only play the note as it is tuned. You can't adjust the note to something slightly sharper or flatter by changing the way you touch the key. You are at the mercy of the tuning. And equal temperament is the way virtually all pianos have been tuned for roughly the past 150 years.

Michael's philosophy of tuning embraces the comma rather than avoiding it through temperament. Not only does he permit the comma to breathe freely in his tunings, he composes music that uses it to advantage.

"I call it the emancipation of the comma," says Michael. "If you think of it in Jungian terms, the comma is our shadow self, our dark side. If you avoid something, it becomes your fate. The comma is the shadow of music. Face it, and you no longer need temperament."

With equal-tempered tunings that avoid the comma, the piano becomes dissonant, producing physical waveforms in the air that are discontinuous—they do not persist or repeat. But in just intonation—the foundation of Michael's "Revelation" tuning—the waveforms are periodic, or continuous—they repeat, and repeat, and they stimulate our nervous systems through a different channel to the brain. To hear them is to have a completely different kinesthetic experience in response to tone.

"Vibration affects the physical body, and composite waveforms trigger a neurologic circuit to the brain. If a periodic waveform triggers the same circuit, you get a feeling of universal truth. Once we embrace the comma, it opens a whole realm of sound that has been ignored in the West for centuries."

"But the Schubert concert tuning is in equal temperament," I persist. "So why am I responding to it in the way that I am?"

"Marc is very aware of all these subtleties I'm talking about. He tunes my piano for my concerts. He's showing you a very high level of refinement. But with just intonation, you will get an even higher level of refinement. Much higher, in fact."

I ask him to show me.

Michael takes me to the ebony Schimmel piano, the one that has been customized for playing in pure intonation. Each note has only one string; this enhances the purity of the tone. There are also many small color-coded buttons sitting over the strings, and these are designed to selectively damp some strings so that they cannot sympathetically vibrate. All is designed to produce the longest-sustaining tone possible, but under the complete control of the pianist as to which tones sustain.

Michael gets out a tuning hammer, and quickly tunes a perfect fifth for me, between C and G. I play it and immediately feel a strong elation. The tone rolls back from the piano's soundboard in a continuous, smooth, glassy wave, then seems to ride out through the air to infinity. There is a purity and a clarity that I find deeply moving.

"What am I hearing?"

"A perfect fifth."

"But, *what am I hearing?*"

We both laugh.

"It's music taking us to another dimension of experience."

Michael tunes several more fifths and then plays them. The sound is a bouquet rising off the soundboard, a perfumed plume. The tones radiate on and on and on.

"May I?" I play a fifth on the keyboard and listen to the sound roll out. "The tones are merging."

"That's right. If you throw a stone in a lake, the ripples that come off the stone are what happens when you have temperament. The sound wavers." He plays an out-of-tune third. "Hear the wavering? Hear how jangly that is?"

Then he plays the fifth again.

"This has no waver—the lake is perfectly still. It's like crystal."

The sound is exhilarating.

"What if someone can't hear?" Of course, I am thinking of my husband, Oliver. "What if their hearing is impaired? Can they still have this experience?"

This sets Michael back a moment, as he thinks it over. "Yes," he says slowly. "I would think they can. It's vibration, and while the principal effect is through the auditory circuits of our brain, we know from experiments with the effect of vibration on sand and water that there is an effect without hearing. When violins are played, the molecular structure of wood changes, and neither sand, nor water, nor wood have ears. So, it's possible that vibrations also affect our nervous systems without us having to hear them."

Next Michael invites me to play the Mason & Hamlin grand that sits behind the Schimmel. This piano is tuned to his "Revelation" tuning, another form of just intonation. I play a scale and it is strange— the C# is lower than the C. I try to play my Chopin B minor waltz, and I bust out laughing. Where the notes should go up, they go down. It seems impossible to play a melody on this piano. It's like being in a fun house at the carnival, or a hall of mirrors, and you can't find your way out, and everything you try to say comes out garbled. The Chopin sounds like utter nonsense.

Michael wants to play *Revelation* for me, so I can hear how this piano is intended to sound, but the abridged version is forty-five minutes long. We decide to get something to eat first. In the kitchen, Michael lays out bread, cheese, and fruit for us. He asks how I am going to solve my piano problem now that I know about the Schubert concert tuning. Perhaps I'm interested in selling the Grotrian and buying the Steinway L?

But even the idea of this makes me freeze. There's more to Marlene than the tuning, I am certain. There is something going on in the belly of my piano, something I have heard in no other piano, not even the L with Marc's tuning on it. I have no idea what this unique quality is, but I do not want to give it up. I tell Michael I'm resigned to getting the Grotrian factory voicing and using my regular tech's tuning. It will be okay.

But this does not settle the question for Michael.

"Couple of ways I could try to solve this," Michael persists, as we eat our cheese and bread. "You could get an Accu-Tuner. An Accu-Tuner can memorize and read the exact frequency on a string. So you have Marc come out to Montana and do a perfect-as-possible tuning, then with the Accu-Tuner you measure the exact frequency of every note. And then either you learn how to tune it yourself, so you can re-create that tuning—it's not so hard—or you get a local tuner who knows how to use an Accu-Tuner. Then you wouldn't have to buy one—they are expensive."

"Is an Accu-Tuner refined enough to record everything that Marc is doing?" I ask, incredulous.

"Yes. It's very refined," says Michael. "Marc creates the tuning by ear to your specific piano, the acoustics in the room, everything. The Accu-Tuner makes a map that re-creates that exact tuning. It's digital— like burning a CD of the tuning. You could put the Schubert tuning on the piano, then ruin it, and then use the Accu-Tuner to make it go back exactly the way it was. It's very precise."

"Can you transfer the tuning from one piano to another?"

"Ah . . . you could . . . but it won't be quite the same, because each piano will have different overtone characteristics. The ideal is to have Marc set up your piano for you, tune and voice it just the way you want, then record it with the Accu-Tuner. But to keep the piano exactly the way you like it, you will need Marc to come out every year, because your voicing is going to change. You don't want anyone else to *touch* your voicing. Marc's the *best* voicer around."

Yes. That's fine. Except it's not practical to expect Marc to come out to Montana. Even if I could afford it. Between his full-time job, his commercial clients, and Connie's health, Marc can't make such a commitment to me, and I wouldn't ask him to. And so there's no point in having Marc voice my piano, because nobody else knows what he does. Unless I know for certain that Tom can put the Schubert concert tuning on my piano using an Accu-Tuner, I don't want *anyone* to touch the new hammers Carl is going to send. Not even Marc.

And yet, might there still be a way to get Marc's tuning on my piano? Maybe Marc could tune and record the walnut Grotrian in Carl's showroom before Carl sends me its hammers? Then at least the tuning would have been done with the actual hammers going into my piano. But I'm not going to belabor this with Michael.

"I wonder how Marc would feel about his tuning being recorded?" I muse aloud.

"He won't mind," Michael says. "Let me talk to him."

✦

Michael sits before the Mason & Hamlin, and I take a seat in the farthest corner from the piano, the better to let the acoustics of the long room mix the sound before it reaches me. Then he begins *Revelation*.

At first the music sounds cacophonous, indistinct, confusing. But then my ear begins to adapt and I sense sound building under the piano's open wing. The tone begins to pour out. Because the soundwaves are consonant, they are free to continue moving and building. They do not jangle against each other and cut each other off, as they usually do in piano music. They spiral and swirl out from under the wing, launching great clouds of tone that seem to increase in density until I feel I am enclosed by a matrix of sound.

And then, bit by bit, I notice the character of the sound changing. First I hear a flute, indistinct, but then more and more clearly a flute. Then, other nonpiano sounds take shape. I hear an oboe, then a horn, then a violin. The flute soars up and down the octaves. A piccolo rings out. French horns join in, a bassoon, trumpets blast into the room in massive waves of sound.

Michael continues playing for so long, I begin to wonder when the music will end. But the longer I sit with the tone cloud, the more I realize that what I hear cannot be accounted for by what Michael is doing. He's only playing a very small area of the keyboard, and yet the entire piano is ringing with overtones so alive, so persistent, it seems like the instrument has been turned inside out. It has a life of its own—the tone cloud reshapes and re-forms into sounds that are not from the piano. The harmonics are generating an orchestra. Either that, or Michael Harrison has ten arms.

In time, as the character of the tone cloud shape-shifts around me, I become entranced and give myself over to the experience of being wrapped inside a tonal maelstrom. The cloud becomes a hurricane, gale force winds roar about me. Finally a whole and complete orchestra is braying from beneath the hood of the instrument.

I'm struck by wonder. The instruments sound like occult manifestations, spectres emerging from the intense frequency waves of the piano's harmonics. The tone cloud continues to evolve, building and building until the excited harmonics produce the sound of a sitar, then a tamboura, and finally, a chorus of angels' voices, ringing and ringing through the room until I think they will blow out the walls and windows. When all the colors of the rainbow have been unleashed in a riot of sound, the tonal thundercloud finally subsides, and at last the work ends.

Michael rises from the piano, his gaunt face flushed with ecstasy.

"How did you create all those other instruments?" I ask, when I have recovered enough from my awe to speak.

"The sympathetic resonances combine and form whole new sounds, like a harmonic recipe," he says. "They are literally recombining and producing the actual harmonics of those instruments. It's physics."

23

Physics and Metaphysics

"What is is *movement."*

—DAVID BOHM, PHYSICIST, *WHOLENESS AND THE IMPLICATE ORDER*

If there is a scientific explanation for our physiological response to tone, for what happened to me when I found my piano—a way to diagram transcendence—then I want that explanation. I begin reading about the physiology of hearing, the physics of sound vibration, psychoacoustics, neuroscience, and finally, quantum physics. Physics and mathematics were never my strong suit at school, but my desire to understand the Marlene Experience drives me on. Soon I find myself in remarkable territory.

Sounds, I learn, exist only in our brains; they are perceptions formed in response to air pressure created by moving objects. When strings, drum skins, or tuning forks vibrate, they disturb air molecules the way a rock disturbs the still waters of a pond. Currents of alternating high and low air pressure ripple through the atmosphere in waves. When these pulses of alternating pressure reach our ears, they are amplified, turned into mechanical energy, then into electrical energy, and then are sent to our brains, where they affect our nervous system.

Inside the ear canal is a column of air, just like in a flute or an organ pipe. This air column vibrates in response to pressure waves, sending pulses to the eardrum. The eardrum converts these pulses to mechanical energy and passes them on to the middle ear. In the middle ear, the pulses drive three small bones, linked together as a series of levers that triple the pulses' power. These intensified vibrations then reach a membrane-covered opening called the "oval window." The oval window concentrates the force of the vibrations further, and by the time they reach the cochlea, the liquid-filled inner ear, their mechanical force has been amplified eight hundred times across a span of only 1.6 inches.

Inside the cochlea, which is about the size of the tip of a little finger, this force becomes hydraulic pressure pulsing through the liquid in the spiral ducts and beating against the membranes of the inner ear, until they reach the most protected area of the body: the organ of corti, a gelatinous mass over an inch long. The organ of corti moves to the rhythm of the pulses. At the end of the organ of corti, a mass of cells nearly touch the tentacles of the auditory nerve. These cells have thousands of fine, soft hairs embedded in a thick overhanging sheet known as the tectoral membrane. When this membrane is set in motion by the fluids pulsing from sound-wave energy, the hairs go along for the ride, and their shearing motions generate electrical signals that stimulate the auditory nerve, and ultimately the hearing centers of the brain.

This electrical energy sends the brain a coded version of the original sound waves—their fundamental frequency, intensity, and timbre. This information then travels to the central nervous system. How sensitive an individual is to this information varies greatly. For someone who has been carefully taught how to listen, subtle differences in frequency and timbre seem significant. But if someone does not have a trained ear, or simply does not value these differences, they may seem insignificant.

Training in music changes the underlying structure of our nervous systems, I learn from an article on the neuroscience of music in the journal *Nature*. The authors theorize that musical vibrations entrain our motor and physiological functions, changing heart rate, respiration, and mood. When listeners experience "chills down the spine" in response to music, neuroimaging shows that the same area of the brain is stimulated that responds to food and sex. They also found this effect transcends our ability to hear and touches our neurobiology directly. Air pressure vibrations can be felt as well as heard.

The deaf can distinguish musical intervals by feeling their vibrations in a wall using their hands and arms. Sound is tactile, as well as auditory; our physical response to sound goes beyond hearing.

The heart, generator of the body's main pulse, normally beats at a frequency of 1 to 1.2 hertz. These beats reverberate throughout the body in the form of electromagnetic energy. Our nervous system is an electrical system, oscillating between motion and rest. When the body is exposed to music, our heartbeats change in response to its rhythm and intensity. Researchers at the University of Oklahoma postulate that sound stimulates involuntary centers of the central nervous system; they respond to the frequency, volume, and timbre of sound waves.

Research cardiologists take these findings very seriously. At Harvard Medical School, Dr. Ary Goldberger found the complex rhythms of healthy hearts are similar to note patterns in classical music. At the Carle Heart Center in Urbana, Illinois, Dr. Abraham Kocheril, chief of cardiac electrophysiology, has harpists play in his operating theater when he performs open heart surgery. Live music may regulate patients' heart rhythms, Kocheril has found. Harps are used in some hospitals to help normalize the heart rates of newborns, reduce patient anxiety, and ease the passing of dying patients.

Dr. Mark Tramo, a neurologist at Harvard and director of The Institute of Music and Brain Science, says entrainment—the influence of one oscillating system over another—may be an explanation for music's healing effect. The oscillating electromagnetic field of the human nervous system is influenced by oscillating sound vibrations, much the way pendulum clocks "learn" to tick in tandem when they are placed in close proximity. Music affects the part of the brain known as the mesolimbic system, which controls emotions and can profoundly influence the heart.

The connection between emotions and music has been explored in depth since the 1960s by neuroscientist, poet, and concert pianist Manfred Clynes. Clynes, a researcher at the department of physiology and biophysics in the Lombardi Cancer Center at Georgetown University, invented the Computer of Average Transients, or CAT, for measuring responses hidden in brain waves, and he used it to study the effects on the brain of seeing the color red. Finding that all human brains have a similar electrical response to the color red, he wondered if the expression of our inner mental states could also be measured. So he invented an output device, called the sentograph, and named the field of inquiry "sentics."

Subjects are asked to express a single emotion through touch, using their finger on a pad. The sentograph draws the shape of the pressure and duration of the touch on a computer screen. Clynes tested subjects in Bali, Japan, Mexico, and America. To his amazement, he found that the touch of each emotion has its own, universally understood character. The shapes the sentograph drew for love, hate, anger, reverence, jealousy were distinctly different from each other, and yet, regardless of the ethnicity, race, or geographic location of his subjects, they produced similar forms for each emotion. Clynes found that the fundamental physical expression of our emotions, through gesture, is universal. These basic shapes of human emotions, called "essentic forms," are alike for everyone.

Clynes remembered reading about the work of German musicologist Gustav Becking, who found that when he listened to music and allowed his finger to describe the character of that music, his response to each composer produced patterns and shapes characteristic of the entire body of that composer's work. He drew these shapes on a piece of paper. Taking a cue from Becking, Clynes hooked himself up to the sentograph and thought his way through works of Beethoven, Mozart, and Schubert. Thoughts of each composer's music resulted in a distinctive shape, unique to that composer.

Clynes then asked pianist Rudolf Serkin to try the experiment. Serkin's touches for Mozart, Beethoven, and Schubert resembled the ones Clynes himself expressed. Clynes repeated the experiment with Pablo Casals and other distinguished musicians. The shapes were alike. He concluded that touch expression and musical expression arise from the same underlying brain function. Our nervous systems, it seems, are designed to express our emotions with universal physical gestures, through motion and touch. Sound waves, initiated by our movements and touch, also move and touch us. Might they also then quite literally convey certain emotions? And might a musician who understands this principle have greater powers of musical communication?

After exchanging a few e-mails with Dr. Clynes, he agrees to accept a telephone call from me. He is eighty-one now, and lives in Sonoma, California. Clynes says he knows well my experience with the Grotrian. He only recently had just such an experience himself with a Bösendorfer in San Francisco. He bought the instrument to make a new recording of Bach's *Goldberg Variations*. He says that his

work with sentics has given him greater authority in his musical interpretations.

"It's puzzling how you can sometimes have a beautiful sound and
you don't know what it is that makes it that way, and then the next day
it is gone," he says sympathetically when I tell him about Marlene.
"What you experienced with the piano is real. People take tone for
granted. Tone is not simply the sum of a bunch of harmonics, but how
they are experienced through time.

"Science can't explain this experience to us, the quality of our feel-
ings, any more than science can tell us why some smells are good and
others bad, or what the redness of red is," the professor continues.
"These are qualia, inventions of nature. We could not invent them.
Our subjective experience is totally objective, it's actually the most
universal. But how we bring that experience to consciousness is a total
unknown. Science does not have even a clue."

I thank Dr. Clynes for his time, and ponder for a while my apparent dead end. If what I am trying to understand is a total unknown to
conventional Western science, then where next do I turn? Over dinner one night, I share my conundrum with friends. They suggest I take
a look at string theory and quantum physics. String theory is an
attempt to have a "theory of everything," a single idea, a master equation that would explain all the laws of the universe, from gravity to the
speed of light. String theory says that reality occurs in parallel dimensions made up entirely of vibrating strands of energy. These vibrations
are a cosmic symphony composing all of reality. This theory is not
testable, nor can it be observed.

But let's say for a moment that string theory is the explanation for
everything, including my experience of the piano I call Marlene. This
would mean that all physical reality—subnuclear, atomic, molecular,
macro—is vibratory. *Everything* oscillates between two states of rest,
like a pendulum, producing sound, some of it outside our range of
hearing. The earth itself has a fundamental frequency of 7.8 Hz as
measured from the electrostatic field between the earth's surface and
the ionosphere, and all the planets have keynotes. All vibrations, be
they sound, photon, electron, neutron, have harmonicity—and they
respond to stimuli. If all matter is vibrating fields of electromagnetic
energy, vibrating at innumerable frequencies, that includes us humans.

Then our bodies *must* be able to respond harmonically to the vibrational frequencies of a piano. And since between the poles of the two notes of an octave, there are an infinite number of frequencies, is it plausible that, as Carl Demler says, we each have our own individual frequency, like a tonal fingerprint? If a piano's unique frequency matches our own, wouldn't we resonate to it, like a crystal goblet vibrating to a soprano's high note? Wouldn't our physiology, our cellular structures, powerfully respond?

And if our bodies can respond harmonically to a *piano's* fundamental frequency, how are we affected, on a vibrational level, by other human beings? Can two individuals literally resonate to each other? Does this explain why we feel immediately at ease with some new acquaintances and uncomfortable with others? Perhaps some married couples become more alike over time because their vibrational frequencies become entrained with one another? When lovers argue, do their vibrations go out of phase? If you spend enough time with anyone, will your individual vibrations entrain with theirs?

I pose these questions to a friend who is a neuropsychologist, and he tells me new research has proven that this does indeed happen: scientists using EEG scans of the brain have documented entrainment between complete strangers meeting for the first time.

I begin reading about vibrational healing. Sound healers believe that we each have our own fundamental tone, and that disease results when we go out of phase with our own frequency. Their remedy is the application of pure Pythagorean intervals, like those in Michael Harrison's piano tuned in just intonation.

I think of some of the friends I have made on Piano World, people who have shared with me privately their own experience of being powerfully affected by the piano. One fell out of binge drinking and into piano playing when he heard Horowitz play Beethoven. Another abandoned his careful plan for suicide after driving past a piano shop and remembering his lifelong dream of playing one. He bought three pianos within twenty-four hours, then two more soon after, and taught himself to play. From that point forward, he wanted to live.

When Darrell and Heather Fandrich visited me, Heather, a former mental health counselor, observed that many of their customers who are most attuned to tone, for whom tone is of critical importance, came from highly dysfunctional families. Perhaps some of us use piano tone as a means of emotional self-healing?

If we conclude from sentics that music is a transducer of our emotions, communicating and amplifying them to an audience, can we also conclude that instruments themselves convey the emotions of those who built and prepared them? Can tunings? And can they heal us?

Music structures time, promoting order in the mind through repetition, whether listening to the repeated theme of a sonata or the repeated vibrations of a single chord. When congruent pure intervals are played, their vibrations are free to keep repeating their movements, and because we make sense of our world through the recognition that arises from repetition, this is deeply satisfying to us.

If consonant harmonic resonance—like the pleasurable harmonies of a barbershop quartet—entrains the vibrations of our cellular structures, does harmony perhaps make these structures more coherent, affecting our biologic and psychological health for the better? We do know, from a study at Massachusetts General Hospital, that dissonant and consonant sounds are processed very differently by the brain: dissonance stimulates anxiety, but consonance generates euphoria.

The intervals in the Schubert concert tuning are as close to consonance as it is possible to achieve in equal temperament. Perhaps the waveforms of this tuning, with its pure double octaves—and Marc's gift for creating pure unisons—resonate in our central nervous systems in a way that the nonperiodic, dissonant waveforms of a conventional piano tuning cannot?

Though these ideas and hypotheses are all new to me, I soon learn that many of them have been around since ancient times. Plato taught that the natural musical proportions of the overtone series describe the vibrations of man's inner nature, and therefore could be used to heal the soul. He defined these proportions using a line divided unequally, such that the relationship between the smaller section of the line and the larger section of the line is the same as the relationship between the larger section of the line and the entire line. The ratio for this relationship is 1:1.618034, also known as the Golden Section, the Divine Proportion, or the Golden Mean.

This ratio describes nature's own matrix of harmonic relationships, and the pure, natural overtones of the harmonic series are only one example. The Golden Section describes the chambers of a nautilus shell, the spiral of seeds in the head of a sunflower, the patterns tree branches make, and even the proportions of the human body: the distance from the foot to the navel, then the navel to the top of the head, and the way the seven layers of our heart muscle are nested together, for example, conform to this ratio. There are musical ratios in the spacing of the hairs on the organ of corti in the human ear, enabling them to resonate to particular frequencies of incoming sound energy. From the shape of galaxies in space, to the essentic form for love, to the structure of the DNA spiral, this proportion describes everything that is naturally harmonious. We live in a Golden Mean–proportioned world.

So it is not surprising that this proportion is the one most naturally pleasing to us. Since man's earliest civilizations, the Golden Section's proportion for width in relation to height has been a standard for buildings, windows, paintings, and picture frames. The Egyptians used it to build the pyramids. The ancient Greeks called it "God's own prescription for beauty," and the fifth-century architect Iktinos used it to design the Parthenon. In the Italian Renaissance, architects used it to design cathedrals like St. Mark's Basilica in Venice. Leonardo da Vinci used it to design the compositions of his paintings. Mozart, who was fascinated by numbers, reputedly used it to write his musical compositions, as did the twentieth-century composer Béla Bartók.

Both the modern grand piano and the pianoforte invented by Bartolomeo Cristofori in 1700, express approximate Golden Section ratios: the width of the treble section in proportion to the width of the bass, the width of the bass in proportion to the total width of the piano. The length of black keys in proportion to the length of white keys. The eight white keys of the octave in proportion to the five black keys. Chord patterns on the piano are full of Golden Section relationships. Fascination with the Golden Section was widespread and intense at the time of the piano's invention, but even if Cristofori had no intention of using the Golden Section, his intuitive feel for this proportion—an intuition we all possess—led him to follow it anyway.

The twentieth-century physicist and philosopher David Bohm spent his life seeking to understand the nature of reality. In his 1980 book *Wholeness and the Implicate Order,* he posits that music makes time's passage audible, and thus gives us a direct experience of reality.

In listening to the movement of individual notes played across time, yet making up a whole of the music, we experience the reality of one moment yielding to the next, to the next, to the next. The motion of the ever-present now becomes an immediate experience, something we can feel with every aspect of our beings. When we play or intently listen to music, we are brought fully into the present, into the unfolding of the now to the now to the now.

Bohm wrote of how ordinary reality is nothing more than static pictures on the screen of our minds, a distortion, a delusion that reality is unchanging, that the past and the future, which actually do not exist, are alive in the present. Music connects us to the "implicate order," the enfoldment of one moment into the next. We must release the notes that have just passed to be fully present with the notes that are being born. We *must* learn to be in the present.

This is the work music performs on us, leading our consciousness to a more perceptive state. The philosopher Hegel thought of music as an analogue of our inner lives—continuously flowing streams of sounds in relation to each other, moving through time.

Bohm's hypothesis makes me think of the days I've spent alone in the mountains, far from any trail, traversing difficult terrain, a heavy pack on my back. One wrong placement of my foot on the boulders and I could die. My attention is fully focused on my steps—first one, then another, then another, all unfolding to a destination. Just as one note follows another to create a work of music, footfall after footfall, my feet carry me through time to create a destination. Footfalls become my entire reality, so completely focused, by necessity, must my attention be. We experience this also in the movement of our breath followed by a breath followed by a breath, should we care to rest our attention on it, and the totality of our breaths is the narrative of our lives, our stories. Footfalls the whole of a journey. Notes the whole of a work of music. Breaths, the whole of our lives. All can be a direct experience of reality—the wholeness in the implicate order.

This seems to me a recipe for sanity in this delusional world. With our attention placed entirely on the unbroken movement of time unfolding, as it must be when we play the piano, our illusions of pain, loss, regret, and the past are shattered.

So far, I have more questions than answers, more theories and suppositions than real knowledge. What should I believe? How shall I make sense of what I have learned? I need to talk to someone who has thought deeply about these ideas, who can explain them to me. I telephone Marc to ask if he knows of anyone who is investigating the phenomenon of how tunings or pianos affect people. I can practically hear his eyebrows rise.

"This is open territory," he says. "How a piano might affect our vibrational energies?" He laughs. "It would take a convention of healers, physicists, physicians, mathematicians, piano technicians, musicians, philosophers all coming together to try to explain this phenomenon. It's a big, deep subject. I certainly don't know of any one interdisciplinary individual who has explored this."

Then Jerry Korten mentions an article in the current *New York Times* science section about a jazz drummer in Queens, New York, who is experimenting with healing human hearts by listening to their "melody," then composing music to correct arrhythmias. Milford Graves is a purveyor of "free jazz" who played with the New York Art Quartet back in the sixties, became a tenured professor of music at Bennington College in 1973, and then a martial arts master, acupuncturist, shaman, and herbalist. He received a Guggenheim Fellowship for his heart research. Well, I think, is this perhaps is an "interdisciplinary individual" who can explain my experience to me?

✦

I take the subway out to Parsons Boulevard, in the Jamaica section of Queens, on a brilliant spring day, and think through my questions carefully. It wasn't easy getting Milford Graves to agree to see me. The *New York Times* article has brought many people to his door, and on the phone Graves emphasized how much he prizes his research time, which he squeezes into the three days a week he is not at Bennington College. I will have to stay focused on what I most wish to know: How is it scientifically possible for music to heal a human heart? Do people have their own, unique frequencies that resonate to certain other frequencies? And most of all—can a piano be an instrument of healing? If so, how, exactly, does that happen?

A bus from the station takes me to a neighborhood of bodegas and 99-cent stores. South Jamaica seems sick with squalor and despair. I get off at the Santana Grocery and begin the long walk down several rough-looking blocks.

Graves's modest three-story home is easy to spot—it's nearly covered with fanciful mosaics made from shards of mirror, rocks, pebbles, pottery, and ceramic tiles. Graves's wife, Lois, opens the door and ushers me onto a tiny stair landing, midway between the kitchen and the basement. She calls down to the cavelike space below, announcing my arrival.

Graves swivels a quarter turn toward me in his purple suede desk chair, his corduroyed knees swinging side to side. "I have to shut something down that I can't have you see," he says. He swivels back to face the computer, where a circuitry diagram is on the screen. I use this as an opportunity to take a look around, and I find myself in the strangest laboratory.

A full human skeleton, covered in multicolored stickers and wires, stands in one corner. Large sheaves of dried herbs and African drums hang overhead from the house's floor joists. A mysterious apothecary—glass jars, bottles, and ceramic jugs holding various herbal concoctions—fills the shelves of an ancient-looking cabinet; some of the labels are in Chinese.

Audio speakers of all sizes and shapes are everywhere. A drum trap set with cymbals is painted in colorful, wild swirls; a carved African figure stands in the belly of the bass drum. EKG wires and leads festoon a green vinyl chair, and electronic monitors are strapped to its arms. On a side table, four stethoscopes are hooked into a computer processor. The chair looks as if it could give life.

But the most mysterious object in this fantastical lair is a plywood box sheathed in brass. Input and output jacks hang loosely from it. A drum is mounted on top, and acupuncture models—an ear, a hand, a human head, and a small, naked human figure—are also attached. This must be the device I read about in the *Times* article. According to the article, Graves listens to the heart rhythms of volunteers for extended periods of time, using his stethoscopes and sensors, which feed pulses into a computer. Software analyzes the data, and Graves focuses on the microrhythms within the electrocardiogram readouts. The computer converts the heartbeats to a higher register that can be heard over special speakers.

"A lot of it is like free jazz," Graves was quoted as saying. "There were rhythms I had only heard in Cuban and Nigerian music." The rhythms and pitches are made by muscle and valve movements in the four chambers of the heart. The pitches correspond to actual notes on a musical scale, and when they are raised several octaves, the sounds become melodic. "It sounds like four-part harmony," Graves said. "You can pinpoint what is wrong by the melody. You can hear something and say, 'Ah, it sounds like a problem in the right atrium.' "

If Graves hears an arrhythmia, he'll manipulate the rhythms on his computer or compose one on his drums, creating a counterrhythm that may nudge the heart back to a normal pattern. Then he puts the corrective rhythm into the volunteer's body, using speakers or acupuncture needles, or both. Graves can even burn a CD of the beat for the patient to listen to at home. According to Graves, this trains the heart to adopt a healthy beat.

Graves's computer screen now shows only the innocent blue desktop, and suddenly I find the professor's vivid, dark eyes gazing into mine.

"Now what can I do for you?" His voice is deep and gravelly, and a little impatient. He's wrapped loosely in a burgundy paisley shirt and pajama-like trousers. His hair fans out as if sparking with electricity. His graying goatee is heading toward Fu Manchu length. His right eyebrow seems raised in skepticism.

Sensing I could be evicted at any moment, I begin with my most important question. The jazzman leans back into his chair and crosses his arms. "I'm not trying to knock your instrument, but the piano has limitations," he says with a syncopation to his speech that sounds like he's rapping. "Drums are my thing. Yes, the piano can heal—any time you are drawn to something, you have similarities to that thing or to the people who created it—the person who tuned it, the person who built it. But the piano isn't biologically correct. What is in between those black and white keys there? I want to get in there. It's better to sing, so you can feel the note, and have an instrument you can sing with. If you want to expand your tonal imagination, the piano cannot travel with you."

Yes, I think, true. You can't intonate on a piano. I'll come at my question a different way.

"How, exactly, does music heal someone?" I ask.

Graves explains that sound waves push on the eardrum, which converts that mechanical movement to electrical energy, which becomes nerve impulses that become energy and movement in the body. "Music is a way of converting energy into nerve impulses, electrical and chemical activity in the body. Just like using an electric charge to revive someone having a heart attack, or giving them electrolytes intravenously to correct a chemical imbalance, or using a nine-volt battery to power a pacemaker. Electricity is what keeps us alive.

"That juice is heavy-duty stuff, man," says Graves. "A nine-volt battery is why someone exists! We make things so complicated, but this is simple stuff. We already have the most advanced technology in us. We're all wireless generators. Voodoo? It's misunderstood. It's wireless communication, it uses the electromagnetic energy in the air. We take in and put out energy. Our minds are amplifiers. Every human folk has had this experience: you think of someone and then they call you. It's all electromagnetic impulses.

"What is this electrical activity or movement in the body? It's *prana, qi,* a lot of African Americans call it *soul.* It's a feeling, it can be conveyed by touch, it's pressure converted to electrical energy. Music is a way of doing that. You can call it spirit, God, it's the electrical activity we need in the body."

Graves says his interest in healing through music began in the dance halls of Jamaica, or "Soulville," as he calls his birthplace. People who were sick reported to him that they felt physically better after his performances, and Graves became fascinated by the effects of music on human physiology.

Now when he performs, he listens first for the fundamental tone of the audience—the sound it makes with its talking and laughter. He says the frequencies of individuals are the harmonics of the crowd's fundamental tone. "Once I get that fundamental, the rest falls into place." Graves will then use that sound as a beginning reference point for his improvisations. He'll reinforce that initial vibration if it is positive, or shift it if he senses that something is out of balance or unhealthy. Through his music he projects positive emotion to his audience, intending to shift them into "an open state of relaxed focus."

"A musician has to be a good person," Graves says. "You tell your story through an instrument. People vibrate, and they vibrate differently. Next time you are in a crowd, you listen for what I'm talking about."

So do we each have our own frequency?

"We have a full spectrum of frequencies. We have to watch how we treat our frequencies. What we imagine, ingest, taste—we have a lot more to learn about biochemistry. We do things that don't let us grow, like watch degraded stuff on TV, eat depleted food, listen to music with a 'heavy' frequency. We don't vibrate like no sine wave. The way we vibrate is *deep*. We have to understand what biological waves are all about."

I tell Graves about my first encounter with Marlene, how I resonated deeply to her, how I fell hard for her. What was it I experienced?

"You experienced the intention of every person who ever worked on that piano," he says. "The person who tuned it, the person who built it. That piano carries their intentions. Intention is everything."

✦

On the train back into Manhattan, the doors open at the Forest Hills station and a gaggle of schoolgirls come aboard, giggling, burbling with good cheer and excitement, making a tremendous racket in the confines of the subway car. Suddenly I remember Graves's imperative to listen for a crowd's frequency. Can I hear the frequency of these fifteen-year-old girls in their school uniforms? High and sweet. Bright yellow, very sunny. Definitely a major key. C-sharp? Yes, I am pretty sure this group's sound is in the key of C-sharp major.

Amazing. I start to listen to the frequencies of everything around me—the clacking on the subway train rails, the rushing roar of crowds surging from the station. I remember sitting by a creek near my home, and realize that the noise of a rushing stream has a fundamental pitch. A new world of perception opens. My reading and thinking begin to crystallize.

When we talk about the "vibe" someone gives off, we are being literalists—vibration *is* what we are experiencing. Why do we inexplicably gravitate to certain people and are repelled by others? We respond to each others' emotional frequencies, whether they mesh well with our own or clash with them.

I now realize I have already experienced what Graves does during his performances: I have consciously put myself in a positive, calm, open frame of mind, and persisted in it, only to see others shift their inner states in response to mine. They become calm when they were agitated, open when they were closed. This phenomenon feels like giving a gift.

If our emotions have universally understood frequencies, if music is a transducer of our emotions, and if our physical bodies respond to emotion expressed through music, resonating like soundboards, then when we listen to music our very cells must entrain with the pulses of the musician's intention. And when we play the piano, we experience the emotional vibration of what was done to that piano, first and foremost the tuning. The Schubert concert tuning is a transmitter of Szott's intention—kindness and humanity—as interpreted and expressed by Marc. The tuning is an emotional gesture of the tuner.

But how is it possible that the *piano itself* carries intention? Is there something in the Grotrian—its scale design, its belly, the tree it was born of—that expresses emotion? There is the sensibility of its designer through the design, certainly. What about the soundboard maker? The bellyman? How is it possible that their intentions, their emotions were carried across the sea to me in the body of a piano? What about the forest where the tree was born, the forester who chose the tree, the logger who cut it? What about the mill workers who sawed the tree, the steel workers who forged the plate, the voicer who put the finishing touches on Marlene before she left the loading dock for America? Did I experience their intentions, too? Does Graves mean this in some literal way? Or metaphorically? And if what he says is true, are these people my fellow travelers and kindred spirits?

Who are they?

24

Braunschweig

"Boys, build good pianos and the rest will take care of itself."

—GROTRIAN-STEINWEG FACTORY MOTTO

Martin Walter dances between three sawhorses in his work station. Each supports an inner rim, the laminated wood frame of a grand piano. Martin swiftly brushes glue onto the top edge of one rim, then clamps a soundboard to it. Grappling a chain and pulley, he lowers a cast-iron plate onto the second rim, then measures the string bearing. His long body is nearly horizontal as he reaches across the plate to pencil a guideline onto the bass bridge for his planer. Into the top edge of the third rim, he routs grooves to receive a soundboard's ribs. All the while, Martin's eyes stare intently through his glasses, his mouth set in pursed concentration, his every movement elegant and precise.

Martin doesn't speak English, and I don't speak German; we have help for that, when we need it. But even without language, he communicates much in the fluidity of his long, pale limbs, in the way his mouth curls into a sly smile, and in his eyes, shining with the joy of mastery. He's boyish: an adolescent's outsized arms, tousled, dark hair, dimples bedded in a nascent stubble, an air of rebellion. But Martin Walter also carries in his gestures a sense of purpose. At twenty-seven, he is already a fine bellyman, consistently bringing forth beauty into the world. Watching him work, I am awed and envious of his sureness, his balletic, insouciant grace among the sawhorses, his obvious, radiant pride in what he does.

"I have this job so deeply in my mind, I could do it blind," he says, a happy smirk on his face.

Martin arrived at the Grotrian-Steinweg piano factory for a three-and-a-half-year apprenticeship when he was seventeen, and he has been here ever since. I arrived at eight o'clock this morning, when I left my hotel and walked across the Braunschweig suburb of Veltenhof to begin my week's stay at Marlene's birthplace.

◆

On the overnight flight from New York to Frankfurt, I slept fitfully, curled up in a coach seat. In the morning, I took the Deutsche Bahn train north. The view of the countryside was lush and velvety in the rain; the leaves unfurled their new spring garments before my window, soothing my tired eyes.

At the Braunschweig station, in my exhaustion, I didn't see anyone looking for me on the platform, so I took a cab to my hotel. Once inside my sparsely furnished room, I collapsed onto the duvet of the twin bed, but then the phone rang. Burkhard Stein, the managing director of Grotrian-Steinweg, had been worried. Did I not see him waiting for me on the train platform, holding up his little "Grotrian" sign?

No matter, he was on his way to take me to dinner.

◆

The Grotrian-Steinweg piano factory is in Lower Saxony, just east of Hanover, in a low modern building nestled beside Autobahn 2, where lorries and cars travel on their way to and from the East—Berlin, the Czech Republic, Slovakia, Poland, Russia. Until 1990, this section of the autobahn was silent, empty. The border with the German Democratic Republic, just a few miles away, was closed and heavily guarded. Since Reunification, 250,000 vehicles a day roar by.

Germany is to piano building what New York is to publishing, the stock market, or theater. Twelve German piano makers and eighteen manufacturers of piano components vie with each other in the world market at the highest possible standard of performance and workmanship. Most of these companies were established in the nineteenth century.

✦

Wood shavings fly through sunbeams pouring down from skylights. Voices echo. Strings snarl to life. Hammers clang, brass on brass. Copper wire whirs 'round steel. Pneumatic air and steam guns hiss. Band saws roar. Fresh sawdust on the concrete floor.

Slowly my eyes and ears adjust to the particulars of where I am. The entire workshop is about eighty yards long by seventy-five yards wide, and divided into staging areas for each step of the piano-making process. Overhead rails run the length and width of the workshop, dangling chains and pulleys for transporting heavy equipment and piano plates. Beyond a Mylar curtain is the carpentry shop where piano case parts are prepared. Massive accordioned hoses siphon sawdust from computer-controlled planers, sanders, and polishers, carrying it for fuel to the plant's boiler. Long beards of glue, dried into stalactites, hang from sawhorses. Air hoses move about on dollies. Strange machines designed and built on-site for soundboard crowning, string winding, and rim pressing surprise me with their exotic, mystifying shapes.

My tour guide is Burkhard Kaemmerling, a *Klavierbaumeister*—a registered master piano maker—and the son of a well-known professor of piano at the University of Hanover and the Salzburg Mozarteum. "I had to practice *a lot*," he says with a roll of his eyes as we march into the main factory workshop.

Kaemmerling, thirty-six, is Grotrian's European distribution manager and master technician, and since his English is as flawless as his understanding of how pianos are made, he is a perfect facilitator of my quest to understand the nature of Marlene's magic.

"This is Herbert Solarski," says Kaemmerling, and we pause so he can shake the woodworker's hand. "He did the lid and case for your piano." Solarski runs a machine with a long belt carrying flat case parts through a polisher. The black, patent-shiny panels for uprights arrive at the far end to a woman who stacks them. Herbert smiles kindly at me. He doesn't speak English. No one here does except the managers.

A young woman, an apprentice wearing protective ear cuffs, winds piano wire onto pins near the stringing station, but most of the workers are men. Most have a few days' growth of beard, some are rather shaggy-haired, and they dress casually in jeans and T-shirts. Kaemmerling, though, is a manager. He is clean shaven, his hair is carefully cut, his posture is perfect, and he wears a neatly pressed oxford-cloth dress shirt. He shakes the hand of every worker we meet. Shaking hands before having a conversation, even if you've already greeted each other that day, is the custom.

Eckhard, a worker with a long Santa Claus beard, cuts a huge sheet of laminated wood into the shape of treble bridges. He does this freehand, on a band saw. He lines up all the bridges and cuts off their ends together, then sets them in a stack to await the drill press.

Waldemar polishes grand piano cases, using a wax-coated flannel wheel spinning at the end of an electric drill.

Another worker strikes nickel-covered steel pins into a bass bridge with a soft copper mallet. "It's very difficult to hit the pins accurately," says Kaemmerling. "We have only two people here who are allowed to do it."

Out on the loading dock, where wood, wire, felt, and iron arrive, and pianos depart, Uwe Gille, the loading dock master, packs up three grand pianos headed for a conservatory in Zagreb. He wraps them in Styrofoam and styrene-lined cardboard, covers their legs and lyres with sheets of Bubble Wrap. Work stops at the factory at 2:40 p.m., Kaemmerling says, but Gille often works past five o'clock. Especially on Wednesdays and Thursdays. Thursdays are shipping days, when the trucks arrive to pick up pianos and carry them anywhere from Greece to Norway. This week will be an exceptionally busy one at the factory, as five concert grands are scheduled to ship. Grotrian produces only twenty concert grands in an entire year, and they take more than eight months to produce. Some have gone to La Scala, the Sydney Opera House, and the Bolshoi Theater in Moscow.

On a typical weekday, the workshop's thirty-eight production workers arrive at 6:20 a.m., work until nine, when they have breakfast in the company break room until 9:20, work until lunch at 12:30, then resume work from one p.m. until they leave at 2:40. Once a week they have a planning meeting. "Management is not invited," says Kaemmerling. "They organize themselves."

A call comes in on Kaemmerling's cell phone—the managers communicate with each other inside the factory in this way—he's wanted in the office. He drops me off in the factory showroom, where I can watch a video on the history of the company.

The showroom walls are covered with enormous gilt-framed oil portraits of the company's owners, beginning with Friedrich Grotrian, and continuing forward through five generations of Grotrians. Friedrich Grotrian was a Moscow music shop owner and piano builder who returned home to his native Braunschweig in the 1850s to manage a large inheritance. There he met and became partners with one Theodor Steinweg, who owned a piano factory founded by his father, Heinrich Engelhard Steinweg. The elder Steinweg built his first piano in 1835, in his kitchen in Seesen, near the Harz Mountains. In 1851, Heinrich emigrated from Braunschweig to New York, where he changed his name to Henry Steinway and established Steinway pianos. In 1865, Theodor left Braunschweig for New York to join his father, and sold the Steinweg family's interest in the Grotrian-Steinweg piano factory to the Grotrians.

A fight over the Steinweg name began in 1895 and continued for decades. Steinway sued to prevent the Grotrian family from using the name Steinweg on their pianos, but lost. In 1919, the Grotrian family changed its name to Grotrian-Steinweg to protect their ownership of the name, but failed to register the trademark in the United States. When, in the 1960s, Knut Grotrian-Steinweg made a deal with Wurlitzer to sell Grotrian-Steinweg pianos in America, Steinway found out and took the company to court in New York. A long battle ensued, and ultimately, Grotrian lost. In the ruling on the final appeal, the New York Supreme Court decided that in the United States only, Grotrian-Steinweg may not reveal that Henry Steinway founded their company, nor may they use the Steinweg name on the fallboard of their pianos. Since 1977, any Grotrian-Steinweg pianos to be sold by authorized dealers in the United States may have only the name "Grotrian" on them.

In 2000, the year my piano was built in this factory, Burkhard Stein became the first managing director in the company's history who was not a member of the Grotrian family. He and Kaemmerling are new blood, a younger, more entrepreneurial generation, trained in business as well as piano technology and design. Though the market has been getting smaller for pianos overall, with intense competition from the Chinese, the new management team streamlined production and reduced costs by giving each worker five or six jobs to do and demanding greater accountability. Grotrian's grand piano production increased 23 percent in 2005, and the company now builds ten percent of Germany's pianos. They say they are intent on increasing their market share in America as well.

"We have a saying here," says Kaemmerling, when he returns and I ask him about the company's prospects in an ever-more competitive global market. "If you see a donkey who is running, don't hit him— let him run." It's a phrase they use as a reminder to let good workers do their jobs, but it could just as easily be applied to the Burkhards Stein and Kaemmerling themselves.

"Take all the pictures you want," says Kaemmerling, as we return to the workshop. "We don't mind. You can't take a picture of what is in here." He taps the side of his head and flashes an engaging grin.

I can see for myself there is a good deal more to piano building than I can learn in a day, a week, or capture in hundreds of pictures. A good deal more than I can explain in a few paragraphs, or even a whole book devoted to nothing but piano building. "Some things not even the top technicians know," Kaemmerling says.

As I look about the workshop, what I don't know makes what I do know seem puny, laughable. What I don't know is an unimaginably vast territory I may never entirely grasp. So I must be discriminating, selective, and efficient about what I try to learn in a week. But I keep taking notes and pictures. Somewhere, here, in this factory, with these workers, is the key to Marlene's magic.

The tour begins in earnest.

◆

Everything in a piano is built around the geometry of the cast-iron plate, Kaemmerling explains. Though Grotrian's grand piano plates are cast, prebored, and shaped by computer using Grotrian specifications, no two are exactly the same. The molten iron cools in its sand cast unevenly, with the part of the plate that is coolest shrinking faster than the warmer areas. This creates uneven tension in the iron, so all plates have a very slight warp in them, and the contour of that warp is unique to each plate. To account for the plate's warp, the rim, soundboard, pinblock, bridges—all the wood components of the belly—must be built around one plate, and all components are given a production number identifying them as belonging to that plate.

Marc Wienert told me he believes that the soul of the piano resides in the plate, not the soundboard, since when old grand pianos are fully rebuilt, only the plate and the case are saved from the original piano. If indeed the shape of each plate is unique, and all else is built from that starting point, it does suggest a plausible explanation for why the unique sound of each piano might be traced to the unique warp of its plate.

Hans Lorenz, who has been at the factory since 1979, uncrates the plates when they arrive from Springfield, Ohio, where the O. S. Kelly Company, a division of Steinway, makes grand piano plates for Grotrian. By the time they arrive, the matte black plates have been allowed to cure for several months. Lorenz inspects, fills, and sands the plates before they enter the production stream, using a pencil-size belt sander to grind down irregularities, and his hands and eyes to judge if every part of the plate meets Grotrian's standards.

Lorenz also helps Martin Walter make grand piano rims, a process requiring at least two people. For the inner rim, twenty-seven single sheets of one-eighth-inch-thick red beech and birch are laminated together in a rim press. The sheets are nearly two feet wide and almost sixteen feet long for the Cabinet grand. The heartwood of these trees is known for its flexibility and durability.

Martin and Hans lay the first sheet of wood on a long gluing table. Martin mixes water with glue powder in a bucket, then pours the mixture into the reservoir of a hand roller. Working quickly, he rolls the glue onto the first sheet, then pulls another sheet down and lays it on top, then glues that one, then lays down another sheet—until the sheets are stacked up like a layer cake. Because the grain of the outer layers runs lengthwise, the sheets are very flexible, and when Martin and Hans each pick up an end, the whole body of the multiple laminations hangs limp between them, like a giant piece of fettuccine.

With the fettuccine suspended just barely above the floor, the men grapple it over to the electric rim press. The press looks like a low piano-shaped table; it is fitted with an aluminum form that gets very hot. The men wrap the laminations around the tail end of the form and clamp them on. Then they turn on the power, and the form, running on a rail, carries the laminations forward into a piano-shaped recess. When the form meets the recess, a hydraulic lock clamps the two shapes tightly together, exerting an even pressure of six tons and heating the wood and glue to 203 degrees Fahrenheit. The boiling glue becomes moldable as it cools. When it is hard, it is one-sixth of the weight of the rim, acoustically inert, and impervious to water, keeping the piano's case stable in the most humid of conditions.

When a new inner rim arrives at Martin Walter's station, first he cuts into the rim's interior wall, creating recesses for solid pine braces, two inches thick each. These braces fit snugly against the rim in a star pattern, stabilizing the piano's shape, so that tuning, regulation, and moving cannot distort it.

Now the rim is ready for bellymaking, the creation of the acoustic box—the architectural foundation of the piano's tone. Martin fits together the soundboard, bridges, pinblock, and plate in an interconnected series of relationships that give the piano its unique character.

◆

When Martin was fourteen, he saw a film about piano building at his school's job center and decided to break with his family's tradition. They had always been bakers.

"At first my parents were shocked, but after a while they got used to the idea, and even thought better of it," says Martin as he clamps a soundboard to a rim. "In my opinion, it's a special job, a rare job. In Germany, it's one of the most prestigious jobs you can find. And in the end, when I passed my exams, they were very proud of me." He wipes his brow, rolls his eyes, and sighs heavily, pantomiming his relief. He's full of comic gestures—a character.

When Martin is at work, he exudes a white-hot kinetic energy. I ask him if he loves his work.

"Absolutely! I'm a fanatic." He flashes an impish grin. "A piano is not just a machine—it's a product of art. It's more than furniture, or a car to drive. No two instruments are the same. Each one has its own character."

"Where does the character come from?"

"It's like the character of wine—where does that come from? It's the same as describing the soul of a person." He looks at me like how could I ask such an obvious question.

"But *why* are they different from each other?"

"That's a very good question. It's the connection between different materials—spruce, copper, red beech, wool. No tree grows like the next tree. Especially the felt of the hammer heads is different. And then there is the difference of the workers. Every worker has their opinions and their experiences that they add. It's a puzzle of different materials, different workers' personalities, and this makes up the puzzle of the piano's character."

As I watch Martin craft that character, it seems to me the transmission of one's intention into the piano is something quite ordinary. Intention is the personality of the builder within the parameters of the design and materials. Think of the piano as a poem. The piano designer is the poet who supplies the words. The materials are pen, ink, and paper. The bellyman is the scribe who manifests the poem in his own hand. And no two people have the same handwriting.

Martin fits a red-painted template to another rim to mark the exact placement for the soundboard. Working with templates is an old German tradition, a way of reducing tolerances and increasing consistency. Grotrian's production patterns were made from the original piano design prototypes and cover virtually every step of the piano making process. Twice yearly, they are checked against the originals to make certain their dimensions have not changed. "One drop of glue can change a measurement by two millimeters," says Kaemmerling. "That is a whole universe in piano making."

"It's a tower," says Martin, as he marks the soundboard placement carefully with T-shaped pins. "One part is built upon the other. Every instrument is a new puzzle, and you have to start from the beginning again. How do you fit all the pieces together? That is what grabs me."

Martin's is a young man's job—a bellyman has to be able to carry more than two hundred pounds—or you have to be a "sporty person," says Martin. "All my teachers say to lift with my knees and I won't have problems." But Martin wants to do more. "I want to know all the steps, not just a part. I want to know the whole piano."

His great ambition is to become a *Klavierbaumeister,* like Kaemmerling, to go to the famed Oskar-Walker-Schule in Ludwigsburg. But it will be difficult for him to pursue this goal for now—there is no one else at the factory who can do his job.

I ask Kaemmerling about the school, which is near Stuttgart. The program is full-time, one year, and before you can attend you must have completed a three-year apprenticeship at a factory, then another three years working with a registered master. Students study physics, finance, and pedagogy—so they can educate their apprentices. They must take a ten-hour written test and a seventy-plus-hour practical test, where they turn a shell of a broken-down piano into a playable instrument.

"The tuition is free, if you qualify," says Kaemmerling. "You have to provide your own tools and materials and pay your room and board. The question is, do you want to be a worker? Or do you want to join the master class?" He repeats this question in German, and smiles encouragingly at Martin.

Martin already knows the answer. He wants to work for himself, he says, and establish his own shop. But right now his salary is needed to help his family, and he can't save for school. "I am eating only white bread to save money," he says with a melodramatic sigh.

◆

When the bellyman has taken his measurements from the cast-iron plate, it goes to a spraying room for painting. The spraying room amazes me. One entire wall is a waterfall, rushing down and running below the floor, under an open grating, a river under the worker's feet. The worker wears a white protective jumpsuit over his clothes, but he hardly has a spot of paint on it. He doesn't wear a mask. As he sprays a fine mist of gold polyurethane from an air pressure pistol, a fan blows air down from a porous fabric ceiling, forcing the paint particles to the floor. They fall through the open grate, into the rushing water, and the water washes them away through a filter, then returns to the waterfall. A toxic waste company collects the residue from the spraying rooms twice a year.

"The environmental laws in Germany are very, very strict," Kaemmerling explains. "This technology cost us five hundred thousand euro. You can't even smell any fumes." It's true. I can't. I think of Marc and his colleagues huffing fumes in New York. This system could save their health.

After the plate is painted, Georgios Sotirelis, a Greek from Athens who has been with Grotrian for thirty-three years, bolts it to the inner rim, glues on red felt strips for the strings to rest on, and drills holes into the pinblock for the tuning pins, using a drill press that moves on a robotic arm. He installs a half round of brass, called a crossbar, just before the string hitch pins, as a termination point for the strings. This crossbar is a critical component of the Grotrian scale design.

A scale design is a composite of many, many small and large choices: how the bridge is pinned, how the ribs are notched, how the sound-board is crowned, just for starters. The totality of these choices expresses the maker's piano tone philosophy. For Grotrian, that philosophy is for a more brilliant tone with lots of colorful harmonics in the treble.

"We want clarity in the tone, so we have short, thick strings under high tension," Kaemmerling explains. This combination requires a stiffer soundboard, with denser annular rings. "A very high crown with high tension in the soundboard and very low downbearing on the bridge creates greater sustain. We want a more powerful tone, with more and higher partials."

Between the brass crossbar and the hitch pins is a section of string that vibrates at a different frequency than the note for the string. When the whole piano is strung, all the strings vibrate at these alternate frequencies creating what Grotrian calls a "mixture scale."

"The mixture scale is like a universal voicing," says Kaemmerling. "It influences the sound, but it itself does not have a special tone. It is a colorful noise, created by various lengths of string parts that cannot be tuned. The different lengths of string cause various small reflections. This adds a background of noise to the clarity of the treble, giving it a more colorful character."

He strums these string sections so I can hear their harmonics. I recognize the sound: This is the tone cloud that blooms up from Marlene's belly. This is the sound of her soul, whispering to me.

The scale design is behind the magic—it is calculated and quantifiable.

◆

We move on to the action department, where Andreas Schecke is installing a damper action, the most challenging part of piano building. While building a Grotrian piano always begins with the cast-iron

plate, all the minute calculations that flow from the plate end with the
dampers. The dampers must absorb any inconsistencies from all the
other components, and the adjustments are very difficult. "You have
to be very accurate," Schecke says. "If you are off by only a quarter of
a millimeter . . . The precision is most difficult."

Dampers are pieces of wool felt that rest on top of the piano
strings and quiet them when a key is released. They move up and
down on a wire, and each wire is bent by hand. "It is really hard to do
it right," says Kaemmerling. "There is no template to guide him."

"You need good control of your fingers, good eyes, good ears," says
Schecke. "There are people who seem to be made for installing
dampers. Others can do it for years and won't get it. Most of all, you
must love the instrument." As he talks, the top of Schecke's shiny egg-
shaped head rises and falls from behind the case of a grand piano, where
he sits on a wooden chair laid on its side before the open keybed.

"We call him 'the rising moon'," Kaemmerling chuckles. "That's
all you can see when you walk by, is his bald head."

Andreas Schecke was born in the Harz Mountains in Wiebenburg,
about thirty miles from Braunschweig. Everyone in his family played
accordion, and it was his own first instrument. But he'd always wanted
to learn piano, and at age fifteen his family gave him the piano lessons
he'd been begging for. His father worked for the railway, but his parents wanted him to have a career in music, so he went to an instru-
ment-maker's school for three years, then apprenticed at Grotrian. He's
been here thirty-three years. "It's my life," he says. "I'm married to
Grotrian."

Schecke says you need good ears to work on a piano action
because then you can hear if just one string isn't damped, or if the
strings aren't level. You can hear if the pitches of the wooden hammer
shanks are not in the right order—Grotrian puts shanks with lower
pitches in the high treble, so they'll make less noise.

"You have to go deep into the details. You need perfectionism.
When I do something, it must be done right. I can't stand half-done
things."

Schecke trades the chair for a swivel stool and sits before a grand
piano action on a worktable. He tests the hammer travel by gently
pressing a key at a time, then he flips back hammers that are not per-

pendicular or not evenly spaced. He heats their shanks with a small brass alcohol lamp that looks as if it should have a genie in it. The alcohol flame is clean and won't blacken the wood of the shank. He bends them into their correct position, judging by eye and by feel.

"The best feeling you get is when you press down a key and it is right. Everything runs like it should, and it all plays wonderful." Schecke doesn't look up as he talks, but he speaks evenly. His affect is one of calm solidity. He's dressed simply, in a black T-shirt and green khakis. His glasses hang down on his nose. His lower lip juts forward with concentration. "When people ask me what I do, and I say 'I am a piano builder,' they say 'Wow!' "

Schecke also prepares pianos for concerts. "If the pianist thanks me afterward, it makes my heart beat faster," he says, pausing to put a fist on his chest. "It's a reason to continue."

"What should pianists understand about your work?" I ask.

Schecke pauses. He must stop to think. "That's difficult to say. It should be the other way around. The pianist tells us what should be done a better way."

◆

The next day the weather is cool and rainy again. I bundle up in my warmest clothes for the short walk to the factory.

Kaemmerling greets me in high spirits. He has found a way to cross the language barrier—we've been having a bit of trouble translating piano parts from German to English. "Look at this!" he says.

He hands me a large workbook called *Piano Nomenclature*. Inside, every part of the piano is named in six languages. Together we consult it for the words we did not know yesterday. Trying to communicate clearly has been challenging. For example, "lacquer" is used to describe everything from paint to polyester to, well, lacquer. There is only one word for all of them in German—*Lack*. And deciphering if the cast-iron plates are sand cast or vacuum cast (sand cast), or if the string scale design is a duplex or not (not), hasn't been easy, either.

Armed with our dictionary, we head back to the action department, where nomenclature was the most troublesome. Schecke is not there, but a number of piano actions in varying stages of assembly are. One of them, I see, has the initials "M. M." written in pencil on the stack. I recognize this signature at once from my own piano. Who is M. M.? I ask Kaemmerling.

"That's Maik Müller. He's away now, joining the technician master class."

There are initials and signatures written all over all the actions. "Everyone who works on them signs them," Kaemmerling explains. "It's the company's inner hieroglyphics."

"Who else worked on my piano?"

"We know exactly who," says Kaemmerling. "We have a file on every single piano ever made by Grotrian. It is confidential, of course."

"May I see it?"

Kaemmerling smiles and tilts his head. He isn't sure. This isn't public information. But after lunch, he presents me Marlene's file with a flourish. He got permission.

MARLENE'S BIOGRAPHY

In the year 2000, the Grotrian-Steinweg Company built 130 grand pianos. Eighty of them were Cabinet grands, and one of those, born in October, was Marlene.

Her production number was 856.

Her plate was cast in Springfield, Ohio, on October 5, 1999.

Hans Lorenz polished and prepared her plate.

Martin Walter built her belly.

Georgios Sotirelis mounted her plate and strung her.

Burkhard Kaemmerling built her action and installed it, tuned her, and prevoiced her hammers.

Andreas Schecke did the finish regulation.

Rolf Bosse did the finish voicing.

Burkhard Stein did the final inspection. The problems he found were very minor—the lock to the fallboard didn't lock, a bit of action adjustment was needed, the pedal was noisy. Schecke corrected them.

So the only person who worked on my piano whom I have not yet met—of those workers who are here—is Herr Bosse. The voicer.

And perhaps he is the person whose work I need to see, whose "intention" I would like to experience, most of all.

◆

Rolf Bosse's workshop is a soundproof, windowless room, lit by a skylight. Today he is at work on a baby grand going to the German ambassador in Kyrgystan. He plays up and down the scale very rapidly with just his middle finger. A piece of chalk in his left hand marks notes that need work. A too-harsh note gets a vertical chalk mark on the back of the key. A too-soft note gets a horizontal line. Then he pulls the action out and needles the felt to soften it, or sands it to brighten the tone. He polishes all the hammers, as a group, with a velvety black carbide paper. This smoothes the wool fibers, giving the tone its characteristic sparkle.

Bosse has been with Grotrian since he was fifteen years old. He began his apprenticeship in 1959. "I thought it would be nice, clean, and interesting work," he says.

Voicing—called *Intonation* or "tone regulation" here—has been primarily Bosse's responsibility at Grotrian for thirty-five years now. Ninety percent of the grand pianos produced by Grotrian are voiced by Rolf Bosse.

I am all attention—seeing what Herr Bosse does could be critical to my future relationship with Marlene. I need this knowledge for the hammers Carl will send me.

No one in this country knows how to voice those hammers, I remember Wally Brooks, the U.S. Abel hammer representative, said to me.

Nobody can voice those hammers like they do in the factory in Germany, Darrell Fandrich told me.

Now I am here. I can see for myself. I take lots of pictures and notes. I will explain every bit of the factory voicing to Tom when I get home.

Bosse is mostly silent as he works. He's stout and square-headed, with a bulldog's jowls, pug-nosed, a rough pelt of short, graying hair, and a brushy mustache. His plaid dress shirt is rolled up at the sleeves. His tired eyes stay on his work.

I ask if he ever uses chemicals on the hammers.

"If needed, we use whatever works," Kaemmerling says. "Ironing, plastic keytops dissolved in acetone. Sometimes we use Styrofoam dissolved in lacquer thinner—it stays elastic and keeps a good dynamic range."

Bosse shows me the iron—a brass spatula he heats with an alcohol lamp, then touches to the strike points. He runs his sensitive hands around the shapes of the hammers.

"Grotrian needs an egg-shaped hammer," he explains. "You want continuous fibers all around the shape. And always voice with three needles. And always shape the hammers as a group, making the tops absolutely equal."

The hammers arrive very hard and need to be "opened up" to get a range of tone. The shoulders are needled because this is where the wool gets the most tightly compressed in the caul when the hammers are made. The first voicing might involve stabbing both shoulders of each hammer sixty to eighty times. Then the action is put in the piano, the piano is played, and the action is pulled and the hammers are needled again. Bosse might remove and replace the action more than twenty times in a voicing session.

Bosse began to learn voicing when he had been at Grotrian eight years. "From the old ones who did this for years and years." He points to a black-and-white photograph pinned to the wall. There is a young Bosse posed beside his elderly teacher, both of them in work aprons, surrounded by a gaggle of eager-faced apprentices. His main teacher was a Herr Feuerhahn, Grotrian's voicer in the mid-twentieth century. "He spent his whole life here as a voicer."

"One must be very, very sensitive to be a voicer," Bosse says. "You must be very critical against yourself and your own work. You need a gift, an ear for what pianists want, and the talent to achieve it. Nobody can really explain to you how to listen."

"How would you describe your ideal piano tone?" I ask.

"Very difficult to describe tone," Bosse says, as he polishes the hammers. "The most important thing is to have a huge dynamic range. You want clarity in the pianissimo, and power in the fortissimo. You can't really make it happen. It's a knack. If I get the right tone, I just got lucky. I'm just happy it happened."

He wipes the chalk marks from the backs of the keys with a square of chamois skin, then levels some strings to the hammers using a bent piece of steel with a hook on the end of it. He says he never shapes the hammers to the strings.

He checks each note again: three quick strokes of his middle finger for each key, fast and mezzo forte. He pulls the action again and taps on one hammer head with a wooden shank. The shanks are out of order—the pitch of one is too high for the treble section. Bosse marks that one with an X. It will have to be changed. I ask him how he knew that.

"I just listen to the piano and I know how it should sound. You can only learn by doing. I show my apprentices how to work, and control and control and control them."

Bosse shows me how he needles the hammers as a group, keeping the needle points away from the strike point by guarding it with his thumb. Using one's thumb as a guide looks very dangerous to me. Quite a bit of blood must have been shed in this room over the years.

He slips the action back in and plays "Somewhere Over the Rainbow" to test the tone. The bass rings a bit. The higher treble is still too bright. Bosse finds the offending notes quickly, marks them, needles them, polishes them. His carbide paper strip fits exactly over three hammers at once. I pick up a piece and turn it over. Six hundred grit. I write it down.

Kaemmerling, noticing my detailed note taking, picks up a loose bass hammer and draws on its sides with a pen, making radiant lines from the molding to the shoulders. "This is where you needle, at this angle," he says. Then he gives me the hammer to keep.

"It's important for a voicer to play the piano," Bosse says. "It takes more than having talent or a feeling for tone."

Kaemmerling, who grew up playing the piano, heartily agrees. "Growing up with music develops the ear. This is most important. But most important to being a voicer is being able to tune. It is impossible to get an idea of the tone on a mistuned piano. It must be an absolutely clean tuning. The unisons have to be clean."

Everyone at Grotrian tunes only by ear, he tells me. The problem with tuning machines, he says, is that there is more than one way to tune a piano. Some want a more mellow sound. Others want a wider stretch. You listen to how the pianist plays, what he plays, what he says he wants. And you must understand how strings behave, how to get equal tension in the whole string. Your ears have to be good enough to hear if the tuning is stable. "Otherwise, it's like there is a cat in the string," Kaemmerling says. "Meow. Meow." He laughs.

Bosse says he is only two years from retirement now.

"Five years!" Kaemmerling argues.

Bosse just smiles to himself. "We shall see."

What does he love most about being a voicer? I ask.

"I love the tone of the piano," he says. "There's a 'sound picture,' the form and character of a grand piano sound. I love when the tone is close to finished. You can hear the sound coming together—this is the most exciting thing. And when the pianists come and say it is beautiful. This is very satisfying.

"But sometimes you finish your work, and you think it's excellent, and someone else doesn't agree. And you have to just deal with it. That's the hardest part." He shrugs. "You can always find imperfections."

I tell Bosse about Marlene, how I fell so hard for her. Why, I ask him, do we respond so powerfully to certain pianos?

"There are lots of things you could not explain," he says in German, his eyes rising from his work to meet mine at last. "Not even if you speak the same language."

✦

On my last full day at the factory, the other Burkhard, Herr Stein, Grotrian's managing director, takes me under his wing. Early that morning, while he attends to some details in the office, I wander back into the showroom, sit before one of three Cabinet grands, and play my Chopin waltz. This piano is very brilliant, much more so than any other Grotrian I have played. I try the other two. One has a mellower tone, and all of them are singing, with a soaring sustain.

But just as I am warming up, Herr Stein finds me, and together we walk briskly through the factory. Stein is a young man, with a soft face that doesn't see enough sunlight, and kind eyes that look tired. He has a demanding schedule, and four young children at home. He is the most formally dressed of anyone here, wearing a button-down dress shirt, a wide, gray tie, and dress slacks. A pen he uses often is clipped to his shirt pocket.

Stein lets us into the "end control" room, a soundproof inner sanctum between the workshop and the loading dock. This is where Stein personally inspects every piano before it leaves the factory.

I learned a bit about Burkhard Stein over dinner the night I arrived. He was born in Marburg, Germany, about 150 miles south of Braunschweig, in 1967. Both his father and grandfather were *Klavier-baumeisters*. The family had a piano store that sold Grotrians.

"I wasn't sure if working in my father's store was right for me," Stein said. He was interested in both business and piano technology, studying at the Ludwigsburg school during the day, and on holidays working toward his MBA at a German business academy. He worked for his father for a year, tuning and repairing, then moved on to Siemens, the electronics concern, selling telephones. Then Knut Grotrian-Steinweg, the last member of the Grotrian family to hold the managing director's position, offered Stein a sales job. Ironically, Knut also had a son who wasn't interested in the family business, so he brought in Stein as the management heir apparent. Stein apprenticed to the business of running Grotrian under Knut for eight years.

"It's very important to have knowledge from experienced old people," Stein says. "Some of our dealers have had relations with us for one hundred years. It's helpful to know their taste and their requests."

But last year, when Grotrian's director of sales died after thirty years with the company, Stein decided it was time to make some changes. "Grotrian has always been a very conservative company. It needed a new generation to get a new position in the market, and our success says we were right." In a market that is growing smaller, Grotrian is increasing production in response to demand and expanding its dealer base. Stein now travels to North America several times a year to promote the piano and find new dealers.

Over dinner, Stein wished to hear my story, how I found my piano and what has brought me to Germany. When I told him about Marlene, and the Schubert concert tuning, and my readings, and Milford Graves's suggestion that I am experiencing the intention of all the people who built my piano, Stein didn't seem at all surprised. "I know such things happen to artists who play piano—it's a very interesting part of my job."

"Why do you think this happens?"

"It's a mixture," he said, in his halting English. "Many people worked on the piano."

But he did not elaborate. He's a taciturn man. Perhaps he couldn't express it further in English. Perhaps I'll see for myself at the factory.

Now we're in the control room to do a final check on an upright headed for Zurich.

"Our dealers have very high expectations," says Stein, removing the front of the piano's case to inspect the soundboard. He finds glue and sawdust there, and marks it with a piece of masking tape. "You will always find something if you look very carefully."

I look, just to be sure, but Stein is not wearing white cotton gloves. Still, his attitude would match them. He makes certain the serial number is the same as the one on the paperwork. The fallboard is marred, it needs a polyester repair. He plays the piano—do all the keys return after they are played? Do all the hammers meet the strings squarely? Are the dampers moving in unison?

He looks at the list of control checks, several pages long, framed and mounted on the wall. He runs his hands lightly across the tops of the keys to feel if they are all the same height. How does the tuning sound? What about the voicing? He marks with chalk the notes he does not like. Were there any special requests from this customer and did they get fulfilled?

On a sheet he marks any issues he has: A screw is not perfectly straight. A damper leaves a string too late. The tuning is out. There is not enough of a gap in the sostenuto pedal.

"We keep a record of who did what, in case there is a complaint. The person who did the work must correct it, and they must sign this sheet when the correction is done. Until then, the movers can't take the piano."

"What happens if the piano isn't ready?"

"Sometimes the movers spend half a day waiting on the loading dock."

Today is Thursday, shipping day. The factory is thrumming in preparation. Tomorrow I leave Braunschweig, and already I feel regret. The factory and the workers have quickly become dear to me. I'll miss the symphony of the workshop: the whining saws, whirring polishers, hissing sprayers, the snarl of drills, the dull roar of conveyor belts carrying piano parts to workstations. I'll miss Bosse and Schecke's patience and kindness. Kaemmerling's kidding around, our friendly banter. Stein's sober and generous hospitality. And perhaps, most of all, I'll miss watching Martin Walter work. Martin's passionate, energizing drive, his graceful, precise bellymaking.

A feeling surges in me—crazy—I want to apprentice here. Is such a thing possible?

Stein smiles. "Sure, we will take you."

"Seriously, what are the requirements?"

There's a two-day test in carpentry, woodcraft, and simple regulation. There is a hearing test—can I hear intervals, and when a piano is in tune? Then, the company evaluates who is most likely to stay on after the apprenticeship, and who fits in. Obviously, I'm not going to be a very strong candidate.

"We need people who are specialists and individualists," Stein explains. "The bellyman has to believe his job is the most important job in the factory. The furniture finisher must think *his* job is most important, because he is preparing the face of the piano as it is seen onstage.

"But they also must fit in together so we don't have shouting and anger—yes, it happens," he says with a nod and a look. "The personal chemistry must be right. Talent for handcrafting is important of course, but a harmonious atmosphere is *as* important. After all, we're producing a harmonious instrument."

Yes. That makes sense. And that harmony is why I feel so comfortable here, so in tune with these people. If I listen to the workshop the way Milford Graves listens to his audiences, the fundamental frequency of this factory, and its harmonics are a positive, uplifting force. Those chords of harmonious intention are part of what I experience when I play Marlene.

◆

Martin Walter was going to show me how he crowns a soundboard today, but when Kaemmerling and I get to his station, Martin announces that the available ribs are the wrong color. They are darker than the soundboards. There will be no soundboard crowning.

"But the ribs are underneath," I protest. "The pianist won't notice."

"*We* will notice," says Kaemmerling. He will show me what he can about soundboards.

Kaemmerling and I enter the hush of the drying room, where the tonewood is stored. The room's humidity is 30 percent, and the temperature is kept between 86 and 104 degrees Fahrenheit. The aim is to keep the wood's moisture near 2 to 3 percent. By keeping soundboards so dry, then later exposing them to a normal 40 to 50 percent humidity, the wood will swell, increasing tension on the board once it is held in place by ribs and rim. The highest possible soundboard tension is a necessity for the Grotrian scale design.

Soundboards arrive at Grotrian as flat panels assembled by Holzwerke Strunz in Bavaria. They are built to Grotrian specifications, with each individual plank selected for its natural tone or frequency, determined by rapping on the wood. The planks are not all the same frequency—that is not possible—but are "homogeneous," the Grotrian website explains. What does homogeneous mean, exactly?

"We have an agreement not to talk about this," says Kaemmerling. "What we can tell you is that we have a method for selecting single pieces of wood by their sound, weight, and elasticity that gets the best results possible. We keep the pitch consistent. With Chinese pianos getting better and better, we still need small miracles, small things nobody else knows, to separate us from other manufacturers."

My guess is they are selecting planks with consonant frequencies, but I do not press the question. Besides, Kaemmerling says, the natural frequency of the soundboard, while important, is not what creates the signature sound—after all, it is not possible to create two soundboards with the same natural tone. What matters is the frequency of the board after it is placed under tension, the "forced" frequency, he calls it. The secret is how to spread the tension around the soundboard, and how much tension is needed to make the board's own frequency neutral, so that the only pitch heard when the piano is played is the frequency of the strings. The board becomes a transducer, like a speaker cone, projecting the sound vibrations of the strings.

Kaemmerling picks up a piece of tonewood, about three-eighths of an inch thick, to demonstrate. He holds it about a quarter of its length from the top and invites me to rap it with a knuckle. It makes a hollow, resonant sound, rather deep. Then he bends the same piece of wood between two hands, creating an arc with it.

"Now tap it again," he says. The frequency is higher. "We deliberately manipulate the natural frequency with crowning and placing it under tension from the strings. If there's no tension, the soundboard won't *swing*."

"Swing? You mean vibrate?"

"Yes! Vibrate! Especially in the treble area, you need maximum tension. This excites higher partials. If the board is too flexible, you lose vibration. Each part of the soundboard must vibrate at the right frequency. The more tension, the less flex, and the higher the frequency, the more responsive the board is to the vibrations of the strings. Compare it to a rubber band. Slack, it makes no sound. But put it under tension and it will play a note."

After the boards arrive from Strunz, Grotrian shapes them in a planer, calibrating the various thicknesses with a computer. Then the manufacturing process uses every possible means to create a very high crown—allowing the dry board to swell with normal room humidity while attached to ribs that are not dry, shaping the board to those ribs in a press, shaping the ribs themselves so they can flex with the soundboard, cutting an angle on the top of the inner rim to support the crown, lacquering just one side of the soundboard to fix it in place while the other side expands. All of these steps create energy in the board, like winding up a spring.

The soundboard press is a convex table made with lengths of inflatable fire hose sandwiched between steel beams that pull down and clamp the ribs onto the board until the glue is set. "This is an old system," says Kaemmerling, lowering and raising one of the clamps. The press was made here in the factory's machine shop. Nobody manufactures them for sale—probably because they last forever.

"The result should not be a surprise," says Kaemmerling. "It's a mix of calculation and trial and error. But however good one's calculations, it's most important to try what you have calculated. Our opinion, and our taste, are what matter in the end."

Kaemmerling says the trees for the soundboards must be very carefully selected.

"If you knock on one of these trees before it is cut, you will hear a very clear difference in the sustaining sound of the tone. You can hear if you have a sound like *pock* or if it is rather like *p-o-o-o-ck*. And this is how to select trees for tonewood.

"But I do not know what Strunz is doing for us—nobody does. Our process is to create the crown, the belly, the soundboard together. What Strunz does—these things are hidden from me. Yes!" he says, when he sees my skeptical look.

"This is like a secret society?" I tease.

"Yes, it is!" He is serious. "No one person knows all of it. Not even me!" And Kaemmerling laughs his good-natured laugh.

25

Austria

When Thomas Hilz's grandfather Carl was alive, and he went to the forests to select trees for tonewood—the wood used to make musical instruments—he walked among the standing giants, knocked on them with a hammer, and listened for a resonant tone. This was more than fifty years ago, Thomas tells me, as he drives us into the Alps of Austria to search for tonewood ourselves. Carl Hilz needed only one hundred trees a year, but today, Thomas Hilz, the owner of Holzwerke Strunz, the world's oldest maker of piano soundboards, needs five thousand trees a year, and if he were to test each live tree by knocking on it, you might never get a piano.

"Now I personally do not know anybody who is knocking trees with a hammer," says Thomas, emphatic and animated when I repeat to him what I have heard. "We all select the trees from looking at them. And if anybody says he does this, I think it is a kind of fairy tale."

Thomas is the seventh generation of his family to make soundboards from the trees of Middle Europe—specifically, European white spruce grown in the mountains of Austria, Germany, and Switzerland. He began selecting tonewood when he was eight years old, on trips to the forest with his father, Adolf. Peering into an unmilled log to discern its tonal qualities is not possible, but Thomas relies on intuition informed by his family's 185-year tradition and his own thirty-one years of experience.

"Sometimes with trees there is a special feeling," he says, as we walk about Reinhard Kirchner's log yard. We followed Reinhard here in Thomas's car, after visiting the forests outside of Filzmoos, where we watched forester Maier Christian select trees, and the loggers cut and skid them. Now Reinhard hopes Thomas will buy some of the one hundred round logs he has preselected. Thomas is his best-paying customer.

The logs are laid out in a long, knee-high, four-yards-wide avenue, their bark peeled, their bodies pressed neatly together, a road of corduroy.

"When I see a log for the first time, it is yes or no," says Thomas, eyeing his prospects as we walk beside the felled trees. "My first decision is always the best one. If it is no, and the supplier says 'Please take it,' I don't like it. No one can change my thinking. If I say it is no, it is no."

"It's hard to convince a piano maker," Reinhard cheerfully agrees as he follows our progress from the opposite end of the trunks. As Thomas examines each log, he calls out to Reinhard his verdict. If it is "Passt" (okay), Reinhard sprays an orange dot of paint on his end of the log, and the letters "str" for Strunz. But more often Thomas says "nix," the local dialect for "nicht."

"I don't like this one, it has too many knots."

"We must teach the trees to grow square, and without knots," calls out Reinhard, who is almost skipping with high spirits. "We must get Nature to grow them the right way!"

Reinhard knows that Thomas will buy only 2 or 3 percent of even the best selection of logs. But this is still very profitable. A soundboard maker will pay a premium for a good tonewood tree, twenty percent more than Reinhard can get from a fine furniture maker or a building contractor.

"The spruce I don't take, Reinhard can sell for window frames," says Thomas. "No problem for him."

But today, Thomas likes many of the logs.

"Perfect," he says, again and again. "This is perfect soundwood tree." He swings a double-headed hammer into the butt of the log, embedding an orange plastic tag with a number on it. Then he turns the hammer about and swings the opposite head into the wood just below the tag. That one embosses his initials, TH, with a satisfying *thock*. The logs he has chosen are almost perfect cylinders, and their annular rings are uniform and tightly spaced.

"Ja, perfect. This is exactly the right grain." He squats and traces it with his forefinger. The growth rings are so densely packed, it is almost impossible to count them. This log is twenty-six inches across. Within that span are approximately 250 evenly spaced growth rings. Year after year, this tree produced regular, even, unconstricted layers of cambium, for 250 years.

In all, Thomas selects twenty-six logs, both first and second quality, a far higher percentage than usual. He pays by the cubic meter, and Reinhard calculates the purchase is 2,571 cubic meters, or 90,794 cubic feet, from which Thomas will build three hundred to four hundred piano soundboards, both uprights and grands.

"In the beginning, he shows the poorest quality, and at the end, the best," Thomas complains, shaking his fist as we return to the car. "I could hit him!"

✦

My adventure at Holzwerke Strunz began in Pocking, Germany, where Thomas's workshop sits beside the Austrian border. Thomas and his wife, Martina, have taken the greatest care of me, treating me like a foreign dignitary ever since I arrived to see where Marlene's soundboard was made. Over dinner last night, Martina, a pixieish interior designer with soulful, evocative eyes, shyly told me the story of how she and Thomas met, eighteen years ago. Her parents' house, in the next village over, caught fire while they were out of town, and Thomas was one of the firemen who answered Martina's alarm. After rescuing the house, he stayed for tea, drinking from a mug with the name "Martina" on it. "Who is Martina?" he asked. They have been together ever since.

Thomas still carries himself with a firefighter's heroic bravado. He's a man who is the master of his universe, and very happy about it, too. The eldest of the couple's two sons, Max, is like Thomas was as a boy, says his mother, always in and out of the workshop, more interested in the business of soundboards than in school.

✦

From Kirchner's yard in Austria, the logs travel by truck to a mill near the German border. The best way to mill tonewood logs for piano soundboards is to quartersaw them. The whole round log is sliced in half, lengthwise, then each half is halved again, also lengthwise. From these quarter rounds, boards are sliced so that the grain appears vertical when they are viewed on edge. This gives the boards the flexibility needed for crowning.

Quartersawing back in the 1820s, when Thomas Hilz's ancestor Peter Strunz founded his company, was done by hand with a pit saw, an enormous blade operated by two men: one stood in a pit, under the log, and another stood atop the log, which was supported by a scaffold. But today, quartersawing a 250-year-old tree requires highly specialized equipment, an enormous investment of capital to procure it, and specialized skills to run it. In Austria, there are only six or seven small, family-owned mills that are capable of delivering this custom cut. Thomas Hilz might use any of them.

"They do a perfect job," Thomas says of the mill we are visiting today. "They handle the wood like it is their own. It's important to have a sawmill owner you can trust."

✦

Johann Esterbauer neatly stacks fresh-cut spruce boards as they roll off his sawmill's conveyor belt. It's a gray, chill spring day, and he wears a gray-striped sweater and a wool cap over his white hair. The lumber is cut in thin wafers, then stacked across slats; this separates the boards, allowing air to circulate. Long past the age of retirement, Esterbauer still spends every day at the mill his son Karl now runs, stacking lumber and handing out chocolates to visitors. He's there because he needs something to do. He's a cheerful man, always joking. He is also one of the wealthiest landholders in this region of Austria, an owner of electric companies, Salzburg luxury rentals, and forests, Thomas tells me.

Esterbauer's computerized saw is only two years old, and the family has invested nearly two million euro in it. The saw is housed under an enormous two-story shed that is open on one side to the lumberyard, where the winter's harvest of spruce logs, piled as high as a house, are defrosting. When Thomas Hilz's logs arrive from Filzmoos, they must be cut right away, before insects can infest them.

Karl Esterbauer operates the saw from inside a glassed-in control tower, perched high under the shed's roof, for an optimal view of the saw. The titanium-tipped band saw is over five feet tall and nearly eight

inches wide, and its enormous teeth could be from the maw of a ferocious prehistoric monster. A 15-ton platform carries the logs into the
saw on a rail. Karl sits in what is known as the "pilot's seat," a high-
backed swivel chair with control consoles built into each of the wide
arms and a computer keyboard before it. A computer monitor hangs
just above Karl's head. The chair's arms are covered in buttons, levers,
joysticks, and dials, all in primary colors. As he rapidly operates the
controls, Karl looks like the captain in a *Star Trek* episode, or perhaps
a puppeteer manipulating his industrial marionettes from behind a
glass curtain.

Karl presses a button, and down below a pair of long mechanical
arms reach out, grab a whole, round log with their sharp, chisel-like
fingers, and drag the log onto the platform. A push of a joystick, and
the platform runs the log into the band saw, slicing it in half lengthwise. Karl must use just the right touch, he explains, or the force of the
moving log will rip the saw to pieces. Another button pushed, and one
half of the log is shoved aside by more mechanical arms. Then a long
knife slices the rough edges of the remaining half, preparing it for the
cutting of the first board.

Once the log is halved, Karl decides if it is suitable for tonewood.
If the wood is clear, knot-free, without any pitch pockets, then he sets
the computer to cut the log into half-inch-thick planks. If the wood
is unacceptable, then the boards will be milled at about an inch thick
and put to other uses.

Nobody knows what is inside a log until it passes through the saw,
and there is always a risk that a log will be bad: poor color, compression rings, too many knots in the outer edge of the tree, or even rot
hidden inside. Even the highest-quality log has areas that are not
usable. At best, only ten percent of a log can be used for pianos, and if
you are making first-quality soundboards, the number is even lower—
perhaps only three to five percent.

✦

The freshly cut planks are carefully stacked on pallets, and the pallets
are hoisted onto a flatbed truck and carried off to Pocking, a small village south of Passau, just west of the Inn River. This is where Thomas's
father and grandfather resettled in 1950, after the Soviet government

took over the family mill and workshop in Aussergefild, Czechoslovakia, about three miles east of the German border, on the river Moldau.

In March of 1945, at the funeral of Thomas's great-grandfather,
the family was ordered by police to leave the country immediately.
The Strunz family goes back some three hundred years in what is now
the Czech Republic, but was then a part of Germany. The family was
very wealthy, and their company, known then as Holzstrunz Aussergefild, had 250 employees and owned forty houses. They were forced to
leave with only the clothes on their backs. Their assets were taken by
the Soviet government, and the factory was burned to the ground.

Thomas's father was only fifteen at the time, and he was permanently traumatized. "Every year on March twentieth he was very sad,"
says Thomas. "It was a catastrophe for him. He never got over it."

Thomas's grandfather Carl Hilz was originally from Bavaria, and
so he moved the family there. He reestablished the company with only
a pit saw, just as Peter Strunz had back in 1820, and resumed the family tradition of building piano soundboards, ribs, and keyboards.
Thomas took over management of the company in 1988, and became
the sole owner in 1995.

He's a stout man of thirty-nine, not tall, not fit, but powerfully built
and with a will of steel beneath his very friendly, engaging, and hyperkinetic personality. Thomas is one of those people who gets more
done in a day than most of us do in a week, and he is an energetic
whirlwind, full of plans, strategies, and near-constant travel to build his
business and promote his company, which he has made the center of
his life since he was in elementary school. While single-handedly running the business, he continues to personally select each and every log
that will become a Strunz soundboard.

When tonewood planks arrive at Strunz, they are air-dried outdoors for three months. Then they are kiln-dried to a moisture content of six percent. From the kiln, the planks are taken by forklift into
an enormous heated warehouse, where they cure for a month. Inside
the warehouse are stacks of wood some twenty feet tall. A behemoth
of a red enamel furnace sits at the center, devouring fuel bricks made
of sawdust and wood chips, waste from soundboard manufacturing.

When the wafer-thin planks are ready, they are twelve to sixteen
feet long. Two workers examine every plank as it travels down the first

conveyor belt, and they mark the knots with large nubs of phospho-rescent crayon. Werner Fraemhofer, who has been with Strunz for thirty-one years, brackets each knot with brilliant orange lines. Halfway down the conveyor, a computerized crosscut saw reads the Day-Glo markings and cuts them. As the boards continue down the conveyor, they are sorted by sensors that trigger mechanical arms. The arms push the boards off the belt into piles of matching lengths.

The planks continue their journey around the workshop on more conveyor belts, through more computer sensors. "Early wood," or the young growth of a tree, is cut away—its wide annular rings are not suitable for soundboards. Waste wood is diverted into a chipper, then made into fuel briquets. The highest-quality planks follow a path to a computer-operated planer, where they are smoothed on four sides.

By now, the best pieces are in many different lengths, and they are ready for soundboard selection. There are four soundboard layout sta-tions, each with a waist-high table and a flat hydraulic press that low-ers onto the table from the ceiling. Each table is surrounded by dozens of smooth white boards of the finest possible grain, standing upright against the station's walls, like a pale forest.

A worker pieces a soundboard together on his layout table, using a stencil as a guide. No two piano makers specify the same grain angle, quality, color, size, or contour specifications for their soundboards. Some want wider or closer grain. Some want redder or whiter color.

For a Grotrian soundboard, the layout worker selects the whitest possible spruce, the closest and most uniform possible grain. "The boards for Grotrian are of the highest quality," says Thomas. "You would need a magnifying glass to count the rings." There are twenty annular rings to the inch, and the wood is flawless.

When all the planks are in place at the grain angle specified on the template, the worker lowers the flat press onto the boards and taps their exposed edges lightly with a rubber mallet, nudging them together. Then he pencils a large *V* across all the boards, stacks the planks atop each other in order, and places the stack on a green metal rack. When the rack holds twelve stacks of planks, it is wheeled to the soundboard composition station.

Fedor Tschense, a Russian émigré who came to Germany after the Velvet Revolution of 1989, makes up grand piano soundboards two at a time. He clamps a stack of planks together, quickly applies white glue to their edges with a roller, then covers a Mylar pattern with the boards, fitting them back together to match the penciled *V.*

Tschense's gray metal worktable, about three feet high, looks like an enormous Peg-Board, perforated with evenly spaced holes. On this table, he holds the soundboard assembly together with air-pressurized clamps from above and on the sides. The side clamps are spring-loaded metal plates. Their housing fits into the table's holes and the plates expand against the edges of the soundboard.

While one board dries, he begins another on an adjacent table. After twenty minutes, the glue is dry, the clamps are all removed, and the board is lifted from the table. With its untrimmed, ragged edges, it looks like a pixilated, or digitized board, without the graceful curves recognizable as the shape of a grand piano.

Tschense sets the boards in a drying rack, where they sit for a day. Then they are passed through a planer to remove the glue and the pencil marks. Pitch pockets are removed at a special station with a hand-held router and patched with wooden plugs. Then the board is planed again.

From here the boards go into an eighty-six-degree Fahrenheit hot room, where they stay until they ship to Grotrian. They are sanded and shaped in a computer-driven planer that contours each soundboard to the specifications of every piano make and model Strunz supplies— 130 different soundboards for twenty-five different piano makers all over the world.

Just before shipping, each soundboard is inspected by the company's foreman, Heinz Seitz, who has been friends with Thomas since elementary school. Seitz tests the soundboards by bending them in every possible direction over a felt-covered hump. This screens out any soundboard that might crack under the pressure of crowning. Against the far wall of the workshop, the finished soundboards are stacked vertically in racks: their destinations are as near as Stuttgart and as far away as Korea.

Each night before retiring, Thomas Hilz enters his workshop alone, looks over the silenced saws, the quiet conveyors, runs a hand over the mute soundboards, thinks of the beautiful music that will emerge from them. Here are the hearts of the world's finest pianos, awaiting their destinies, soon to begin beating. Thomas puts his shop to bed, tucks it in tenderly. "It's like my heart," he says. "The most important thing in life is to love your work."

After seeing Grotrian soundboards made, I had planned to treat myself to a visit to the ancient trading city of Passau, where the Danube and the Inn rivers meet, and from there travel to Mozart's birthplace in Salzburg, then on to hear music in Vienna. But Thomas Hilz has other plans for me.

"If you really want to understand tonewood, you must meet my friend Mr. Fuchs, in Mittenwald," says Thomas. He pronounces the name "Fox." "His family has been selling tonewood for violins since even before my family. He and I have a business relationship—he takes the older trees for violins, and I take the younger ones for pianos—but we are also friends, and I haven't seen him for fourteen years. I will take you to him myself."

Mittenwald is in southernmost Bavaria, several hours in the opposite of my intended direction. Yes, of course, I will certainly go to Mittenwald and visit Mr. Fuchs—after I've seen Vienna. But Thomas must go to Berlin later in the week. He must take me now. You don't need to drive me, you have already done so much, I say. But Thomas has decided, and he is a force of nature. My protests are to no avail. Early the next morning he loads my bag into the trunk of his car, and off we go to Mittenwald.

26

Mittenwald

We drive through sheets of rain, climbing ever higher into the mountains. We sway around roller-coaster turns, past lakes and farms with their small dairy sheds cast about green meadows, awaiting the cows of summer. We rise through tall, straight stands of spruce until finally we are up among naked, dramatic, snow-covered peaks in a landscape too forbidding, it would seem, for human habitation. Near evening we arrive in a latter-day Shangri-la.

Mittenwald is a tiny village clinging to the edge of a hanging valley in the Alps, in the shadow of the Karwendel Range, almost on the Austrian border. For centuries it was a toll station where the nobility taxed traders traveling to and from Italy. For three hundred years, it has been Bavaria's Cremona, a center of violin making. Mozart's own violin was made here by a descendant of Matthias Klotz, who began the tradition. This region was a natural place for violin makers to settle, as the ancient maples and slow-growing spruce in these mountains made superb violin backs and tops. Though most of the tonewood today comes from other parts of the Alps, there are still violin makers and luthiers everywhere in Mittenwald, carrying on the traditions begun by their great-great-grandfathers.

Spring arrives late at this elevation. The trees are bare, the air is chilly. But purple flowers hang in cascades over the banks of the clear creek that wends its way through the town, and the pastel colors—roses and yellows and corals—of the ancient buildings are cheering. Most houses are decorated in the Bavarian style, with enormous murals painted on exterior walls. There are angels, saints, and scenes from the Bible; there are scenes from the mountains—stags, goats, and sheep. Every window is framed by elaborate scrollwork, painted in exacting detail. This is kitsch at its very highest.

At the center of the village, rising up against a backdrop of snowy peaks, is the community's heart—a pink church some three hundred years old. Before the church is a tall statue in bronze of Matthias Klotz, whittling a violin into being.

Thomas and I pull up to the Hotel Reiger, where I check into a room with a view of the Karwendel from the bathtub. Imposing mountains are everywhere in one's face in Mittenwald. Hastily, I wash up and change clothes, then come back down the stairs to the hotel restaurant, where Thomas and his friend Norbert Fuchs are already conspiring over a bottle of wine.

Fuchs is a huge man of seventy, tall and broad-backed, with a full head of gleaming white hair, grizzled eyebrows, and a worldly, heavy-featured face. He's loud and domineering, like the old, retired German men I've encountered on the trains, holding forth with each other around tables, cacophonous lords of their own conversational universe.

Fuchs announces, in rapid-fire English, that he has only just returned from the Caucasus, a trip he makes once a month to acquire some of the world's finest and most ancient maple trees for violin making. This is a treacherous journey: first he drives for sixteen hours to the Ukrainian border, where he must change to a Russian car.

"You can't take a German car there—it's all Mafia, terrorists, very dangerous, we have to pay them all the time," he says to Thomas as he bends intently over the table, cupping his wineglass in two large hands. "After we reach the Russian border, we drive another twenty-four hours."

"Don't you worry about your safety?" I interject.

"They won't bother me." Fuchs waves a dismissive hand. "I am so old." He smiles, big yellow teeth.

"How do you bring the trees here?"

"It's illegal to bring out whole trees. They have to be milled there. They speak dialects." Fuchs turns back to Thomas again. "Even if you speak Russian, you wouldn't understand them."

Fuchs speaks in English. Thomas answers him in German. I think that Thomas must be tired of speaking English all day, but this makes it hard for me to participate in the conversation. Fuchs, as if perhaps reading my mind, turns to me and tells the story of how he first came to Mittenwald.

Norbert Fuchs's tonewood company, Brüder Fuchs, has been in his family for seven generations, supplying stringed instrument makers since 1778. The firm was in Eger, Czechoslovakia, until 1946, when the Americans arrived in the wake of the Second World War. Fuchs's mother made the mistake of cooking for the Americans, and when the Russians took over, nine months later, the family was forced to leave. Some uncles were in Mittenwald, and with so many violin makers there, this was a natural place to reestablish the business. At the time, Fuchs was in school, and he did not understand a word of German.

The next day I visit Fuchs's tonewood warehouse and manufactory. "Ask me anything!" he roars between incoming cell phone calls. "I've been doing this business for fifty-eight years!" He shows me boxes of violin parts—fiddleheads, backs, necks, sides, tops. He has twenty-four different types of routers to make every part of a violin, and he can make five hundred necks in one day, he shouts. Six minutes to press a violin back! One hundred thousand premade sets of violin parts a year!

Inside the main building, there are sections of tree trunks as enormous as billiard tables, 450 years old. For the first 150 years, the growth rings are so tight, I can't distinguish the separate lines. "I take the big ones, Thomas takes the little ones," Fuchs says. "For the violins, all the pieces must be from the same tree."

Fuchs walks outside to show me future violin backs made from wedges of tiger maple. He moves with a cowboy's lateral gait, not a swagger but an old man's totter. The wedges are stacked outside for two or three years to cure before they are sold. Then a violin maker may cure them another five to twenty-five years—or even longer. He picks up a wedge from the drying stack and knocks it with his knuckle. He hands it to me—it is very heavy. "All the grain must be straight!"

I ask him why spruce and maple are best for violins. "Ask the violin makers!" he booms, throwing one arm to the sky.

I leave him to his multiple dealings on his cell phone, and Fuchs's daughter gives me a ride to meet a violin maker, Ranier Leonhardt, who is also director of the local violin-making museum.

Leonhardt's workshop is in a courtyard on the edge of town.

Everything here appears to be made by hand, from the doorknocker to the courtyard fountains to the diorama of a violin maker's workshop under glass in the foyer, to the exquisite ceremonial face masks hanging on a workshop wall. These are used for an annual festival, part of a long tradition specific to Mittenwald.

I ask Leonhardt what he thinks happens when someone falls in love with a violin, and he quickly refers me to someone else. "You must ask my colleague Anton Sprenger about that," he says, shaking his head, looking amused. "Here is his number."

I return to the hotel and call the number but there is no answer. So I walk about the village, browse in the Apotheke, have some tiramisu gelato at a café. Violin music flows from open workshop windows through the streets. The weather is warming up. It is so lovely in Mittenwald that I decide to extend my stay into the weekend. The one clerk at the hotel who speaks English says it is no problem.

I change into my hiking shoes and climb into the surrounding mountains. Soon I am in a tamed wilderness, with paved footpaths, religious crèches everywhere, and a restaurant at the top of a mountain peak. Ancient maples turn their graceful, bare arms up to the iron-gray sky. Heather is in bloom. The craggy peaks are so close, they seem to kiss my cheeks. I am inspired by the beauty, and I forget all about the frustration of being hijacked here. I feel a sense of locking into place, of being connected. I could be in Montana. The loggers near Filzmoos could be my smokejumper friends, with their wilderness derring-do. I am at home.

Hiking back to the village in the late-afternoon light, I notice my perceptions have sharpened. Hellebore and cherry trees bloom in the gardens. Firewood is stacked neatly on the sidewalks before the row houses. Apostles shed tears of blood and their broken limbs hang awkwardly; painted statues of Mary stand in private crèches, hundreds of lit candles flickering before them. The violin music leads me on again, and as I pass the pink church in the heart of the village, I see a tiny sign—*Anton Sprenger, Geigenbaumeister*—and an arrow pointing down a narrow street. I follow the direction of the arrow, and soon find myself alongside a creek. Children stop their play and look up at me as I gaze about the greening countryside. I let myself in the low gate, into a small yard.

◆

At once I hear, through stained glass windows, Bach being played on a violin. The door to Anton Sprenger's workshop stands open, and when I look in, the sound of the violin makes my nerves thrum; I feel the hairs on my arms stand up. The violinist sees me and lowers his bow.

"Bitte, sprechen Sie englisch?" I say.

"Ja. Can I help you?"

"Your colleague Ranier Leonhardt sent me to you. He said you would be the right person to speak with about how people respond to musical instruments. I am sorry to interrupt. Please, continue playing."

"Yes, thank you," says Anton Sprenger with an abrupt nod and a flashing smile. "I have only just finished making this violin. It is the first time I play it. I am very pleased." And he draws the violin up under his chin again and puts the bow to the strings.

At the draw of the bow, the room is filled with tremendous resonance. The sound vibrates powerfully through my entire body, waves of tone set off strong physical sensations. The low notes saw through my bones. The high ones tear my heart in half. Before I even realize what is happening, tears course down my cheeks.

Not fair! Not fair! I think, embarrassed. The violin is too beautiful. And then, I give in, I give myself over to the sound, and openly weep. My heart, my whole being, opens wide, becomes radiant with light. I look at Anton in wonder. How could his playing affect me like this?

Anton at last lowers his bow and sets the violin on a quilted mat on his workbench. We are silent, simply looking at each other, allowing the resonance of the music to fade. Finally, I say, "What a privilege to hear this instrument!"

"Ja, I think it turned out well." The calm smile again. "I am happy."

"What did I just experience?"

"It is very difficult to explain," the violinmaker says, taking a seat on his work stool, putting one foot on a rung. He is surprisingly young for someone who has mastered the art of violin making. He is thirty-five. He has close-cropped, dark hair, healthy apple cheeks, a short goatee, and shining eyes. He wears a green work apron, and his shirtsleeves are rolled up. He rests a hand atop each knee, elbows akimbo.

"It's a puzzle of many things. There are more things on this earth than exist in front of our eyes, and with this opinion, I make such quality of instruments," he says.

"How do you think your intention affects the way people experience your violins?" I take a seat on a folding chair and look expectantly at Anton's face, which is absorbed in thought.

"This is not easy to talk about, because if people don't know about the power of the universe, they tell me I am silly." He shrugs. "I felt such things even as a boy, but I was told I was wrong. You know, I had to learn to trust myself. Not easy. You have to feel it. That is the important thing."

I point to my still damp cheeks and laugh. "I guess I must feel it!" He laughs too.

"There was a girl who came here from Japan. She tried one violin and she couldn't stop playing it. She was supposed to leave Mittenwald that day, but she had to stay the night because she played the violin for eight hours. And she was always crying."

I explain that as much as I might yearn to, I cannot play one of his violins. I play the piano. I had an experience like this with a piano. That is why I am here. I want to understand how a tree becomes an instrument, how the soul of a tree becomes the soul of an instrument, and why it affects us so.

"A lot of people come here to talk about these things, not to buy a violin!" He laughs again. "I am a point of a network. I put people on track. You are not the first or the only person to come here with these questions. Often, I am the last violin maker they visit in Mittenwald. For me, it is more important to talk about these things than to sell violins."

"So what do you tell them? What is your explanation?"

"I think the starting point is the mind, how you think. It is best to think 'I do this because I like it.' 'I want to be better today than yesterday and make the best violins I can make.' And, in my mind, I am in the Renaissance; I don't feel like a modern violin maker. I go into the world like the best Italian violin maker from 1750. I hear the music from this time. I don't use power tools anymore, I don't need them, I can work anywhere—on top of a mountain, like five hundred years ago."

Also, Anton says, where he lives is important. "The landscape, the traditions, your family—all of that gets into your instrument." His family has made violins in Mittenwald for 180 years, though the line has been passed from uncle to nephew, rather than father to son.

"Next, is to make a violin from a piece of wood—that is so fantastic for me. It was a tree, a *live tree*. Here." He picks up a heavy block of dark wood and dangles it on his knee. "This is a piece of wood from three hundred fifty years ago, from a church. The tree grew for five hundred years. Think how long ago that was! From a tree, you make something that vibrates so warm, for such a long time. It is the maximum you can make from a tree."

But, he says, the tree is only one small part of the equation.

"There is lots of science and nature involved. The biochemical and the biophysical have to come together. All things are vibration." He picks up a small jar from his workbench; it is half-filled with clear liquid. He hands the jar to me. A square of white paper is taped to the jar, and on the paper the number "8" is written. But it is not just a number. It is a winding line of the words "love" and "gratitude" in German, repeated in the shape of the number eight, the symbol for infinity.

"Eight is the highest vibration," says Anton. "This is the lacquer I put on my violins. The number eight changes the vibration of the lacquer, it harmonizes it. You should put it on your computer, on all electrical things. I always use this number."

I swirl the lacquer. Vibration. Numerology. Where have I heard about these things before? I feel as if I have come full circle. But Anton Sprenger is no anthroposophist, he assures me. He's a Catholic who believes in Jesus. He uses holy water from the pink church to wet-sand his violins.

"That is so strange," I say, as I watch the lacquer run down the inside of the glass. "You know, my grandpa used to use the number eight as a symbol for 'I love you.' He always signed his letters to us '8.' And it is the day of my birthday."

"Yes," says Anton, taking the jar back and putting it away. "When people come here they are often connected to this number. It is in their phone number, or their address." He opens a drawer and shows me the business cards he has collected. They are from all over the world. "My customers are special. They believe in this, I think. They are sensitive. They feel the energy. If you put the power of the universe in the instrument, it's like a magnetism."

"Is it who you are that they are responding to, do you think? If they fall in love with your violin, are they like you in some way?"

"Oh, yes. It's my way of life. And then when people play my instruments, that energy comes back to me, from all over the world. Every day and night my energy is on the earth. In Taiwan, someone is playing a concert, while in the United States people are sleeping. This is fantastic for me to think about. Also violins have a long life, they cannot die. If you make good violins, they will play for five hundred to a thousand years. I think of this all the time.

"So I have a responsibility for the energy of the violins. I have to prepare myself carefully. It's a lot of pressure. For this reason, I only work when my energy is good. The quality of the violin is higher if I make only one, and only when my energy is high.

"When I feel bad, I go into the mountains, go to a lake, be out in nature. This is like a battery—I get energy from the mountains, air, sun, trees, water. It is very important for me to do this. Also, I sit with my family every day at the table, and it is harmonious. This is very important. And I think where I live is very important. Mittenwald is a very special area."

Yes, I think, it is. I resonate to this place, like I do to the mountains of Montana. Like I did in the forest in Austria where the tree that became Marlene was cut. And in the factory in Braunschweig, with the craftsmen who built her.

One scientist I asked about the Marlene Experience said he'd like to have the Nobel Prize he'd win for being able to answer my questions. But somehow, after my audience with Anton Sprenger, I don't need the answers so much anymore. Besides, all my critical faculties, my skepticism have ultimately proved useless. Understanding the power of music is not about thinking. It's about feeling. On the eve of my return home, I'm fulfilled in some strange way by the unanswerable, the inexplicable.

I was a tribe of one when this journey began, and at its end, I am one among the many who lose their heads and follow their hearts. It is enough to have found so many kindred spirits in this world. Now I'll settle for simply getting my piano back.

27

Healing Marlene

We had a plan. Marc was going to tune the walnut Grotrian in Carl's showroom to the Schubert concert tuning, record it on an Accu-Tuner, and send me the frequency numbers. Then Carl was going to send me the walnut Grotrian's hammers on shanks. Tom would install them and tune my piano using Marc's numbers on his Accu-Tuner. If all went well, I'd have the instrument I fell in love with in the showroom in my living room at last.

But the course of piano love never did run smooth between Marlene and me, and when I get home, I find the plan has developed a few snags.

For starters, I can't find Carl. The last time I spoke with him was months ago, when we had dinner together and he offered to send me the hammers on shanks. I've called the store several times, but he is never in, and he hasn't called me back. While Carl's offer is radical in its generosity—not to mention probably a poor business decision—I haven't been able to come up with a better idea. I return from Europe to find the piano in worse condition than ever—a snarling, dissonant mess. I have to do *something*.

Then Marc begins to waver. He doesn't want to learn how to use an Accu-Tuner, and he doesn't want another technician to see the numbers for the Schubert concert tuning.

"I'm afraid they'll decide I'm full of crap," he confesses. "That tuning is something subtle, in a world where subtlety isn't valued." Instead, he wants to split the cost of an Accu-Tuner with me, have me learn how to use it so I can coach him over the phone, and then we can ship the Accu-Tuner back and forth to each other. It all sounds much too complicated to me, but Marc insists. "Otherwise," he says, "I might be giving something away I wish I hadn't. Anyway, I need to know when Carl is sending you the hammers out of that piano."

"I haven't been able to reach him. It's a bit strange."

"Well, you know, his mother died."

"Oh, no!"

"I hear he took it hard. He spent three days alone in a room with her, trying to contact her in the spirit world. But this was some time ago."

I manage to find Carl's cell phone number, and this time he picks up.

"Carl, I am so sorry about your mother."

"Yes, well," he says. His voice sounds faint, ephemeral. "We should celebrate when someone leaves this life. It is when they are born that we should grieve."

Gently, I ask him about the hammers on shanks. Has he heard anything from Grotrian? Will they send them?

"It didn't happen," he says, his voice growing even fainter. "I forgot all about it. I will call them at five o'clock tomorrow morning and take care of it."

The next day we talk again and Carl confirms I'll have the hammers in three weeks. I call Tom Kuntz and schedule his visit to Missoula.

Then Marc begins calling frequently. He frets over Carl remembering what to do; he feels I don't stay on top of Carl enough. He agonizes over the Accu-Tuner. He wants me to guarantee him I'll be happy with the tuning.

"Marc, if you aren't comfortable, let's not do it," I tell him. "I'll live with what I get with the new hammers and Tom's tuning. I'd love to have Marlene back, but if the logistics are too much—"

"No, no, no, no! It's fine, I *want* to do this. I want to find out if it will work," says Marc.

But the next day, he calls again: "I want to know if I record the tuning, is it going to solve your problem?" he demands.

"I don't know! How can I know that?" I say, exasperated. "I can't predict the future!"

"Why don't you believe the new hammers and the tuning will give you what you want?" he insists. His voice grows shrill. "You are setting the clock back to zero. You get to hit the reset button and start over. You are only a set of hammers away from a new musical instrument. Of *course* this will give you what you want!"

"It's not that I don't believe," I explain, trying to control my mounting impatience. "It's just that I'm staying neutral until I hear it for myself."

"Oh my *God*!" Marc gasps.

"What?"

"I didn't realize! I went out to Montana to help Carl because he is my friend. I made it sound good so you wouldn't send the piano back, but—"

"Right, it didn't solve the problem. I've had the piano for three years, and out of all that time maybe it's been right for a month. So yes, I'm staying neutral. I'll believe it when I hear it."

"You are staying neutral while you are walking down Death Row!" he yells, sounding almost hysterical. "And you're just hoping that the electricity won't work when they pull the switch!"

Death Row! I can hardly believe the melodrama.

"You should have returned this piano long ago," he continues. "It's my fault that you didn't! I talked you out of it. I've been leading you along through this process, not understanding what you were going through. But I do now."

"Well, you told me how torqued out pianists get, and then no one wants to work with them, so I didn't talk about it."

"Look," he continues, his tone still edgy. "You can walk bravely now! The electricity will go out! I know you, I know what you respond to. The new hammers will work for you. The tuning will work. I believe in the numbers.

"I feel stupid now! Worrying about the numbers and who has them!" His voice is full of anguish. "I don't care who has them. I can hire someone to take the numbers from the tuning."

"I can pay for that."

"Nononononono," he says. "It's nothing."

We hang up at last. I slump over my desk, wrung out from the exchange. He is so intense! Then the phone rings. It's Marc again.

"Will you be home two weeks from Saturday?"

"Yes."

"I can fly to Missoula then."

"No, Marc, that's crazy."

"Look. The tuning really should go directly onto your piano. That's the right way to do it."

I feel a shot of panic. What is he thinking? Does he think he's going to voice the hammers? He'll want to use his softening chemicals! Then I really will be back to the beginning.

"Marc, I can't let you do that!"

"I'm coming out there! I'm going to make this right. You've been through enough! You could go bankrupt at this rate, trying to figure this out."

"Marc! This is *crazy*!"

"I've got a plane reservation up on my laptop right now. Say the word and I'll push the button."

"No."

"What do you mean, *no*?"

"I mean, I can't let you do this. I can't fly you out here, I can't pay you for your work, or your expenses."

"You don't have to. This is something *I* need to do." His voice is almost manic. "*I* need to make it right."

I hesitate just a moment. Marc takes the opening.

"This will be perfect," he says. "This way, if Carl hasn't sent the hammers out in time for Tom to put them on, I'll bring them with me and I can do it."

"Let me think about it."

"*Perri!*"

"Let me think about it."

"Okay," he says. "You have until tonight."

I am shaking when I hang up. Now what do I do? I can't let Marc touch those hammers. I've already been through so much. I don't know if I can trust anyone with the piano anymore. I lie down on the sofa and try to calm myself. But as soon as I close my eyes, a voice floats up inside me: *Let him come. Let him help you.* Really? I sit up. *It's okay to let him to help you.*

The phone rings. It's only four p.m., but it is Marc again. He is being impatient.

"Look, I have to do this now. Just say the word and I've got a reservation."

"Okay. Okay, you can come. But no voicing."

"*What?!* Listen, the tuning doesn't work without the voicing."

"I know." I choose my words carefully. "I know that. But the problem is, Marc, your voicing without your tuning doesn't work for me. We've seen that. And the tunings don't last very long. Until we are certain your tuning can be duplicated with the Accu-Tuner, I don't want the hammers voiced."

"I won't use chemicals. I promise. Just needles."

"Marc, I live so very far away from you. I have to take this slow."

"Okay. No voicing. Can I reserve this flight now?"

◆

The hammers were gone from your piano on Sunday!

It's an e-mail from Jerry Korten. I told Jerry about our original plan, and he must have gone to Beethoven's hoping to hear the Schubert concert tuning on the walnut Grotrian. He's played this piano before. At the time, he said to me, "If Carl had had this piano when I was shopping, I wouldn't have had to buy mine in Germany."

Tom is installing them on my piano as I write this, I type back. *I don't know yet how they will sound. He's regulating the height at the moment.*

OH MY GOD I CAN HARDLY STAND IT! is Jerry's reply.

Neither can I. Ever since Tom arrived this morning, I've been almost hopping out of my skin.

Watching Tom Kuntz set up his tools and take apart the piano has become a familiar and comforting ritual. This morning he's full of good humor and teasing little jokes.

Tom's cell phone rings. He looks at it, but doesn't pick it up until the ringing stops. Then he says into the unconnected receiver: "Hello? The White House? The president wants his piano tuned today? Uh, you mean George Bush? You tell George Bush he'll have to wait until tomorrow. I'm tuning *Perri Nye's* piano today." He gets from me the laugh he was angling for.

I tell Tom that if these new hammers don't solve the problem, I am going to take a sledgehammer to the piano and throw it in the river. "Oh, no you won't!" says Tom. "I'll take it off your hands. I'll be very happy to have this piano."

So much has happened in the past six months since Tom was last here to tune, there is so much to tell him, I don't know how he'll get any work done. I tell him about the Schubert concert tuning. I show him my pictures and notes from the Grotrian factory on how to voice the hammers. I tell him about my scheme with Marc to record the tuning so we can put it on my piano. I ask Tom, would he be willing to use that tuning?

"Sure! I'm very curious to hear it. Of course, I've had people rave to me about tunings and I think they are awful," he warns. "But then, I don't have to like it. It's your piano."

He plays a riff on the Grotrian. The piano has a buzzy, grating sound, truly awful. Putting in the new hammers will be like giving the piano a brain transplant. I can hardly wait.

Tom explains that the hammer swap will require intensive action regulation to compensate for the fact that the hammers are now in a different piano belly. All the parts need to be adjusted to one another. It will take several hours.

Carl shipped the hammers in a padded metal case. I open it now and remove the Bubble Wrap to reveal the contents—hammers glued to shanks, each hinged to a flange, nested together in precise rows. Tom lays them neatly on the coffee table, one by one, keeping them strictly in order, from treble to bass. We stand back and admire them for a moment.

"So," Tom says. "Do you want me to put them all on? Or do you want to listen to first this one, then that one? Maybe keep some of the ones that are already on the piano?" He's tweaking me.

"Let's not be crazy about this," I say, laughing.

"Oh, okay. Good!" He grins.

He pulls the piano's action, turns it around so he can use the keybed as a workbench, and unscrews every other hammer flange from the action rail, treble section first. He replaces each missing hammer with a new one, and adjusts all the hammers and shanks in the section until they are moving and angled correctly. Then he repeats with the remaining hammers. I dance around him while he works, hang on the piano's rim to watch and ask questions, then realize I must be being a pest.

"Tom, feel free to banish me at any time."

"Oh, you're fine!"

I go into my office and try to work. But I can't work. I have to go back into the living room.

"I think this is going to work!" Tom says. "Why didn't I suggest we do this in the first place? How stupid."

When all the new hammers are in the piano, they look out of alignment. "They'll look better when they're regulated," Tom says.

We take a break for lunch.

At Tom's favorite lunch spot, the Hob Nob Cafe, we sit at a sidewalk table, enjoying the sunshine and the view of the surrounding mountains, still covered in snow. Tom tells me about his recent visit to Italy, where he spent a week at a special seminar for technicians at the Fazioli factory. He shows me a tiny bubble level they use there for leveling strings. The highlight of his trip, he says, was getting to play their ten-foot-two-inch concert grand in a hall at the factory with specially designed acoustics.

"That was really something!" He stops eating his quesadilla and throws himself backward in his chair, as if being hit by a missile. "The vibrations just go right inside you." He puts his arms out to play some air piano and shivers all over as if he is receiving an electric shock. "Oh, man! It was the ultimate."

"So is the Fazioli now your favorite piano? What about the Mason?" I tease.

"The Mason & Hamlin is my favorite *American* piano," Tom counters. "The Fazioli is my favorite *Italian* piano." He named his new dog Fazioli.

Back at the house, Tom adjusts the blow distance—how far the hammers must travel to hit the strings. He checks the hammer alignment and the spring tension. "These are very straight shanks," he says. "Not a big deal to straighten these out."

But there are many more tiny, minute adjustments to make, each one repeated eighty-eight times. "Here, watch me adjust these little buttons," he says, taking a long metallic tool, kind of like a dental pick, and poking it through the holes of the capstans. "I'm going to make the touch very responsive by adjusting these guys. Then in time, the felt will wear down, and you'll need me to do it again."

Tom asks if we can have some music. "Put on that Moravec guy."

Of course, I have to tell Tom about my meeting with Moravec in

Munich, at a concert I attended at the stately and austere Herkules Hall in the Residenz palace, after I left Mittenwald.

It was a rainy spring night, and the program was Chopin and Debussy. Moravec is known as the ultimate master of the delicate touch. He's a small portrait pianist, favoring the performance of short works that showcase the beauty of tones. That night he made the Hamburg Steinway concert grand sound like liquid silver. But some notes were harsh. I could not help but wonder why he did not back off them more—perhaps the piano was voiced too bright for him?

After the concert, I stood in the reception line for a long time, waiting for him to sign my program. Moravec's wife stood protectively behind his right shoulder, keeping well-wishers who ventured too close at bay. When finally it was my turn, I thanked him for the concert as he wrote out his signature in a powerful cursive. Then I asked, how had he liked the voicing of the piano onstage?

"Voicing!" he said, looking up at me in surprise. His pleasant affect vanished, and his hairless, egg-shaped head turned scarlet. His wife leaned in between us, as if I were a would-be assassin. "You want to know about *voicing*? That is a very technical subject." His Czech accent was crisp. "That is about how you get the freedom to produce the music. If you have the voice of the notes one way here, one way there, how can you make the music sound the way it should? I worked with a technician for *two hours* because that piano is too bright, and it still isn't right! *Voicing!* It's *never* right. It's a forgotten art."

✦

Five hours have gone by. At last all the hammers are regulated—time to tune. As Tom tunes, I can hear the tone is very different. Cooler in color. It may need some warming up, but I can worry about that later. This time, I'm going to give myself a chance to get used to whatever I get, before I take any irreversible steps. When the tuning is done, Tom invites me to play.

I am struck first by the clarity and beauty of the treble. It speaks out with the slightest touch, immensely responsive, effortless. I play the Chopin. The melody sparkles, it's luminous.

It isn't Marlene, but it's very beautiful, and Tom did a superb job with the action. The touch is now better than ever. The tone is very even, complex, rich with saturated color. What will Marc's tuning sound like on these hammers? Other than a bit of edginess, they are quite lovely just the way they are.

Then Tom takes a turn, playing some mellow jazz.

"It's going to need some more regulation, and some touch-up voicing," he says. "But this is all I have time for today." He has to get back to Coeur d'Alene because he's playing string bass with his jazz trio tonight.

I open my checkbook and ask him how much. He asks for the usual, and I know this job is not the usual, so I write the check for more.

"Tom, why do you drive all the way over here?"

"It's interesting. I learn things. Besides, I'll go just about anywhere to tune. It's part of the adventure."

✦

Marc will be here in only a few days to put the Schubert concert tuning on the piano and record it. When I call him to report on the installation of the hammers and tell him how beautiful the piano sounds now, he demands to know what I paid Tom.

"That was a giveaway," he says, sounding almost angry. I don't bother reminding him that we don't pay New York prices in this part of the world. "After I do my tuning for you, will this be complete?"

"I don't know, Marc. How can you think I would know that?"

"That's not an acceptable answer. You know enough at this point to know the answer."

I have only two questions, I tell him: Will I like the piano well enough with these hammers and his tuning? And will it again be the piano I fell in love with?

"No," he says with an abruptness that almost sounds like fury. "It can't be that piano."

We hang up. Lately, these telephone calls with Marc exhaust me. What will it be like having him here for three days?

28

Marc's Return

He stands at the curb, waving, a large wheeled case on at his side, dressed all in black, wearing his telephone headset, as usual. I pull up to the airport arrivals exit and together we muscle the heavy case into the back seat of my Toyota. "I could hijack a plane with what is in this bag," says Marc, reporting on airport security's reaction to his technician's tools. He climbs into the front seat, and we look at each other for a moment of silent recognition. All at once, I am deeply glad Marc is here. He's the one person who understands better than anyone the piano road I've traveled. And he came because he feels called to be here—there can be no other reason. I am grateful for this gesture, though I still have my doubts about the wisdom of permitting it. Will Marc really be able to resist voicing my piano?

Marc didn't boost my confidence on that score at all when he telephoned me a few hours ago while on layover in Minneapolis.

"How much time am I going to spend working on your piano today?" he asked. It's a question I could not possibly answer: Why was he asking? I told him I want to live with the new hammers for a while before I decide if they need any voicing. But Marc wants to do his thing.

"You realize that the tuning happens in conjunction with the voicing?"

Yes, Marc, I know.

"I don't know what this tuning will sound like on hammers that don't have my voicing."

"We'll find out when you tune it," I said, feeling the muscles in my neck tense. "I don't want to touch the hammers."

"I don't usually work that way," he pushed. "I tune, I voice, I tune, I voice."

I didn't reply, hoping silence would communicate my resolve better than words had so far. The problem is the opposite of what Marc thinks—the problem is what his voicing sounds like without his tuning. That is how Marlene sounded when she arrived, and it is how she will sound in future if Marc voices her again, unless he stays in Montana so he can tune the piano every few days.

The end of Marlene's saga will *not* be when Marc restores her to her glorious showroom self for just one day. The end of the story will be when the piano has a beautiful yet stable voice, one that is neither dull nor shrill, that maintains itself from day to day. The new hammers have already brought the piano very close to this ideal. Marc's tuning will be the final polish, the icing on the cake—but I do not want him cutting into that cake. Besides, Marc hasn't even heard them yet. He doesn't know what voicing they do or don't need. And he's not listening to me. I am a little pissed off—he agreed to not voice before he bought his plane ticket. I resolve to be firm: no needles, no chemicals, no nothing. If I have to throw him out of the house, I will.

◆

"This is not very out of tune."

We're in my living room, and Marc is playing a few chords on the Grotrian. "And the voicing isn't so bad that it's going to interfere with what I want to do."

"There's a few little things that bother me," I say, bringing him a glass of water while he unpacks his tools. "But then, I'll play the piano again the next day, and I don't hear any problem. So I don't want to rush into anything."

He plays octaves, tenths, and seventeenths, listening to the relationships between the notes. I love hearing him play these familiar chords, they've become, for me, Marc's signature sound. Marc rapidly flies up a series of major chords into the high treble.

"That's wild!" he exclaims in a whisper.

"What?"

"Whoo, whoo, whoo, whoo." He makes a whispery whooshing noise, like wind blowing through grasses, sighing through tree boughs.

"Is that good or bad?"

"It's not good or bad!" There's joy and pleasure in his voice. "It's just a sound your piano makes."

"A friend of mine says there's fairies in there."

"Oh! I totally agree!" Marc laughs. He bangs on a bunch of high treble keys in rapid succession. And I hear the delicate *whoosh* rising off the soundboard in the wake of the notes, like sparkling confetti or a cloud of fireflies glimmering. The colorful mixture scale.

It's the piano's belly making that sound, says Marc. It's the chemistry between the plate, the rim, the soundboard, and the bridge. "They all come together so that the sound vibrates freely, so that you get a large amplitude. And it's at the beginning of its golden period where you've got plenty of amplitude at the moment of attack, but a great sustain with a double swell of sound. Eventually, your sustain will continue to improve, and your amplitude will start to diminish, and you will no longer have the same dynamic range you had, but you'll have the most incredible *cantabile,* and then eventually it'll just sort of slow down, so that it doesn't have the vigor anymore to give any kind of punch at the moment of attack, and it'll sound stringier and stringier at that point."

"Is that the life cycle of a soundboard?"

"Yeah."

"Where's my soundboard in the cycle?"

"I think it's at the beginning of its idealness. 'Cause I don't remember it having quite the bloom three years ago that it does now. And I've got a pretty good memory. I remember it being tighter. Like it went booooom, not bo-ou-ou-ou-m. Like that. If you see what I mean." He pounds some more chords in the treble. "Don't listen to what I play, listen to what comes after—it's just billowing out of your piano, releasing sound instead of driving sound out, a symphony of every sound you can possibly imagine."

"To me it sounds like there's a living entity in there, a disembodied soul."

"That only happens with the best bellies."

Marc puts his temperament strip into the piano, isolating the center strings of the trichords, and begins tuning.

"Just by the way," he says, playing octaves and wiggling the tuning lever, "I rarely do this tuning."

"I thought it was *my* tuning!"

"Right. Because this one is really, really distinctly crafted to please your ear. But there are other people that really love this. There are."

"So why do you call it the Schubert concert tuning?"

"If I say 'it's a tight double-octave tuning,' well, that doesn't mean anything to anybody. But if I say, it's a tuning that makes Schubert sound beautiful, well, then people can relate to that."

"So what does Schubert need to sound beautiful?"

"The tuning isn't busy. It doesn't distract you in any way. It just sort of glows."

"Kind of like calm water instead of ripples?"

"Yeah, right, exactly. Here, I'll show you."

Marc changes the tuning on just the top note of an octave, a pair of Cs. I hear the shift immediately. The chord changes from having a shimmering, serene, ethereal quality to become brassy, excited, more extroverted. I recoil. He switches it back.

"The 'Moonlight' Sonata, right?" The sound is pure, clear, sustaining. He changes it again. The top note goes jangly, then disappears. "Hear the beating?"

"I like mine better!" I laugh.

"There's no beat with yours, it's just a roll."

"It's so subtle, just a different quality or color, but they are both in tune."

"Exactly. It's all taking place in a little microworld about this big." He pinches his fingers together. "But the totality is huge! This is just one version of the lie that it's in tune."

I wonder, will the Accu-Tuner accurately measure such subtle differences?

Marc completes the tuning very quickly, and it's time for me to play. I do not have a moment's concern that the tuning will be anything less than perfection, but Marc stands by nervously. He seems not sure that he was able to pull off, yet again, the tuning I fell for.

There is no doubt when my hands touch the keys. I feel a rush of joy at the tones emanating from the belly—subtle, warm, and complex, with an added sparkle of shooting stars on top—I recognize the signature at once. I launch into the Mozart Andante, and the piano becomes an ecstasy machine, an opiate drip, a ride into an altered state.

The tuning is transcendent, and I feel exalted. This has nothing to do with my skill as a pianist, or Mozart's gifts as a composer, but is the effect of the specific frequencies Marc chose, and how they combine with each other. This relationship between all the beats within the beats of interacting partials is called the "stretch characteristic," he says. "It's an inner vibrato I use to control the voice of the piano."

"Marc, you are a magician," I say, hanging my head over the keys, overcome with the beauty of the piano. "Too bad it doesn't stay like this."

"It can't," says Marc. "Pianos tear themselves apart; every time the hammer strikes the strings, it's destructive. You are captivated by a brief moment in time."

Tuning is all we are going to do for today. Marc has dinner plans with an old friend who is driving over from Bozeman. My assignment for tonight is to figure out how to use the Accu-Tuner so we can record the tuning tomorrow. Marc clearly wants to have as little to do with the electronic tuning device as possible—he has no desire to learn how to use an ETD. Marc leaves the machine and its instruction booklet with me, but I can hardly make heads or tails of it.

The Accu-Tuner is a small blue box you set on the piano's plate. It has a microphone to pick up the tones, a digital readout to display the frequencies of the tones, and a bull's-eye circle of five swirling lights that slow and then stop when the frequency of the piano's tone and the frequency numbers on the display match up. I decide to call Tom and ask him how to use it.

"It's very important how you stop the lights. You have to be very consistent," Tom says. "The trick is a nice clear tone, and do it exactly the same length for each note. The higher up you go, the faster you have to repeat the notes. Make sure the lights really stop. You want four or five lights lit up, then you've nailed it. Strike the key with a nice blow, mezzo forte, not real hard. And not more than two seconds. Take your reading *after* the initial attack."

Then he tells me how to store each number. The machine automatically moves up to the next note as each note is stored. "The manual *is* hard to understand. Call Rick Baldassin or Jeff Stickney if you get into trouble tomorrow."

I should have thought to hire Jeff to come and record the tuning, I now realize, but I had no idea recording an aural tuning would be so difficult for an inexperienced person, and it is too late to call him now.

The next morning, I pick up Marc from his hotel and bring him home. While I make coffee, he touches up yesterday's tuning, lining up the unisons. Then he asks me to play the piano again to make sure this is the tuning we want to record.

"It's going to be up to your guy to make the unisons." He means Tom. "And he may make unisons differently than me. There's no way for the machine to record how I tune unisons." We still don't know how important the unisons are to what I experience with this tuning.

I play the piano and it sounds just as wonderful as yesterday—time to record. I turn the machine on, and the lights swirl around their bull's-eye. Marc explodes in a fury.

"WHY ARE THOSE LIGHTS SPINNING!" He sounds like a madman, and I recoil in shock.

"I'm just following directions. See? Here." I show him the manual. He calms down a bit.

"You have a better intuitive sense of this machine than I do."

"I just read the manual," I say, innocently, still shocked at Marc's vehemence. He's reacting to the ETD as if it is a viper.

"I read it too! I read everything! That machine is a mystery to me!" He sounds very upset. "I would never buy that machine. Absolutely not! It's better if I just focus on the tuning to get what you want."

"I think you should focus on the tuning," I say quietly. He returns to refining the high treble.

I calibrate the machine to Marc's A4 = 441. This is where the piano settled a long time ago, and Marc will leave it there for the sake of tuning stability. He checks the double octaves again, up and down the piano. They sound so warm and rich. "Okay!" Marc exclaims. He is pleased.

We start with the first note on the piano, A0. I press the key down and let the note decay.

"No. *No.*" Marc says irritably. "You have to keep playing it. See what I mean? It seems simple, doesn't it? I'm going to start over." He grabs the Accu-Tuner and starts punching buttons on it. "You're not in the right mode. I've been through this a million times."

"All right."

"Not that I enjoyed it! Let me tell you." He is seething. "I think this thing is a piece of . . . I won't say any more."

Marc bangs and bangs on the note. "It's not hearing the E3 partial!"

I push the buttons to get the lights to stop, then write the numbers on the display down on a pad. But Marc isn't satisfied.

"Let's not make this more complicated than we have to," I implore.

"I'm sorry, but I read that manual and I've still got about ten thousand unanswered questions. Okay? That is not a good manual. Nowhere do they recommend what partials to use. Nowhere!"

I get up to call the Accu-Tuner company. Tom gave me the number, but there is only an answering machine. Of course, I think. It's a Saturday morning. "We have a few urgent questions," I say into the company's voice mail.

"So it's worth doing this?" Marc rails at me when I return. He is still sitting at the piano, banging on the Accu-Tuner's buttons. He's actually having a fit. "Because I'm not enjoying this."

I am about ready to strangle him right there on the piano bench. None of this was even my idea. If Michael Harrison hadn't suggested recording the tuning, I would have asked Marc to explain the stretch characteristic to Tom, and that would have been the end of it. When he insisted he wanted to record the tuning, I tried to talk him into hiring someone else to do it. I also tried to talk him out of coming all the way out here. But here we are. And he's behaving abominably. I want to rail right back at him, *Don't blame me!* But I bite my tongue.

The phone rings. It's Paul Sanderson, one of the owners of Accu-Tuner, returning my call. Paul walks us through the entire operation on the phone. Bit by bit, Marc's mood lightens as he gets the knack of how to use the machine, and by the time we reach the treble of the piano, taking turns hitting the note, adjusting the ETD to make the lights stop, writing down the name of the note, the partial we used, and the frequency, he's laughing again.

But he still hates the machine. "It's like going to church to know God," he says with disgust.

Now we have the numbers for all eighty-eight keys. For a break we take Tucker on his daily walk. Out in the sunshine and fresh air,

moving our limbs, the old dog lumbering along behind us, the afternoon's tension ebbs away and we let it go.

I had asked Marc to find out more about Szott, the Polish immigrant at Steinway whose signature tuning inspired the Schubert concert tuning. Now Marc tells me he called an old friend at Steinway
who knew Szott much longer than Marc did. Ishmael Cunha, who
still tunes for Steinway's Concert and Artist department, remembered
the old tuner well.

Edward Szott was from Kraków and learned to tune in Germany.
Prior to fleeing Cold War–era Poland and joining Steinway New York
in 1985, he was the tuner for the Kraków Radio Symphony Orchestra. Kraków is also where he lost half of one leg when an armored
tank crushed the car he was driving.

Szott worked as a tuner for Steinway's retail department but was
never one of its stellar lights. His tunings were not generally appreci-
ated because he was unable to make them stable; his Polish tuning
hammer was not a refined enough tool, Ishmael suspects. The tunings
were "so beautiful and amazing," Marc says, the octaves perfectly clean
and clear, but they would quickly melt away.

"They were tremendously atmospheric," Marc recalls. "I still hold
the sound of one particular tuning on one particular day inside me. I
sat down in front of a piano he had tuned, and said, 'God I wish I could
tune like that.'

"I still go back to that feeling when I tune. Szott was the first person who keyed me in to how critical stretch characteristic is. I had the
epiphanous moment when I really understood."

Szott did not speak English well and was unable to communicate
to Marc how he created his tuning, but Marc was able to figure it out,
though he says he isn't sure if he's ever created exactly what Szott did.

Szott met a very sad end. Two days before Christmas 1991, Ed
Szott was leaving the subway station at West Fifty-seventh Street to go
to work at Steinway Hall when he collapsed and died on the stairs in
the middle of the morning rush. His heart had given out. He left
behind a wife and young daughter in Brooklyn, and only a paltry death
benefit to support them. "It's still terrible to think about," Ishmael said,
sounding as shaken as if Szott's death were only yesterday.

It was Szott's tuning Marc thought of when a German client told

him the kind of tuning she wanted. She knew about stretch characteristic, and she launched Marc in a new direction. He began experimenting. He made tunings to describe each of the four seasons. He
made tuning portraits of friends. When he came to Bozeman, a competitor disparaged his work by calling him a "Picasso tuner" because
of Marc's experiments with stretch.

"I was willing to open up my approach to what it means to be in
tune," says Marc. "It always comes back to the lie, and how you use
falseness to create an experience of truth. Some tuners think there is
only one right tuning. They do excellent and tremendously musical
and stable tunings and yet they think there is only one way."

"So what does it mean exactly when you say the piano is in tune?"
I ask, turning us back toward the house.

"Well," says Marc. "It doesn't mean anything!" He laughs his wild
laugh. " 'In tune' means some kind of perfect thing, and that's a big lie.
It's alive. It doesn't stay where you put it for very long. That's it! Nothing you can do about it."

✦

Back at the house and on to the next step: checking the tuning against
the ETD. This will tell us if we recorded it accurately.

For the third time, Marc touches up the unisons. He's making the
tuning as stable as possible so that even if Tom does not return for
months, I'll be able to enjoy the tuning for a long time. Then he puts
the temperament strip back in and we fire up the Accu-Tuner.

"So, what's the reading for A-zero?"

I play A0.

"It stopped!" Marc's voice is full of delight. "It can't get any sweeter
than that!"

"Okay! Let's try another one."

"Move up an octave."

I play A1.

"Eeeww!" I say when the EDT's lights don't come to a full stop.

"Don't go *eeeww!*" Marc sounds indignant. "That's stopped. Let me
tell you, it's well within the parameters."

I play A3. The lights waver again. I feel dismay. What if it doesn't
work after all?

"Marc, this is not what we were going for when we were measuring. We had the lights completely stopped. Did your unison touch-up change it?"

"No. No, no, no, no. I didn't even touch those notes. We're not playing it ten times. I'm just playing it once and getting a feel."

I play A4.

"Five lights! That's what we *were* doing. And ripping our hair out. I'm just doing one check." He bangs the note once, hard. "See? The light *stopped*. That's good enough for me!"

But the next A, A5, has moved a little bit. And so have the other notes in the treble. Marc touches up just that A. "It's not that far off," he says. "I don't want to disrupt the whole piano. I've worked hard to stabilize it like it is."

"Okay."

But I'm still worried that if it isn't exactly precise, the sound won't be the same. This gets Marc agitated again. "I'm telling you, it's thousandths of a semitone. It's not even as far off as my tuning fork is. Stop worrying about a thousandth of a semitone."

"You think we should keep the numbers we have?"

"Yeah, I do. I made it stop."

"Okay." I give up.

"I made it stop!" says Marc when he sees my shrug.

"And it still sounds good," I say, trying to be reasonable. The piano sounds gorgeous, actually.

"Yeah. It truly does. It's not any different."

Marc rips out the temperament strip and invites me to try the treble section with the unisons in play. It is beautifully in tune. Shimmering, gossamer, sparkling perfection.

"It does sound clean."

"Yeah. I'm telling you, the ear does not hear a thousandth of a semitone. It just doesn't." He puts the strip back in. "Let's just keep going right up the scale. And I'm not going to go *eeeww* every time I see the lights move."

We finish our test sample. The treble has drifted just slightly. Marc says it's from the slight change in humidity since this morning. "As far as I'm concerned, we're totally in the pocket. I think it's gonna work!"

He hits another note. The lights stop cold.

"Dead on! *Yeah!*"
"We did it!"

✦

I didn't exactly forget that Marc is a sophisticated gourmand who spent his childhood summers in the south of France with his maternal grandfather, going to the market every day and preparing traditional French cooking at home—I was thinking only of thanking him with the best Missoula can offer. But when Oliver, Marc, and I walk into Pearl, a country French restaurant named after the owner, and Marc takes in the décor and the menu, I do remember, and I get a bit nervous. I hope he won't find the Missoula version of French cuisine as repugnant as he finds the Accu-Tuner version of an in-tune piano.

I needn't have worried. Marc raves about the wine list, the menu, the setting, and the service. We give him carte blanche, and he samples several wines, an array of appetizers, including duckling foie gras with cherry compote and port syrup, then mulls with indecision over the entrees before ordering grilled beef filet with brandy-infused green peppercorn sauce, and two desserts. The wine sends him into a cascade of superlatives. When the foie gras arrives, he takes a taste and swoons in disbelief, full of praises.

"This is completely authentic! What a find this place is!"

He regales us with fond memories of his childhood vacations in France, and describes in painstaking detail the elaborate feasts he and Connie concoct at home. He's clearly as particular about his food as he is about piano tone.

Hours later, we walk Marc to his hotel, and then slowly back to Oliver's Jeep in the fading evening light. "It was worth the price of the food just to listen to him talk about it," says Oliver, slipping an arm around me. Oliver, my stalwart partner who has unselfishly seen me through this long and sometimes arduous journey, has only generous things to say. I squeeze him tight, an embrace of gratitude. Yes, I think, he's right. Marc Wienert, talking about anything, is inimitable.

✦

When I pick up Marc in the morning, he is happy and relaxed; we return to our old camaraderie. The pressure is off now, and he admits the entire visit had him in a sweat. "This has been like facing two doors," he says. "Behind one is the tiger, and behind the other is the maiden." On top of his worries that the tuning wouldn't work on a piano he hadn't voiced, and his frustrations with the Accu-Tuner, he explains, he also was not too happy about putting numbers on his tuning. "That's like rendering Walden Pond no longer bottomless."

"Well, I can understand that. It's like quantifying the ineffable."

"Yeah, I felt funky about doing that."

"But just because something is quantified, it isn't any the less wonderful," I say. "Besides, I kind of doubt anyone will really be able to duplicate the tuning just the way you do it. I bet it's like handwriting—even a forged signature isn't quite as authentic in feel as the original."

When we arrive at the house, Marc touches up the unisons on the piano again, though there isn't much to do. He tests the numbers on the Accu-Tuner against the notes on the piano one more time, just enough to reconfirm what we already know—his job is done.

He asks me to play the piano for him, and I play the Mozart Andante and Allegretto from K. 330. The tuning leaves nothing to be desired. It is luminous, perfect.

Now the only unknown is what the piano will sound like when Tom uses the numbers to duplicate the tuning, several months from now. There is minor voicing to be done, I can hear an edginess on some notes still. And Marc hears that some strings need to be leveled. But he says he can't work on that, or it will upset the tuning. "I'll leave that to your guy," he says. "That's his territory. My goal was to give you the tuning and the numbers."

I turn on the bench, away from the piano, to face Marc sitting on the sofa. "Don't you think you can fix just that one little string?" I say, bouncing my finger on the offending note.

"Look, I didn't come out here to be your practical piano tuner," he says mildly. "The whole purpose of what we're doing is for you to decide if you're keeping this piano. I came out to resolve the existential issue."

"It's resolved."

"So you love your piano again?"

"I have the most beautiful piano on earth. And that was not something I could say with any kind of conviction for quite a while."

"I know. And I'm experiencing a big relief! I'm sure not as big as yours!" He laughs.

"You know, it doesn't seem quite real to me," I say. "I'm still not ready to trust the piano will stay this way. This whole experience has been a little traumatic."

"Yeah. I understand," Marc says. "Unfortunately, your experience is not unique. Truly not. People go on monumental quests to find the perfect piano, thinking what you see is what you get—they're not even thinking 'It's gonna sound different in my home.' Much less are they thinking it's going to evolve as soon as they start playing it. Much less that it's going to be totally transformed once their own technician is working on it as opposed to the store technician.

"All these factors remain totally unconsidered in the minds of most piano buyers. And then they say, 'Well, I'm not going to be satisfied unless you can fix this one note.'" He plugs his index finger down on an imaginary note. "Then I know that those people are in for a disastrous, horrible relationship with their instrument for the rest of their lives.

"So here's my idea—to open a psychological practice for piano owners. I think I could do more beneficial work that way than I can by working on their pianos. I'd have a setup of several pianos, all the same make and model, voiced and tuned different ways, and teach them about the differences and what to expect."

"No doubt you'd be on the tough-love side of the profession," I tease.

"Yeah! I'm the Dr. Phil of the piano world!—*What were you thinking!?*"

"I love it! Dr. Marc!"

✦

We get to the airport early, and sit in the car by the departures entrance, watching the private planes take off and land at the adjacent municipal airport. Marc talks of his upcoming vacation to France, of his plans to launch a rebuilding facility at the Manhattan School of Music. But soon it is time to go, and we know we may not see each other again for a very long time.

I help him extract his rolling tool case from the back of the car.

He extends his arms for a good-bye hug. "We went on a journey together to find the source of vibration, and we made some interesting discoveries," says Marc.

"Yes, and I still haven't sorted out what they mean."

"Me either."

I start toward the car, key in hand, but then turn back to face him. "Marc, why did you come out here?"

"Because I love you," he says sweetly. "I was taking a risk that the tuning wouldn't work, but it was so simple for me to do, and so critical for you. Once I realized that it was the tuning that mattered, I knew you were dead in the water if I didn't come. I felt called into service to do that."

"You could have put the tuning on the piano in New York and sent the numbers."

"What if I did that and it still didn't work? Then I'd have to come out anyway, and it would have been that much more you'd have been put through. No. You'd been through enough."

"But why me? I'm just some amateur pianist who isn't even very good. I'm only just learning."

"I don't care. Doesn't matter to me. You play with feeling and you are obviously tremendously musical even if you don't have the technique to express all of what you hear. What you want out of a piano isn't what most pianists are looking for, anyway. Most pianists aren't trying to ride the crest of the wave of the expanding universe. But for me, this is all the really real stuff. And I want to collaborate with someone who really believes.

"You are a truly worthy curator of your instrument. You are sophisticated and picky and you know exactly what you want—and I know how to satisfy you. I mean, nobody needs me as much as you! You have the ability to embrace the process as deeply as the technician who is doing the work. That's why so many techs want to help you—your odyssey is archetypal—it resonates in a mythological way, so mythological figures appear—Steve Brady, Darrell Fandrich, Tom Kuntz—these people who come here and want to work with you—that's why. You are on a Promethean journey, and so Prometheus will be there.

"Put it another way—when you want something badly enough, life delivers."

✦

I drive slowly home, so profoundly touched by Marc's words, and his gift of the tuning, I feel I can hardly speak. If finding and buying a piano is like love and marriage, then this tuning is Marc's wedding present to Marlene and me, a unique creation for us, so that we can live a long and happy life together. The tuning makes our relationship whole: it's the tuning that belongs on this piano, it uniquely describes me and this piano—with it, we can build a wonderful relationship. At last, I let myself trust in my future with this piano, and it's a delirious feeling. I rush back into the house to play her again and open myself wide to the experience.

Astonishing. The bass is a bass I haven't heard before. Clear, rich as chocolate, luscious, warm, powerful. This can't be real, can't be my piano. My hands hover over the keys in a disbelieving moment. Then I play again. Each and every note responds to my touch with precisely the timbre I intend, changing color with each change in the stroke. I run up the entire chromatic scale just for the sheer pleasure of feeling the tones race through my body. Then I take out the Brahms Intermezzo I have just begun to learn, Opus 118, no. 2. Brahms should love that chocolaty bass.

The piano seems to play itself, and soon I am lost in its world of sound. The tone leads me to a place of pure being, where the music simply is.

✦

Tom knocks. I turn to see him behind the full-panel glass of the front door, shading his eyes to peer in with his left hand and waving with a trill of fingers on his right, looking lanky and very summery in his khaki shorts, polo shirt, and sandals. The heat of late July blasts in with him. He sets his tool kit beside the piano bench and opens its latches with a snap.

"So this is the famous Schubert concert tuning," says Tom, taking the pages of numbers from the piano's music desk and scanning them with eyebrows raised, a slight tone of friendly derision in his voice.

"How do the numbers look?" I ask. Will he think they look wrong?

"I don't know until I try them." He puts the pages down. "So, Marc flew out here just to tune this piano?"

"Yes."

"Wow! You got da power! You know, a lot of techs would take offense being asked to put somebody else's tuning on a piano."

"I know. I really appreciate that you are willing to do this."

"Oh, it doesn't bother me at all. I don't have a big ego like some of these guys."

"Maybe they are like that because piano technicians don't get enough respect?" I'm echoing Marc, who describes techs as neuro-surgeons on a plumber's salary.

Tom's eyebrows go up again. He pulls the music desk off the piano. "If a person is happy in themselves, that's the best place to be," he says. He unrolls his tuning hammer from its canvas case. "Because you can't make the world happy. Okay, let's get to it."

Tom's Accu-Tuner rolls its lights. They spin and wink in response to every word I say. "We took the numbers just the way you told us: mezzo forte, four to five lights stopped."

"Uh-huh. Wow, look at this, it's pretty much dead-on, right where he left it. You just need the pitch up slightly and touch up the unisons. That was a good tuning he gave you."

We sit together before the piano. Each time Tom plays a key, I read aloud the note name, the name of the partial, and the frequency number. Then Tom nudges the tuning hammer. I have my eyes closed, listening. I hear the tone go in and out of alignment, a *wowwowwow* flutter that tuners call "beats." The number of flutters slows and quickens as Tom moves the hammer.

"You could learn how to do this, you know," Tom says to me. "You could get an Accu-Tuner and a hammer and touch these up yourself." I listen to the beats slow as Tom eases a string into the correct tension. I'm listening for that pure, unruffled, glossy tone, crystalline and singing. Then when I hear Tom play the next note up the scale, I open my eyes and read him the next number from the page.

"I don't think so," I say, still looking from the page to the numbers on the ETD, just to be sure they are right. Marlene's DNA is what these numbers are. Can't let them get scrambled. I check them off the list so I don't make a mistake. "I'm afraid I'd ruin my pinblock. Besides, I'm told touching up unisons is the hardest part of tuning."

We make rapid progress. Tom pauses to play some fourths. "I see what he was going for. That's nice. Really nice. He did this aurally? This guy is a really good tuner. He sets a nice temperament. He would have passed the exam with this." Tom administers the Piano Technicians Guild exam for our region. "The Guild tuning is different. They want you to stretch and stretch the intervals. I like this much better. This suits my ear better."

Now we're at the top of the keyboard, tuning the last undamped notes, where there is no sustain and the piano sounds rinky-tink. The numbers are up and down, they don't follow the unbroken, predictive curve of an ETD tuning. "That's the way his ear hears. Plus a slight amount of change up at this end of the keyboard is a lot. It moves five cents if you barely move the pin. And you can hardly hear the change up at this end, whereas five cents down in the tenor you hear a lot."

We're at the last note, way up at the top of the scale where I almost never play. C8 is the last note on the piano. Tom sets it to Marc's numbers and then taps the key several times, listening. "That's great by ear. He nailed that C8. That's incredible."

Tom plays some chords. Then he plays "Over the Rainbow." The piano soars.

Now it's time to tune the unisons by ear. I close my eyes again, listening, listening for the beats to fade, for the tone to become utterly clean and pure, and then I hear Tom move beyond beatless, into a search for sustain, going for the greatest sustain possible within a beatless note. Each note sings out, rises like vapor, traveling out over the soundboard, full and pregnant until, finally, at long last, it fades off into nothingness.

This is going to be a great tuning.

When he's finished, I play Debussy's "Rêverie," the perfect piece to bring out the sparkle of the treble.

"Tom! It's so beautiful!" I lean back from the bench to throw him a look of gratitude. He's packing up his tools. "Thank you!"

"Better than new!" he exclaims, like he always does.

❖

But this visit of Tom's is months in the future. Tonight, while Marc is winging his way home, I lift the fallboard again to just be with my piano. Chopin sparkles. Schumann sings. But Brahms brings out the best in her, with a tone so rich, deep, dark, complicated, and colorful, I cannot tear myself away. Is it Marlene? Almost, but better than the original Marlene, with an even more incredible range of tonal color than she ever had before. I lean into the sweet pealing of her voice, let my hands fall heavily, reveling in the purity of the tone even at *fortissimo,* letting myself go into the sound, into the music, immersed in her tonal perfume.

Dinnertime passes, and I play. Oliver heads for bed, smiling at the rapture in my face, and on I play. I exhaust my repertoire, and then I begin it again, and then I play arpeggios, and then intervals, tenths and seventeenths to remind me of Marc, the familiar sound of him setting his tuning temperament, his signature sound, just to luxuriate in the tone, wallow in tone. It grows late. In between the notes are deep middle-of-the-night silences. I stop to listen.

My piano. Really. In my living room. Worth every penny. Worth every moment of the years of agony and the odyssey of discovery. She is here. She has been here all along.

I know she won't sound like this but for an evening. The thousands of moving parts can only sustain correct relationships with each other briefly. Each depression of the key and strike of the hammer sends the strings back down their inevitable path of imperfection. A freshly tuned piano is a golden coach that turns back into a pumpkin with the dawn.

Then, in time, the piano technician returns, straightens her up and sets her right, and for a few brief hours she wears her golden lamé cloak, blazing like a comet across the sky, only to quickly fade back into darkness. She is a shooting star, and I must be fully present in the moment to wish on her. If I want to enjoy Marlene in her ephemeral state of great beauty, I cannot wait until morning. I must seize the moment.

And so I keep playing.

In the months and years to come, after Marc's tuning has been put on this piano many times, after the hammers have been played in, voiced just a little, then played in some more, the tuning put on again and yet again, the piano reaches homeostasis—a place of stability, where her magic is no longer ephemeral, but a constant that changes only imperceptibly over time. She reaches a golden period, Marlene, a voice of shooting stars whenever I choose to play her, a source of inspiration and renewal for months and years at a time. But for now, still in her infancy, she remains a fleeting dream.

And so I play on into the night.

So brilliant she sounds, I have not even noticed that her lid is closed. But I do now, and I get up and lift her wing as high as it will go, raising the longest prop stick so that the full force of her perfect frequencies will wash over me. And so it is that when I sit down again, and begin the Brahms Intermezzo for yet another reprise, I become the other wing. And together, my piano and I take flight.

ACKNOWLEDGMENTS

This book could not have been written without the gifts of time, love, energy, advice, and talent generously offered by an enormous number of people. My debt to them is no less significant though there is not enough space here to name them all.

My agent, Nick Ellison, has served as a wise and trusted advisor, formidable champion, and good friend. His assistant Alexandra Lee provided a thoughtful critique and, along with Colin Shepherd, helped the logistical wheels run smoothly.

My editor at Scribner, Colin Harrison, has been a patient and insightful literary midwife throughout the writing and editing of this book. Working with Colin has been an extraordinary experience that I will always cherish. No writer could hope for a more compassionate, intuitive, and gifted editor.

Also at Scribner, my heartfelt thanks to editorial assistant Karen Thompson, production editor Dan Cuddy, designer Kyoko Watanabe, and publicists Molly Dorozenski and Jennifer Bernard for their hard work and professionalism. I know there are many others at Scribner who gave their all, and my thanks to them as well.

My husband, Oliver Wendell Holmes, is *Grand Obsession*'s true hero. He has my enduring gratitude for his patient and unshakable faith in me. He served as my first reader and my most unflinching critic. When Wendell was fascinated by the book's chapters, even though he had lived through their often painful details—and was quite sick of hearing about pianos already—I knew my writing had passed its most rigorous test. Wendell made many and difficult sacrifices so that I could write this book, and he made them with love, grace, and a sense of humor.

Of all this book's many friends and supporters, none has given more than Kim Brizzolara. She hosted me in New York for weeks at a time, read and critiqued the manuscript, and freely shared her always clear-eyed perspective. I am forever grateful for her friendship.

I'm also indebted to Richard Blood and Judith Crist, who championed this project from its inception. Dick Blood touched me many times with his gruff encouragement, all the more meaningful because of his fearsome reputation as an uncompromising critic. Both he and Judith offered bracing and valuable advice.

Many others made indispensable contributions: Lois Schlyer transcribed some thirty hours of taped interviews. Pam Voth provided my cover photograph. Paula Parcheta, Carol-Lynne Toleno, Frank White, and Marilyn Beech cared for my body and spirit, served as sounding boards for my ideas, and read early drafts. Lisa Rogak, Marty Nemko, and M. J. Rose offered their expertise. William Dietrich and James Johnson's enthusiasm for the initial idea incited me to pursue it. Greg and Dorothy Patent provided a place to write. Other friends and colleagues who offered guidance and support include Emily Benedek, Amber Husbands, Thomas McNamee, Robert Frenay, Constance Barrett, Connie Poten and Andy Sponseller, Clara Erickson, Phil O'Connell, Diane Haddon, Linda Raye, Rick Wheeler, David Burton, Jerry Korten, and Norbert Marten.

My gratitude as well to everyone who appears in this story. My thanks above all to Marc Wienert, who inspired this book and without whom it could not have been written. In Europe, the managers and workers at the Grotrian-Steinweg factory in Braunschweig, Germany, Thomas and Martina Hilz of Pocking, Germany, and Piera Ciresa and Fabio Ognibeni of Tesero, Italy, were most generous with their knowledge, time, and hospitality. My thanks also to Carl Demler and his staff at Beethoven Pianos in New York, Darrell and Heather Fandrich of Stanwood, Washington, Del and Barbara Fandrich of Centralia, Washington, Frank Baxter and the pianophiles of Piano World, and the many gifted piano technicians who guided me on this journey. Michael Harrison especially gave generously of his time and patience to teach me about the physics of tuning and review the manuscript.

My brother, Michael Knize, gave generously of his love and support, showed up when it mattered, and bore gifts that made a difference. TANA, Mike.

Last, but very far from least, my love and thanks to my father, Leon Knize, who passed on to me his passion for music and trained my ear to appreciate it. Surely there can be no greater gift from a parent to a child.

ABOUT THE AUTHOR

PERRI KNIZE is an award-winning environmental policy reporter whose articles and essays have appeared in *The Atlantic Monthly*, *Audubon*, *Sports Illustrated*, *Condé Nast Traveler*, and *Outside*. She was educated in philosophy and Russian at the University of Michigan, studied piano at the Mannes College of Music, worked as a poster and book designer in Manhattan, volunteered as a wilderness ranger on the Beaverhead National Forest in southwest Montana, and received her Master's degree in journalism at Columbia University. She has been a reporter at *New York Newsday* and *Newsweek*, a freelancer for *The New York Times*, and has taught journalism at the University of Montana. She lives with her husband in Montana.